Cisco Secure Firewall Module (FWSM)

Ray Blair, CCIE No. 7050
Arvind Durai, CCIE No. 7016

Cisco Press

Cisco Press
800 East 96th Street
Indianapolis, IN 46240 USA

Cisco Secure Firewall Services Module (FWSM)

Ray Blair, Arvind Durai

Copyright© 2009 Cisco Systems, Inc.

Published by:
Cisco Press
800 East 96th Street
Indianapolis, IN 46240 USA

Printed in the United States of America

First Printing September 2008

Library of Congress Cataloging-in-Publication Data:

Blair, Ray, 1965-

Cisco secure firewall services module (FWSM) / Ray Blair, Arvind Durai.

p. cm.

ISBN-13: 978-1-58705-353-5 (pbk.)

ISBN-10: 1-58705-353-5 (pbk.)

1. Computer networks—Security measures. 2. Firewalls (Computer security) 3. Cisco Systems, Inc. I. Durai, Arvind. II. Title.

TK5105.59.B563 2009

005.8—dc22

2008030575

ISBN-13: 978-1-58705-353-5

ISBN-10: 1-58705-353-5

Warning and Disclaimer

This book is designed to provide information about the Firewall Services Module, using practical design examples. Every effort has been made to make this book as complete and as accurate as possible, but no warranty or fitness is implied.

The information is provided on an "as is" basis. The authors, Cisco Press, and Cisco Systems, Inc. shall have neither liability nor responsibility to any person or entity with respect to any loss or damages arising from the information contained in this book or from the use of the discs or programs that may accompany it.

The opinions expressed in this book belong to the author and are not necessarily those of Cisco Systems, Inc.

Trademark Acknowledgments

All terms mentioned in this book that are known to be trademarks or service marks have been appropriately capitalized. Cisco Press or Cisco Systems, Inc., cannot attest to the accuracy of this information. Use of a term in this book should not be regarded as affecting the validity of any trademark or service mark.

Corporate and Government Sales

The publisher offers excellent discounts on this book when ordered in quantity for bulk purchases or special sales, which may include electronic versions and/or custom covers and content particular to your business, training goals, marketing focus, and branding interests. For more information, please contact:

U.S. Corporate and Government Sales   1-800-382-3419   corpsales@pearsontechgroup.com

For sales outside the United States please contact:

International Sales   international@pearsoned.com

Feedback Information

At Cisco Press, our goal is to create in-depth technical books of the highest quality and value. Each book is crafted with care and precision, undergoing rigorous development that involves the unique expertise of members from the professional technical community.

Readers' feedback is a natural continuation of this process. If you have any comments regarding how we could improve the quality of this book, or otherwise alter it to better suit your needs, you can contact us through email at feedback@ciscopress.com. Please make sure to include the book title and ISBN in your message.

We greatly appreciate your assistance.

Publisher	Paul Boger
Associate Publisher	Dave Dusthimer
Cisco Representative	Anthony Wolfenden
Cisco Press Program Manager	Jeff Brady
Executive Editor	Brett Bartow
Managing Editor	Patrick Kanouse
Development Editor	Dan Young
Senior Project Editor	Tonya Simpson
Copy Editor	Barbara Hacha
Technical Editors	Sunil Gul Wadwani, Bryan Osoro
Editorial Assistant	Vanessa Evans
Designer	Louisa Adair
Composition	Mark Shirar
Indexer	John Bickelhaupt
Proofreader	Kathy Ruiz

CISCO.

Americas Headquarters	Asia Pacific Headquarters	Europe Headquarters
Cisco Systems, Inc.	Cisco Systems (USA) Pte. Ltd.	Cisco Systems International BV
San Jose, CA	Singapore	Amsterdam, The Netherlands

Cisco has more than 200 offices worldwide. Addresses, phone numbers, and fax numbers are listed on the Cisco Website at **www.cisco.com/go/offices.**

CCDE, CCENT, Cisco Eos, Cisco Lumin, Cisco Nexus, Cisco StadiumVision, the Cisco logo, DCE, and Welcome to the Human Network are trademarks; Changing the Way We Work, Live, Play, and Learn is a service mark; and Access Registrar, Aironet, AsyncOS, Bringing the Meeting To You, Catalyst, CCDA, CCDP, CCIE, CCIP, CCNA, CCNP, CCSP, CCVP, Cisco, the Cisco Certified Internetwork Expert logo, Cisco IOS, Cisco Press, Cisco Systems, Cisco Systems Capital, the Cisco Systems logo, Cisco Unity, Collaboration Without Limitation, EtherFast, EtherSwitch, Event Center, Fast Step, Follow Me Browsing, FormShare, GigaDrive, HomeLink, Internet Quotient, IOS, iPhone, iQ Expertise, the iQ logo, iQ Net Readiness Scorecard, iQuick Study, IronPort, the IronPort logo, LightStream, Linksys, MediaTone, MeetingPlace, MGX, Networkers, Networking Academy, Network Registrar, PCNow, PIX, PowerPanels, ProConnect, ScriptShare, SenderBase, SMARTnet, Spectrum Expert, StackWise, The Fastest Way to Increase Your Internet Quotient, TransPath, WebEx, and the WebEx logo are registered trademarks of Cisco Systems, Inc. and/or its affiliates in the United States and certain other countries.

All other trademarks mentioned in this document or Website are the property of their respective owners. The use of the word partner does not imply a partnership relationship between Cisco and any other company. (0805R)

About the Authors

Ray Blair is a consulting systems architect and has been with Cisco Systems for more than eight years, working primarily on security and large network designs. He has 20 years of experience with designing, implementing, and maintaining networks that have included nearly all networking technologies. His first four years in the high-technology industry started with designing industrial computer systems for process monitoring. Mr. Blair maintains three Cisco Certified Internetwork Expert (CCIE) certifications in Routing and Switching, Security, and Service Provider. He also is a Certified Novell Engineer (CNE) and a Certified Information Systems Security Professional (CISSP).

Arvind Durai is an advanced services technical leader for Cisco Systems. His primary responsibility has been in supporting major Cisco customers in the Enterprise sector, some of which includes Financial, Manufacturing, E-commerce, State Government, and Health Care sectors. One of his focuses has been on security, and he has authored several white papers and design guides in various technologies. Mr. Durai maintains two Cisco Certified Internetwork Expert (CCIE) certifications in Routing and Switching and Security. Mr. Durai holds a Bachelor of Science degree in Electronics and Communication, a Master's degree in Electrical Engineering (MS), and Master's degree in Business Administration (MBA).

About the Technical Reviewers

Sunil Wadwani, M.S, M.B.A, is a technical marketing engineer for the Security Technology Business Unit (STBU) at Cisco. Sunil is a 20-year veteran of the technology field with experiences in the design, development, and provisioning of networking products. His career in Cisco began in 1992, when he was part of a design team developing the first version of the Cisco 7200 router. Sunil's primary responsibiliy today as a technical marketing engineer requires him to advise customers and sales engineeers on some of the deployment aspects of security products such as VPN, firewall, and IPS.

Sunil has an M.S in Computer Engineering from the University of California, Irvine, and an M.B.A from Santa Clara University. He lives in Saratoga, California with his wife Shalini and two sons, Shiv and Kunal.

Bryan Osoro, CCIE No. 8548, is a systems engineer with Cisco and has covered the small/medium business, large enterprise, and some service provider networks in the Pacific Northwest for the past five years. He also has spent time working in the TAC organization supporting a variety of technologies, including the PIX and VPN security devices. Mr. Osoro has been responsible for designing highly complex network environments with strict requirements for availability and reliability. He currently maintains four CCIE certifications in Routing/Switching, Security, Service Provider, and Voice. He is also a Certified Information Systems Security Professional (CISSP) and holds the Juniper Networks Certified Internet Specialist (JNCIS-M) certification.

Dedications

Ray Blair: As with everything in my life, I thank my Lord and Savior for his faithful leading that has brought me to this place. This book is dedicated to my wife, Sonya, and my children, Sam, Riley, Sophie, and Regan. You guys mean the world to me!

Arvind Durai: This book is dedicated to my wife, Monica, who pushed me in this endeavor, supported me during the long hours, and helped me achieve this goal—and to my son, Akhhill, who always gave me the extra energy that recharged me to work on this book.

To my parents, for providing me with values and opportunities.

To my brother and family, my parents-in-law, and brother-in-law and family for all their support and wishes.

Thank you, God!

Acknowledgments

Ray Blair:

This project was a significant undertaking, and without the support of those mentioned below as well as many others, this would not have been an achievable goal. I am very grateful for all your help and support in completing this book!

To my nontechnical wife, who was the initial reviewer, who suffered through reading technical material, finding errors and phrasing that didn't make sense, I will always remember your sacrifice and commitment to the success of this book—thank you!

Thanks to my children, Sam, Riley, Sophie, and Regan, for your patience in the many hours I spent working on this book and tolerating the "We'll do it after I get this book done" response. Let's go fishing!

Arvind, your excellent technical knowledge and the great working relationship that we have always enjoyed made writing this book a pleasure. I look forward to many more years as your colleague and friend.

Arvind Durai:

Thanks to my wife, who reviewed all my chapters several times during each stage of the book and gave me suggestions for improvement. She spent numerous late nights and early mornings working on the book review with me. I never felt alone. Thank you!

I would like to thank Andrew Maximow (director, Cisco Advanced Services), Uwe Fisher (manager, Advanced Services), and Naheed Alibhai (manager, Advanced Services) for supporting me in this effort. I also want to extend my thanks to all my peers with whom I worked on customer designs.

Ray, this book has been a great partnership. Your technical knowledge is awesome. You have been a great friend and colleague, and it is always a pleasure working with you.

Thanks to everyone who supported me directly or indirectly in every phase of the book. Without all your support, this book would not have been possible.

Our special thanks to:

We are very grateful to Bryan Osoro and Sunil Gul Wadwani. Without the talent of these two technical reviewers, the book wouldn't have been possible.

A big thanks to the product, development, and test teams within Cisco that provided answers to questions and prereleased code for testing: Reza Saada, Chandra Modumudi, Donovan Williams, Muninder Sambi, Munawar Hossain, Christopher Paggen, and Ben Basler.

The Cisco Press team was very helpful in providing excellent feedback and direction; many thanks to Brett Bartow, Christopher Cleveland, Dan Young, and Tonya Simpson.

Thanks to all our customers with whom we have worked. Each customer scenario inspired us to write this book.

Contents at a Glance

Contents

Icons Used in This Book

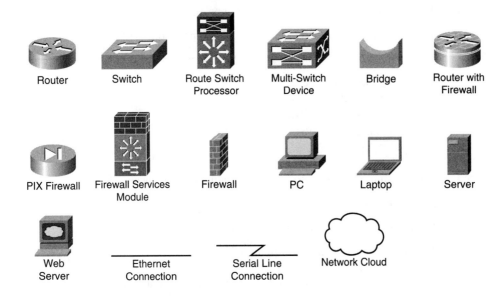

Command Syntax Conventions

The conventions used to present command syntax in this book are the same conventions used in the IOS Command Reference. The Command Reference describes these conventions as follows:

- **Boldface** indicates commands and keywords that are entered literally as shown. In actual configuration examples and output (not general command syntax), boldface indicates commands that are manually input by the user (such as a **show** command).
- *Italic* indicates arguments for which you supply actual values.
- Vertical bars (|) separate alternative, mutually exclusive elements.
- Square brackets ([ ]) indicate an optional element.
- Braces ({ }) indicate a required choice.
- Braces within brackets ([{ }]) indicate a required choice within an optional element.

Introduction

Firewalls are one of the main components used in securing a network infrastructure, and having an in-depth understanding of how these devices function is paramount to maintaining a secure network.

This book was written to provide an understanding of the functionality of the Firewall Services Module (FWSM), from both a hardware and software perspective and to be a practical design guide with configuration examples for the design, implementation, operation, and management of FWSM in various deployment scenarios.

Who Should Read This Book?

This book is targeted at individuals who would like an in-depth understanding of the FWSM. It is focused primarily for those who design, implement, or maintain the FWSM, such as security/network administrators. To get the most value from the material, the reader should have at least an intermediate knowledge of networking and security.

How This Book Is Organized

This book is organized into five sections that cover the basic introduction of firewalls, initial and advanced configurations, design guides and configuration examples, and features and functionality introduced in FWSM version 4.x code:

- **Chapter 1, "Types of Firewalls":** This chapter explains the functionality of the different types of firewalls.

- **Chapter 2, "Overview of the Firewall Services Module":** This chapter covers specifications, installation information, performance, and virtualization; shows a comparison of IOS FW, ASA, and FWSM; and also explains the hardware and software architecture.

- **Chapter 3, "Examining Modes of Operation":** This chapter examines the modes of operation (transparent/routed) and explains the advantages of each.

- **Chapter 4, "Understanding Security Levels":** This chapter explains how traffic flows between interfaces, using both NAT and PAT and routed and transparent modes.

- **Chapter 5, "Understanding Contexts":** This chapter provides an overview of the benefits of contexts and how to manage them.

- **Chapter 6, "Configuring and Securing the 6500/7600 Chassis":** This chapter explains how to configure the host chassis to support the FWSM.

- **Chapter 7, "Configuring the FWSM":** This chapter covers the initial configuration of the FWSM.

- **Chapter 8, "Access Control Lists":** This chapter examines the use of ACLs.

- **Chapter 9, "Configuring Routing Protocols":** This chapter explains the use of routing protocols on the FWSM.

- **Chapter 10, "AAA Overview":** This chapter covers the principles of using authentication, authorization, and accounting.
- **Chapter 11, "Modular Policy":** This chapter covers the use of class and policy maps.
- **Chapter 12, "Understanding Failover in FWSM":** This chapter explains the use and configuration of using multiple FWSMs for high availability.
- **Chapter 13, "Understanding Application Protocol Inspection":** This chapter covers the use and configuration of application and protocol inspection.
- **Chapter 14, "Filtering":** This chapter examines how traffic can be filtered using filter servers and how Active X and Java filtering function.
- **Chapter 15, "Managing and Monitoring the FWSM":** This chapter covers the different options of managing and monitoring the FWSM.
- **Chapter 16, "Multicast":** This chapter explains the interaction of multicast with the FWSM and provides some practical examples.
- **Chapter 17, "Asymmetric Routing":** This chapter provides an explanation of asymmetric routing and how it can be configured.
- **Chapter 18, "Firewall Load Balancing":** This chapter covers the options of how to increase performance using multiple FWSMs.
- **Chapter 19, "IP Version 6":** This chapter explains IPv6 and how it is configured on the FWSM.
- **Chapter 20, "Preventing Network Attacks":** This chapter examines how to mitigate network attacks, using shunning, antispoofing, connection limits, and timeouts.
- **Chapter 21, "Troubleshooting the FWSM":** This chapter explains how to leverage the appropriate tools to solve problems.
- **Chapter 22, "Designing a Network Infrastructure":** This chapter covers an overview on placement of the FWSM in the network.
- **Chapter 23, "Design Scenarios":** This chapter provides many practical examples of how the FWSM can be configured.
- **Chapter 24, "FWSM 4.x Performance and Scalability Improvements"**: This chapter covers the performance improvements in 4.x code.
- **Chapter 25, "Understanding FWSM 4.x Routing and Feature Enhancements":** This chapter explains the use of commands introduced in 4.x code.

PART I

Introduction

CHAPTER 1

Types of Firewalls

By definition, a firewall is a single device used to enforce security policies within a network or between networks by controlling traffic flows.

The Firewall Services Module (FWSM) is a very capable device that can be used to enforce those security policies. The FWSM was developed as a module or blade that resides in either a Catalyst 6500 series chassis or a 7600 series router chassis. The "tight" integration with a chassis offers increased flexibility, especially with network virtualization and the incredible throughput that is not only available today but will increase significantly with the introduction of the 4.x code train.

The look and feel of the FWSM is similar to that of the PIX and ASA. These products are all part of the same family, originating with the PIX and the "finesse" operating system. If you have had any experience with either the PIX or ASA, you will find comfort in not having to learn another user interface.

Having a good understanding of the capabilities offered by the different types of firewalls will help you in placing the appropriate type of firewall to best meet your security needs.

Understanding Packet-Filtering Firewalls

Packet-filtering firewalls validate packets based on protocol, source and/or destination IP addresses, source and/or destination port numbers, time range, Differentiate Services Code Point (DSCP), type of service (ToS), and various other parameters within the IP header. Packet filtering is generally accomplished using Access Control Lists (ACL) on routers or switches and are normally very fast, especially when performed in an Application Specific Integrated Circuit (ASIC). As traffic enters or exits an interface, ACLs are used to match selected criteria and either permit or deny individual packets.

Advantages

The primary advantage of packet-filtering firewalls is that they are located in just about every device on the network. Routers, switches, wireless access points, Virtual Private Network (VPN) concentrators, and so on may all have the capability of being a packet-filtering firewall.

Routers from the very smallest home office to the largest service-provider devices inherently have the capability to control the flow of packets through the use of ACLs.

Switches may use Routed Access-Control Lists (RACLs), which provide the capability to control traffic flow on a "routed" (Layer 3) interface; Port Access Control Lists (PACL), which are assigned to a "switched" (Layer 2) interface; and VLAN Access Control Lists (VACLs), which have the capability to control "switched" and/or "routed" packets on a VLAN.

Other networking devices may also have the power to enforce traffic flow through the use of ACLs. Consult the appropriate device documentation for details.

Packet-filtering firewalls are most likely a part of your existing network. These devices may not be the most feature rich, but when you need to quickly implement a security policy to mitigate an attack, protect against infected devices, and so on, this may be the quickest solution to deploy.

Caveats

The challenge with packet-filtering firewalls is that ACLs are static, and packet filtering has no visibility into the data portion of the IP packet.

TIP   Packet-filtering firewalls *do not* have visibility into the payload.

Because packet-filtering firewalls match only individual packets, this enables an individual with malicious intent, also known as a "hacker," "cracker," or "script kiddie," to easily circumvent your security (at least this device) by crafting packets, misrepresenting traffic using well-known port numbers, or tunneling traffic unsuspectingly within traffic allowed by the ACL rules. Developers of peer-to-peer sharing applications quickly learned that using TCP port 80 (www) would allow them unobstructed access through the firewall.

NOTE   The terms used to describe someone with malicious intent may not be the same in all circles.

- A cracker refers to someone who "cracks" or breaks into a network or computer, but can also define someone who "cracks" or circumvents software protection methods, such as keys. Generally it is not a term of endearment.

- A hacker describes someone skilled in programming and who has an in-depth understanding of computers and/or operating systems. This individual can use his or her knowledge for good (white-hat hacker) or evil (black-hat hacker). Also, it describes my golf game.

- A script kiddie is someone who uses the code, methods, or programs created by a hacker for malicious intent.

Figure 1-1 shows an example of a packet-filtering firewall, a router using a traditional ACL in this case, access-list 100. Because the ACL is matching traffic destined for port 80, any flows destined to port 80, no matter what kind, will be allowed to pass through the router.

Figure 1-1   *Packet-Filtering Firewall*

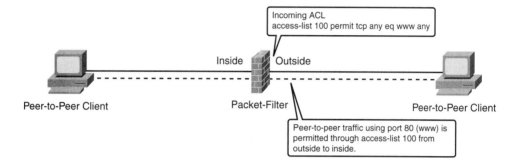

Given the issues with packet filtering and the fact that they're easy to circumvent, you may dismiss using them entirely. This would be a huge mistake! Taking a holistic approach and using multiple devices to provide defense in depth is a much better strategy. An excellent use of packet filtering is on the border of your network, preventing spoofed traffic and private IP addresses (RFC 1918) from entering or exiting your network. In-depth ACL configuration is beyond the scope of this book, but a good reference is RFC 2827.

Understanding Application/Proxy Firewalls

The following section uses the Open System Interconnection (OSI) model in the description of application/proxy firewalls and warrants a brief review. The OSI model describes how information is transmitted from an application on one computer to an application on another. Each layer performs a specific task on the information and passes it to the next layer. This model helps explain where functions take place.

The seven layers of the OSI model are as follows:

- **Layer 7 is the application layer:** It is the user interface to your computer (the programs), for example, word processor, e-mail application, telnet, and so on.

- **Layer 6 is the presentation layer:** It acts as the translator between systems, converting application layer information to a common format understandable by different systems. This layer handles encryption and standards such as Motion Picture Experts Group (MPEG) and Tagged Image File Format (TIFF).

- **Layer 5 is the session layer:** It manages the connections or service requests between computers.

- **Layer 4 is the transport layer:** It prepares data for delivery to the network. Transmission Control Protocol is a function of Layer 4, providing reliable communication and ordering of data. User Datagram Protocol is also a role of Layer 4, but it does not provide reliable delivery of data.

- **Layer 3 is the network layer:** It is where IP addressing and routing happen. Data at this layer is considered a "packet."

- **Layer 2 is the data-link layer:** It handles the reliable sending of information. Media Access Control is a component of Layer 2. Data at this layer would be referred to as a "frame."

- **Layer 1 is the physical layer:** It is composed of the objects that you can see and some that you cannot, such as electrical characteristics.

TIP   Use the following mnemonic to remember the OSI model: All People Seem To Need Data Processing.

Application firewalls, as indicated by the name, work at Layer 7, or the application layer of the OSI model. These devices act on behalf of a client (aka proxy) for requested services. For example, open a web browser and then pen a web page to www.cisco.com. The request is sent to the proxy firewall, and then the proxy firewall acting on your behalf opens a web connection to www.cisco.com. That information is then transmitted to your web browser for your viewing pleasure.

Advantages

Because application/proxy firewalls act on behalf of a client, they provide an additional "buffer" from port scans, application attacks, and so on. For example, if an attacker found a vulnerability in an application, the attacker would have to compromise the application/proxy firewall before attacking devices behind the firewall. The application/proxy firewall can also be patched quickly in the event that a vulnerability is discovered. The same may not hold true for patching all the internal devices.

Caveats

A computer acting on your behalf at the application layer has a couple of caveats. First, that device needs to know how to handle your specific application. Web-based applications are very common, but if you have an application that's unique, your proxy firewall may not be able to support it without making some significant modifications. Second, application firewalls are generally much slower than packet-filtering or packet-inspection firewalls because they have to run applications, maintain state for both the client and server, and also perform inspection of traffic.

Figure 1-2 shows an application/proxy firewall and how a session is established through it to a web server on the outside.

Figure 1-2   *Application/Proxy Firewall*

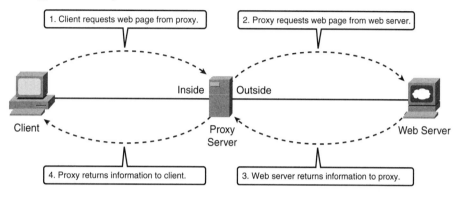

The step-by-step process, as shown in the figure, is as follows:

Step 1   The client attempts to connect to the web server located on the outside. For example, a user enters **www.cisco.com** in a web browser.

Step 2   The proxy server receives the request and forwards that request to the appropriate web server (www.cisco.com).

Step 3   The web server receives the request and responds back to the proxy server with the requested information.

Step 4   The proxy server receives the information and forwards it to the originating client.

NOTE   For simplicity's sake, Domain Name Service (DNS), Address Resolution Protocol (ARP), and Layer 2/3 information is not discussed in this example. This also assumes that the client web application has been configured with the appropriate proxy information.

Application/proxy firewalls can be very effective devices to control traffic flow and protect clients from malicious software (malware) and outside attacks. These firewalls must also run applications similar to the clients, which can also make them vulnerable to application attacks.

Understanding Reverse-Proxy Firewalls

Reverse-proxy firewalls function in the same way as proxy firewalls, with the exception that they are used to protect the servers and not the clients. Clients connecting to a web server may unknowingly be sent to a proxy server, where it services the request on behalf of the client. The proxy server may also be able to load balance the requests to multiple servers, consequently spreading the workload.

Advantages

To be really effective, reverse proxies must understand how the application behaves. For example, suppose you have a web application that requires input of a mailing address, specifically the area code. The application firewall needs to be intelligent enough to deny information that could cause the server on the far end any potential issues, such as a buffer overflow.

NOTE   A buffer overflow occurs when the limits of a given allocated space of memory is exceeded. This results in adjacent memory space being overwritten. If the memory space is overwritten with malicious code, it can potentially be executed, compromising the device.

If a cracker were to input letters or a long string of characters into the ZIP code field, this could cause the application to crash. As we all know, well-written applications "shouldn't" allow this type of behavior, but "carbon-based" mistakes do happen, and having defense in depth helps minimize the human element. Having the proxy keenly aware of the application and what's allowed is a very tedious process. When any changes are made to the application, the proxy must also change. Most organizations deploying reverse-proxy firewalls don't usually couple their proxy and applications so tightly to get the most advantage from them, but they should.

Another advantage of a reverse-proxy firewall is for Secure Sockets Layer (SSL) termination. Two significant benefits are that SSL does not burden the application server, because it is very processor intensive, and when decryption is done on a separate device, the plain-text traffic can be inspected. Many reverse-proxy firewalls perform SSL termination with an additional hardware module, consequently reducing the burden on the main processors. Figure 1-3 shows an example of a client on the outside (Internet, for example) requesting information from a web server.

Figure 1-3   *Reverse-Proxy Firewall*

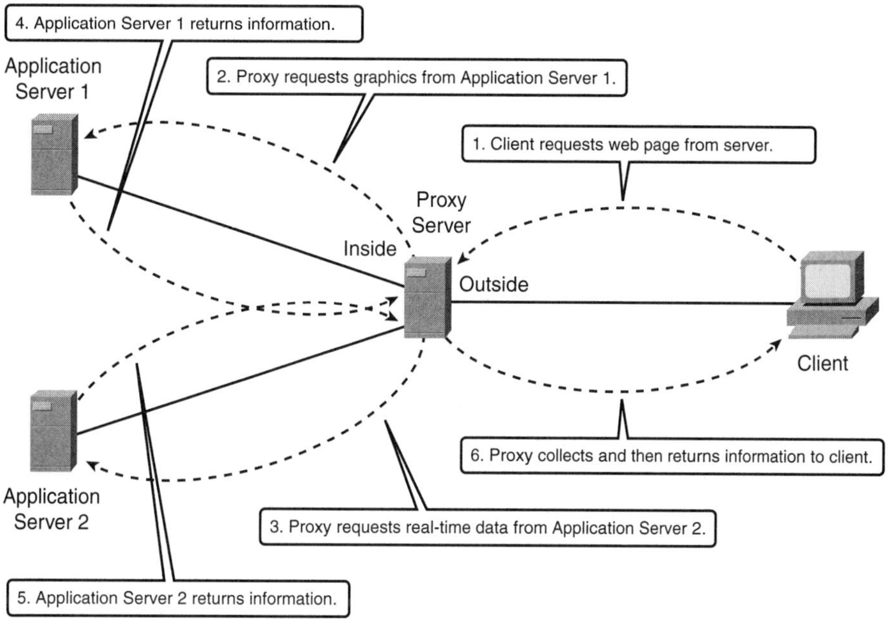

4. Application Server 1 returns information.

Application
Server 1

2. Proxy requests graphics from Application Server 1.

1. Client requests web page from server.

Proxy
Server

Inside

Outside

Client

6. Proxy collects and then returns information to client.

Application
Server 2

3. Proxy requests real-time data from Application Server 2.

5. Application Server 2 returns information.

The step-by-step process, as shown in the figure, is as follows:

Step 1   The client opens a web browser and enters the URL that directs
                  them to the associated proxy web server, requesting information.

Steps 2 and 3 The proxy server can have multiple locations from which to glean
                  information, in this example, it requests graphics from Application
                  Server 1 and real-time data from Application Server 2.

Steps 4 and 5 The proxy server prepares the content received from Application
                  Servers 1 and 2 for distribution to the requesting client.

Step 6   The proxy server responds to the client with the requested
                  information.

As you can see by the previous example, the function of a reverse-proxy server is very
beneficial in distributing the processing function over multiple devices and by providing an
additional layer of security between the client requesting information and the devices that
contain the "real" data.

Caveats

The same caveats that apply to proxy firewalls also apply to reverse-proxy firewalls, but with a much higher degree of visibility. Because reverse-proxy firewalls are generally providing a service to customers outside the organization, when access to these services is lost so is revenue in the form of access to critical information, such as patient data or product information. With that consideration, it's even more imperative to keep these services running.

Reverse-proxy firewalls aid in protecting and load balancing servers; they also provide a barrier between clients and critical applications through proxy services. Well-written proxy servers significantly reduce the risk of a security breach.

Utilizing Packet Inspection

Packet-inspection firewalls look at the session information between devices. Session information is typically protocol, new or existing connection, source and destination IP address and port numbers, IP checksum, sequence numbers, and application-specific information, such as command and response conditions in Simple Mail Transfer Protocol (SMTP).

A typical flow of traffic from client to server starts with a client initiating the connection to the IP address of the web server destined for port 80 (HTTP). The packet-inspection firewall determines whether that packet is allowed through the firewall based on the current rule-set. If the firewall has the capability to look into the data portion of the IP packet and determine whether it is legitimate Hypertext Transfer Protocol (HTTP) traffic, this process is considered a "deep-packet" inspection because it validates the payload. If all the requirements are met, a flow entry is created in the firewall based on the session information, and that packet is allowed to pass through the firewall. The web server receives the packet and responds accordingly. Return traffic is received by the outside interface of the firewall. The firewall determines whether the return traffic is allowed by comparing the session information (source and destination IP, port numbers, sequence numbers, and so on) with the information contained in the local translation table. If the return traffic matches the previous requirements, the IP payload can be inspected to validate appropriate HTTP compliance (deep-packet inspection), and then it is forwarded to the client.

Figure 1-4 illustrates a graphical representation of the process.

Figure 1-4   *Packet-Inspection Flow Diagram*

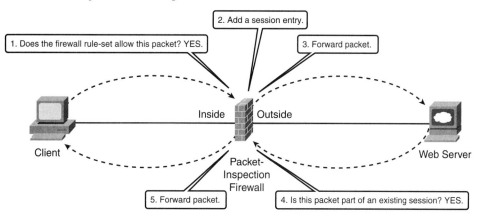

Packet-inspection firewalls are generally much faster than application firewalls because they are not required to host client applications. Most of the packet-inspection firewalls today also offer very good application or deep-packet inspection. This process allows the firewall to dig into the data portion of the packet and match on protocol compliance, scan for viruses, and so on and still operate very quickly.

Reusing IP Addresses

A feature that is common among all firewalls is Network Address Translation (NAT) and Port Address Translation (PAT) . NAT obfuscates the IP address scheme you are using internally, and the PAT function helps minimize the use of public address space.

Figure 1-5 shows how a firewall can be used to provide NAT and/or PAT functionality.

Figure 1-5   *IP Address Reuse*

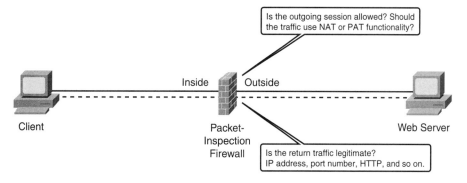

NAT

NAT provides the capability to change the source and/or destination IP address. This is common when private address space is used internally. NAT has a one-to-one relationship between inside and outside IP addresses.

Figure 1-6 shows two clients located on the inside of the firewall. Client 1 has an IP address of 192.168.1.2 and Client 2 has an IP address of 192.168.1.3. A NAT pool of addresses has been assigned to the firewall using IP addresses 172.16.1.2 through 172.16.1.254.

When Client 1 attempts to connect to the Internet, the firewall has been configured to take an IP address from the pool and change the client's source address to the address from the pool. Notice that when the connection passes through the firewall, the source address changed from 192.168.1.2 to 172.16.1.2 (the first address in the pool).

When Client 2 establishes a connection through the firewall, it will get the second address from the pool. As you can see, the size of the pool is directly proportional to the number of clients allowed through. When the 255th client attempts to make a connection through the firewall, the pool of addresses will have been completely allocated and the connection will be denied. This problem will be addressed in the next section, "PAT."

NAT functionality can also be configured statically, called "static" NAT (can you believe it). This feature permanently maps inside to outside or outside to inside addresses. This allows connections from the outside to be established to the inside, using a mapped IP address.

Figure 1-6   *NAT*

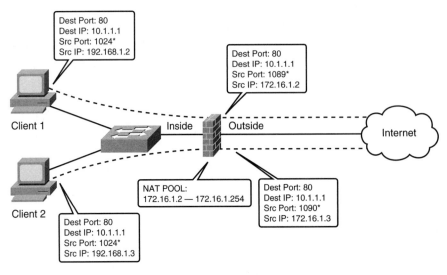

* Indicates an ephemeral port, which is a temporary port not currently
  in use. For Windows the ports are 1024 to 4999.

The use of shared NAT pools conserves valuable public IP address space and also supports applications that aren't very well behaved and opens random ports for communication. Static NAT will not conserve public IP addresses, but it provides a mechanism for clients on the public network (Internet) to access services that are privately addressed.

PAT

PAT, on the other hand, has a one-to-many IP address relationship. A common implementation is using a private address space internally but having only one public IP address; this could be the case on your home network. Translations are performed at the transport layer of the OSI model.

Figure 1-7 is similar to Figure 1-6, except that instead of a pool of addresses on the firewall, the firewall has been configured to translate the client addresses to the outside IP address of the firewall.

When Client 1 connects through the firewall, the firewall changes the source address of 192.168.1.2 to 172.16.1.1.

When Client 2 connects through the firewall, the firewall changes the source address from 192.168.1.3 to 172.16.1.1.

Both clients use the same IP address. If you are wondering how the firewall knows where to send the data back to, that is where the source port numbers come into play. The firewall creates a table that maps the appropriate source IP and port numbers to the translated source IP and port number. That way, when traffic returns to the shared outside address of 172.16.1.1, it knows the appropriate destination.

Figure 1-7 *PAT*

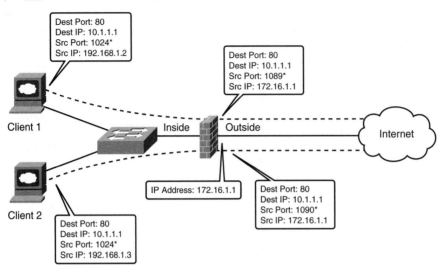

* Indicates an ephemeral port, which is a temporary port not currently
in use. For Windows the ports are 1024 to 4999.

As you can see, PAT gives you much better scalability from an IP usage standpoint, consequently reducing the number of public IP addresses required on the Internet. You will also see in Chapter 4, "Understanding Security Levels," how PAT can be used by clients to access multiple resources using the same IP address.

Summary

Three basic types of firewalls —packet filtering, application, and packet inspection—are designed to control traffic flows. The previous descriptions provide general functionality of the operation of these types of firewalls. Individual vendors may employ additional features; you should refer to their documentation for specific information.

You might be wondering where the FWSM fits. The FWSM is a packet-inspection firewall with many more bells and whistles that will be explained in the following chapters.

CHAPTER 2

Overview of the Firewall Services Module

The Firewall Services Module (FWSM) is a very sophisticated combination of hardware and software. The better understanding you have of the attributes and architecture, the better your ability to design, deploy, manage, and troubleshoot a security infrastructure.

Specifications

The FWSM is a single line-card/module that can be installed in either a 6500 series switch or 7600 series router (one to four modules are supported in a single 6500 or 7600 chassis—assuming slots are available). Dynamic routing is also supported through Routing Information Protocol (RIP), Open Shortest Path First (OSPF), or Border Gateway Protocol (BGP) stub in single-context mode. Enhanced Interior Gateway Routing Protocol (EIGRP) will also be supported in the 4.x code train. Table 2-1 and Table 2-2 provide additional requirements and specifications.

Table 2-1 *General Requirements*

Specification	Description	
Dimensions	1.18×15.51×16.34 inches (30×394×415 mm)	
Device requirements	6500 or 7600	
Environmental Considerations		
Humidity	10% to 90% noncondensing	
Storage temperature	–40°F to 167°F (–40°C to 75°C)	
Operating temperature	32°F to 104°F (0°C to 40°C)	
Heat dissipation	733.29 BTU/Hr	
Modules per switch	4	
Power requirements	4.09A, 171.78W	
Slot requirements	Any—except supervisor slot(s)	
Supported IOS for 3.1	Sup 720, 32	Sup 2
IOS	12.2(18)SXF and above	12.2(18)SXF and above

continues

Table 2-1   *General Requirements (Continued)*

Specification	Description	
IOS Modularity	12.2(18)SXF4 and above	Not supported
Catalyst OS	8.5(3) and above	8.5(3) and above
Weight	Minimum: 3 lb (1.36 kg) Maximum: 5 lb (2.27 kg)	

Table 2-2   *General Specifications*

Specification	Description
Backplane connection	6G/s with fabric module 32G/s with shared bus
Licensed features	Contexts 20, 50, 100, and 250 GTP/GPRS
Jumbo support	8500B packet
Memory	1GB RAM 128MB Flash
Security contexts	3

As you can clearly see from the specification in the previous two tables, good things do come in small packages!

Installation

Before you begin the installation of the FWSM, you should not only have a Phillips screwdriver and an antistatic strap, but if you are putting it in a production device, you should have a plan. Take into consideration the additional power required for the FWSM, which slot it should be placed in, whether the FWSM has a configuration that may cause a network outage, and so on.

Because the FWSM doesn't have external connections, consider placing it between modules that have many physical connections to provide an additional space to route cables. Also, if you ever plan to use a redundant supervisor, avoid slots that would be used for the redundant supervisor, if possible.

WARNING   Only qualified individuals should install or remove an FWSM. Serious injury or death could occur. Whenever you are working with AC or DC power, safety is always a concern.

Always use an appropriately connected grounding mechanism, such as a wrist strap, to prevent electrostatic discharge (ESD), and touch only the bottom edge of the module. If ESD precautions are not employed, you could damage circuitry, which may not be apparent immediately.

To install FWSM, follow these steps:

Step 1   Select a vacant slot.

Step 2   Remove the existing filler-plate by taking out the two Phillips screws.

Step 3   Open the ejector levers on the FWSM.

Step 4   Align the slides on the FWSM with the slot guides on both sides (top and bottom for Network Equipment Building Systems [NEBS]) of the chassis. That's shiny side down or left for NEBS.

Step 5   Insert the FWSM into the chassis until the ejector levers begin to close.

Step 6   Close both ejector levers simultaneously until they are flush with the front of the FWSM.

Step 7   Tighten both captive screws on the FWSM.

The FWSM supports hot swapping, which allows you to install or remove the module while the chassis is powered. To reduce injury and minimize any potential damage, it's always best to power down the chassis before installing or removing the module.

In addition, when removing the FWSM from the chassis, either depress the Shutdown button on the FWSM or issue the following command on the host chassis to gracefully shut down the FWSM:

```
Host-chassis# hw-module module <slot-number> shutdown
```

Verify that the status LED on the FWSM is either orange or off before removing the module.

Although we are all in a hurry to get our tasks completed, replacement and removal of valuable equipment should always be something we take great care with. Take your time; planning will save you pain in the long run.

Performance

The FWSM has both application and protocol inspection engines for stateful inspection of traffic and can handle up to 1,000,000 connections at a connection rate of 100,000 per second. A single FWSM supports more than 5 gigabits (Gbs) of throughput and more than 20 Gbs with four modules in a chassis. The FWSM supports 250 virtual contexts, which are unique firewall instances that can be in either a routed mode, transparent mode, or a combination of each. Table 2-3 and Table 2-4 show many of the capabilities and limitations of the FWSM.

Table 2-3   *Single/Multiple Context Mode.*

Specification	Single	Multiple
Authentication, Authorization, and Accounting (AAA) connection rate	80/sec	80/second shared
Access Control List (ACL) flow logging	32K	32K shared
Alias statements	1K	1K shared
Address Resolution Protocol (ARP) entries	64K	64K shared
Domain Name System (DNS) inspection rate	5K/sec	5K/sec shared
Global statements	4K	4K shared
Inspection statements	32	32/context
Multicast: Forwarding Information Base (FIB) entries	5K	N/A
Multicast: Internet Group Management Protocol (IGMP) groups	5K	N/A
Multicast: Protocol Independent Multicast (PIM) routes	12K	N/A
Network Address Translation (NAT) statements	2K	2K shared
Packet reassembly	30K	30K shared
Route table entries	32K	32K shared
Shun statements	5K	5K shared
Static NAT statements	2K	2K shared
Trivial File Transfer Protocol (TFTP) sessions	999,100	999,100 shared
User authenticated sessions	50K	50K shared
User authorization sessions	150K, 15/user	150K shared, 15/user

Table 2-4 *Single/Multiple Context Rule Limits (Based on 12 Partitions)*

Specification	Single	Multiple
AAA rules	6451	992
Access Control Entry (ACE)	72,806	11,200
ACE downloadable	5K	5K
Established rules	460	70
Filter rules	2764	425
Hypertext Transfer Protocol (HTTP), Internet Control Message Protocol (ICMP), Telnet, and Secure Shell (SSH) rules	1843	283
Policy NAT ACE	283	283
Inspect rules	5529	850

Although the FWSM has tremendous capabilities, recognize the limitations and avoid getting into a situation where the FWSM has been oversubscribed. For more information on ACL and ACE improvements using the 4.x code train, refer to Chapter 24, "FWSM 4.x Performance and Scalability Improvements."

Virtualization

Virtualization or multiple-context mode allows the FWSM to be logically separated into multiple unique firewall instances as shown in Figure 2-1. These individual instances or contexts have a unique set of policies, IP addressing, static routes, and configurations. Because each context is unique, using the same IP addresses is allowed. This provides tremendous flexibility when adding new services or customers that may need to be separated from other contexts because of a security policy or for management reasons.

Using virtualization, you can consolidate multiple firewall appliances into a single line-card on the host chassis. Considering that the FWSM supports up to 250 contexts, how much rack space, power, and cooling will that eliminate?

Many organizations are employing virtualization techniques, such as Multiprotocol Label Switching-Virtual Private Network (MPLS-VPN), Virtual Routing and Forwarding (VRF)-lite, and generic routing encapsulation (GRE), to logically separate applications, services, job functions, to provide a public transport, and so on. This gives them the advantage of not having to create a new physical infrastructure or manage complex access lists every time a function needs to be isolated from the others.

Virtualization techniques are not only being deployed in the campus and wide-area network (WAN), but also within the datacenter to logically isolate applications and services. Using the FWSM in this scenario is particularly advantageous because of the amount of space and power it saves.

Figure 2-1   *Virtualization (Multiple-Context Mode)*

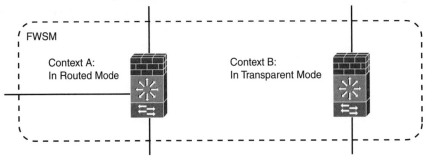

Comparing the FWSM to Other Security Devices

You should consider several factors when choosing the appropriate device to provide firewall functionality. These factors include the applications and security policies that need to be supported, device capabilities, future feature requirements, longevity of the product, cost, reuse, familiarity with the equipment, operational integration, training, and so on. Addressing the technical aspect is as follows—you are on your own for the rest!

The FWSM, Internetwork Operating System Firewall (IOS FW), Private Internet Exchange (PIX), and Adaptive Security Appliance (ASA) all provide similar capabilities in the support of stateful application and protocol inspection, Network Address Translation (NAT) and Port Address Translation (PAT), routing, content filtering, and user authentication and authorization. The FWSM does not support Virtual Private Network (VPN) termination except for use in management, whereas the PIX, ASA, and IOS-based devices all have that capability.

Obviously, creating a feature list that is completely inclusive is beyond the scope of this book. The objective is to provide a general guideline for selecting the appropriate platform to match the solution.

Choosing the appropriate security device requires that you not only have a good understanding of the scope of the project but of the capabilities of the hardware, too. Keeping up to date on the technologies will definitely help you be successful.

IOS FW

Routers starting with the 800 series through the 7600 (SX code) and including the 7200 and 7300 series and the 6500 series switch support IOS FW.

NOTE   Be sure to check the appropriate documentation for the specific hardware and software you plan to deploy.

IOS FW is usually deployed on branch office routers by customers that are looking for a one-box solution. IOS provides many other capabilities, such as voice gateways, GRE, Internet Protocol Security (IPsec), Advanced Encryption Standard (AES), Secure Sockets Layer (SSL), Virtual Private Network (VPN), Multiprotocol Label Switching (MPLS), extensive routing protocol support, and so on. By combining these additional features, routers running IOS FW provide incredible flexibility and the option to quickly add new services as business requirements change.

IOS FW is a general-purpose firewall and not as robust as the purpose-built FWSM; therefore, it cannot match the performance capabilities and features like stateful failover.

In addition to the firewall feature set, IOS provides incredible flexibility and should be kept in your arsenal to defend your network.

PIX

The origin of the FWSM is the PIX, which finds its roots in the Finesse operating system. Many similarities exist between the FWSM, PIX, and ASA, including inspection engines, configuration of access lists, privileged levels, interface security levels, and so on. The most significant differentiator besides the form factor is that the FWSM does not support VPN (IPsec, AES, and SSL) termination.

If you are considering a PIX today, a better solution would be the next-generation appliance, the ASA.

ASA

In addition to the capabilities of the PIX, the ASA also has the capacity of supporting the Advanced Inspection and Prevention Security Services Module (AIP-SSM). This is an inline Intrusion Protection System (IPS) used to detect and drop malicious traffic. The Content Security and Control Security Services Module (CSC-SSM) is the other module supported in the ASA. It provides antivirus, antispyware, antispam, antiphishing, and file and URL blocking, as well as URL and content filtering.

Placement of the ASA is generally at the network edge in small, medium, and large network deployments. With its integrated capabilities, it makes an excellent security device for protecting services such as e-mail servers, web servers, user traffic, and so on.

With the integration of the FWSM in the 6500 or 7600, locating these device within the datacenter or protecting resources internal to the network is very common.

Taking a holistic approach to firewall security and leveraging the capabilities of the IOS FW, PIX, ASA, and FWSM provide a defense-in-depth security strategy. A complete defense-in-depth strategy is beyond the scope of this book. For additional information on the Security Architecture for Enterprise (SAFE) documentation, go to http://www.cisco.com/go/safe.

Hardware Architecture

The architecture of the FWSM consists of four major components: Network Processors (NP) 1A (NP1A) and 1B (NP1B), Network Processor 2 (NP2), and the Processor running the FWSM code (FWSM-complex).

The FWSM is connected to the backplane of the 6500 or 7600 through a full-duplex 6-gigabit EtherChannel (GEC), totaling 12 gigabits of bandwidth using marketing math. A 3 Gb connection is established to NP1A and also to NP1B from the backplane.

One item of consideration is the use of GEC to load-share traffic. The GEC load-sharing algorithm by default for non-IP traffic is an exclusive-OR (XOR) of the source and destination Media Access Control (MAC) addresses, and for IP traffic it is an XOR of the source and destination IP addresses. This will cause the traffic flow from a single source to a single destination to use only one of the gigabit connections. If you are testing performance numbers, recognize that you will need multiple source/destination pairs for traffic to load-share across the GEC.

To determine how the EtherChannel is configured, use the **show etherchannel load-balance module** command as shown in Example 2-1.

Example 2-1 *Determining EtherChannel Configuration*

```
6500# show etherchannel load-balance module module-number
EtherChannel Load-Balancing Configuration:
        src-dst-ip
        mpls label-ip

EtherChannel Load-Balancing Addresses Used Per-Protocol:
Non-IP: Source XOR Destination MAC address
  IPv4: Source XOR Destination IP address
  IPv6: Source XOR Destination IP address
  MPLS: Label or IP
```

NP1A and NP1B can handle 3 million packets per second and perform Layer 2 checking by verifying that the destination of the frame is either the MAC address of the FWSM or a broadcast/multicast address. They also verify whether the destination IP address of the packet is associated with the FWSM.

Routing protocol packets and any non-Transmission Control Protocol (TCP)/User Datagram Protocol (UDP)/ICMP traffic will be sent to the FWSM-complex. A session lookup is done on TCP/UDP/ICMP traffic, and if session information is not available, one of four of the following will occur:

- If the packet is not a TCP Synchronize Sequence Number (SYN) (the first packet in the TCP 3-way handshake), it will be dropped.
- If the packet is UDP or TCP SYN, send it to NP2.

  If the packet is ICMP, verify against ACL or permit ICMP statement.

- If the packet is routing information, send it to FWSM-complex.
- If the packet is a fragment, send it to the virtual reassembly process on NP1A/B.
- Control messages are also sent to NP2.

If the session information is available, take the following action:

- If the packet requires "protocol-inspection," send it to the FWSM-complex.
- If the packet is network management associated with the FWSM, send it to NP2.
- If the packet is a fragment, send it to the virtual reassembly process on NP1A/B.
- Perform a packet rewrite and if necessary, modify TCP information and checksum (TCP protocol-inspection), execute NAT/PAT rewrite, add Layer 2 information, and send it to the host-chassis. Any traffic that follows this flow is said to be in the "fast or accelerated path."

NP2 can sustain 100K new connections per second. It also matches against ACL entries, performs route lookup, maintains the AAA cache, TCP intercept, Reverse Path Forwarding (RPF) checks, and translation address pool allocation. Traffic that follows this flow is in the "session management path."

Packets received from NP1A/B that can be processed on the NP2 will be returned to NP1A/B. Packet forwarding is based on the following criteria:

- If the packet is part of an existing session, TCP intercept, AAA updates, and so on are performed.
- If the packet has no session (TCP SYN, UDP, ICMP echo request), ACL checking, Destination Network Address Translation (DNAT), RPF check, route lookup to determine destination interface security level, and address pool allocation are performed. If it passes the previous checks, connection state information is built on NP1A/B (fast path) and if not, the packet is dropped.

- If the packet is destined for the FWSM-complex, a congestion control check is done to verify that the load of the FWSM-complex is able to handle the additional information, and if appropriate it's forwarded; otherwise, the packet is dropped.

The FWSM-complex performs Layer 7 protocol inspection, maintains routing information and neighbor adjacencies, and handles failover and the management interface. Because this is the software component of the FWSM, performance is dependent on the configuration and traffic patterns. Any processing done in the FWSM complex is in the "control plane or slow path."

NOTE   Traffic processed on NP1A or NP1B is considered "fast path." Traffic processed on NP2 is considered the session management path," and traffic processed on the FWSM-complex is "slow path."

Figure 2-2 shows a block diagram of the FWSM hardware. NP1A and NP1B are connected to the backplane of the 6500 via a 6-gigabit EtherChannel. They have connections to NP2 and the shared bus for all the processors. NP2 and the FWSM complex share a local bus.

Figure 2-2   *FWSM Hardware Architecture*

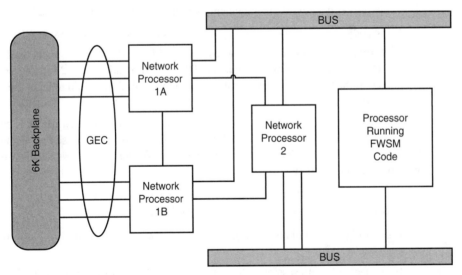

From a hardware perspective, the FWSM is a fairly complex animal. Understanding the packet flow through the FWSM and where each function is applied will give you a better understanding on where to place the FWSM in your network and help you to troubleshoot problems much faster.

Software Architecture

The other component to any computer-based system is the software. No matter how sophisticated your hardware may be, if it does not have an operating system, it is probably good only as a heater or paperweight.

Fortunately, the FWSM has lots of features that you can take advantage of and many "nerd knobs" that you can tweak. Understanding how the software handles traffic is fundamental, and you should spend a considerable amount of time in the next section to become very familiar with the software characteristics.

Input packets are first checked for fragmentation and, if required, will be reassembled before delivering to the "Mgmt/Routing" decision process. This process determines if the packet is routing information or is a management packet, such as telnet, SSH, or Hypertext Transfer Protocol Secure (HTTPS). If the packet matches this criterion and passes the interface ACL, it is sent to the session management process and handled accordingly.

If not, the third decision process (TCP/UDP/ICMP) separates non-TCP/UDP/ICMP packets from those requiring Destination Network Address Translation (DNAT), RPF check, and address pool allocation. An ACL check is also performed to validate the packet.

If the packet is part of an existing session, it is directed to the NAT process and sent out; otherwise, an ACL check is performed and if necessary the protocol-inspection process. The protocol-inspection process, previously known as the "fixup" protocol, inspects and modifies packets that require special attention, such as the following:

- **Computer Telephony Integration Quick Buffer Encoding (CTIQBE):** CTIQBE is a Cisco proprietary VoIP protocol used for Telephony Application Programming Interface (TAPI) and Java Telephony Application Programming Interface (JTAPI) to communicate with Call Manager.

- **Domain Name System (DNS):** DNS is used to convert a hostname or domain name into an IP address.

- **File Transfer Protocol (FTP):** FTP is a communication protocol used for exchanging files between computers.

- **General Packet Radio Service (GPRS) Tunneling Protocol (GTP):** This is used to carry signaling and user traffic between nodes.

- **H.323:** H.323 is the International Telecommunications Union (ITU) recommended method for multimedia communication.

- **Hypertext Transfer Protocol (HTTP):** HTTP is a protocol used for the transfer of information.

- **Internet Control Message Protocol (ICMP):** ICMP is used to exchange control, error, and information messages.

- **Internet Locator Service (ILS):** ILS is used to support Microsoft NetMeeting clients.

- **Media Gateway Control Protocol (MGCP):** MGCP is used for signaling and control in VoIP applications.
- **Network Basic Input/Output System (NetBIOS):** NetBIOS is a mechanism used for computers to communicate within the same Layer 2 network.
- **Point-to-Point Tunneling Protocol (PPTP):** PPTP is a tunneling protocol used to extend Point-to-Point (PPP) sessions across an IP network.
- **Remote Shell (RSH):** RSH is a UNIX command used to remotely execute commands.
- **Real-Time Streaming Protocol (RTSP):** RTSP is used to control data delivery of real-time traffic.
- **Session Initiation Protocol (SIP):** SIP is a signaling protocol used for multimedia sessions.
- **Skinny Call Control Protocol (SCCP):** SCCP is a Cisco proprietary protocol used for communication in VoIP applications.
- **Simple Mail Transfer Protocol (SMTP)/ Extended Simple Mail Transfer Protocol (ESMTP):** These two protocols are used for the sending and receiving of e-mail messages.
- **Simple Network Management Protocol (SNMP):** SNMP is a protocol used to manage and monitor network devices.
- **Structured Query Language SQL*Net/Net8:** These are used in client/server applications for database access.
- **Sun's Remote Procedure Call (SunRPC):** SunRPC is a function that allows a procedure to be run on another computer; it was developed by Sun Microsystems.
- **Trivial File Transfer Protocol (TFTP):** TFTP is a mechanism to transfer information.
- **X Display Manager Control Protocol (XDMCP):** XDMCP is used to set up X sessions with remote systems.

These applications either have embedded IP addresses in the data portion of the packet, open secondary channels, or require additional inspection of the data portion of the packet. Unless the firewall is aware of these "special applications," they may not work properly or may allow unnecessary access to applications.

As you might have noticed from the flow, packets that are part of an existing session are *not* checked by an ACL. What this means from an implementation perspective is that if you allow traffic to pass from one interface to another, it will be initially checked by an ACL, but the return traffic now part of a session will not be checked. Remember this aspect when allowing access to services or applications.

You can place these services on a specific interface and create a static entry that allows traffic from a lower interface (in regard to the security level, see Chapter 4, "Understanding Security Levels," for details) to a higher interface (in regard to the security level, which is where the services are located) without creating any ACL on the higher-level interface. Traffic will return because of the established session. Recognize also that traffic will not be allowed to initiate from the higher-level interface without an ACL. This function enhances the security of those devices by minimizing any carbon-based (human) configuration errors and not allowing someone with access to one of these devices to establish outbound connections for illegitimate purposes.

Figure 2-3 shows an overview of the decision process, which should help you understand the flow.

An ACL is still required when going from a higher-level interface to a lower-level interface. The point is that traffic matches an existing session first.

With an understanding of how, through which components, and in what order traffic passes through the FWSM, you will substantially increase your success in design, implementation, and troubleshooting.

Summary

The FWSM is a firewall line-card hosted in a 6500 series switch or 7600 series router chassis. It uses a 6-gigabit EtherChannel to connect to the host-chassis backplane, eliminating the need for any external connections. You can leverage your investment in hardware by virtualizing up to 250 firewall instances, reducing the number of appliances, saving rack space, and minimizing heating and cooling. Understanding the hardware and software capabilities is paramount to a successful implementation.

Figure 2-3 *FWSM Software Architecture*

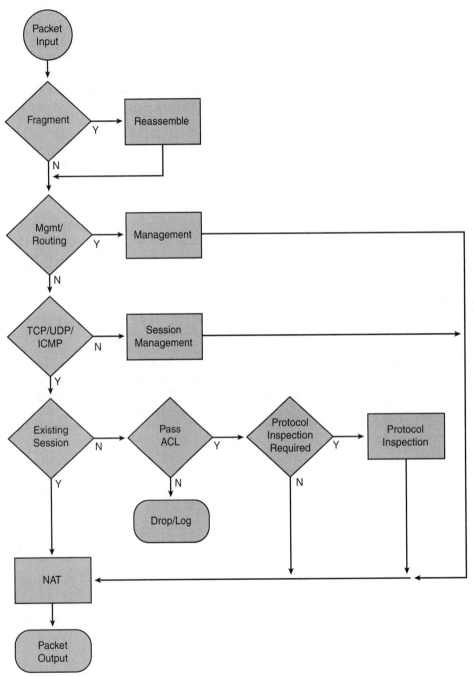

CHAPTER 3

Examining Modes of Operation

The Firewall Services Module (FWSM) has the capability to function in two modes: transparent and routed. With the introduction of version 3.1, mixed-mode operation is also supported. This allows the capability to have both transparent and routed contexts operate simultaneously on the same FWSM.

Working with Transparent Mode

The transparent mode feature on the FWSM configures the firewall to act in a Layer 2 mode, meaning that it will bridge between networks. Transparent mode helps provide a seamless transition when adding the FWSM into an existing infrastructure, by eliminating changes to the existing IP addressing scheme that otherwise would be needed.

With the FWSM configured for transparent mode, it acts as a "bump in the wire." This configuration, known as a bridge group, supports only an inside and outside interface, essentially bridging the networks together, as shown in Figure 3-1. Up to eight bridge groups are supported on the FWSM, unless it's configured for multiple contexts; then it's eight bridge groups per context. Any attempt to configure more than eight will result in the following error message:

```
ERROR: Maximum number of interfaces already configured.
```

EtherType Access Control Lists (ACL) allow non-IP protocols such as Internetwork Packet Exchange (IPX), AppleTalk, Multiprotocol Label Switching (MPLS), and even bridge protocol data units (BPDU) to pass through the FWSM. These unique access lists allow EtherType values of greater than 0x5FF, with the exception of BPDUs, which carry spanning-tree information. BPDUs allow switches on the inside and outside interface to form spanning-tree adjacencies, consequently making the FWSM appear as a physical wire, at least from a spanning-tree perspective.

Figure 3-1 *FWSM in Transparent Mode*

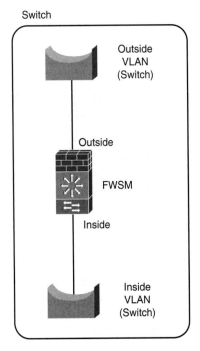

For example, if an EtherType ACL is created to allow MPLS traffic through the FWSM, no inspection of the MPLS traffic will occur. Even though MPLS frames carry IP traffic, the MPLS header must be removed before inspection can occur.

WARNING Be aware that traffic is not inspected if it matches an EtherType ACL.

Techniques for inspecting MPLS frames are discussed in Chapter 22, "Designing a Network Infrastructure," and Chapter 23, "Design Scenarios."

IP traffic and Address Resolution Protocol (ARP) (EtherType 0x0806) frames cannot be denied by an EtherType ACL; even with a specific match to EtherType 0x0800 for IP and 0x0806 for ARP, the traffic will still flow through the FWSM. Does this sound like a security risk?

IP and ARP frames cannot be denied by an EtherType ACL.

IP traffic must be explicitly permitted through the use of an extended access list. By default, all IP traffic is denied.

ARP traffic is handled by ARP inspection and will compare the IP address, Media Access Control (MAC) address, and source interface of ARP frames with the static entries in the ARP table (these entries are created manually). In the event of a mismatch, that frame will be dropped. If there isn't a match in the ARP table, there is a configurable option to forward the ARP frame out other interfaces. Use the following command to enable that feature:

```
FWSM (config)# arp-inspection interface_name enable flood
```

NOTE   ARP inspection applies to all bridge groups.

To manage the FWSM or the transparent context by means other than connecting through the host-chassis, a management IP address must be assigned to the Bridge-Group Virtual Interface (BVI) that's associated with the bridge group of the interfaces. The management address must also be a valid address related to the IP network and not an IP version 6 (IPv6) address.

If you have not used transparent mode in the past, this is one of those features to have in your "tool bag." With the capability to have both routed and transparent support on the same FWSM, it offers tremendous functionality.

Advantages

Operating the FWSM or context in transparent mode provides three significant advantages:

- The FWSM can be placed inline with the existing network.
- Routers on the inside and outside of the bridge group can establish a neighbor relationship via an Interior Gateway Protocol (IGP).
- Multiple types of traffic are supported.

Placing the FWSM inline results in minimal reconfiguration of other devices within the network. Because the FWSM operates in a bridge mode, it can be easily placed directly in front of or behind the default gateway, as shown in Figure 3-2, and IP addressing will not be required to change.

Figure 3-2 *Transparent Mode Inline Operation*

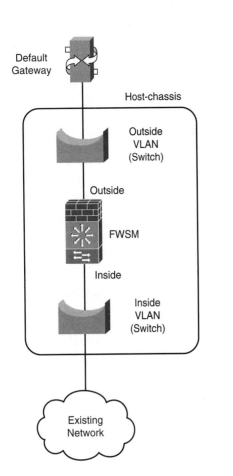 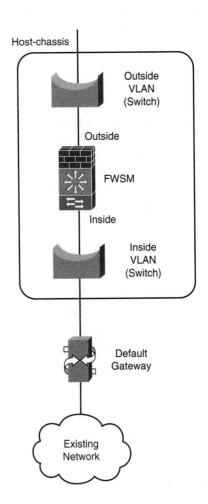

Establishing a neighbor relationship between routers on the inside and outside of the transparent firewall, as shown in Figure 3-3, eliminates the need to run a dynamic routing protocol on the FWSM. Because the FWSM doesn't support a dynamic IGP routing protocol in multiple-context mode, this is a great solution. Using a dynamic routing protocol also allows the IGP to quickly determine whether the path through the FWSM is operational. Taking advantage of multi-VPN routing/forwarding instance (VRF) or MPLS, the 6500 or 7600 Multilayer Switch Feature Card (MSFC) can support routing processes minimizing the need for additional routers.

NOTE Use VRF-lite to create routing instances on the inside and outside.

Figure 3-3   *Transparent Mode IGP Support*

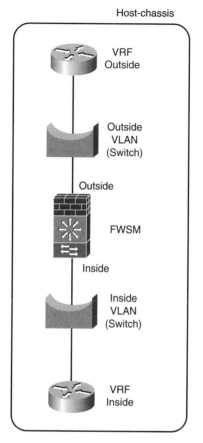

Host-chassis

VRF
Outside

Outside
VLAN
(Switch)

Outside

FWSM

Inside

Inside
VLAN
(Switch)

VRF
Inside

NOTE   Intermediate System to Intermediate System (IS-IS) and Cisco Discovery Protocol (CDP) are not supported with transparent firewalls.

If you are supporting traffic types other than IP (for example, IPX or allowing multicast through the FWSM with minimal configuration), transparent mode is an easy solution. Other options could include Policy-Based Routing (PBR), generic routing encapsulation (GRE), Multi-Topology Routing (MTR), and so on; however, these might require additional hardware and make the network configuration more difficult to manage.

Disadvantages

The three primary disadvantages of using transparent mode are the following:

- It may increase the size of your spanning-tree domain.
- Bridge groups cannot share an interface.
- Supervisor acceleration with 4.x code will not initially support transparent mode.

Adding to the size and complexity of a spanning-tree domain is never a good idea. Spanning-tree faults are very challenging to troubleshoot and with the addition of the FWSM, it will compound the difficulty. Don't get scared away yet—you can minimize the spanning-tree domain by adding a Layer 3 device (router or routing functionality) to the inside and outside interfaces. Using the MSFC and VRF-lite as shown in Example 3-3 will not require additional hardware.

In routed mode, VLAN interfaces can be shared. For example, you may have a situation where multiple contexts share the outside interface. In transparent mode, bridge-group interfaces cannot be shared. The solution is to connect multiple bridge-group interfaces to a Layer 3 device, such as the MSFC or external router.

If you plan to take advantage of the supervisor-based acceleration, explained in Chapter 24, "FWSM 4.x Performance and Scalability Improvements," the context will need to be configured in routed mode, at least until that feature has been added for transparent mode.

Traffic Flow

Access lists (EtherType and extended) authentication, authorization, and accounting (AAA) control what traffic is initially allowed to flow through the FWSM. Network Access Translation (NAT) translates IP addresses, and application layer protocol inspection inspects the traffic.

Consider the topology shown in Figure 3-4.

Figure 3-4   *Transparent Mode Example 1*

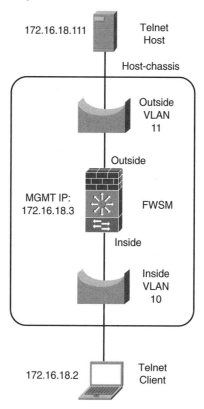

Example 3-1 shows the (nondefault) simple configuration for the FWSM.

Example 3-1   *ACL Example from Inside to Outside Using Transparent Mode*

```
FWSM Version 3.2(1)
!
firewall transparent
!
interface Vlan10
 nameif INSIDE
 bridge-group 10
 security-level 100
!
interface Vlan11
 nameif OUTSIDE
 bridge-group 10
 security-level 0
!
interface BVI10
 ip address 172.16.18.3 255.255.255.0
!
access-list TELNET extended permit tcp any any eq telnet
access-group TELNET in interface INSIDE
```

When a Telnet connection is established from the inside to the outside, the following occurs:

1 Given that the client (172.16.18.2) is not aware of the MAC address of the destination host (172.16.18.111) and vice versa, it will first send an ARP request.

2 When the FWSM receives the frame on the inside interface, the MAC address of the client is added to the MAC address table; it then forwards the ARP request on the outside interface.

3 The host on the outside replies to the ARP request.

4 When the FWSM receives the ARP response frame, it adds the MAC address for the destination host to its MAC address table and forwards the response out the inside interface to the originating client (172.16.18.2).

5 The host now begins the Telnet session by sending a SYN packet to the host on TCP port 23.

6 Because this is the first packet of a connection, the FWSM performs ACL check, AAA, and so on (refer to Chapter 2 for details) to validate that the packet is allowed through.

7 Assuming the packet is allowed, the FWSM records the session information and forwards the request on the outside interface.

8 The return traffic (SYN, ACK) from the host received at the FWSM is allowed to pass without an additional ACL lookup because it is an established connection.

9 The FWSM forwards the packet (SYN, ACK) to the client.

10 With an ACK response from the client, you can leave the rest up to your imagination.

Consider the topology shown in Figure 3-5.

Figure 3-5   *Transparent Mode Example 2*

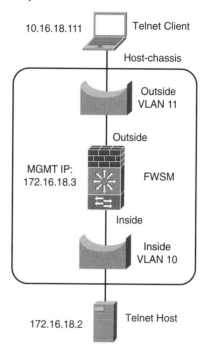

This example has a client on the outside initiating a Telnet connection to a device on the inside using static NAT, with the configuration in Example 3-2 on the FWSM (nondefault).

Example 3-2   *ACL Example from Outside to Inside Using Transparent Mode*

```
FWSM Version 3.2(1)
!
firewall transparent
!
interface Vlan10
 nameif INSIDE
 bridge-group 10
 security-level 100
!
interface Vlan11
 nameif OUTSIDE
 bridge-group 10
 security-level 0
!
interface BVI10
 ip address 172.16.18.3 255.255.255.0
!
access-list TELNET extended permit tcp host 10.16.18.111 host 10.16.18.2 eq telnet
static (INSIDE,OUTSIDE) 10.16.18.2 172.16.18.2 netmask 255.255.255.255
access-group TELNET in interface OUTSIDE
```

When a Telnet connection is initiated from an outside client to the inside device, the following occurs:

1 Given that the client (10.16.18.111) is not aware of the MAC address of the destination host (NAT 10.16.18.2) (real 172.16.18.2) and vice versa, it will first send an ARP request.

2 When the FWSM receives the frame, the MAC address of the client is added to the MAC address table.

3 The FWSM responds to the ARP with its local Bridge Virtual Interface (BVI) as the destination MAC address to 10.16.18.2.

4 The client on the outside now begins the Telnet session by sending a SYN packet to the host on TCP port 23.

5 Because this is the first packet of a connection, the FWSM performs ACL check, AAA, and so on (refer to Chapter 2, "Overview of the Firewall Services Module," for details) to validate that the packet is allowed through.

6 Assuming the packet is allowed, the FWSM records the session information and sends an ARP request for MAC address of the host 172.16.18.2 sourced from the BVI IP/MAC address.

7 The host replies to the ARP and the FWSM adds the MAC address to the MAC address table.

8 The FWSM translates the destination address from 10.16.18.2 to 172.16.18.2 and forwards the packet out the inside interface.

9 The return traffic (SYN, ACK) from the host is received at the FWSM, where the source is translated from 172.16.18.2 to 10.16.8.2. Then that packet is allowed to pass without an additional ACL lookup because it is an established connection.

10 The FWSM forwards the packet (SYN, ACK) to the client on the outside interface.

One very important point is critical to the connection being established. Both the client and the host must have routes to each other.

Additionally, you may have noticed that no ACLs exist on the inside interface. Because the connection is being established from the outside and the return traffic is part of an existing translation, it doesn't go through the ACL check process. This is a great way to configure access to resources from the outside but minimize the impact on the host in the event someone may have access to the console. Connections can't be established from the inside through the FWSM; consequently, other damaging applications can't be easily downloaded.

The way the FWSM handles traffic was explained in Chapter 2, and the practical examples just shown should give you a very good understanding on how access lists behave and how you can best take advantage of them to secure your infrastructure. One of the most important things to remember is that if a packet matches an existing flow, the ACL is never checked.

Multiple Bridge Groups

An efficient way to leverage the FWSM is through the use of multiple bridge groups. Bridge groups are Layer 2 firewall instances within a context. A maximum of eight bridge groups are supported on the FWSM in single context mode. Each bridge group is unique, having an individual inside and outside bridged connection. Figure 3-6 illustrates multiple bridge groups.

Figure 3-6   *Multiple Bridge Groups*

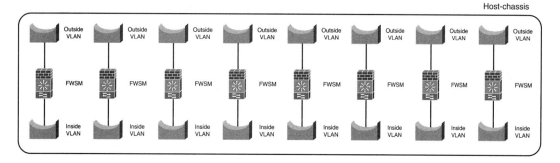

Although the bridge groups are isolated from each other, they share the same AAA configuration and logging information. This may not be acceptable in situations where security policies are distinctive to individual groups, departments, agencies, and so on, or where complete isolation is mandatory.

Management of a bridge group requires the assignment of an Internet Protocol version 4 (IPv4) address. To access the FWSM bridge group from a location other than the directly attached network, a static route must be added.

When the FWSM is configured for multiple contexts, eight bridge groups are supported per context. This provides tremendous scalability, as Figure 3-7 illustrates.

Figure 3-7 *Multiple Bridge Groups with Multiple Contexts*

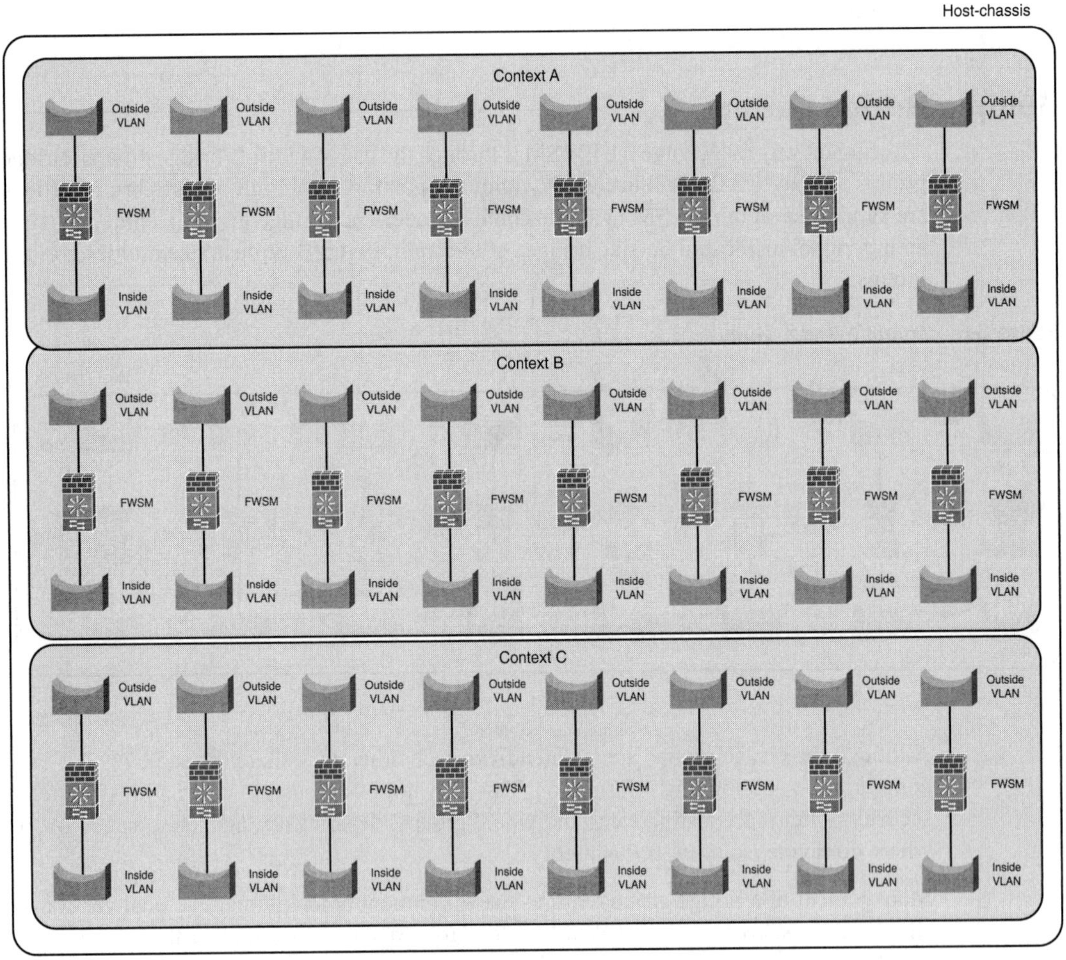

Rather than having to purchase a license for each bridge group, a license is per context. Doing the math shows that if you have 20 context licenses, you can support 160 bridge groups. This should give you plenty of growth potential.

Working with Routed Mode

With the FWSM configured for routed mode, as shown in Figure 3-8, it acts as a Layer 3 hop between networks, essentially performing like a router with advanced security features. Each network interface is unique to a subnet and requires an IP address that doesn't overlap

IP address space assigned to any other interface in single-context mode or within that particular context in multi-context mode.

Figure 3-8   *Routed Mode*

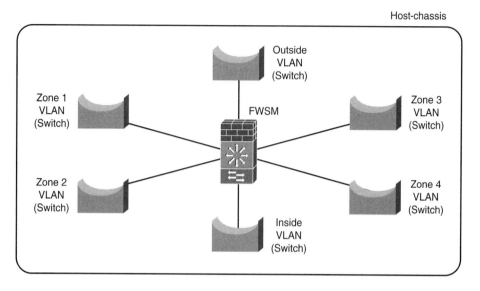

Open Shortest Path First (OSPF) and Routing Information Protocol (RIP) routing protocols are supported in single context mode only, with support for Enhanced Interior Gateway Routing Protocol (EIGRP) in version 4.x. Static and Border Gateway Protocol (BGP) stub routing are allowed in multi-context mode. For additional information, routing protocols are explained in detail in Chapter 9, "Configuring Routing Protocols."

NOTE   Only static and BGP routing protocols are supported in multi-context mode.

Use caution when enabling routing protocols on the FWSM. Make sure the routing protocols are authenticated. Also, if you are exchanging routing information from another domain, it is best to have unique routing instances on the untrusted interfaces and redistribute specific information between the two. This minimizes the impact of some nefarious individual injecting routing information in the FWSM and causing a denial of service (DoS).

Advantages

The two primary advantages of using routed mode are the capability to support multiple interfaces and the capability to route between those interfaces.

As shown previously in Figure 3-8, multiple interfaces provide the capability to connect multiple networks at Layer 3 and apply security policies that permit or deny particular traffic flows.

With the FWSM configured as a device supporting dynamic routing, routing updates can be exchanged dynamically between devices on multiple subnets. In the event of a link or device failure, notification is sent to the other devices participating in the routing updates, and network convergence can be achieved quickly. Remember, OSPF and RIP are supported only in single-context mode with the 3.x code train.

The use of a dynamic routing protocol can be extremely advantageous, especially when it is being used on the internal network—for example, the datacenter. Using a single routing protocol makes it easier to manage; it will be able to quickly react in the event of a topology change and eliminate the need for spanning tree as a failover mechanism.

Disadvantages

The primary disadvantages of using routed mode are the following:

- Limited routing protocol choices exist when using multiple-context mode and single-routed mode.
- The configuration can become very complex.
- Multicast support is limited.

If you plan to use multiple contexts, you can choose between static routes and BGP stub. Significant limitations to BGP stub exist (see Chapter 9, "Configuring Routing Protocols," for details), and static routes do not have the capability to propagate routing changes when a next-hop device is unavailable.

If single-routed mode is used, all the access lists for every interface, both inbound and outbound, appear in the configuration. The larger the configuration, the easier it is to overlook configuration mistakes. Careful attention needs to be exercised when adding, removing, or modifying ACLs.

Multicast support is limited to eight outgoing interfaces. In transparent mode, the FWSM does not need to participate in multicast.

Traffic Flow

In the example that follows, a client on the inside is connecting to a host (WWW server) on the outside using PAT on the outside interface, as shown in Figure 3-9.

Figure 3-9 *Routed Mode Example*

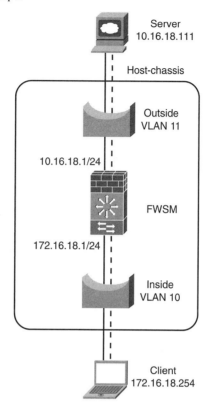

Example 3-3 shows the nondefault configuration of the FWSM.

Example 3-3 *PAT Example from Inside to Outside Using Routed Mode*

```
FWSM Version 3.2(1)
!
interface Vlan10
 nameif INSIDE
 security-level 100
 ip address 172.16.18.1 255.255.255.0
!
interface Vlan11
 nameif OUTSIDE
 security-level 0
 ip address 10.16.18.1 255.255.255.0
!
access-list HTTP extended permit tcp 172.16.18.0 255.255.255.0 any eq www
global (OUTSIDE) 1 interface
nat (INSIDE) 1 172.16.18.0 255.255.255.0
access-group HTTP in interface INSIDE
```

Given that this is a new connection and the FWSM, client, and host are not aware of one another, the following occurs:

1 The client (172.16.18.254) begins by sending an ARP request for the network gateway (172.16.18.1).

2 The FWSM adds the MAC/IP address pair of the client to its local ARP table and responds to the ARP request with its MAC address.

3 The client on the inside now begins the HTTP session by sending a SYN packet to the host on TCP port 80.

4 Because this is the first packet of a connection, the FWSM performs an ACL check, AAA, and so on (refer to Chapter 2 for details) to validate that the packet is allowed through.

5 Assuming that the packet passes the ACL check and is allowed, the FWSM records a session and sends an ARP request for the MAC address of the host 10.16.18.111.

6 The host responds with its MAC address, and the FWSM adds the MAC/IP address pair to its local ARP table.

7 The FWSM changes the source address of the client to the outside interface of the FWSM (10.16.18.1) and forwards the packet out the outside interface.

8 The host responds with an SYN/ACK to 10.16.18.1, and the FWSM changes the destination IP from 10.16.18.1 to 172.16.18.254 and forwards the packet out its inside interface. Because this is part of an existing session, the outside interface ACL is not checked.

9 The client receives the SYN/ACK and responds, consequently completing the three-way handshake.

Summary

The FWSM has the capability to operate in a routed mode or in transparent mode. Using 3.1 code, both functions are supported simultaneously, offering maximum flexibility. Transparent mode appears as a Layer 2 bridge and minimizes IP address changes when inserting into an existing network. In single-routed mode, the FWSM supports OSPF, RIP, static routes, BGP stub, and with the release of the 4.x code train, EIGRP will also be supported. When the FWSM is operating in multi-context routed mode, the routing options are limited to static routes and BGP stub.

References

RFC 826, "Ethernet Address Resolution Protocol"

Stevens, W. R. *TCP/IP Illustrated,* Volume 1: The Protocols. Reading, MA: Addison-Wesley, 1994.

CHAPTER 4

Understanding Security Levels

The fundamental premise of a firewall is to enforce security policies within a network or between networks. The FWSM uses security levels as a basic principle for the differentiation of interfaces in which the security policies are applied. This chapter helps to explain the intricacies of security levels and how they can be used to enforce your specific security requirements.

Security levels are numeric values between 0 and 100, assigned to an interface, with 0 being the least secure and 100 being the most secure. These values help to define a level of trust associated to an interface, specifically in how it relates to interfaces of different values. For example, the outside interface generally has a value of 0 and the inside a value of 100. An easy way to remember is 0 for outside. Security levels and names are required parameters for the FWSM to function.

NOTE   To help remember that 0 is the lowest security level, just think O (zero) for outside.

To assign a security level to an interface, use the following command:

```
FWSM(config-if)#security-level <0-100>
```

If the FWSM is configured for transparent mode, the security level is significant only if the same value is used on both interfaces. This will result in traffic being denied with the following message:

```
Deny inbound (No xlate)
```

For those who read the next section and wonder if the **same-security-traffic permit inter-interface** command works in transparent mode—it does. As a "best practice," use a security level of 0 for the outside and 100 for the inside.

In routed mode, it is also possible to configure the same security level on multiple interfaces. This also allows the capability to configure more than 100 interfaces on the FWSM. When this occurs, the interfaces with the same security levels are unable to exchange traffic. If this is not the desired behavior and traffic needs to be exchanged between interfaces with the same security-level, use the following command:

```
FWSM(config)#same-security-traffic permit inter-interface
```

A good use of the same security level on multiple interfaces is if multiple departments, agencies, companies, and so on exist that require access through the FWSM but not to each other. This minimizes the configuration because additional access control lists (ACL) are not required to disable communication between same-level interfaces.

The use of security levels is fundamental in the function of the FWSM. It helps to control the flow of traffic between interfaces of different levels and also between interfaces of the same level by either permitting or denying the traffic flows by default.

Traffic Flow Between Interfaces

If you are already familiar with Private Internet Exchange (PIX) or the Adaptive Security Appliance (ASA) code, you will notice a significant difference in that the FWSM requires ACLs on the higher-level interface for traffic to pass through to a lower-level interface. The PIX/ASA allows this behavior by default.

Traffic filtering is performed on both higher-to-lower and lower-to-higher security levels.

NOTE   Unlike the PIX or ASA, the FWSM requires an ACL on the higher-level inbound interface to permit traffic flow.

Only two inspection engines have dependencies on security-levels: Network Basic Input/ Output System (NetBIOS) and OraServ. NetBIOS inspection is used for outbound connections only, and OraServ inspection only permits the data connection from a lower to higher security level.

If the same security level is used on multiple interfaces, filtering, inspection, and the established command can be used bidirectionally.

To allow traffic to pass through the firewall from a higher-level interface to a lower-level interface in routed mode, the only requirements are IP addresses assigned to the interface, security level assignment, interface names assigned, and an ACL on the ingress side of the higher-level interface.

For transparent mode, the requirements are security level assignment, interface names assigned, both inside and outside interfaces assigned to the same Bridge Virtual Interface (BVI), and an ACL on the ingress side of the higher-level interface. As a best practice, add an IP address on the BVI interface for network management.

When you begin to configure the FWSM and attempt to pass traffic from a higher-level interface to a lower-level interface and it does not work, make sure you have an ACL in the higher-level interface that matches the traffic you are sending.

Network Address Translation/Port Address Translation

Network Address Translation (NAT) is the function of changing the source address and/or the destination address of an IP packet. NAT must also be performed in both directions. For example, if a connection is attempted from a client to a host and the client's IP address has been modified or translated, the host returns traffic to the translated address.

When a connection is attempted from the client to the host, as shown in Figure 4-1, the following NAT function occurs:

Step 1   The client with the IP address of 10.1.8.6 is attempting to connect to the host with the IP address of 172.16.8.27.

Step 2   The FWSM receives the packet and changes the client's address (source address) to 172.16.8.200, creates an entry in the connection table, and forwards that packet out the outside interface.

Step 3   The host receives the packet and responds back to the NAT IP address of 172.16.8.200.

Step 4   When the FWSM receives the packet, it changes the destination from 172.16.8.200 to the client's IP address of 10.1.8.6 and forwards that packet out the inside interface.

Figure 4-1   *NAT*

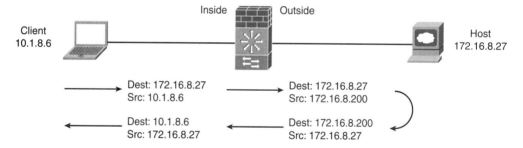

Port Address Translation (PAT) is the process of NAT (changing the source address, destination address, or source and destination addresses of an IP packet) combined with changing the source port number, destination port number, or both the source and destination port numbers.

Figure 4-2 shows an example of two clients sharing a single IP address (PAT) and how the connections are established. Both clients attempt to access the same host on the outside with an IP address of 172.16.8.200.

Client 10.1.8.6 example follows:

Step 1 The client initiates a connection to 172.16.8.200 using a source port generated by the client's operating system of 1024.

Step 2 The FWSM receives a packet from the client with an IP address of 10.1.8.6, and the FWSM changes the source IP address to 172.16.8.200 and the source port number to a value assigned by the FWSM. In this example, the port number assigned is 1116.

Step 3 The FWSM creates an entry in its local connection table and forwards that packet out the outside interface.

Step 4 The host receives the packet and responds to the translated IP address of 172.16.8.200 with a destination port of 1116.

Step 5 The FWSM receives the packet and modifies the destination IP address and port according to the information stored in the connection table. In this case the destination IP address is the client's IP address of 10.1.8.6, and the port number is 1024.

Step 6 The FWSM sends the packet out the inside interface to the client.

Client 10.1.8.7 example follows:

Step 1 The client initiates a connection to 172.16.8.200 using a source port generated by the client's operating system of 1024.

Step 2 The FWSM receives a packet from the client with an IP address of 10.1.8.7; the FWSM changes the source IP address to 172.16.8.200 and the source port number to a value assigned by the FWSM. In this example, the port number assigned is 1128.

Step 3 The FWSM creates an entry in its local connection table and forwards that packet out the outside interface.

Step 4 The host receives the packet and responds to the translated IP address of 172.16.8.200 with a destination port of 1128.

Step 5 The FWSM receives the packet and modifies the destination IP address and port according to the information stored in the connection table. In this case, the destination IP address is the client's IP address of 10.1.8.7 and the port number is 1024.

Step 6 The FWSM sends the packet out the inside interface to the client.

Both clients are using PAT to the same outside address and connecting to the very same host. The information within the packet that makes the connections unique is the port number.

Figure 4-2   *PAT Permits Multiple Devices to Share a Single IP Address*

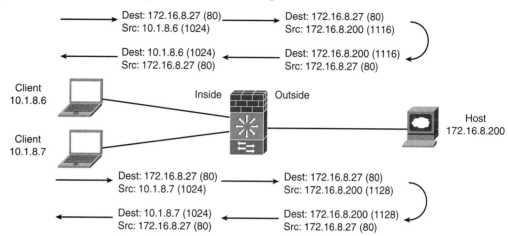

Both NAT and PAT reduce the number of Internet-accessible IP addresses, help provide additional security by obfuscating internal IP addresses, and can be used to solve problems from overlapping IP address space.

Although NAT and PAT have some significant advantages, as just shown, no good thing comes without a price. Applications that maintain IP information in the data portion of the IP packet, such as NetBIOS over Transmission Control Protocol/Internet Protocol (TCP/IP) (NBT), where NetBIOS frames are encapsulated in TCP/IP packets, and IP protocols without ports, similar to Encapsulation Security Payload (ESP), which uses IP protocol 50, may not function properly.

Fortunately, inspection engines incorporated in the FWSM and encapsulation methods for IP Security (IPsec) help to minimize the burden.

A resource limit of 266,144266,144 concurrent translations exists. The FWSM will create a NAT session for every connection traversing interfaces. To minimize the impact, NAT translations can be disabled for connections not requiring NAT capability. This is accomplished with the following command:

```
FWSM(config)# xlate-bypass
```

Finally, the NAT process can be configured to change the IP address to any valid IP address. It is not necessary to use an IP address assigned to the specific interface, but it is important for the devices being accessed to have a route to that specific address or range.

In most cases today, applications and protocols are better behaved, and for those that are not, the inspection engines within the FWSM will help mitigate the shortcomings. The advantages of using PAT to help reduce the depletion of valuable Internet IP address space is one very significant reason to take advantage of PAT.

Static NAT

Static NAT is used to create a permanent IP address mapping of a specific IP address (real IP address) or range to the translated address (global IP address) or range. The static mapping can be used only by the real address and not shared by other devices. When the real IP address originates traffic, it will use the static mapping only. The configuration command for a static map is as follows:

```
FWSM(config)# static (internal_if_name, external_if_name) | Global address overload
    from interface | Real IP address of the host or hosts | netmask netmask
```

For example:

```
FWSM(config)# static (INSIDE,OUTSIDE) 192.168.18.55 172.16.18.21 netmask
    255.255.255.255
```

This command maps the inside address of 172.16.18.21 to the outside address of 192.168.18.55. This means that if a device in the inside with IP address 172.16.18.21 establishes a connection through the FWSM, the address that it will be translated to would be 192.168.18.21. If the appropriate ACLs permit ingress traffic on the outside interface, a device on the outside would be able to establish a connection to 192.168.18.21, which would be translated to an inside address of 172.16.18.21.

NOTE   Make sure no duplicate IP addresses exist on the outside that would correspond to an inside address (inside 172.16.18.21 and outside 192.168.16.21), or you may be spending some time troubleshooting.

In Figure 4-3, the client on the inside has the capability to access the host on the outside, and the host on the outside has the capability to access the client on the inside.

Access from the client to the host is as follows:

Step 1   The client with the IP address of 172.16.18.21 is attempting to connect to the host with the IP address of 192.168.18.254.

Step 2   The FWSM receives the packet and changes the client's source address to 192.168.18.21, creates an entry in the connection table, and forwards that packet out the outside interface.

Step 3   The host receives the packet and responds to the translated IP address of 192.168.18.21.

Step 4   When the FWSM receives the packet, it changes the destination from 192.168.18.21 to the client's IP address of 72.16.18.21 and forwards that packet out the inside interface.

Access from the host to the client is as follows:

Step 1   The host with the IP address of 192.168.18.254 is attempting to connect to the client. With static NAT configured on the FWSM, the host will need to access the client's translated address, which is 192.168.18.21.

Step 2   The FWSM receives the packet and changes the destination address of 192.168.18.21 to the client's address of 172.16.18.21, creates an entry in the connection table, and forwards that packet out the inside interface.

Step 3   The client receives the packet and responds to the host's unchanged IP address of 192.168.18.254.

Step 4   When the FWSM receives the packet, it changes the client's source address from 172.16.18.21 to 192.168.18.21 and forwards that packet out the outside interface.

Did you notice that the host in the previous example believes that it is communicating with the client on the local subnet? The host would not even need to have a default gateway to make this work properly.

Figure 4-3   *Static NAT*

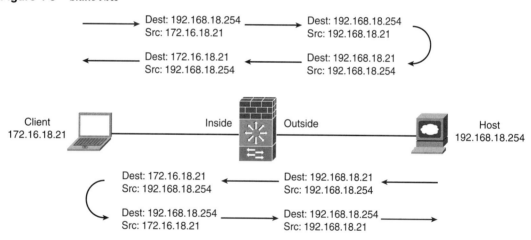

Additionally, groups of address can be translated with a single command:

```
FWSM(config)# static (INSIDE,OUTSIDE) 192.168.18.0 172.16.18.0 netmask
    255.255.255.0
```

Another capability is outside static NAT. This allows the mapping of an inside address to an outside address, as follows:

```
FWSM(config)# static (OUTSIDE,INSIDE) 172.16.18.254 192.168.18.254 netmask
    255.255.255.255
```

When a connection is attempted from the client to the host, as shown in Figure 4-4, the following outside NAT function occurs:

Step 1   The client with the IP address of 172.16.18.21 is attempting to connect to the host. With outside static NAT configured on the FWSM, the client will need to access the host's translated address, which is 172.16.18.254.

Step 2   The FWSM receives the packet and changes the destination address of 172.16.18.254 to the host's address of 192.168.18.254, creates an entry in the connection table, and forwards that packet out the outside interface.

Step 3   The host receives the packet and responds to the client's original IP address of 172.16.18.21.

Step 4   When the FWSM receives the packet, it changes the source IP address from 192.168.18.254 to the translated IP address of 172.16.18.254 and forwards that packet out the inside interface.

Figure 4-4   *Static Outside NAT*

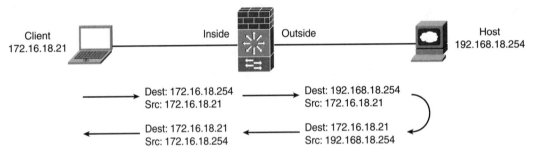

If you don't use this command very often, it might be difficult to remember. Here's a way that helps: for inside NAT, use **static** *inside-outside outside-inside* and for outside NAT, use **static** *outside-inside inside-outside*.

TIP   If you can remember that for inside NAT, use **static** *inside-outside outside-inside* and for outside NAT, use **static** *outside-inside inside-outside*, it might keep you from having to look up the **static** command every time you need to use it.

Because there is a static mapping of the address, devices on the lower-level interface can access the device on the higher-level interface. The appropriate ingress ACL entry on the lower-level interface is also required.

Some additional command parameters deserve an explanation at this time. These include the number of simultaneous TCP connections, the number of embryonic connections, Domain Name Service (DNS), norandomseq, Transmission Control Protocol (TCP), and User Datagram Protocol (UDP) options.

Number of Simultaneous TCP Connections

The number of simultaneous TCP connections is a parameter configured using the static command. The numeric value is specified as shown by the following command:

```
FWSM(config)# static (INSIDE,OUTSIDE) 192.168.18.0 172.16.18.0 netmask
  255.255.255.0 <0-65535>
```

The numeric value of 0 to 65535 specifies the maximum number of TCP connections either to or from the real IP address. For example, if the number of TCP connections is set to 10, and 8 inbound (from outside to inside) TCP connections are created, that device would be able to establish only two outbound (from inside to outside) connections.

If the TCP connection is unused (idle) longer than the timeout period specified by the **timeout conn** command, it will be closed. There may be situations where applications start an initial TCP connection but remain open for some time. If it is longer than the timeout period, this may cause the application to stop responding. As a solution, the timeout period can be increased.

When additional connections are attempted, the FWSM will block them and provide the following logging message:

```
%FWSM-3-201002: Too many tcp connections on xlate
```

Controlling the maximum number of established TCP connections can be a useful tool in protecting hosts or other resources on the network.

Number of Embryonic Connections

The number of embryonic connections is a parameter configured using the static command. The numeric value is specified after the number of simultaneous connections, as shown by the following command:

```
FWSM(config)# static (INSIDE,OUTSIDE) 192.168.18.0 172.16.18.0 netmask
  255.255.255.0 <0-65535> <0-65535>
```

The embryonic option is a subset of the number of TCP connections option and defines the number of TCP connections from 0 to 65535 that have not completed the three-way handshake. When the embryonic connection limit is reached, the FWSM will respond with SYN cookies to the hosts SYN requests. This will help mitigate a denial of service (DoS) attack on the device associated with the real IP address by not allowing the device itself to use up additional resources to handle the incoming SYN requests.

Are you asking yourself, "What are SYN cookies?" No chocolate chips in these, but they're just as good if you are a firewall.

When the FWSM receives a SYN request and the embryonic connection limit has been reached, the FWSM responds to the originating client with a SYN-ACK and an encrypted hash value of particular fields of the IP packet in the data portion of the packet; it then removes the SYN connection from the local translation table.

If the client responds with an ACK that contains the appropriate hash value, the FWSM initiates a connection to the device associated with the real IP address and binds the sessions. This process also minimizes the impact on the FWSM by dropping connections that may be from a DoS attack.

DNS

To rewrite the DNS record, you configure the option using the static command, as follows:

```
FWSM(config)# static (INSIDE,OUTSIDE) 192.168.18.0 172.16.18.0 netmask
  255.255.255.0 dns
```

Use the DNS option when translating to a device where client access is coming from multiple interfaces and the device and DNS server are on separate interfaces—for example, if a client and host are both on the inside interface and the DNS server is located on the outside (potentially an Internet DNS server). If the client attempts to access the host via a DNS entry without the DNS option, it will receive the IP address from the DNS server associated with the translated address on the outside. When the client attempts to access the host, the FWSM will deny the connection because of hairpinning the traffic on the outside interface. With the DNS option enabled, when the client requests the IP address of the host from the DNS server, the FWSM will modify the entry of the host to that of the inside (real) address. The client can then connect directly to the host without going through the FWSM.

This feature may be needed when you are using private address space internally and should be something you put in your memory bank for future reference.

Norandomseq

To disable TCP sequence number randomization, you configure that option using the static command, as follows:

```
FWSM(config)# static (INSIDE,OUTSIDE) 192.168.18.0 172.16.18.0 netmask
  255.255.255.0 norandomseq
```

TCP sequence numbers are used for the setup of a TCP three-way handshake. When a client communicates with a host, it sends an Initial Sequence Number (ISN). The host responds to the client with its own ISN and the original ISN in the packet. The problem lies with the hosts not performing an adequate function on randomizing the ISNs. Many operating systems use a constant to derive the "random" number. This obviously makes the "random" number easy to guess, and consequently allows an attacker to exploit.

Fortunately, the FWSM randomizes the TCP ISN of outbound traffic by default. Using the "norandomseq" option will turn off randomization and subject TCP connections to sequence number attacks—obviously not recommended.

For additional information on ISN, read RFC 1948.

TCP

The number of simultaneous TCP connections is a parameter configured using the static command. The numeric value is specified as shown by the following command:

```
FWSM(config)# static (INSIDE,OUTSIDE) 192.168.18.55 172.16.18.21 netmask
  255.255.255.255 tcp <0-65535>
```

This is the same option as "<0-65535> number of simultaneous TCP connections (tcp_max_conns)". When using the following command:

```
FWSM(config)# static (INSIDE,OUTSIDE) 192.168.18.55 172.16.18.21 netmask
  255.255.255.255 <0-65535>
```

Either method will result in the same command displayed in the configuration.

For example, when configuring the number of simultaneous TCP connections using the following command:

```
FWSM(config)# static (INSIDE,OUTSIDE) 192.168.18.55 172.16.18.21 netmask
  255.255.255.255 50 25
```

The configuration will be displayed as shown next:

```
FWSM(config)# static (INSIDE,OUTSIDE) 192.168.18.55 172.16.18.21 netmask
  255.255.255.255 tcp 50 25
```

Using the optional "tcp" parameter is up to you; the resulting configuration will be displayed with the "tcp" identifier shown.

UDP

The number of simultaneous User Datagram Protocol (UDP) connections is a parameter configured using the static command. The numeric value is specified as shown by the following command:

```
FWSM(config)# static (INSIDE,OUTSIDE) 192.168.18.55 172.16.18.21 netmask
  255.255.255.255 udp <0-65535>
```

The UDP option limits the number of UDP connections to and from the real IP device. The maximum number of connections is 65,536, which can also be represented by 0.

UDP is a connectionless method of communication, meaning that unlike TCP it has no built-in mechanisms such as sequence numbers and acknowledgments to keep track of session information. UDP data may be received out of order, not received at all, or possibly duplicated.

You might be asking, "Then isn't a 'UDP connection' an oxymoron?" Yes it is, but the FWSM maintains information based on the source and destination IP addresses and source and destination port numbers. In terms of the FWSM, this is referred to as a *connection*.

Static PAT

Static PAT is a very efficient way to utilize valuable public IP addresses. Static PAT is configured very similarly to static NAT, but as the name implies, it also provides the capability to translate based on the port number. For example, a single outside (global) IP address could be mapped to multiple inside (real) addresses using a port map.

The following commands use a single outside address (192.168.18.55) that clients can access; based on the port number accessed, it will redirect the connection to a variety of inside devices. A client can telnet to 192.168.18.55 on port 2023 and access the inside device 172.16.18.21, or telnet to 192.168.18.55 on port 3023 and access the inside device 172.16.18.253. Last, a client can open a web connection to 192.168.18.55 and access 172.16.18.83 on the inside.

```
FWSM(config)# static (INSIDE,OUTSIDE) tcp 192.168.18.55 2023 172.16.18.21 telnet
    netmask 255.255.255.255
FWSM(config)# static (INSIDE,OUTSIDE) tcp 192.168.18.55 3023 172.16.18.253 telnet
    netmask 255.255.255.255
FWSM(config)# static (INSIDE,OUTSIDE) tcp 192.168.18.55 www 172.16.18.83 www netmask
    255.255.255.255
```

Figure 4-5 shows an example of three clients on the outside of the FWSM connecting to three hosts on the inside of the FWSM. All the hosts are sharing a single IP address (PAT) and all are offering services.

Client 1 connects to Host 1 using Telnet:

Step 1   The client initiates a Telnet connection to the translated IP address of 192.168.18.55 using a destination port of 2023.

Step 2   The FWSM receives a packet from the client with a destination IP address of 192.168.18.55 and destination port of 2023. The FWSM changes the destination IP address to 172.16.18.21, the destination port number to 23 (Telnet), and changes the source port number to a value assigned by the FWSM. In this example, the port number assigned is 1114.

Step 3   The FWSM creates an entry in its local connection table and forwards that packet out the inside interface.

Step 4   The host receives the packet and responds to the original client's IP address of 192.168.18.48 with a destination port of 1114.

Step 5   The FWSM receives the packet and modifies the source IP address to 192.168.18.55 (the translated address), the destination port number to 1024, and the source port number to 2023, according to the information stored in the connection table.

Step 6   The FWSM sends the packet out the outside interface to the client.

Client 2 connects to Host 2 using Telnet:

Step 1   The client initiates a Telnet connection to the translated IP address of 192.168.18.55 using a destination port of 3023.

Step 2   The FWSM receives a packet from the client with a destination IP address of 192.168.18.55 and destination port of 3023. The FWSM changes the destination IP address to 172.16.18.253, the destination port number to 23 (Telnet), and changes the source port number to a value assigned by the FWSM. In this example, the port number assigned is 1167.

Step 3   The FWSM creates an entry in its local connection table and forwards that packet out the inside interface.

Step 4   The host receives the packet and responds to the original client's IP address of 192.168.18.83 with a destination port of 1167.

Step 5   The FWSM receives the packet and modifies the source IP address to 192.168.18.55 (the translated address), the destination port number to 1024, and the source port number to 3023, according to the information stored in the connection table.

Step 6   The FWSM sends the packet out the outside interface to the client.

Client 3 connects to Host 3 using WWW:

Step 1   The client opens a browser and enters the IP address of 192.168.18.55 (the translated address) using a destination port of 80 by default.

Step 2   The FWSM receives a packet from the client with a destination IP address of 192.168.18.55 and destination port of 80. The FWSM changes the destination IP address to 172.16.18.83, the destination port number remains the same, but the source port number is changed to a value assigned by the FWSM. In this example, the port number assigned is 1143.

Step 3   The FWSM creates an entry in its local connection table and forwards that packet out the inside interface.

Step 4   The host receives the packet and responds to the original client's address IP address of 192.168.18.99 with a destination port of 1143.

Step 5 The FWSM receives the packet and modifies the source IP address to 192.168.18.55 (the translated address) and the destination port number to 1024, according to the information stored in the connection table.

Step 6 The FWSM sends the packet out the outside interface to the client.

Although multiple devices on the inside provide services using the same IP address on the outside, distinction is made by the specific port numbers. Here is another great use of PAT saving Internet address space and reducing the risk to the host by allowing access to only one specific port.

Figure 4-5 *Static PAT*

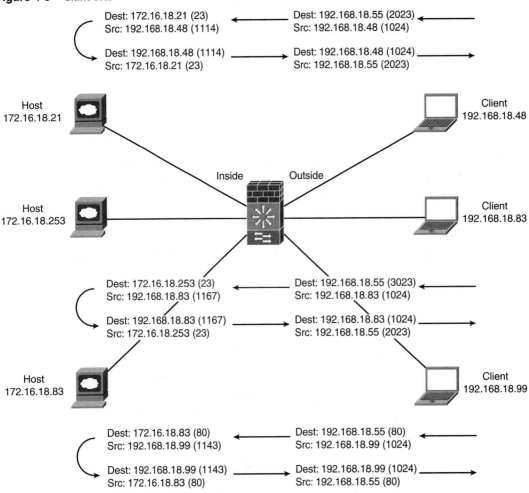

Dynamic NAT

With dynamic NAT, a pool of IP addresses is created using the **global** command. The FWSM then allocates these addresses to devices allowed to use the address pool. The benefit of using a pool is that real IP addresses will be translated to global IP addresses on a one-to-one basis. This provides the capability to support applications that require an individual IP address assignment and also allows for oversubscription of the pool. When a device with a real IP address initiates a connection, the FWSM assigns an IP address from the pool and maps it to the real IP address. When the pool of addresses have been depleted, no other connections are allowed, and the FWSM logs the following message:

```
%FWSM-3-305006: portmap translation creation failed
```

To alleviate the previous message, an additional PAT address can be added using the following commands:

```
FWSM(config)# global (OUTSIDE) 1 192.168.18.3-192.168.18.103
FWSM(config)# global (OUTSIDE) 1 192.168.18.104
```

When the NAT pool has been depleted, new connections will use the PAT address originating from 192.168.18.104.

Both dynamic NAT and PAT provide additional security by denying ingress traffic from the outside interface. Because no permanent IP address assignments exist, the FWSM will not translate an initial connection from the outside to the inside even with a wide-open ACL on the ingress of the outside interface.

Dynamic PAT

Dynamic Port Address Translation (PAT) is the process of NAT (changing the source address, destination address, or source and destination addresses of an IP packet) combined with changing the source port number, destination port number, or both the source and destination port numbers.

PAT translates real inside addresses to a single outside address. This allows many users on the inside to access resources on the outside using only a single IP address, consequently reducing the number of Internet IP addresses required. The disadvantage is that some applications may require a static port assignment and will not function properly using PAT.

Using PAT minimizes the depletion of valuable Internet IP addresses. If applications require a static IP address for security purposes or application requirements, configure those clients or hosts accordingly.

NAT Control

The FWSM configured with an inbound access list will allow traffic to flow from a higher-level to a lower-level interface. To force the FWSM to NAT traffic flows between these interfaces and provide additional security, the NAT control feature can be used. It requires real IP addresses to use a NAT function when traversing the FWSM from a higher-level interface to a lower-level interface. Traffic between same-level interfaces is permitted without NAT, assuming the "same-security-traffic permit inter-interface" has been implemented.

NAT control is implemented with the following command:

```
FWSM(config)# nat-control
```

If NAT control has been configured and a connection is attempted without a corresponding NAT statement, the FWSM will log the following message:

```
%FWSM-3-305005: No translation group found
```

If you are using NAT/PAT exclusively on the FWSM, it is always a good idea to add that extra measure of security. The NAT-control feature will mitigate the risk of devices being permitted across the FWSM from a higher-level interface to a lower-level interface without passing the NAT process.

NAT Bypass

There may be situations where NAT may be desirable for some hosts or applications and others where it is not, especially if NAT control has been enabled. There are three mechanisms to bypass the NAT function: NAT 0 or identity NAT, static identity NAT, and NAT exemptions.

NAT 0 or Identity NAT

NAT 0 allows for an individual or range of real IP addresses to be translated to a lower-level interface without translating the IP address. Sound strange? This provides the capability to pass the NAT-control requirement but not actually translate the real address. This connection must be established from the higher-level interface. Traffic originating from the lower-level interface is not allowed.

The NAT 0 function can be used by specifying the source addresses or through the use of an ACL that provides granularity to both source and destination IP address and source and destination port numbers.

```
FWSM(config)# nat (INSIDE) 0 172.16.18.21 255.255.255.255
```

Static Identity NAT

Static identity NAT is similar to NAT 0 in that the real IP address is not translated, but static identity NAT allows connections to be established from the lower-level interface and provides for port-level mapping.

A client on the inside can establish a connection to one host (192.168.18.254) on the outside using one address and to another host (192.168.18.253) using another address. Example 4-1 shows a static identity NAT example.

Example 4-1   *Static Identity NAT Example*

```
access-list HTTP-to-HOST extended permit tcp any host 192.168.18.254 eq www
access-list TELNET-to-HOST extended permit tcp any host 192.168.18.253 eq telnet
global (OUTSIDE) 1 192.168.18.55
global (OUTSIDE) 2 192.168.18.77
nat (INSIDE) 1 access-list HTTP-to-HOST
nat (INSIDE) 2 access-list TELNET-to-HOST
```

Figure 4-6 shows an example of a client with the address of 172.16.18.21 establishing a HTTP connection to a web server on the outside. The policy on the FWSM changes the client source address to 192.168.12.55. When the same client connects to a router at 192.168.18.254, a different policy will NAT the client address to 192.168.18.77.

This feature gives a tremendous amount of control in how translations are established, depending on the source and/or destination IP address and source and/or destination port numbers.

Figure 4-6   *Dynamic PAT*

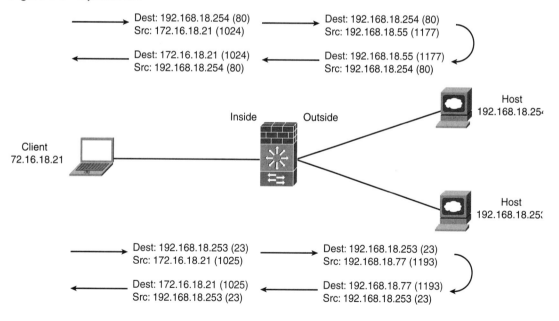

Summary

Security levels play a significant role in the FWSM. Many features and functions depend on the relationship of traffic flows from higher-level to lower-level interfaces, from lower-level to higher-level interfaces, and between the interfaces with the same security level. Network Address Translation (NAT) and Port Address Translation (PAT) are used to change IP addresses and/or port numbers. These features minimize the number of Internet-accessible IP addresses, add additional security by obfuscating internal IP addresses and can be used to solve overlapping IP address problems. There are several "nerd knobs" used to control how NAT and PAT behave, including connection limits, NAT 0, identity NAT, and so on.

References

RFC 1631—*The IP Network Address Translator (NAT)*
RFC 2663—*IP Network Address Translator (NAT) Terminology and Considerations*
RFC 1827—*IP Encapsulating Security Payload (ESP)*
RFC 1948—*Defending Against Sequence Number Attacks*

CHAPTER 5

Understanding Contexts

A context on a Firewall Services Module (FWSM) is analogous to a virtual machine in VMware or to a switch that supports multiple VLANs. Although you are using the same physical hardware, you can logically separate the firewall functionality into unique instances. This is also known as virtualization. Each context has a unique set of interfaces, rules, and/or policies applied.

Mixed mode contexts are also allowed, which enables the support of transparent and routed mode contexts simultaneously.

Figure 5-1 illustrates three separate contexts: "Context A," a routed mode firewall with seven interfaces, "Context B," a routed mode firewall with four interfaces, and "Context C," a transparent mode firewall. These contexts can be managed separately with completely distinct configurations.

Virtualization gives you the advantage of the separation of multiple physical devices but provides tremendous flexibility that you will learn about in this chapter.

Figure 5-1   *Context Overview*

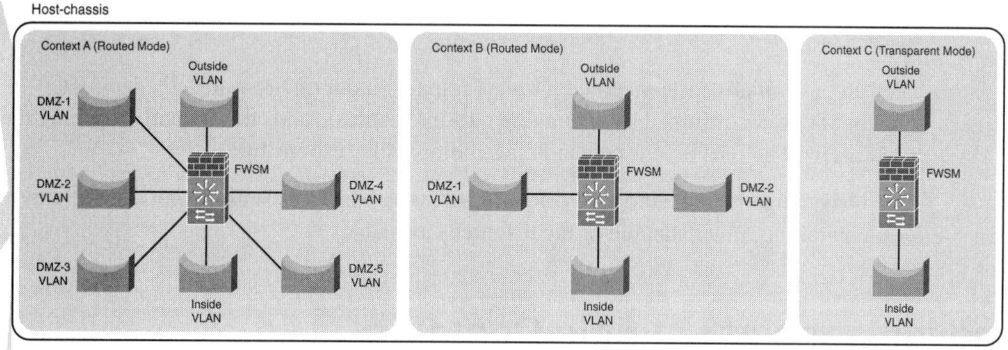

Benefits of Multiple Contexts

The benefits of using multiple contexts are the logical separation of security policies and leveraging the investment in hardware.

Separating Security Policies

Many organizations support multiple customers, departments, agencies, applications, and so on that not only require unique security policies but also require separation of those security policies. These security policies may be managed by different groups, which may need to be isolated.

Managing a single context with a single configuration and multiple groups will create a very complex rule set. Mistakes are more likely when working with a complex configuration. Separating the configurations into smaller more manageable components will make the job of administration much easier and consequently make your network more secure.

There might be other more compelling arguments to separate contexts, which could be driven by industry compliance or government regulations. Whatever the reason, supporting multiple firewall instances on the FWSM is a simple process.

Leveraging the Hardware Investment

Rather than install a new firewall every time a new customer, department, agency, application, and so on is added, creating a new context is very simple and does not require any additional rack space. The footprint of a device is a huge concern in locations where customers lease space by the rack unit (RU). Multiple contexts do not require additional space.

The "green" initiative is concerned with the impact on our environment. Reducing the amount of power consumed by leveraging multiple contexts and consequently reducing the hardware will help us do our part in being ecologically responsible.

If you have already made the investment in hardware, it makes sense to get your money's worth by taking full advantage of the resources available.

Disadvantages of Multiple Contexts

With the previous section touting what an incredible device the FWSM is, you are probably ready to install several of them right now. If you can believe it, there are some limitations. These are throughput, being limited to 1 gigabit/sec per flow, and the reduction in allocation of resources, because they are now shared. Fortunately, these issues will be addressed, at least to some degree, in Chapters 24, "FWSM 4.x Performance and Scalability Improvements," and Chapter 25, "Understanding FWSM 4.x Routing and Feature Enhancements."

Adding and Removing Contexts

The first step in adding contexts is to configure the FWSM for multiple-context mode using the following command:

```
FWSM(config)# mode multiple
WARNING: This command will change the behavior of the device
WARNING: This command will initiate a Reboot
Proceed with change mode? [confirm]
```

If you have a configuration worth saving, be sure to create a backup.

The number of security contexts is based on the license key. To verify the number of supported contexts on the FWSM, use the following command:

```
FWSM# show version
```

Look for the line that indicates the number of contexts:

```
Security Contexts         : 50
```

The primary context used for administration is the admin-context. From this context, access to the system execution space and all other contexts are available. Although the admin-context behaves like a regular context, extra precaution should be taken if you use it for anything other than a way to access management functions. As a best practice, use the admin-context for management only!

WARNING   The admin-context has full access to all the other contexts, extra precaution should be exercised if you use it for anything other than management access.

To specify which context will be the admin-context, use the following command:

```
FWSM(config)# admin-context ADMIN
```

The **ADMIN** name is a user-defined variable and can be named anything within the confines of the FWSM supported characters. That is, up to 32 characters in length and the words "system" and "null" are reserved.

NOTE   Throughout this book you might have noticed that user-defined parameters in configurations are capitalized. This makes the configuration much easier to understand, especially for those who are not as familiar with the FWSM configuration.

To create the admin context, use the following command:

```
FWSM(config)# context ADMIN
```

Again, the name that is defined must match the previous command.

Assign interfaces to the ADMIN context with the following command:

```
FWSM(config-ctx)# allocate-interface vlan# name_of_interface
FWSM(config-ctx)# allocate-interface vlan# name_of_interface
```

If the previous command is used with the optional "visible" parameter, the virtual local area network (VLAN) identifiers are displayed.

The **config-url** specifies the location of the configuration file. Unique to the admin-context is the requirement to have the configuration file stored locally. Other contexts may have configurations stored on Hypertext Transfer Protocol (HTTP), Hypertext Transfer Protocol Secure (HTTPS), Trivial File Transfer Protocol (TFTP), File Transfer Protocol (FTP) servers, or on the local flash.

```
FWSM(config-ctx)# config-url disk:/ADMIN.CFG
```

Interface assignment must happen before the **config-url**. If **config-url** loads the configuration file and the interfaces are not defined, commands specific to the interfaces will not function properly.

Configuring the FWSM to support multiple contexts is relatively easy, but don't forget that a reboot is required. Pay close attention to the "admin" context because it provides full access to all other contexts and shouldn't be used for controlling user traffic.

Adding a Context

Now that the admin-context has been created and a way exists to administer the FWSM directly, additional contexts can be added. Each new context will now have the benefit of unique policies associated to control the flow of traffic, besides being able to be managed individually.

New contexts are added with the following commands:

```
FWSM(config)# context context_name
FWSM(config-ctx)# allocate-interface vlan# name_of_interface
FWSM(config-ctx)# allocate-interface vlan# name_of_interface
FWSM(config-ctx)# config-url location_of_file file_name
```

The number of contexts you are allowed to create is based on the "Security Contexts" license; use the **show version** command if you are curious how many you can create. Don't forget to add the **config-url** statement, or you will not be able to manage the context.

Removing a Context

Be extremely cautious when removing contexts, or you may be scrambling to get services back up and functional. There is one command to remove a context, as follows:

```
FWSM(config)# no context context_name
WARNING: Removing context 'context_name'
Proceed with removing the context? [confirm]
Removing context 'context_name' (4)... Done
```

If you do inadvertently remove a context and need to get it back, hopefully you saved the configuration file. When you re-create the context, the previous configuration will be installed when you add the **config-url** statement—just be sure to have the interfaces allocated or the entire configuration will not be added.

Storing Configuration Files

The configuration file can be stored on the local flash, FTP, HTTP, HTTPS, or TFTP servers. If the configuration files are stored anywhere other than the local flash, the server(s) must be accessible by the admin-context.

The location of the configuration file is stored under the context as follows:

```
FWSM(config)# context context_name
FWSM(config-ctx)# config-url location_of_file file_name
```

The usage for the options are the following:

Flash

> disk:/[*path*/]*filename*]

FTP

> ftp://[*user*[:*password*]@]*server*[:*port*]/[*path*/]*filename*[;*type=xx*]
> type=*xx*, where xx represents one of the following options:
> ap - ASCII passive mode
> an - ASCII normal mode
> ip - Binary passive mode
> in - Binary normal mode

HTTP and HTTPS

> http[s]://[*user*[:*password*]@]*server*[:*port*]/[*path*/]*filename*]

TFTP

> tftp://[*user*[:*password*]@]*server*[:*port*]/[*path*/]*filename*[;int=*interface_name*]
> If the TFTP server is connected beyond a Layer 3 boundary, the interface parameter will override the route statement and send traffic out the specified interface.

To display a list of contexts that have been created, from the system execution space use the following command:

```
FWSM# show context [name | detail | count]
```

Following is an example of an admin context and two user contexts. Both **ADMIN** and **CustA** are in routed mode, and **CustB** is in transparent mode. Notice also the VLAN assignments and the URL location.

```
FWSM# show context
Context Name    Class       Interfaces          Mode        URL
*ADMIN          default     Vlan10,Vlan11       Routed      disk:/ADMIN.cfg
 CustA          CRITICAL-A  Vlan12,Vlan13,Vlan14 Routed     disk:/CustA.cfg
 CustB          NON-CRITIC  Vlan15,Vlan16       Transparent disk:/CustB.cfg
Total active Security Contexts: 3
```

You have several options for where to save the configuration file. The most important item to mention is that you should always maintain a current copy of the configuration in the event of a catastrophic failure.

Changing Between Contexts

Changing between contexts is a very simple process. The **changeto** command has two options: changing to the system execution space using the following command:

```
changeto system
```

or changing to a user-defined context, including the admin-context, with the following command (the context name is case sensitive):

```
changeto context context_name
```

To change between contexts, you must have initially connected to the admin context or the system execution space from the switch.

If command authorization has been configured on the target context and adequate privileges are not available, you can change login user with the **login** command.

In a context, you can verify which context you are currently in by looking at the prompt and the **show context detail** command, which provides details including the state of the context, where the configuration file is maintained, the assigned interfaces, and the resource management class:

```
FWSM/CustA(config)# show context detail
Context "CustA", is active
  Config URL: disk:/CustA.cfg
  Interfaces: Vlan12, Vlan13, Vlan14
  Class: default, Flags: 0x00001855, ID: 2
```

Comparing the output with the system configuration section for that context, you notice that the interfaces use the VLAN description, this is because of the keyword **visible**.

```
context CustA
  allocate-interface Vlan12 visible
  allocate-interface Vlan13 visible
  allocate-interface Vlan14 visible
  config-url disk:/CustA.cfg
```

Context for **CustB** does not use the visible option; consequently, the interfaces use names defined in the system configuration.

```
FWSM/CustB(config)# show context detail
Context "CustB", is active
  Config URL: disk:/CustB.cfg
  Interfaces: INSIDE_CustA, OUTSIDE_CustA
  Class: default, Flags: 0x00001855, ID: 3
```

This is the system configuration for context CustB:

```
context CustB
  allocate-interface Vlan15 INSIDE_CustA
  allocate-interface Vlan16 OUTSIDE_CustA
  config-url disk:/CustB.cfg
```

As an administrator of the FWSM using the command-line interface (CLI), the **changeto** command will become second nature. Depending on how you would like to view the interfaces of a context, you can use the "visible" option to display the actual VLAN identifier. This may save you a couple of commands to verify the associated VLANs in a context.

Understanding Resource Management

Resource management is one of the most critical aspects to the administration of the FWSM. Although the FWSM is a very high-performance device, it does have a finite limit of resources. As contexts are added, it becomes even more imperative to understand and allocate resource appropriately, or some services may suffer.

Classes are used to specify resource limits. After the limits have been defined, they can then be associated to a context or group of contexts. The FWSM will not prevent you from oversubscribing resources! This can be beneficial if you are providing firewall services for contexts that are not mission critical or where a service level agreement (SLA) does not warrant providing that degree of service.

WARNING   Resources associated with a group of contexts can be oversubscribed.

All contexts are assigned to the "default" class, which has unlimited access to the FWSM resources, unless explicitly changed. When new classes are created and options have not been defined, the undefined values are taken from the "default" class. For example, if you create a new context and configure only options for the number of Adaptive Security Device Manager (ASDM) connections, all the other parameters are inherited from the "default" class.

To create a class, use the following command in the system execution space:

```
FWSM(config)# class class_name
```

The **limit-resource** options are available for the total number using the **limit-resource** command with the option keyword, and the rate per second, using the **limit-resource rate** command with the option keyword for the following parameters:

- **ASDM:** Adaptive Security Device Manager, graphical user interface (GUI)
- **All:** All resources
- **Conns:** The total number of connections allowed
- **Fixups:** The legacy name for inspection
- **Hosts:** The number of host entries
- **IPsec:** The number of Internet Protocol Security (IPsec) sessions for management
- **Mac-addresses:** The number of Media Access Control (MAC) address entries
- **SSH:** The number of Secure Shell (SSH) sessions for management
- **Syslogs:** The number of syslog events
- **Telnet:** The number of Telnet sessions for management
- **Xlates:** The total number of translations allowed

Now that the class has been created, it can be applied to a context using the following commands in system execution space:

```
FWSM(config)# context context_name
FWSM(config-ctx)# member class_name
```

As you begin to utilize resource on the FWSM to its full potential, how they are allocated among classes and how contexts are associated with each class become important.

Memory Partitions

The FWSM has a pool of resources (memory) in which to allocate ACL memory to partitions. In multicontext mode, there are 12 memory partitions and two trees used for security policy rules exclusively: Uniform Resource Locator (URL) filtering statements, configured inspections, established rules, authentication, authorization, and accounting (AAA) authentication policies, remote access to the FWSM (SSH, Telnet, HTTP), Internet Control Message Protocol (ICMP) to the FWSM (configured using the ICMP CLI), policy

Network Address Translation (NAT) configuration, and access list entries. Each of the 12 partitions receives an equal distribution of those resources. There are primary (active) and backup trees that maintain the information in the partitions. The backup tree is a mirror of the active tree. It is switched to active mode after the compilation process is running. This process can run in the background without interrupting traffic currently switched by the FWSM. When the compilation has finished, trees are switched back again.

Starting with release 2.3, it is possible to modify the ACL memory space carving scheme. Instead of the default 12-pool model + 2 trees for downloadable ACLs, the administrator can choose to divide the space as business needs require.

A detail item list is located in Table 2-4 of Chapter 2, "Overview of the Firewall Services Module." Looking at the output of the **show resource acl-partition** from the system execution space, as demonstrated in Example 5-1, you can see that 14,173 rules are supported for each partition of the 12 partitions and that the three contexts that have been created each use one-twelfth of the total pool.

Example 5-1 *Default Access Control List (ACL) Resource Allocation*

```
FWSM# show resource acl-partition
Total number of configured partitions = 12
Partition #0
        Mode                     : non-exclusive
        List of Contexts         : ADMIN
        Number of contexts       : 1(RefCount:1)
        Number of rules          : 17(Max:14173)
Partition #1
        Mode                     : non-exclusive
        List of Contexts         : CustA
        Number of contexts       : 1(RefCount:1)
        Number of rules          : 17(Max:14173)
Partition #2
        Mode                     : non-exclusive
        List of Contexts         : CustB
        Number of contexts       : 1(RefCount:1)
        Number of rules          : 0(Max:14173)
Partition #3
        Mode                     : non-exclusive
        List of Contexts         : none
        Number of contexts       : 0(RefCount:0)
        Number of rules          : 0(Max:14173)
Partition #4
        Mode                     : non-exclusive
        List of Contexts         : none
        Number of contexts       : 0(RefCount:0)
        Number of rules          : 0(Max:14173)
Partition #5
        Mode                     : non-exclusive
        List of Contexts         : none
        Number of contexts       : 0(RefCount:0)
        Number of rules          : 0(Max:14173)
Partition #6
```

continues

Example 5-1 *Default Access Control List (ACL) Resource Allocation (Continued)*

```
        Mode                    : non-exclusive
        List of Contexts        : none
        Number of contexts      : 0(RefCount:0)
        Number of rules         : 0(Max:14173)
Partition #7
        Mode                    : non-exclusive
        List of Contexts        : none
        Number of contexts      : 0(RefCount:0)
        Number of rules         : 0(Max:14173)
Partition #8
        Mode                    : non-exclusive
        List of Contexts        : none
        Number of contexts      : 0(RefCount:0)
        Number of rules         : 0(Max:14173)
Partition #9
        Mode                    : non-exclusive
        List of Contexts        : none
        Number of contexts      : 0(RefCount:0)
        Number of rules         : 0(Max:14173)
Partition #10
        Mode                    : non-exclusive
        List of Contexts        : none
        Number of contexts      : 0(RefCount:0)
        Number of rules         : 0(Max:14173)
Partition #11
        Mode                    : non-exclusive
        List of Contexts        : none
        Number of contexts      : 0(RefCount:0)
        Number of rules         : 0(Max:14173)
```

Partitions 3 through 11 are just sitting there waiting for a context to be added. Yes, it is a waste of valuable resources if you do not plan to add more contexts. If there is a possibility of running out of resources, the partition space can be reallocated using the **resource acl-partition** command and specifying the number of partitions. This command requires a reboot of the FWSM.

After a reboot, the resource allocation has changed significantly: It went from 14,173 to 46,077, as Example 5-2 shows.

Example 5-2 *Modified Access Control List (ACL) Resource Allocation*

```
FWSM# show resource acl-partition
Total number of configured partitions = 3
Partition #0
        Mode                    : non-exclusive
        List of Contexts        : ADMIN
        Number of contexts      : 1(RefCount:1)
        Number of rules         : 18(Max:46077)
Partition #1
        Mode                    : non-exclusive
        List of Contexts        : CustA
```

Example 5-2 *Modified Access Control List (ACL) Resource Allocation (Continued)*

```
          Number of contexts       : 1(RefCount:1)
          Number of rules          : 18(Max:46077)
    Partition #2
          Mode                     : non-exclusive
          List of Contexts         : CustB
          Number of contexts       : 1(RefCount:1)
          Number of rules          : 0(Max:46077)
```

Notice that the partition 0,1, and 2 have ADMIN, CustA, and CustB assigned (respectively). You can specify which context is associated with a partition using the **allocate-acl-partition** command in the system execution space under a context.

```
context CustB
   allocate-acl-partition 2
```

What happens when another context is added? Glad you asked! It will share the resources of the next partition in the list. In this case it would be partition 0. Now, two contexts are sharing a partition. Because resources are allocated on a first come, first served basis, if one of the contexts is hogging resources, the other one is out of luck. Use caution when modifying these parameters.

```
Partition #0
      Mode                     : non-exclusive
      List of Contexts         : ADMIN, CustC
      Number of contexts       : 2(RefCount:2)
      Number of rules          : 19(Max:46077)
```

Now that the allocation has changed, you may be wondering how those resources are actually used. This can be viewed using the **show resource rule** command, as shown in Example 5-3.

Example 5-3 *Resource Rule Allocation*

```
FWSM# show resource rule

            Default  Configured  Absolute
 CLS Rule    Limit      Limit       Max
----------+----------+----------+---------
 Policy NAT    921        921       3333
 ACL         34560      34560      34560
 Filter       1382       1382       2764
 Fixup        4608       4608       9216
 Est Ctl       230        230        230
 Est Data      230        230        230
 AAA          3225       3225       6450
 Console       921        921       1842
----------+----------+----------+---------
 Total       46077      46077

Partition Limit - Configured Limit = Available to allocate
     46077       -      46077      =         0
```

Now you can see exactly how memory is allocated for each resource. Your next question might be, "Can I reallocate those resources as well?" The answer is yes.

To determine where the resources are being allocated, use the **show np 3 acl count** command and specify the partition number, as shown in Example 5-4.

Example 5-4 *Resource Rule Allocation*

```
FWSM# show np 3 acl count 1
-------------- CLS Rule Current Counts --------------
CLS Filter Rule Count       :          0
CLS Fixup Rule Count        :       3767
CLS Est Ctl Rule Count      :          4
CLS AAA Rule Count          :         24
CLS Est Data Rule Count     :          0
CLS Console Rule Count      :         18
CLS Policy NAT Rule Count   :          0
CLS ACL Rule Count          :      22400
CLS ACL Uncommitted Add     :          0
CLS ACL Uncommitted Del     :          0
```

If you need to increase a particular value for a feature, use the **resource rule** command in the system execution space. After the option parameter, you can use a numeric value or the keywords current, default, or max. The following options are available:

- **NAT:** The number of NAT entries
- **ACL:** The number of ACL entries
- **Filter:** The number of filter rules
- **Fixup:** The legacy name for inspection
- **Established (EST):** The number of established commands
- **AAA:** The number of AAA rules
- **Console:** The number of management access and ICMP rules

Following are some specifics when you use this command:

- You cannot exceed the "absolute max" for any value from the show resource rule command.
- When resources are reallocated, the total cannot exceed the "total default limit" from the "show resource rule" command. For example, if you need to add 1000 ACL rules, you will need to decrease the total of the other options by 1000.
- A change will affect all partitions! Make sure that a change in parameters will not adversely impact the FWSM.
- The changes take effect immediately.

Software release 3.1 significantly increases memory utilization—up to a 31 percent improvement. Table 5-1 provides a comparison between 2.3(4) and 3.1(2):

Table 5-1   *Memory Utilization: Software Release 2.3(4) and 3.1(2) Comparison*

Release 2.3(4)	Release 3.1(2)
FWSM# **show np 3 acl stats**	FWSM# **show np3 acl stats**
---------------------------	---------------------------
ACL Tree Statistics	ACL Tree Statistics
---------------------------	---------------------------
Rule count : 0	Rule count : 0
Bit nodes (PSCBs): 0	Bit nodes (PSCBs): 0
Leaf nodes : 0	Leaf nodes : 0
Total nodes : 0 (max 143,360)	Total nodes : 0 (max 184,320)
Leaf chains : 0	Leaf chains : 0
Total stored rules: 0	Total stored rules: 0
Max rules in leaf : 0	Max rules in leaf : 0
Node depth : 0	Node depth : 0

Summary

Virtualization is one of the fundamental elements of the FWSM. It provides the ability to logically separate firewall instances into contexts, consequently providing separation of policies and leveraging the investment in hardware. Be aware that a finite number of resources can be allocated to contexts; this may require some thoughtful consideration before implementation.

Initial Configuration

CHAPTER 6

Configuring and Securing the 6500/7600 Chassis

The FWSM isn't just a Power Sucking Alien (PSA) in the 6500/7600 chassis (host-chassis), it plays a critical role in the overall solution to securing your infrastructure. Proper "care and feeding" of the host-chassis is paramount, and following the best practices in this chapter will help to minimize a potential compromise of your network.

Understanding the Interaction Between the Host-Chassis and the FWSM

With the integration of the FWSM in a host-chassis, it becomes imperative to secure the host device. This is because the delineation of interfaces on the FWSM is associated with the virtual local-area network (VLAN) interfaces of the switch. The separation is logical not physical. If a misconfiguration occurs on the switch, traffic from a less secure interface (outside) may have uninhibited access to a more secure interface (inside). For this reason, you must consider the switch configuration and access to the host-chassis as critical as the FWSM configuration and access to the FWSM.

The host-chassis provides power and connectivity for the FWSM. In Chapter 2, "Overview of the Firewall Services Module," you learned that the FWSM is connected to the backplane of the host-chassis through a full-duplex 6-gigabit EtherChannel (GEC) connection and consumes 171.78 watts of power. The GEC is the communication mechanism between the two devices. Consider the host-chassis as an extension of the FWSM through the use of VLANs. VLANs from the host-chassis are assigned to the FWSM, and a Layer 2 connection is established across the GEC. Figure 6-1 shows a logical representation of how the FWSM connects to VLANs within the host-chassis.

Figure 6-1 *FWSM/Host-Chassis Overview*

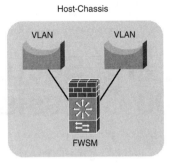

As you can see from Figure 6-1, VLANs are logically associated to the FWSM, but all traffic traversing the FWSM must use the GEC for ingress and egress flows. This configuration could also be considered a FWSM on a stick.

The VLAN can then be associated to a Switched Virtual Interface (SVI) or routed interface on the Multilayer Switch Feature Card (MSFC), as shown in Figure 6-2. This interface has the IP address assignment and would act as the next-hop address.

Figure 6-2 *Switched Virtual Interface*

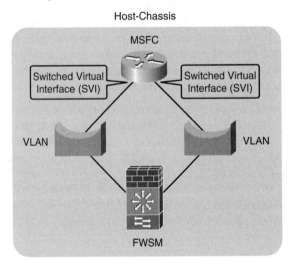

By default, you can assign only one FWSM VLAN to an SVI. This is to prevent you from bypassing the FWSM and routing across the MSFC. The MSFC is the Layer 3 device on the host-chassis that handles routing. If it becomes necessary to bypass the firewall, use the

firewall multiple-vlan-interfaces command in configuration mode. When entering this command, you will be greeted with the following message:

```
host-chassis(config)# firewall multiple-vlan-interfaces
Warning: enabling multiple VLAN interfaces may result in traffic bypassing the FWSM
- use with caution!
```

WARNING   Heed the warning! Bypassing the FWSM may not be the intended result you are looking for.

When the multiple-vlan-interfaces feature is configured, traffic may have an alternative path between networks using the MSFC. This would circumvent any security policies that are applied on the FWSM.

Figure 6-3 illustrates how the traffic flowing between the two clients bypasses the FWSM.

Figure 6-3   *FWSM Bypass*

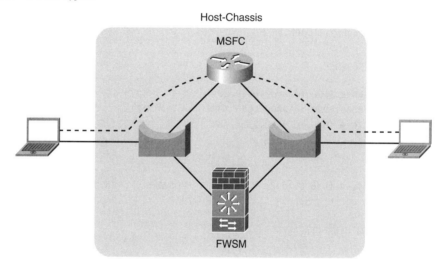

This configuration may be used to direct Novell Internetwork Packet Exchange (IPX) traffic, specific applications, or hosts through the MSFC. This can be accomplished by using Policy Based Routing (PBR), essentially creating a rule set that matches specific traffic and sends that traffic through another path. For additional information on PBR, take a look at the Cisco Press book *Routing TCP/IP*, Volume I.

If you take a holistic view of the FWSM and the host-chassis together, and consider them a "single" unit, it will provide you with a better understanding of how to secure your infrastructure. Remember that you can take advantage of the routing resources of the MSFC, bridging capabilities of the VLANs and the FWSM.

Assigning Interfaces

For the FWSM to communicate to other devices on the network, a connection must be made from logical interfaces of the FWSM to VLANs assigned to the host-chassis.

Referring to Figure 6-3, notice that the FWSM is logically connected to VLANs. This is accomplished through the following process.

Step 1 Determine in which slot the FWMS is installed with the **show module** command:

```
host-chassis# show module
Mod Ports Card Type                        Model               Serial No.
--- ----- ------------------------------- ------------------- -----------
  1   48  48 port 10/100 mb RJ-45 ethernet  WS-X6248-RJ-45    SAD03150942
  5    2  Supervisor Engine 720 (Active)    WS-SUP720-3BXL    SAD080705DC
  9    6  Firewall Module                   WS-SVC-FWM-1      SAD0707015S

Mod MAC addresses                   Hw    Fw           Sw           Status
--- ------------------------------- ----- ------------ ------------ -------
  1 00d0.c0c8.3080 to 00d0.c0c8.30af 1.0  4.2(0.24)VAI 8.5(0.46)RFW Ok
  5 000d.6536.1390 to 000d.6536.1393 3.0  7.7(1)       12.2(18)SXF9 Ok
  9 0002.7ee4.f640 to 0002.7ee4.f647 1.1  7.2(1)       3.2(1)       Ok

Mod  Sub-Module            Model             Serial        Hw    Status
---- --------------------- ----------------- ----------- ------- -------
  5  Policy Feature Card 3  WS-F6K-PFC3BXL   SAD0808084G  1.1    Ok
  5  MSFC3 Daughterboard    WS-SUP720        SAD0807060G  2.0    Ok

Mod  Online Diag Status
---- ------------------
  1  Pass
  5  Pass
  9  Pass
```

The output of the **show module** command shows that the FWSM is installed in slot 9.

Step 2   Create VLANs on the host-chassis, using the **vlan** command in configuration mode:

```
host-chassis(config)# vlan 10-20
```

This **vlan** command creates VLANs 10 to 20.

If you are using VLAN Trunking Protocol (VTP), VLANs can be added only to devices that are "servers" or operating in "transparent" mode.

Use the **show vtp status** command to determine which mode the host-chassis is in:

```
host-chassis# show vtp status
VTP Version                       : 2
Configuration Revision            : 0
Maximum VLANs supported locally : 1005
Number of existing VLANs          : 16
VTP Operating Mode                : Transparent
VTP Domain Name                   :
VTP Pruning Mode                  : Disabled
VTP V2 Mode                       : Disabled
VTP Traps Generation              : Disabled
MD5 digest                        : 0xB4 0xCB 0x9F 0x39 0x03 0x38 0x6C 0xCE
Configuration last modified by 127.0.0.51 at 0-0-00 00:00:00
```

If necessary, use the **vtp mode** command in configuration mode to change the behavior.

Step 3   Associate the newly created VLANs with a VLAN group.

VLAN groups are used to organize the distribution of VLANs across single or multiple FWSMs, and maximum of 16 groups are allowed. A VLAN is unique to a firewall group, and a group or multiple groups can be associated to single or multiple FWSMs. A group number is any numeric value from 1 to 65535, and the VLAN range includes VLANs 2 to 1001 and 1006 to 4094:

```
host-chassis(config)# firewall vlan-group vlan_range
```

For example, the following command assigns VLANs 10 through 20 to vlan-group 9:

```
host-chassis(config)# firewall vlan-group 9 10-20
```

Step 4 Assign the VLAN group(s) to a specific FWSM:

```
host-chassis(config)# firewall module slot_number vlan-group
group_or_group_range
```

In the following case, the FWSM is installed in slot 9 (see Step 1) and the VLAN group associated to it is vlan-group 9:

```
host-chassis(config)#firewall module 9 vlan-group 9
```

There is no correlation between using the same vlan-group as the slot number; it just makes it easier from an administrative view to correlate the VLAN group to the FWSM.

Step 5 Verify the configuration with the **show firewall vlan-group** and the **show firewall module** commands:

```
host-chassis# show firewall vlan-group
Display vlan-groups created by both ACE module and FWSM


Group    Created by      vlans
-----    ----------      -----
    9          FWSM      10-20


host-chassis# show firewall module
Module Vlan-groups
------ -----------
  09   9
```

From the output of the previous commands, VLANs 10 to 20 are assigned to group 9, and group 9 is assigned to module 9.

To assign VLAN interfaces to the FWSM, see Chapter 7, "Configuring the FWSM."

The host-chassis provides a great deal of flexibility in how the FWSM communicates with the outside world. As you consider how to implement the FWSM in your network, be sure to take advantage of the routing and switching capabilities of the host-chassis.

Securing the 6500/7600 (Host-Chassis)

The following section is intended to give you an overview of the features that need to be deployed to ensure a secure infrastructure. It is beyond the scope of this book to provide an in-depth understanding of each feature. You should refer to the appropriate switch/router documentation for specific details. The National Security Agency (NSA) has a guide to securing routers that would be a good place to start (http://www.nsa.gov/snac/routers/cisco_scg-1.1b.pdf).

You can secure the host-chassis in several ways, including the following:

- Controlling Physical Access
- Being Mindful of Environmental Considerations
- Controlling Management Access
- Disabling Unnecessary Services
- Controlling Access Using Port-Based Security
- Controlling Spanning Tree
- Leveraging Access Control Lists
- Securing Layer 3
- Leveraging Control Plane Policing
- Protecting a Network Using Quality of Service

Controlling Physical Access

Anyone with physical access to the equipment has the ability to quickly perform a Denial of Service (DoS) attack by turning off the power, moving cables, removing line cards, and so on. It is critical to restrict access to individuals who cannot be trusted to behave appropriately.

Equipment can be protected inside locked cabinets, equipment rooms with controlled access by using badge readers or keys, and securing physical cabling within conduit. Other mechanisms that may detour inappropriate activity are closed-circuit TV, motion detectors, lighting, and so on.

If a physical attack occurs and you need to recover, having current documentation of the network, physical connectivity information, and up-to-date configurations of the equipment will significantly help in rebuilding your infrastructure.

Being Mindful of Environmental Considerations

Although not directly related to security, proper heating, cooling, air cleanliness, and conditioned power play a significant role in the availability of the equipment. If the equipment is not working because of the environment, then there is no need to worry about good security. For more information on some of the environmental considerations for the FWSM and the appropriate documentation for the host-chassis, see Chapter 2.

- **Be certain that the equipment operates well within the listed specifications for heating and cooling:** For example, if your 6500/7600 is located in a data center, you may consider using a chassis that has front to rear airflow.

- **Maintain a clean datacenter or server room:** If the host-chassis is in a location without appropriate filtering, dust, chemicals, or debris may enter and cause problems with the electronics.

- **Ensure that voltage and/or current levels are stable:** Fluctuations in voltage and/or current either above or below the recommended levels may also cause some interesting side effects, causing a service outage. Use an appropriate Uninterruptible Power Supply (UPS) and/or line conditioner to control voltage/current levels.

When protecting services that you are offering to consumers, it's not just about firewall rules. You need to consider all factors and manage the risks accordingly.

Controlling Management Access

Methods for accessing the FWSM, include Telnet, Secure Shell (SSH), direct console access, access from the host-chassis, and Hypertext Transfer Protocol over Secure Sockets layer (HTTPS). If someone with malicious intent were to gain access to the FWSM using any of these methods, they could potentially gain unfiltered access to resources within your network. Access methods need to be highly controlled. This becomes even more significant when numerous individuals are accessing the same equipment.

Mechanisms using authorization, authentication, and accounting leveraging a central policy server, such as Terminal Access Controller Access Control Server+ (TACACS+) or Remote Authentication Dial-In User Service (RADIUS), reduce the overhead in managing local users on individual devices and allow an administrator to quickly modify privileges of users from a single location.

TIP   Secure Shell Version 1 (SSH) has vulnerabilities and should never be used to manage devices. Use SSHv2 instead.

Remote access protocols that include encryption, such as SSHv2 and HTTPS, minimize the possibility of eavesdropping; using those in conjunction with One Time Passwords (OTP) considerably help protect remote access to the device.

Simple Network Management Protocol (SNMP) versions 1 and 2 provide weak security and should be avoided if possible. SNMP version 3 adds security mechanisms, such as message integrity, authentication, and encryption, and provides a more secure mechanism for management. Other precautions should also be taken, such as the following:

- Use SNMP for read-only access, not write access on the host-chassis. The FWSM does not allow write access.

- Use very complex passwords that are device specific.

- Use an access list on the SNMP-server community attribute to allow only specific management devices.
- Monitor authentication-failure violations.
- Change the password often!

TIP Complex or secure passwords contain combinations of special characters—for example, "! % & } ~ @" and so on, in addition to letters and numbers. The password should be at least eight characters in length and preferably more. Passwords should also not be a word or name, and you should avoid using numeric or special-character substitutions—for example, "cisco" to "c1$c0".

Login banners do not provide any type of security, but they may assist a potential attacker in gathering information about your organization. Avoid displaying company information or phone numbers, using a welcoming comment, or providing any information that would benefit would-be attackers or make them think it is permissible to access your device. Using a message that indicates that unauthorized access is prohibited, that access to this is monitored, and that unlawful use of this device may result in legal action may help your case in the event of malicious use.

HTTP and HTTPS should also be disabled unless necessary. In that event, use HTTPS with an access class allowing only specific devices; use an authentication, authorization, and accounting (AAA) server for authentication, limit the number of connections, and use a nonstandard port for access.

Use SSHv2 for remote access with an AAA server for authentication whenever possible. SSH incorporates authentication and encryption and provides a secure mechanism for access to the device. If you use SSH exclusively, configure the Virtual Terminal (VTY) lines to permit only SSH connections with the **transport input ssh** command. This will provide an extra measure of security; remember "defense in depth"!

You can use several methods to manage the host-chassis and/or the FWSM. The primary concern is to make sure only authorized individuals can gain access by using the most secure communication mechanisms and strong passwords. You should also be familiar with the command-line interface (CLI) using SSHv2 in the event other methods are not available.

Disabling Unnecessary Services

The following services *may* not be needed. Before you make any changes to a "live" network, be sure you know what the results will be.

- Cisco Discovery Protocol (CDP) is a Layer 2 protocol that is used to provide information about other CDP devices that are directly attached. It is a tremendous tool for troubleshooting but should be disabled on interfaces that have only host devices attached.

- Finger is used to gather information about users logged into a host and is rarely used on an IOS-based device.

- Internet Control Message Protocol (ICMP) redirects are used to tell a device to use a different router to reach the destination. If you have subnets with a single router or routers using Hot Standby Routing Protocol (HSRP), Virtual Router Redundancy Protocol (VRRP), or Gateway Load Balancing Protocol (GLBP), you can potentially disable ICMP redirects.

- ICMP unreachables are sent to the source in the event of a dropped packet. This is generally unnecessary and may overwhelm a switch or router.

- IP BOOTP (Internet Protocol Bootstrap Protocol) server is typically not a service used and should be disabled.

- IP source routing allows the sender to dictate the path that traffic will take to the destination. This function is generally used with malicious intent and should also be disabled.

- Internet Protocol version 6 (IPv6) may open additional vulnerabilities and can be turned off if not in use.

- Network Time Protocol (NTP) should be configured specifically for a time source and should be authenticated, otherwise disable the service.

- Packet Assembler/Disassembler (PAD), unless you are running X.25 and know what PAD is, it should be turned off.

- Proxy Address Resolution Protocol (ARP) is a function in which the router replies to local ARP requests from the source on behalf of the destination. This is generally not a good practice and measures should be taken to eliminate this function.

- Transmission Control Protocol (TCP) and User Datagram Protocol (UDP) small services, including echo, chargen (character generator), and discard should also be disabled.

- Trivial File Transfer Protocol (TFTP) server should be used only on a temporary basis and should be disabled after use.

Often, services may be running on the host-chassis that are completely unnecessary. These services could potentially allow unauthorized access to the device or provide an avenue for someone with malicious intent to create a DoS attack. For the best possible protection, turn off unused services.

Controlling Access Using Port-Based Security

Vendors, partners, consultants, employees, and so on bringing in unauthorized devices might need access to resources on your network or to use your network as a transit to the Internet. These individuals may not always be inclined to ask permission before making a connecting to your network. If they have an opportunity to connect, there is a potential to spread malicious software (malware), either intentionally or unintentionally, and/or allow them the opportunity for other harmful activities.

Controlling which devices that are authorized to have access and those that are not can be a significant concern. Several mechanisms provide the capability to automatically authenticate a device and/or user access to the network. Some of these include Network Admission Control (NAC), 802.1x, MAC-based authentication, web-based proxy authentication, and so on. If you are doing this manually, be sure to turn off 802.1Q trunking to client devices. Doing so will minimize any impact they may have on other VLANs. Also turn off access to ports that are not in use.

Your business requirements will define which mechanism is best for your organization. The key is to control access to the network to legitimate devices and restrict their access to specific services.

Controlling Spanning Tree

Spanning tree is a Layer 2 protocol used to prevent loops within the network. Several flavors of spanning tree exhibit different characteristics and require special attention.

The use of spanning tree as a method for high availability is a controversial issue, but years of experience troubleshooting spanning-tree problems and the difficulties associated with it determine that it is best to avoid using spanning tree as a mechanism for failover, especially given the complexities with running Per VLAN Spanning-Tree (PVST), Per VLAN Spanning-Tree Plus (PVST+), Rapid Per VLAN Spanning-Tree Plus (RPVST+), Multiple Spanning-Tree Protocol (MSTP), 801.d, and so on, and the interoperability issues that you may face. You should consider using Layer 3 connections and using a routing protocol for better control of traffic and significantly superior tools for troubleshooting your network infrastructure. Don't turn spanning tree off, but use it as an insurance policy in the event of a physical or logical network misconfiguration.

If you must use spanning tree for failover, be sure to understand, document, and appropriately configure the devices within your infrastructure to best utilize the forwarding interfaces of spanning tree. Other mechanisms that should also be employed to minimize any ill effects that spanning tree may cause are the following:

- Loop guard, which performs additional bridge protocol data unit (BPDU) checks and will place a port in an inconsistent state in the event of BPDU detection of the root from a root port or alternative root port.

- BPDU guard, which detects incoming BPDUs and will disable the port.

- Root guard, which checks incoming BPDUs and if they are superior to the existing root, will place the port in an "inconsistent" state.

- Controlling VLANs on specific ports minimizes the impact of spanning tree over switches that may not need to participate in that specific VLAN. Consequently, this will reduce the size of the spanning-tree domain and make the infrastructure easier to manage.

If possible, use Layer 3 routing protocols for high availability. When spanning tree is the only alternative mechanism, be sure you understand and control your network infrastructure to minimize any adverse effects.

Leveraging Access Control Lists

Access Control Lists (ACL) provide an additional level of protection by limiting specific types of traffic. The three types of ACLs are as follows:

- VLAN Access Control Lists (VACL) are Layer 2 ACLs applied to a VLAN to control MAC-layer, IP, and Internet Packet Exchange (IPX) traffic.

- Routed-interface Access Control Lists (RACL) are traditional ACLs applied to a routed interface.

- Port Access Control Lists (PACL) control ingress traffic on Layer 2 ports.

- Although you would consider using ACLs primarily on the FWSM, they can also be used on the host-chassis to control management access, mitigate "spoofed" traffic, and so on, as an extra level of defense against attacks.

Securing Layer 3

Malicious attacks can be directed at routing protocols, and unless security precautions are implemented, this could be an area of exploit or DoS attack. Several routing protocols, including Enhanced Interior Gateway Routing Protocol (Enhanced IGRP), Border Gateway Protocol (BGP), Intermediate System-to-Intermediate System (IS-IS) Protocol, Open Shortest Path First (OSPF) Protocol, and Routing Information Protocol version 2 (RIPv2), support neighbor authentication using Message Digest 5 (MD5) hash authentication. Because the routing updates are sent with a "hash," it makes attacking the routing protocol very difficult.

Unicast Reverse Path Forwarding (uRPF) provides a check of the source of the traffic to determine whether there is a valid route. For example, if a malicious attacker on subnet 192.168.2.0/24 was sending traffic originating from subnet 10.2.2.0/24, the uRPF check will determine that no valid route exists from the source network (10.2.2.0/24), and that traffic will be dropped.

Failure to provide adequate security at Layer 3 could potentially allow a malicious individual to inject routing information into the network, consequently redirecting traffic flows that could bypass the FWSM to other security devices.

Leveraging Control Plane Policing

Although both the 6500 and 7600 perform hardware-based forwarding, the first packet of a session is sent to the Route Processor (RP). If a significant number of new flows are being established, usually from malicious activity such as port scans or a DoS attack, the central processing unit (CPU) of the supervisor on the host-chassis can become overwhelmed. If this occurs, critical functions become impaired, and a loss of service occurs that may affect other devices in the network as well. These can include Hot Standby Routing Protocol (HSRP), spanning tree, routing protocols, traffic forwarding, and so on.

With the addition of the Control Plane Policing (CPP) feature, attacks on the CPU can be minimized. A new interface called the control plane was created. It enables you to deploy specific QoS parameters to minimize the impact of malicious traffic, and even traffic that would not be considered malicious, such as SNMP queries, but that could potentially overwhelm the processor.

Protecting the CPU of the host-chassis from a direct or inadvertent attack could be the difference in providing services to customers or not. Be sure to take advantage of the CPP feature to minimize CPU overload.

Protecting a Network Using Quality of Service

You might not consider QoS a security mechanism, but having the ability to control the flow of particular traffic minimizes the impact that malicious traffic will cause. Implementing QoS requires a detailed understanding of the applications running on your network. When known applications can be given the appropriate bandwidth and priority, and other traffic is given a small portion of bandwidth with very low priority, network impacts will be minimized.

For additional information on QoS, see the Cisco Press book titled *End-to-End QoS Network Design*.

QoS may be one of the least-used security methods, but it provides a very effective means to control how much and which type of traffic you want to allow. When you are considering how to effectively implement security policies, don't forget about QoS.

Employing Additional Security Features

Autosecure is a good tool to set a baseline for securing the host-chassis. It will disable nonessential system services and enable some limited security best practices.

NOTE   Be sure to review the configuration changes that Autosecure makes and augment it with other practices outlined in this chapter.

The *Cisco AutoSecure White Paper* can be found at the following location: www.cisco.com/en/US/prod/collateral/iosswrel/ps6537/ps6586/ps6642/prod_white_paper09186a00801dbf61.html

---

Service password encryption will encrypt most passwords in the configuration file and minimizes the impact of "shoulder surfers" and anyone who may have access to the configuration file.

Unknown unicast flood control prevents the forwarding of traffic for frames that do not have a destination Media Access Control (MAC) entry in the Content Addressable Memory (CAM) table of the switch. This requires you to configure static MAC entries on the switch for valid MAC entries.

Recognize that security is one aspect of creating an infrastructure that provides access to resources. Reliability, availability, manageability, and scalability are of great concern as well. Taking a holistic approach to your network will ultimately give your customers a much better network experience.

Summary

The FWSM and the host-chassis provide an integrated solution for the implementation of your security policy. Protecting the host-chassis should be considered as important as securing the FWSM. You should take advantage of several mechanisms to protect the host-chassis, including controlling physical access and environmental considerations to leveraging the integrated security features, such as port security, ACLs, QoS, and so on. Taking full advantage of the capabilities of the host-chassis and considering the FWSM as an integrated solution will allow you to reap the benefits of this security solution.

References

RFC 742—NAME/FINGER Protocol

RFC 864—Character Generator Protocol

RFC 951—Bootstrap Protocol

RFC 1027—Using ARP to Implement Transparent Subnet Gateways

RFC 1157—Simple Network Management Protocol (SNMP)

RFC 1812—Requirements for IP Version 4 (IPv4)

RFC 3411—Simple Network Management Protocol (SNMP) Version 3

RFC 3418—Simple Network Management Protocol (SNMP) Version 2

RFC 2131—Dynamic Host Configuration Protocol (DCHP)

CHAPTER 7

Configuring the FWSM

This chapter takes you through the steps needed to configure the Firewall Services Module (FWSM). This chapter also covers the different FWSM mode configurations: routed, transparent, single context, and multiple contexts.

The FWSM is an inline module in the switch chassis. To configure the FWSM, switch configuration is a necessity because it relates the switch to the FWSM. The configuration of FWSM covers the details of firewall rules, policy, redundancy, and so on.

The configuration of the FWSM is a two-fold process:

Step 1   Configure the FWSM in the switch.

Step 2   Configure the FWSM for security rules.

The sections that follow describe this two-fold process in greater detail.

Configuring FWSM in the Switch

The configuration of the switch for the FWSM is important because it builds the VLANs that are added between the switch and FWSM. These VLANs will be trunked between the switch and FWSM.

Follow these steps in the first configuration:

Step 1   **Verify which module has the FWSM:** This is shown in the output of the **show module** command, as demonstrated next:

```
cat6k6a# sh module
Mod Ports Card Type                            Model            Serial No.
--- ----- ---------------------------------   ---------------  ----------
  1    2  Supervisor Engine 720 (Active)      WS-SUP720-BASE   SAD081502C1
  2   48  48-port 10/100 mb RJ45              WS-X6148-RJ45V   SAL0741MY2T
  4    6  Firewall Module                     WS-SVC-FWM-1     SAD10050ABP
```

```
Mod MAC addresses                            Hw    Fw      Sw            Status
--- -------------------------------------    ---   ------  -------------  -----
 1  000d.6536.321c to 000d.6536.321f  3.1   7.7(1)  12.2(18)SXE5  Ok
 2  000d.edb5.e090 to 000d.edb5.e0bf  1.4   5.4(2)   8.5(0.46)ROC Ok
 4  0016.9daa.72c8 to 0016.9daa.72cf  4.0   7.2(1)   3.1(4)5      Ok

Mod Sub-Module              Model           Serial        Hw    Status
--- --------------------    -------------   ------------  ----  ------
 1  Policy Feature Card 3   WS-F6K-PFC3A    SAD081500HS   2.2   Ok
 1  MSFC3 Daughterboard     WS-SUP720       SAD081409SM   2.2   Ok
 2  Inline Power Module     WS-F6K-PWR                    2.0   Ok

Mod Online Diag Status
--- --------------------
  1 Pass
  2 Pass
  4 Pass
cat6k6a#
```

The highlighted portion in the output shows that the FWSM is in the module 4.

Step 2 **Assign VLANs to the FWSM:** The FWSM does not use external interfaces. The interfaces used in the FWSM are Virtual Local Area Networks (VLAN). These VLANs create a relationship between the switch and the FWSM.

For more details about EtherChannel connections to FWSM refer to Chapter 6, "Configuring and Securing the 6500/7600 Chassis." This gives a description of the EtherChannel connection between the FWSM and the switch.

The firewall VLANS are defined through the **vlan-group** command on the switch. This command enables the VLANs on the firewall.

Guidelines for assigning VLANs on FWSM are as follows:

— Assign the VLAN for the FWSM before it is applied to the Multilayer Switch Feature Card (MSFC).

— Reserved VLANs cannot be used.

— VLAN 1 cannot be used.

— If FWSM failover is used within the same switch chassis, do not assign the VLAN(s) reserved for failover and stateful communications to a switch port. However, if you are using failover between two separate chassis, you must include the VLANs in the trunk port between the chassis because VLANs need to be dedicated for failover purposes and should not be used for any other functionality.

— As soon as the configuration for VLANs is enabled in the **vlan-group** command on the switch, the VLAN information from the supervisor database is sent to the FWSM.

The following list of commands needs to be enabled on the Policy Feature Card (PFC) for adding the VLANs to the FWSM:

(a) Configure the VLAN group with respect to the module slot for the FWSM:

```
firewall module module_number vlan-group firewall_group
```

(b) Configure the VLANs that will represent the security zones in the FWSM:

```
firewall vlan-group firewall_group VlANs
```

NOTE	To determine the module number, type the **show module** command.

For example:

```
firewall module 4 vlan-group 1
firewall vlan-group 1  50,51,100,101,325
```

For security reasons, only one Switch Virtual Interface (SVI) can exist between the FWSM and the switch by default. This means that for all the VLANs defined in the FWSM, only one VLAN can have an SVI interface in the switch.

The designs in the data center with Multiprotocol Label Switching (MPLS)/Layer 3 VPN technology will need to have two SVIs. This is covered in Chapter 23, "Design Scenarios."

For this case, it is desirable to have more than one SVI interface in the MSFC, for the VLANs defined in the FWSM. The command to enable this feature is

```
firewall multiple-vlan-interfaces
```

The command syntax for switch configuration to enable VLANs in the FWSM follows:

```
firewall multiple-vlan-interfaces
firewall module 4 vlan-group 1
firewall vlan-group 1  50,51,100,101,325
```

This section covers configuring the switch for FWSMs functionality. The configuration provides the VLANs that can be used in the FWSM. In this section, it is important to understand how the traffic enters and exits the FWSM. The VLANs must be carefully configured; otherwise, the traffic can bypass the FWSM.

Exploring Routed Mode

In routed mode, the FWSM acts like a Layer 3 device, and all the interfaces in the FWSM need to have an Internet Protocol (IP) address. The interfaces can be in any security zone: inside, outside, or demilitarized zone (DMZ). The firewall configuration is in routed mode and needs IP addresses and IP routing enabled on the interfaces. The routed mode can be in single context or multiple context mode. Figure 7-1 illustrates the high-level details of each mode.

Figure 7-1 *High-Level Topology View of FWSM in Routed Mode*

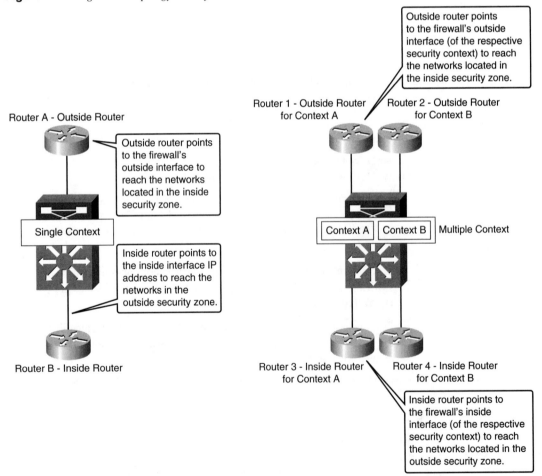

This section covers the details of different modes supported in the FWSM. It is very important to understand the basics of each mode.

In a routed mode, FWSM will not allow non-IP traffic to pass through the firewall. The routed mode can be represented in two modes: single and multiple contexts.

- **Single Context Mode:** A single context mode will have single security policy. The features unique to a single context mode, which cannot apply to the multiple context mode, are the following:

    — FWSM can participate in multicast domain.

    — Routing protocol support is available in single context mode.

- **Multiple Context Mode:** A single FWSM can be partitioned into multiple security contexts. Each of the security contexts will have separate firewall security policies. By this, a single FWSM is virtualized to facilitate multiple security policies. Some of the points to be noted for multiple context mode are the following:

    — The FWSM cannot take part in multicast domain.

    — Routing protocol support for the FWSM is not available in multiple context mode.

    — Active/Active redundancy can be enabled with Asymmetric routing. This cannot be done in the single context mode. These features are supported in the 3.x release.

Routed mode can support both single and multiple context modes. The configuration of single or multiple context modes depends on the design requirements. It is very important to understand the limitation of single and multiple context modes to make the correct design decision.

Exploring Transparent Mode

The firewall is not seen as a Layer 3 hop. The FWSM has a Layer 2 adjacency with the next hop devices. The firewall can be referred to as a bump in the wire.

The transparent firewall also facilitates the flow of IP and non-IP traffic. To place the firewall between two Layer 3 devices, no IP readdressing is required. It is also easy to establish routing protocol adjacencies through a transparent firewall. Likewise, protocols such as Hot Standby Routing Protocol (HSRP) or Virtual Router Redundancy Protocol (VRRP) can run through the security device. Non-IP traffic such as IPX, bridge protocol data units (BPDU), or even MPLS can be configured to pass through the firewall, with a simple Ether-type–based access list. Network Address Translation (NAT) can be enabled in 3.1 and later codes. Transparent mode can also be represented in a single or multiple context mode.

Figure 7-2 represents transparent mode in a single context and multiple context environment.

Figure 7-2 *High-Level Topology View of Firewall in Transparent Mode*

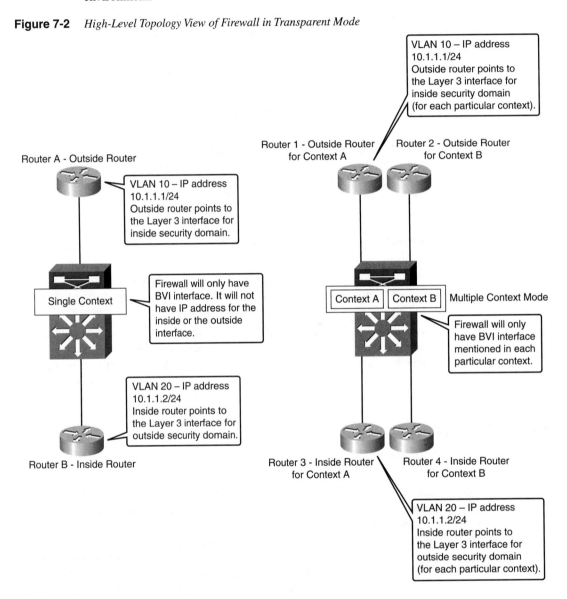

This type of firewall can fit in any design. It easily becomes a part of the network because no considerations are needed for routing or changing the default route address for the servers, when Layer 2 transparent firewalls are introduced in the network.

Using Multiple Context Mode for FWSM

In the multiple context mode for FWSM, the firewall is virtualized into multiple security domains. This facilitates virtualization of the security domains with firewalls.

Prior to multiple context mode, multiple security rules were written in a single firewall rule set, which made the firewall rule set configuration more complex. With multiple context mode, a more granular approach to the rule set can be achieved, where each individual rule set is treated as a separate entity. The changes made in one context will not affect the other policies. Multiple context mode helps in integration of security virtualization with network virtualization.

Each context has its own security policy, interfaces, and administrators. Multiple context mode is similar to having multiple standalone firewall devices, where each firewall represents a security policy and has separate incoming and outgoing interfaces.

The following features will not be available in multiple context firewalls compared to single context firewalls:

- Support for dynamic routing protocols (BGP stub mode or static routes in multiple context mode is supported)
- Multicast routing support (multicast bridge support is available in transparent mode)

In a multiple context mode, the administrator has configurations of a standalone firewall, such as security policy, interfaces, and almost all the options you can configure on a standalone device. You can store context configurations on the internal flash memory or the external flash memory card, or you can download them from a Trivial File Transfer Protocol (TFTP), File Transfer Protocol (FTP), Hypertext Transfer Protocol (HTTP), or Hypertext Transfer Protocol over Secure Socket Layer (HTTPS).

In a multiple context mode, it is very important to understand the types of contexts available and their uses. The next section explains the different context configurations.

Context Configurations

A context has the configuration of the security policy for a specific security domain in the firewall. Administrators can configure all options as a standalone device. A context will have interfaces (VLANs), and each interface is in a security zone based on the rule set. A context is like a physical firewall with separate interfaces and separate security policy in a virtual environment. In the FWSM, in multiple context mode, you can have multiple contexts with different firewall characteristics.

System Context Configurations

The system context adds and manages the context configuration. The system context does not have any interface allocation; it defines the VLANs for the respective contexts. The definition of other contexts is given in system context. Failover command configuration is enabled in the system configuration.

Admin Context Configurations

In the admin context, the user can log in and access the system and other contexts. The user can be granted privileges over all the contexts, and the administrator can restrict a few of these privileges based on the user access criteria. The admin context must reside on flash memory, not remotely. Admin context is created automatically, resides in the flash memory, and is called admin.cfg.

Packet Classifier in FWSM Context Mode

One of the modes in which FWSM can be deployed is the shared outside interface mode. The outside interface is shared between multiple contexts. This translates to one interface for all the contexts in the outside security zone. The packet destined to the outside interface must traverse to a specific context, which has the state information built into it. The traffic is not allowed to traverse the FWSM context if no state information exists. This is for the packets flowing from the lower security zone to the higher security zone. Therefore, in a common shared interface, it is important for the packet to flow to the correct context. The packet classifier takes care of this flow from a shared interface to the respective context that has the state information for the flow. Figure 7-3 illustrates the firewall with a shared outside interface for multiple context mode.

Figure 7-3 *Packet Classifier in FWSM Context Mode*

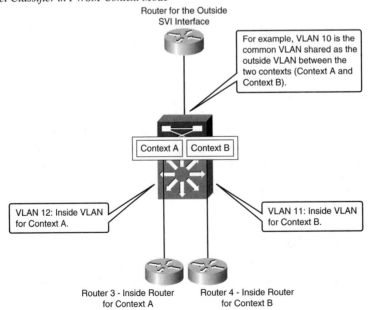

In the example shown in Figure 7-3, VLAN 10 is the outside interface for context A and context B. When the packet in the return path from the outside security zone enters context B, the packet passes through VLAN 10. The state table is built during the initial packet flow from the inside to the outside security zone. At the FWSM, the packet passes through a packet classifier. The packet classifier forwards the packet to the context B and then to VLAN 11.

The purpose of the classifier is to determine the context to which the packet needs to be sent when the packet arrives on a shared interface. The source-destination-flow identification in a VLAN cannot be based on a MAC address. For example, a packet flowing from the outside to the inside interface of context B arrives first at VLAN 10 and will have the MAC address of VLAN 10. VLAN 10 is shared between the two contexts (sharing the common outside interface) in this example. The classifier intercepts the packet and performs a destination IP address lookup. The main field that is looked up is the destination IP field. The classifier has knowledge of the subnets located behind the security context through xlate and static translations. The classifier does not have knowledge of the routing statements of each context. Using the static and xlate table in the context, the packet comparison for the destination is done and is forwarded to the correct context. In this way, packets can flow from one context to the other, even if there is one shared outside interface representing each of the contexts.

Understanding Resource Management in Contexts

If no resource management is done in a multiple context mode, the context resides in the default class and can access unlimited resources. The following sessions are allowed in the default class per context:

- **Telnet sessions:** 5 sessions
- **SSH sessions:** 5 sessions
- **IPsec sessions:** 5 sessions
- **MAC addresses:** 65,535 entries

When resource management is enabled, resource restriction is done from the default resource available. Chapter 5, "Understanding Contexts," provides more details for resource management and memory partition.

Configuration Steps for Firewall Services Module

This section discusses three main configuration examples:

- Type 1: Single Context Routed Mode
- Type 2: Single Context Transparent Mode
- Type 3: Multiple Context Mixed Mode

Type 1: Configuring Single Context Routed Mode

This section covers the configuration of a single context routed mode. There are three main steps for configuring a single context routed mode in the FWSM. These are sequential steps that must be followed in the same order.

Step 1   Configuring the PFC. This step covers the configuration of the switch in relation to the FWSM configuration.

The following command is used to enable multiple SVIs in relation to FWSM:

```
firewall multiple-vlan-interfaces
```

This command is needed only if VLAN 9 and VLAN 10 have SVI interfaces in the PFC. If two SVIs are needed for security segregation, the administrator can configure the SVI in two separate VRFs (Virtual Routing and Forwarding).

The following command is used to configure the VLAN group used in the FWSM:

```
firewall module 3 vlan-group 1
```

The module information is based on the output of the **show module** command.

The following command is used to configure the VLANs in the VLAN group:

```
firewall vlan-group 1  9,10
```

VLANs used in the FWSM and the failover VLANs should be configured in this command. In multiple context mode, all the VLANs in different contexts should also be configured to the VLAN group defined in the **firewall module 3 vlan-group 1** command.

When the SVI of the inside and outside interfaces are defined on the same PFC, a form of segregation is required to prevent the traffic from bypassing the FWSM. In the traditional model, it is recommended to define either the inside or the outside VLANs SVI in the PFC. The VLAN that does not have SVI defined in the PFC will have the Layer 3 interface enabled in the Layer 3 next hop device.

NOTE   The SVI configuration or the Layer 3 interface configuration for the respective inside and outside interface is not shown in this section.

Step 2   Access the FWSM from the switch and configure the mode on the FWSM:

```
6504-E-2# sess slot 3 pr 1
```

The slot number of the FWSM can be identified from the **show module** command output in the PFC.

Verify the functionality of FWSM using the following commands:

```
FWSM# show mode
 Security context mode: single
 The flash mode is the SAME as the running mode.
FWSM# show firewall
Firewall mode: Router
FWSM#
```

The **show mode** and the **show firewall** commands verify whether the firewall is in the single context routed mode.

Step 3   Configure the FWSM (basic configuration).

This section covers the configuration of the FWSM.

— Configure the interfaces:

```
interface Vlan9
 nameif outside
 security-level 0
 ip address 11.1.1.10 255.255.255.0
 !
interface Vlan10
 nameif inside
 security-level 100
 ip address 172.1.1.10 255.255.255.0
 !
```

Make sure the IP addresses defined in the FWSM corresponds to the next hop Layer 3 address of the respective interfaces. The **nameif** command is used to configure the security domain, and the security-level defines the level of security for the domain (security-level 100 is the most secure).

— Define the access list:

```
access-list ANY extended permit ip any any
access-group ANY in interface outside
access-group ANY out interface outside
access-group ANY in interface inside
access-group ANY out interface inside
```

This is a generic access list, which permits all the traffic.

— Configure the maximum transmission unit (MTU), no failover, and Internet Control Message Protocol (ICMP) for inside and outside interfaces (configured only in lab environment).

```
mtu outside 1500
mtu inside 1500
no failover
icmp permit any outside
icmp permit any inside
```

— Define the respective routes:

```
route outside 0.0.0.0 0.0.0.0 11.1.1.3 1
route inside 172.1.0.0 255.255.0.0 172.1.1.3 1
```

Static routes must be configured representing each security domain.

— Configure NAT.

To configure NAT without any translation, enter the following command:

```
nat (inside) 0 0.0.0.0 0.0.0.0
```

To configure NAT translation with PAT, enter the following commands:

```
global (outside) 1 interface
nat (inside) 1 172.1.0.0 255.255.0.0
```

Type 2: Configuring Single Context Transparent Mode

In the transparent mode, the FWSM is a bump on the wire. The next-hop devices will have only a Layer 2 relationship with the FWSM. This section shows the steps for the configuration of the transparent mode in a single context mode.

Step 1 Configure the Policy Feature Card (PFC).

Step 1 covers the switch configuration in relation to the FWSM:

```
firewall multiple-vlan-interfaces
firewall module 3 vlan-group 1
firewall vlan-group 1  9,10
```

The details are similar to the explanation provided in Step 1 of the Type 1 example. In transparent mode, there can be only two interfaces for a context.

Step 2 Access the FWSM from the switch and configure the mode on the FWSM:

```
6504-E-2# sess slot 4 pr 1
```

The slot number of the FWSM is identified from the **show module** command output in the PFC.

Step 3 Verify the mode and functionality of the FWSM from the output shown next:

```
FWSM# sh mod
Security context mode: single
The flash mode is the SAME as the running mode.
FWSM# sh firewall
Firewall mode: Transparent
```

The FWSM is in single context transparent mode.

Step 4 Configure the FWSM.

This section covers the FWSM configuration and its five essential elements.

— Configure the interfaces:

```
interface Vlan20
nameif outside
bridge-group 1
security-level 0
!
interface Vlan21
 nameif inside
 bridge-group 1
 security-level 100
!
```

The Layer 3 interface defined in the Layer 3 router will be in a different VLAN but the same IP subnet. The **bridge-group 1** bridges VLAN 20 and VLAN 21. VLAN 20 is defined as an outside interface, and VLAN 21 is defined as an inside interface.

```
!
interface BVI1
 ip address 1.1.1.254 255.255.255.0
```

Bridge-Group Virtual Interface (BVI) is used to access the transparent firewall for management purposes.

— Define the access list:

```
access-group 101 in interface outside
access-group 100 in interface outside
access-group 100 out interface outside
access-group 101 in interface inside
access-group 100 in interface inside
access-group 100 out interface inside
access-list 100 extended permit ip any any
access-list 100 extended permit udp any any
access-list 101 ethertype permit bpdu
```

This is a generic access list, which permits all the traffic. The access list will cover the rule set defined for the FWSM.

— Configure the MTU, no failover:

```
mtu outside 1500
mtu inside 1500
no failover
```

```
Configure the MTU of the interface to 1500.
```

— Define the respective routes needed for management traffic.

```
route outside 0.0.0.0 0.0.0.0 1.1.1.1 1
```

The default route for management traffic is configured with a next hop of 1.1.1.1 in the outside security domain.

NOTE   While configuring the transparent mode in FWSM, it is important to specify the MAC address and the CAM entries on the Layer 3 next hop device of FWSM.

The following are two examples:

Layer 3 Device A (PFC) at the Outside Security Domain

```
! IP address of the next hop for the outside security domain
interface Vlan20
 mac-address 0000.0000.0001
 ip address 10.10.1.1 255.255.255.0

! Specify the IP address and MAC address at the first hop layer 3 interface
! of the inside security domain
arp  10.10.1.21 0000.0000.0001 ARPA
```

Layer 3 Device B at the Inside Security Domain

```
! IP address of the next hop for the inside security domain
 interface Vlan21
 mac-address 0000.0000.0021
 ip address 10.10.1.21 255.255.255.0
! Specify the IP address and MAC address defined at the first hop interface
! of the outside security domain
arp  10.10.1.21 0000.0000.0002 ARPA
```

Type 3: Configuring Multiple Context Mixed Mode

The multiple context configuration shown in this section is with mixed mode; one of the contexts is in transparent mode, and the other is in routed mode. The configuration for multiple context mode is divided into four steps. Figure 7-4 shows the mixed mode configuration of Figure 7-4.

Figure 7-4   *Mixed Mode Configuration of FWSM*

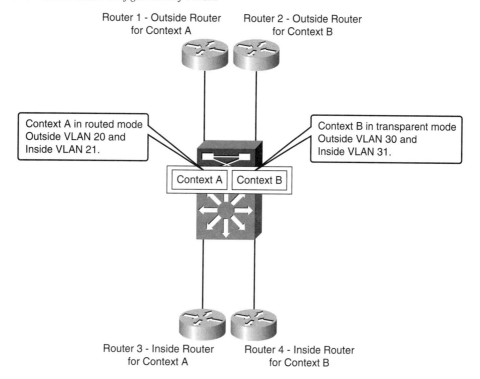

Step 1   Configure the PFC.

This step covers the configuration of the switch in relation to the FWSM configuration:

```
firewall multiple-vlan-interfaces
firewall module 3 vlan-group 1
firewall vlan-group 1  30,31,20,21
```

The explanation is similar to the explanation for the Step 1 configuration in Type 1 example.

Step 2 Access the FWSM from the switch and configure the multiple context mode on the FWSM.

```
6504-E-2# sess slot 4 pr 1
```

The following configuration verifies the functionality of the FWSM with respect to the mode:

```
FWSM# sh mod
Security context mode: multiple
The flash mode is the SAME as the running mode.
FWSM# sh firewall
Firewall mode: Router
```

The command used to change the mode of the FWSM to multiple context mode is

```
FWSM(config)# mode multiple
```

Step 3 Configure the FWSM.

This step shows the configuration of the system context; VLANs in the FWSM are configured and context allocation is done.

— Configure the system configuration:

```
interface vlan 20
interface vlan 21
interface vlan 30
interface vlan 31
context customerA
  description This is the context for customer A
  allocate-interface Vlan20
  allocate-interface Vlan21
  config-url disk:/contexta.cfg
!
context customerB
description This is the context for customer B
allocate-interface vlan30
allocate-interface vlan31
config-url disk://contextb.cfg
```

NOTE   Make a note of the system configuration. The failover configuration should be enabled in this context. This section does not cover failover configuration. For information about failover configuration, see Chapter 12, "Understanding Failover in FWSM."

Step 4   The next two sections cover the configuration of the contexts. The configuration for customer A is in routed mode and for customer B is in transparent mode.

Routed context example for customer A:

To access the context for customer A from the system configuration, the command to be used is

```
FWSMB# changeto context customerA
```
— Configure the interface for context A:

```
interface vlan 20
    nameif outside
    security-level 0
    ip address 10.1.1.2 255.255.255.0
interface vlan 21
    nameif inside
    security-level 100
    ip address 10.1.2.1 255.255.255.0
```

NOTE   If DMZ exists, the interface has to be defined. For failover, the standby IP address must be configured for the interface IP addresses.

— Define route information:

```
route outside 0.0.0.0 0.0.0.0 10.1.1.1 1
```

NOTE   Static route is configured here. Routes can be specified based on the interface name defined in the context. For example, you can have route statements for the inside routes: **route inside 191.1.1.1 255.255.255.255 10.1.2.2.**

— Define translations:

```
nat (inside) 1 10.1.2.0 255.255.255.0
global (outside) 1 10.1.100.0-10.1.100.29
! This context uses dynamic NAT for inside users that
! access the outside security domain
static (inside,outside) 10.1.100.30 10.1.2.75 netmask 255.255.255.255

! Outside user to access the internal server
```

— Define access lists:

```
access-list INTERNET extended permit ip any any
access-group INTERNET in interface inside
access-list SECRULES extended permit ip any any
access-group SECRULES in interface outside
```

Transparent configuration example for context B:

To access the context for customer B from the system configuration, the command to be used is

```
FWSMB# changeto context customerB
```

— Configure transparent mode.

```
firewall transparent
```

— Configure the interfaces.

```
interface Vlan30
 nameif outside
 bridge-group 1
 security-level 0
 !
interface Vlan31
 nameif inside
 bridge-group 1
 security-level 100
 !
```

The Layer 3 interface defined in the Layer 3 router will be in a different VLAN but the same IP subnet.

```
interface BVI1
 ip address 10.100.1.254 255.255.255.0
```

— Define the access list.

```
access-group 101 in interface outside
access-group 100 in interface outside
access-group 100 out interface outside
access-group 101 in interface inside
access-group 100 in interface inside
access-group 100 out interface inside
access-list 100 extended permit ip any any
access-list 100 extended permit udp any any
access-list 101 ethertype permit bpdu
```

This generic access list permits all the traffic.

— Configure the MTU and no failover.

```
mtu outside 1500
mtu inside 1500
no failover
```

— Define the respective routes for FWSM management traffic.

```
route outside 0.0.0.0 0.0.0.0 10.100.1.1 1
```

Summary

After reading this chapter, you should be able to configure the FWSM. The key topics of FWSM configuration covered in this chapter are the following:

- Switch level configuration for FWSM
- Configuration of single context routed mode
- Configuration of single context transparent mode
- Configuration of multiple context mixed mode

CHAPTER 8

Access Control Lists

Access control lists (ACL) filter traffic for a function. The function can be to deny or permit the traffic, to classify the traffic for network address translation (NAT), or to set the traffic to a particular queue, based on quality of service (QoS). ACLs are used in Cisco IOS and firewalls to filter traffic.

Security rules to permit or deny networks or any users are defined by an ACL on a Firewall Services Module (FWSM). The FWSM does not allow any traffic unless it is specified (this is regardless of the security domain). Following are the uses of the access list in the FWSM:

- **Provides network security rule definition:** The rules for one security domain to access the other security domain are described using access lists.

- **Allows for authentication, authorization, and accounting (AAA) network access:** Access lists are used to define the traffic for the cut-through proxy feature. This feature is covered in Chapter 10, "AAA Overview."

- **Allows Virtual Private Network (VPN) access:** Defines the host that can access the FWSM through VPN.

- **Used in configuring network address translation:** Identifies NAT for specific source or destination IP addresses.

- **Used in configuring modular QoS:** Identifies traffic for modular QoS policies.

- **Used in redistribution of routing protocol:** Access lists filter subnets that are redistributed between routing protocols.

Understanding the concept of access lists is important to configure various features in the FWSM. Access lists add to the working of important features in the FWSM.

Introducing Types of Access Lists

This section covers the three major types of access lists. Each type of access list plays an important role in enabling the functionality of specific features in the FWSM.

The three main types of access lists are as follows:

- **Standard access list:** Standard access lists are used in commands to identify the destination IP addresses only. This is normally used in Open Shortest Path First (OSPF) protocol redistribution in FWSM.

  ```
  hostname(config)# access-list access_list_name standard {deny | permit} {any |
      ip_address mask}
  ```

- **Extended access list:** In this type of access list, ports, protocols, and Internet Control Message Protocol (ICMP) types can be specified using an **access-list** command. For security policy, all the fields can be used to control the traffic flow. One access list of each type (extended and EtherType) can be applied to each direction of an interface. The same access lists can be applied on multiple interfaces. With an extended access list, you can schedule the enabling of the access list through the **time-range** command. Any access list can be changed without altering the security structure of the access lists applied to enforce a security policy, using the line number. In an extended access list, you can add an access list with the **inactive** keyword. The access list, though configured, will be in an inactive state. To remove the inactive state, add the access list without the **inactive** keyword.

  ```
  hostname(config)# access-list access_list_name [line line_number] [extended]
      {deny | permit} protocol source_address mask [operator port] dest_address mask
      [operator port | icmp_type] [inactive]
  ```

- **EtherType access list:** This type of access list is defined by a 16-bit hexadecimal number. It is used to support Ethernet V2 frames. 802.3-formatted frames are not supported by this type of access list. The only exception is bridge protocol data unit (BPDU), which is handled by the access list. The FWSM receives trunk port (Cisco proprietary) BPDUs from the switch. Trunk BPDUs have virtual local-area network (VLAN) information inside the payload, so the FWSM modifies the payload with the outgoing VLAN if BPDUs are allowed. In a failover mode, it is best practice to allow BPDUs through both the interfaces. (Layer 2 loops will be seen if BPDUs are not allowed in a failover mode.) For a security rule to be applied on an inside and outside interface, the access list needs to be applied to both the interfaces for the packet to pass through. For EtherType access lists, the implicit deny at the end of the access list does not deny IPv4 traffic or Address Resolution Protocols (ARP). The implicit deny at the end of the access list also does not block any IP traffic that was previously allowed with an extended access list. IPv4 and ARP traffic cannot be controlled with an EtherType access list.

  ```
  hostname(config)# access-list access_list_name ethertype {permit | deny} {ipx |
      bpdu | mpls-unicast | mpls-multicast | any | hex_number}
  ```

Extended access list is commonly used in FWSM with object group and line number. Details of object group are covered in the later part of this chapter. EtherType access list is used in FWSM, in transparent mode.

Understanding Access Control Entry

Access control entries (ACE) are defined in hardware for access list entries. An access list can be made up of one or more ACEs defined in the hardware. For each access list defined, each ACE is appended directly unless a line number is specified. The order of ACE is very important. When a packet arrives, the FWSM checks the packet against each ACE order to determine whether the packet can pass through. In the beginning of the order, if deny all is configured, all the packets will be denied regardless of the security policy.

Table 8-1 documents the rules for FWSM in the 3.x code release.

Table 8-1   *Rules Allocation per Feature for Single and Multiple Context Modes*

Rules	Single Context Mode	Multiple Context Mode (Max Per Partition) with 12 Pools
AAA rules	6451	992
ACEs	74,188	10,633
established commands	460	70
Filter rules	2764	425
ICMP, Telnet, SSH[1], and HTTP rules	1843	283
Policy NAT ACEs	1843	283
Inspect rules	4147	1417
Total rules	**92,156**	**14,173**

[1]SSH = Secure Shell

In the FWSM, if a resource limitation exists with the number of ACEs and you need to add additional ACEs, the additional ACE will destroy the existing ACE structure. The complete ACE structure will be removed if you add any additional ACE after resource capacity for the rules is reached. For more information about the resource tuning in the firewall, see Chapter 5, "Understanding Contexts."

Some quick commands to check the rules used in the FWSM are as follows:

- In single context mode or within a context, enter the following command:

  ```
  hostname(config)# show np 3 acl count 0
  ```

- In multiple context mode system execution space, enter the following command:

  ```
  hostname(config)# show np 3 acl count partition_number
  ```

These two commands are helpful in understanding the resource utilization for the FWSM. It is important to understand the resource utilization because this helps in planning for future resource allotment for new rule sets. Refer to Chapter 5 for more details in resource planning.

Understanding Access List Commit

The FWSM waits until the last entered access list and then activates the access list by committing to the network processor (NP). During the commit, if an access list is added, the FWSM aborts the commit and again starts the commit process. The message that appears after the commit is completed is as follows:

```
Access Rules Download Complete: Memory Utilization: < 1%
```

Understanding Object Groups

Object groups allow the administrator to use access lists, based on a grouping that identifies the common use of a policy. With object grouping, you can classify elements of an access list in a group and can have multiple elements referenced in separate groups. These groups can be referenced in the access list for defining the security policy. The grouping can be done based on the following criteria:

- Protocol
- Network
- Service
- ICMP type

The object group can be used with an extended access list statement. The resource limit of ACE for FWSM applies to the expanded access lists. This ACE limitation applies to the object group. When the rules in the object group are applied, the rules are committed as expanded ACE.

Consider the following examples of object grouping:

- **Example 1:** The customer has multiple VPN devices in the inside or the demilitarized zone (DMZ) security domain. Each of the VPN concentrators takes care of a separate department and has a separate admin control for each department. In the FWSM, instead of defining authentication header (AH), encryption service payload (ESP), and UDP port 500 for each VPN concentrator, these ports and protocols can be put in one object group and referenced in an access list for each VPN concentrator in the respective security domain.

- **Example 2:** The customer has a common security policy for Internet access for the applications residing in the different DMZ zones. These DMZ zones can have a common security policy represented in an object group.

Object groups help simplify and organize the security rule set in the FWSM. This feature will make the rule set easy to understand or integrate with new rule sets.

Monitoring Access List Resources

When a log message is enabled for ACE, every time the ACE is hit (the ACE is used here to deny a network), a log 106100 message is created. The FWSM has a maximum of 640,000 flows for ACE. To avoid the central processing unit (CPU) spikes on concurrent flows, the FWSM places a limit on the deny flow. The FWSM does not place a limit on the permit flows. The deny flows can be exploited by a Denial of Service (DoS) attack. Restricting the number of deny flows prevents unlimited consumption of memory and CPU resources. When the maximum number of deny flows is reached, the FWSM issues a system log message 106100:

```
%XXX-1-106101: The number of ACL log deny-flows has reached limit (number).
```

The deny flow limit can be configured in the FWSM:

```
FWSM(config)# access-list deny-flow-max number
```

The maximum number of default concurrent deny flows that can be created is 4096 (the number can be 1–4096).

The time for reporting the syslog message and actual deny flow can be configured as follows:

```
FWSM(config)# access-list alert-interval secs
```

The default value of reporting is 300 sec, and the range is between 1–3600 sec.

Configuring Object Groups and Access Lists

Several types of object groups and access list configurations exist: protocol type, network type, service type, nesting type, and EtherType.

Working with Protocol Type

In the protocol type of object grouping, protocols can be grouped as an object group and can be referenced in an access list.

- Protocol type of access group:

```
FWSM(config)# object-group protocol prot-A
FWSM(config-protocol)# protocol-object tcp
FWSM(config-protocol)# protocol-object udp
```

Working with Network Type

In the network type of object grouping, IP subnets or hosts can be grouped in an object group. This object group can be reused in various access lists.

- Network type of object group:

```
FWSM(config)# object-group network-A
FWSM(config-network)# description Privileged users
FWSM(config-network)# network-object host 10.1.2.1
FWSM(config-network)# network-object host 10.1.2.18
FWSM(config-network)# network-object host 10.2.14.34
```

Working with Service Type

In the service type grouping, application services can be grouped in an object group and can be reused in multiple access lists.

- Service type of object group:

```
FWSM(config)# object-group service services1 tcp-udp
FWSM(config-service)# description DNS Group
FWSM(config-service)# port-object eq domain
```

Working with Nesting Type

In the nesting of object groups, multiple object groups can be defined. These object groups can be referenced in a parent object group. The parent object group is a collection of child object groups and will be referenced in an access list.

- Nesting type of object groups:

```
FWSM(config)# object-group network deptA
FWSM(config-network)# network-object host 10.11.1.15
FWSM(config-network)# network-object host 10.11.1.19

FWSM(config-network)# object-group network deptB
FWSM(config-network)# network-object host 10.12.1.8
FWSM(config-network)# network-object host 10.12.1.2

FWSM(config-network)# object-group network deptC
FWSM(config-network)# network-object host 10.13.1.3

FWSM(config)# object-group network USERS
FWSM(config-network)# group-object deptA
FWSM(config-network)# group-object deptB
FWSM(config-network)# group-object deptC
```

Object group definition in ACE:

```
FWSM(config)# access-list ACL_IN extended permit ip object-group USERS host
    10.100.100.100
```

Working with EtherType

In transparent mode, you can have EtherType classification grouped in an object group and referenced in an access list.

- EtherType access list example:

```
FWSM(config)# access-list ETHER ethertype permit ipx
FWSM(config)# access-list ETHER ethertype permit bpdu
FWSM(config)# access-list ETHER ethertype permit mpls-unicast
FWSM(config)# access-list nonIP ethertype deny 1256 *
FWSM(config)# access-group ETHER in interface inside
```

* The EtherType access list denies EtherType 0x1256.

NOTE   When allowing mpls-unicast through transparent Layer 2 firewalls on the policy feature card (PFC), the command that needs to be enabled is

```
PFC(config)# mpls ldp router-id interface force
```

or

```
PFC(config)# tag-switching tdp router-id interface force
```

- The following is an example of applying inbound or outbound access lists:

The traffic flow control with access lists can be done in two ways on an interface: inbound control or outbound control. Inbound control provides control on the traffic entering the interface, and the outbound control provides control on the traffic leaving the interface to the next hop device.

You can use inbound and outbound directions to control the flow of traffic with access lists. This mainly depends on the security policy. If the security policy can be complied with one direction of access lists in all interfaces, the other direction (inbound or outbound) can have a **permit ip any any** statement.

In Example 8-1, the inbound access list is allowed with **permit ip any any** and the outbound access list has a specific network based on the security policy that is allowed to traverse the network.

Example 8-1   *Shows Inbound Access List with permit ip any any*

```
ContextA(config)# access-list IN extended permit ip any any
ContextA(config)# access-group IN in interface inside
ContextA(config)# access-group IN in interface outside
```

Example 8-2 shows the outbound access list in the inside and the outside interfaces to have configuration of the security policy (allowing only specific subnets).

Example 8-2 *Outbound Access List in the Inside and Outside Interfaces*

```
ContextA(config)# access-list OUT-Inside extended permit tcp 10.1.1.1 0.0.0.255 any
ContextA(config)# access-group OUT-Inside in interface inside

ContextA(config)# access-list OUT-Outside extended permit tcp any host 201.1.1.1
  eq www
ContextA(config)# access-group OUT_Outside in interface outside
```

The direction to have a specific allow statement depends on the security zone. In Example 8-2, the access list is applied to the inside security zone. This is the most secured domain among other interfaces. Incoming traffic is trusted and allows any traffic to pass through. The outbound traffic is made specific.

In the outside interface, the inbound access list must be specific and granular, and the outbound access list in the outside interface can permit traffic to flow out of the outside interface. The access list and the direction of applying the list depend on the security policy. For no reason should optimization of access list security policy rules be compromised.

Summary

This chapter covers types of access lists. There are three main types of access lists in FWSM: standard, extended, and EtherType. ACE is a component that defines the access list in hardware. It is important to understand ACE for resource management of access lists and rules. Object grouping helps define and structure the security policy into objects that can be reused in the access lists. This makes the security policy in the firewall easy to understand, for future integration of new policies or rules.

CHAPTER 9

Configuring Routing Protocols

This chapter gives a snapshot of routing protocol concepts and their support on the Firewall Services Module (FWSM). It also covers configuration of each routing protocol on the FWSM with design examples.

Packet flow to and from the firewall depends on the routing of the packets from one security domain to the other. It is important to have symmetry in routing between the firewall and the Layer 3 device in each security domain. This helps in aligning and placing the firewalls at various locations on a network, such as the edge of the Internet or in a data center.

Routing in the FWSM follows the security policy before the packet is sent to the next hop address. The FWSM uses the XLATE table and the routing table to select an egress interface to forward the packets. After the egress interface is known, the next hop address is determined based on the routing table. The packet forwarding in the FWSM is a two-step process:

Step 1 Select the egress interface.

If the XLATE table exists, the interface is selected from the XLATE table. If there is no XLATE entry, but static translation exists, the egress interface is selected using the static translation (no routing table is used). For dynamic outbound Network Address Translation (NAT), initial outgoing packets are routed using the route table after the XLATE entry is created. The incoming return packets are forwarded using existing XLATE entry only. For static NAT, incoming packets that are destination translated are forwarded using existing XLATE or static translation rules.

Step 2 Select the next hop address.

After selecting the egress interface to determine the next hop address, an additional lookup is performed in the routing table. The next hop has to be reachable through the egress interface selected in step 1. If no routes in the routing table explicitly belong to the selected interface in step 1, the packet is dropped. If the route for the corresponding next hop IP address exists through the selected egress interface, the packet will then be forwarded.

When the FWSM is configured with dynamic routing protocol, the packets are forwarded based on the XLATE creation to select the egress interface and then use routing protocol lookup for determining the next hop address. If a route flap happens, when using a dynamic routing protocol, the forwarding state will be determined based on the existing XLATE table. The new route table forwarding occurs only after the XLATE entry corresponds (dynamic outbound NAT is used) with the values of the new routing table, after the flap. Therefore, it is desired not to have route flaps in the FWSM. Generally, the FWSM will have only a single interface exit to the security domain, where the egress interface selection for the next hop address will always be the same.

NOTE	Load balancing is possible through multiple next hop addresses using the same egress interface for destined traffic. Load balancing cannot be done for the same destination using multiple egress interfaces.

Supporting Routing Methods

The following routing protocols are supported in the FWSM:

- Static routes
- Default routes
- OSPF
- RIP
- BGP stub

The next section in the chapter covers the features of each routing protocol supported in the FWSM with configuration examples for common design scenarios.

Static Routes

Static routing in the FWSM functions similar to the **ip route** statement in a Cisco router. The route will remain in the gateway even if the next hop is unavailable. For the same destination, a maximum of three equal cost routes can be in the FWSM. Note that for the traffic to be forwarded, the egress interface of the three equal cost routes for the destination has to be the same. Equal Cost Multipath (ECMP) can be specified only through one interface. The traffic will be distributed equally among gateways based on the algorithm and hash. The command to configure a static route in FWSM is

```
FWSM(config)# route if_name destination_ip mask gateway_ip [distance]
```

The following example creates a static route that sends all the traffic destined for 10.2.1.0/ 24 to the router interface 192.1.1.1, connected to the outside interface of the FWSM:

```
FWSM(config)# route outside 10.2.1.0 255.255.255.0 192.1.1.1 1
```

While configuring redundancy, you can use static routes in the FWSM to point to the active HSRP gateway address of the Layer 3 next hop device. A static route from the Layer 3 next hop device points to the primary FWSM interface. With static routes, failover and redundancy symmetry are maintained with the Layer 3 network.

Default Routes

A default route is a gateway of last resort, when no other more specific route exists in the routing table. It is configured with 0.0.0.0/0 representing the network address and the use of a valid Layer 3 next hop address.

You can define a maximum of three default routes in the same security domain. If multiple default routes exist, the traffic is distributed based on the specified gateways.

To configure a default route, enter the following command:

```
hostname(config)# route if_name 0.0.0.0 0.0.0.0 gateway_ip [distance]
```

NOTE   The default route used in the FWSM in transparent mode is for the management traffic only.

Open Shortest Path First

This section gives a basic snapshot of the Open Shortest Path First (OSPF) Protocol and configuring the OSPF Protocol on the FWSM.

OSPF is a link state routing protocol developed by the Internet Engineering Task Force (IETF). An OSPF can operate within a hierarchy. An autonomous system (AS) is the largest entity within the hierarchy, which is a collection of networks under a common administration that share a common routing strategy. OSPF is an IGP routing protocol and uses the Dijsktra algorithm to calculate the shortest path first (SPF) for route computation. Routing from one area to another will have to pass through the backbone area (area 0), which gives OSPF two levels of hierarchy for routing. SPF is independently performed for each area. The routing protocol supports classless interdomain routing (CIDR) and variable length subnet masking (VLSM). Routing decisions are made based on the cost of the links. All links have a cost, and the total path cost from source to destination is used to make routing decisions at the first hop router.

SPF Algorithm

The SPF algorithm is calculated for an area. All the routers in the area share the same database. The OSPF database is built based on link-state advertisement (LSA). OSPF uses LSAs to advertise the networks configured in the node to other nodes in the area. Some of the information in an LSA includes the interface and subnet of the node. A network change triggers an LSA. The periodic refresh is sent every 30 seconds (default value).

The following are some of the OSPF routing protocol packets:

- **Hello:** Hello uses multicast for all routers (224.0.0.5). In a LAN, the hello is 10 seconds, and in a non-broadcast multi-access (NBMA) network, the hello is 30 seconds. This is used to form adjacency between routers and maintain neighbor relationship.

- **Database Descriptor:** Gives the topology information of the database and is exchanged when adjacency is established.

- **Link State Request:** If a router receives a database request with new information, this request is sent to the neighbors to get more details.

- **Link State Update:** This is a response to the link state request. Several LSAs are included within a single link state update packet.

- **Link State Acknowledgment:** This acknowledges a link state update.

OSPF Network Types

There are five OSPF network types:

- **Broadcast multi-access:** Any LAN or Ethernet segment represents this type of OSPF network. In this network, OSPF will have a designated router (DR) and a backup designated router (BDR). The designated router is responsible to maintain the OSPF topology. DR and BDR elections are done based on OSPF priority. A DR is selected based on the highest OSPF priority. In case of a tie, the router with the highest router ID wins the election. BDR is used as a DR in case the designated router fails. The default for interface OSPF priority on Cisco routers is one. The routers send their advertisement to the DR using 224.0.0.6 multicast group.

- **Point-to-point:** One router is directly connected to the other router. For example, a serial link connection between the two routers is a point-to-point link. There is no DR/BDR election in this network type.

- **Point-to-multipoint:** This is a single interface that connects to multiple destinations. There is no DR/BDR election. OSPF sends its messages using multicast.

- **Non-Broadcast Multi-access (NBMA):** Typically seen in Frame Relay circuits when multiple sites are connected to a hub with a single interface. All the interfaces will have a single IP subnet. DR/BDR election takes place here.

- **Virtual Links:** When an area does not have connection to the backbone (all areas defined in the OSPF process should have connection to the backbone), a virtual link needs to be configured between the area and the backbone (area 0).

Concept of Areas

OSPF uses a hierarchy for route exchanges in a domain. An area is a group of routers in the OSPF domain that exchanges and maintains the LSA database. The concept of areas in OSPF builds a two-level hierarchy for routing. Route exchanges from one area to the other is through area 0, which is the backbone for the OSPF network. Figure 9-1 shows the concept of areas and its components.

Figure 9-1   *Hierarchy in OSPF*

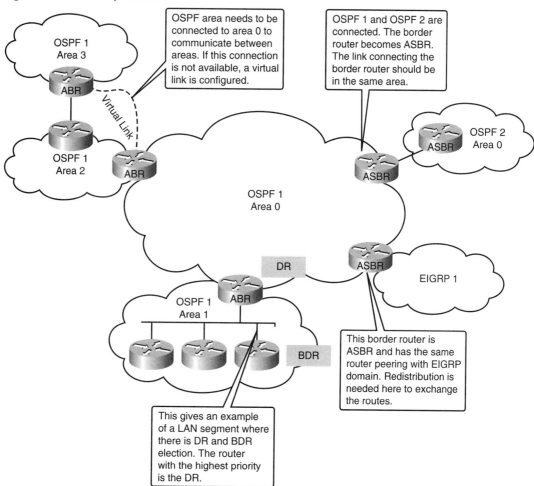

There are different types of routers in an area, and each has a different functionality:

- **Internal routers:** Routers that are inside an area.

- **Area Backbone Router (ABR):** This connects one or more areas to the backbone (area 0) and acts as a gateway for inter-area traffic.
- **Autonomous System Router (ASBR):** Any redistribution of routes makes a router an ASBR. They act as gateways for external traffic.
- **Backbone Router:** All areas are connected to area 0 (also called the backbone). The routers within this area are referred to as the backbone router.

NOTE   The ABR routers must have a link in area 0.

OSPF Link State Advertisement

OSPF routers use LSAs to advertise their networks. Figure 9-2 shows the different types of LSAs in an OSPF network.

Figure 9-2   *LSA Types and Stub Area*

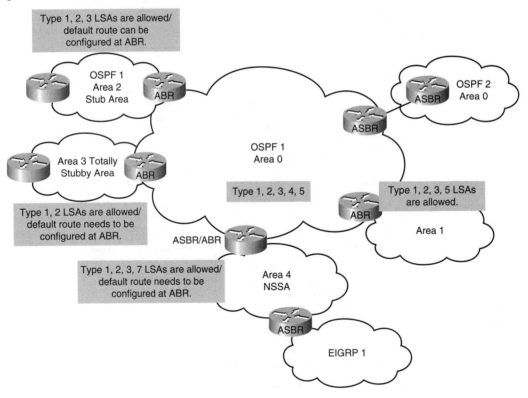

- **Router link LSA:** Every router in a particular area will generate this LSA. This LSA type will be sent to all the routers in the same area to maintain the database for SPF calculation. This type of LSA is identified as Type 1 LSA.

- **Network link LSA:** This LSA is originated by a DR. This LSA advertises the multi-access network and all routers attached to the network. This is a Type 2 LSA.

- **Network summary link LSA:** Describes the destination outside the area and is flooded throughout a single area originated by an ABR. This is a Type 3 LSA.

- **AS external ASBR summary link LSA:** This is originated from the ABR and contains the metric cost from the ABR to the ASBR. It is identified as a Type 4 LSA.

- **External link LSA:** This is originated from the ASBR routers. The route information in this LSA is the destination learned from another routing process (autonomous system). The external metric field in this LSA describes whether the route is external type 1 or external type 2. The difference between the two types is in the way the cost of the route is calculated. The cost of a type 2 route is always the external cost, irrespective of the interior cost to reach that route. A type 1 cost is the addition of the external cost and the internal cost used to reach that route. This is identified as a Type 5 LSA.

- **NSSA External LSA:** When an external route is redistributed in the OSPF NSSA area, Type 7 LSAs are created by ASBRs in NSSA. Type 5 LSAs are not allowed in the NSSA area, so the NSSA ASBR generates a Type 7 LSA instead, which remains within the NSSA. This Type 7 LSA gets translated back into a Type 5 LSA by the NSSA ABR.

Types of Stub Area in OSPF

The types of stub areas in OSPF are as follows:

- **Stub area:** The ABR will not send external LSAs to the routers configured as stub. All the routers in the stub area should have all the interfaces configured as stub. In this case, the hello flag with E bit changes to 0.

- **Totally stubby area:** No external routes or Type 3 LSAs are allowed. The routers inside the area get the default route to make the routing decision.

- **Not so stubby area:** Type 5 LSAs (external routes) are not allowed in a stubby area. Not so stubby area (NSSA) must be configured to support external routes in a stubby area. This is featured in RFC 1587.

OSPF in FWSM

The FWSM can run only two OSPF processes simultaneously. OSPF restricts the FWSM to have overlapping IP addresses. This is traditionally possible through NAT. It is common to see one OSPF process used in each of the two security domains. The redistribution is possible only between two OSPF processes representing each security domain. Static routes can also be redistributed into the OSPF process. Redistribution between RIP and OSPF routes cannot be configured. OSPF and RIP cannot be enabled together in the FWSM.

OSPF Features Supported in FWSM

The following are the important features of OSPF supported in FWSM:

- Only two OSPF processes are supported in the FWSM.
- Redistribution is possible between the two OSPF processes or static routes only.
- Support of virtual link.
- Authentication via message digest algorithm 5 (MD5).
- Supports inter-area, intra-area, and external routes (Type 1 and Type 2).
- OSPF LSA flooding.
- FWSM can be a DR or BDR.
- Advertisement of static and global address translations.
- Stub and not-so-stubby areas.
- Advanced LSA filtering—Type 3 filtering.

OSPF Configuration in FWSM

A number of OSPF features can be enabled in the FWSM. This section covers the commands for configuring the features on the FWSM.

Interface-Based Configuration for OSPF Parameters

The following are some of the OSPF parameters that can be modified on an interface:

- **OSPF cost:** Specifies the cost of sending a packet on an OSPF interface.
- **Priority:** Used in DR/BDR election.
- **Retransmission Interval:** Specifies the number of seconds between LSA retransmissions for adjacencies belonging to an OSPF interface.
- **Transmit delay:** Estimates the number of seconds required to send a link-state update packet on an OSPF interface.
- **Hello Intervals:** The time interval between the OSPF hello packets.

- **Dead Intervals:** Specifies the time interval that a device should wait before it declares a neighbor OSPF router down.

- **Authentication parameters:** MD5 is specified to authenticate messages exchanged between devices.

These OSPF parameters are configured in the Example 9-1.

Example 9-1 *Interface-Based Configuration for OSPF Parameters*

```
FWSM(config)# router ospf 1
FWSM(config-router)# network 10.1.0.0 255.255.0.0 area 0
FWSM(config-router)# interface vlan91
FWSM(config-interface)# ospf cost 30
FWSM(config-interface)# ospf retransmit-interval 15
FWSM(config-interface)# ospf transmit-delay 10
FWSM(config-interface)# ospf priority 30
FWSM(config-interface)# ospf hello-interval 10
FWSM(config-interface)# ospf dead-interval 40
FWSM(config-interface)# ospf authentication-key cisco123
FWSM(config-interface)# ospf message-digest-key 1 md5 cisco123
FWSM(config-interface)# ospf authentication message-digest
```

Summarization

For summarization between OSPF areas, routes are represented as Type 3 LSA. The following example shows the configuration of summarization in an area:

```
FWSM(config)# router ospf 2
FWSM(config-router)# area 1 range 10.1.0.0 255.255.0.0
```

When routes are redistributed into the OSPF process, the routes are represented as Type 5 LSA. The following example shows the summarization of the external routes, using the **summary-address** command:

```
FWSM(config)# router ospf 2
FWSM(config-router)# summary-address 10.1.0.0 255.255.0.0
```

Stub Configuration

The following example shows the FWSM configured as ABR:

```
FWSM(config)# router ospf 1
FWSM(config-router)# area 1 stub no-summary
```

The following example shows the FWSM configured as a part of the OSPF stub area:

```
FWSM(config-router)# router ospf 1
FWSM(config-router)# area 1 stub
```

NSSA Configuration

If the FWSM is the ABR, configure the following command:

```
FWSM(config-router)# area 1 nssa no-summary
FWSM(config-router)# area 1 nssa default-information-originate
```

If the FWSM is a part of the OSPF NSSA area, configure the following command:

```
FWSM(config-router)# area 1 nssa
```

Default Route Information

In OSPF, it is necessary to specify a default route in the routing information base (RIB). When **default-information originate** is enabled in the OSPF process, a default route is generated to the OSPF neighbor routers, and the OSPF router becomes an ASBR. The command to configure default route information is

```
FWSM(config-router)# default-information originate [always] [metric metric-value]
[metric-type {1 | 2}] [route-map map-name]
```

By enabling the **default-information originate** with the **always** keyword, the FWSM will add the 0.0.0.0 route and advertise the route to its neighbors even without the route existing in the RIB. The routes can be redistributed as external Type 1 or Type 2 routes.

Timers

The two timers that can be adjusted in OSPF in the FWSM are *spf-delay* and *spf-holdtime*. Spf-delay is the delay time between when the OSPF process receives the topology change and when it starts the SPF calculation. The default for this is 5 seconds. Spf-hold time is the minimum time between two consecutive SPF calculations. The default is 10 seconds.

The command to configure the spf timers is the following:

Step 1   Enter the OSPF process.

```
FWSM(config)# router ospf process_id
```

Step 2   Configure the SPF delay and hold timers:

```
FWSM(config-router)# timers spf spf-delay spf-holdtime
```

The timers for spf-delay and spf-holdtime ranges from 0 to 65535.

Other timer values that can be changed in OSPF are covered in the "Interface-Based Configuration for OSPF Parameters" section in this chapter.

OSPF Design Example 1

As shown in Figure 9-3, in this example, the same OSPF process routes between the DMZ and the inside security domains. The FWSM is in a single context routed mode. The configuration does not have MD5 enabled. It is a good practice to enable MD5 authentication. Example 9-2 shows the FWSM configuration.

Figure 9-3 *OSPF Single-Process Between Two Security Zones*

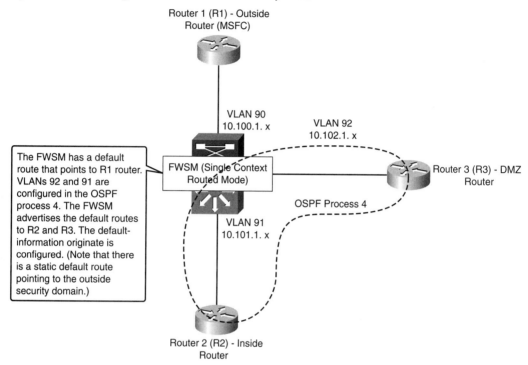

Example 9-2 *FWSM Configuration*

```
FWSM(config)# show run
: Saved
:
FWSM Version 3.1(3)6
!
hostname FWSM
enable password 8Ry2YjIyt7RRXU24 encrypted
names
! Configure the outside interface
interface Vlan90
 nameif outside
 security-level 0
 ip address 10.100.1.2 255.255.255.0
! Configure the inside interface
interface Vlan91
 nameif inside
 security-level 100
```

continues

Example 9-2 *FWSM Configuration (Continued)*

```
 ip address 10.101.1.2 255.255.255.0
! Configure the dmz interface
interface Vlan92
 nameif dmz
 security-level 50
 ip address 10.102.1.2 255.255.255.0
!
passwd 2KFQnbNIdI.2KYOU encrypted
ftp mode passive
! Configure the access list. Note that the access list should be configured based
! on the security policy
access-list 100 extended permit ip any any
access-list 101 extended permit ip any any
access-list 102 extended permit ip any any
access-list 106 extended permit ip any any
pager lines 24
mtu outside 1500
mtu inside 1500
mtu dmz 1500
no failover
icmp permit any outside
icmp permit any inside
icmp permit any dmz
no asdm history enable
arp timeout 14400
nat-control
! Configure NAT for the security domains defined
nat (inside) 0 0.0.0.0 0.0.0.0
nat (dmz) 0 0.0.0.0 0.0.0.0
! Apply access list to the interfaces in the security domain
access-group 100 in interface outside
access-group 100 out interface outside
access-group 106 in interface inside
access-group 101 out interface inside
access-group 102 in interface dmz
access-group 102 out interface dmz
! Configure default route pointing to the outside next hop address
route outside 0.0.0.0 0.0.0.0 10.100.1.1 1
! Configure OSPF defined in each security domain. Configure the router Id. The
! default-information originate command will generate a default route in DMZ and
! inside security domains, based on the static route configured in the FWSM
! towards the outside security domain
router ospf 4
 network 10.101.0.0 255.255.0.0 area 0
 network 10.102.0.0 255.255.0.0 area 0
 router-id 10.101.1.2
 log-adj-changes
 default-information originate
!
timeout xlate 3:00:00
timeout conn 1:00:00 half-closed 0:10:00 udp 0:02:00 icmp 0:00:02
```

Example 9-2 *FWSM Configuration (Continued)*

```
timeout sunrpc 0:10:00 h323 0:05:00 h225 1:00:00 mgcp 0:05:00
timeout mgcp-pat 0:05:00 sip 0:30:00 sip_media 0:02:00
timeout uauth 0:05:00 absolute
no snmp-server location
no snmp-server contact
snmp-server enable traps snmp authentication linkup linkdown coldstart
telnet timeout 5
ssh timeout 5
console timeout 0
!
class-map inspection_default
 match default-inspection-traffic
!
policy-map global_policy
 class inspection_default
  inspect dns maximum-length 512
  inspect ftp
  inspect h323 h225
  inspect h323 ras
  inspect netbios
  inspect rsh
  inspect skinny
  inspect smtp
  inspect sqlnet
  inspect sunrpc
  inspect tftp
  inspect sip
  inspect xdmcp
!
service-policy global_policy global
prompt hostname context
Cryptochecksum:1296bbc15e71a27c5087f81eae48b43c
End
```

The following examples are the outputs for the configuration shown in "OSPF Design Example 1." Example 9-3 illustrates checking the routing table at the FWSM.

Example 9-3 *Checking the Routing Table at the FWSM*

```
FWSM(config)# show route

O    172.17.1.1 255.255.255.255 [110/11] via 10.102.1.1, 17:02:07, dmz
O    172.16.1.1 255.255.255.255 [110/11] via 10.101.1.1, 17:02:07, inside
C    10.102.1.0 255.255.255.0 is directly connected, dmz
C    10.101.1.0 255.255.255.0 is directly connected, inside
C    10.100.1.0 255.255.255.0 is directly connected, outside
S*   0.0.0.0 0.0.0.0 [1/0] via 10.100.1.1, outside
```

The highlighted portion in the output of this **show route** command indicates the networks learned from OSPF neighbors as **O**, directly connected routes at the FWSM as **C**, and static routes configured in the FWSM as **S**. Example 9-4 illustrates checking the OSPF database at the FWSM.

Example 9-4 *Checking the OSPF Database at the FWSM*

```
FWSM(config)# show ospf 4 database


         OSPF Router with ID (10.101.1.2) (Process ID 4)


               Router Link States (Area 0)

Link ID         ADV Router      Age      Seq#        Checksum Link count
10.109.1.1      10.109.1.1      1087     0x80000029 0x3ca5    2
10.101.1.2      10.101.1.2      1411     0x8000002b 0x43f2    2
10.102.1.1      10.102.1.1      1291     0x8000002b 0x e14    2

               Net Link States (Area 0)

Link ID         ADV Router      Age      Seq#        Checksum
10.101.1.1      10.109.1.1      1857     0x80000020 0x5fc9
10.102.1.1      10.102.1.1      1550     0x80000020 0x470a

               Type-5 AS External Link States

Link ID         ADV Router      Age      Seq#        Checksum Tag
0.0.0.0         10.101.1.2      1411     0x80000026 0x8e89    4
```

The output shown in Example 9-4 gives the LSA types in the OSPF process learned via the OSPF neighbors. Example 9-5 shows the partial output of the **show ip route** command at the DMZ router.

Example 9-5 *Displaying the IP Route at the DMZ Router*

```
Gateway of last resort is 10.102.1.2 to network 0.0.0.0

     172.17.0.0/32 is subnetted, 1 subnets
C       172.17.1.1 is directly connected, Loopback201
     172.16.0.0/32 is subnetted, 1 subnets
O       172.16.1.1 [110/12] via 10.102.1.2, 17:01:34, Vlan92
     10.0.0.0/24 is subnetted, 2 subnets
C       10.102.1.0 is directly connected, Vlan92
O       10.101.1.0 [110/11] via 10.102.1.2, 17:01:34, Vlan92
O*E2 0.0.0.0/0 [110/1] via 10.102.1.2, 17:01:34, Vlan92
```

Note that the highlighted portion of the default route (O*E2) is learned from the FWSM. This is an external Type 2 route.

Example 9-6 shows the partial output of the **show ip route** command at the inside router.

Example 9-6 *Displaying the IP Routes at the Inside Router*

```
Gateway of last resort is 10.101.1.2 to network 0.0.0.0

     172.17.0.0/32 is subnetted, 1 subnets
O       172.17.1.1 [110/12] via 10.101.1.2, 17:01:25, Vlan91
     172.16.0.0/32 is subnetted, 1 subnets
C       172.16.1.1 is directly connected, Loopback200
     10.0.0.0/24 is subnetted, 2 subnets
O       10.102.1.0 [110/11] via 10.101.1.2, 17:01:25, Vlan91
C       10.101.1.0 is directly connected, Vlan91
O*E2 0.0.0.0/0 [110/0] via 10.101.1.2, 17:01:32, Vlan91
```

Note that the highlighted portion of the default route (O*E2) is learned from the FWSM.

OSPF Design Example 2

As shown in Figure 9-4, in this example, the same OSPF process routes between the DMZ and the inside security domains. A separate OSPF process is used to route packets to the outside security domain. This example provides redistribution between the OSPF processes. The FWSM is in a single context routed mode. Note that only two OSPF processes can be configured in a single context routed mode. The configuration does not have MD5 enabled. It is a good practice to enable MD5 authentication. Example 9-7 shows the FWSM configuration in single context routed mode.

Figure 9-4 *Dual OSPF Processes Between Security Domains*

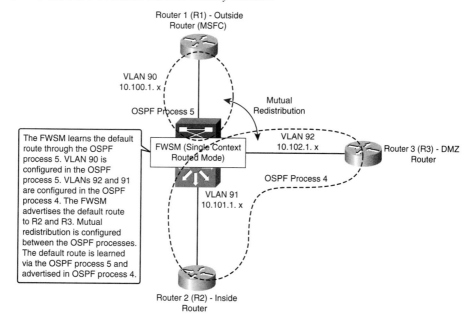

Example 9-7 *FWSM Configuration in Single Context Routed Mode*

```
FWSM# show run
: Saved
:
FWSM Version 3.1(3)6
!
hostname FWSM
enable password 8Ry2YjIyt7RRXU24 encrypted
names
! Configure the outside interface
interface Vlan90
 nameif outside
 security-level 0
 ip address 10.100.1.2 255.255.255.0
! Configure the inside interface
interface Vlan91
 nameif inside
 security-level 100
 ip address 10.101.1.2 255.255.255.0
! Configure the DMZ interface
interface Vlan92
 nameif dmz
 security-level 50
 ip address 10.102.1.2 255.255.255.0
!
passwd 2KFQnbNIdI.2KYOU encrypted
ftp mode passive
! access list will be defined based on security rule set.In this configuration.
! Access list is defined for all the traffic to pass through the FWSM
access-list 100 extended permit ip any any
access-list 101 extended permit ip any any
access-list 102 extended permit ip any any
access-list 106 extended permit ip any any
pager lines 24
mtu outside 1500
mtu inside 1500
mtu dmz 1500
no failover
icmp permit any outside
icmp permit any inside
icmp permit any dmz
no asdm history enable
arp timeout 14400
nat-control
! Configure NAT for each security domain defined in the FWSM
nat (inside) 0 0.0.0.0 0.0.0.0
nat (dmz) 0 0.0.0.0 0.0.0.0
! Apply the access list to the interface
access-group 100 in interface outside
access-group 100 out interface outside
access-group 106 in interface inside
access-group 101 out interface inside
access-group 102 in interface dmz
```

Example 9-7 *FWSM Configuration in Single Context Routed Mode (Continued)*

```
access-group 102 out interface dmz
! Configure OSPF and advertise the networks in the inside and dmz security domains.
! Redistribute the OSPF process of the outside security domain (ospf 5) to ospf 4
router ospf 4
 network 10.101.0.0 255.255.0.0 area 0
 network 10.102.0.0 255.255.0.0 area 0
 router-id 10.101.1.2
 log-adj-changes
 redistribute ospf 5 subnets
 default-information originate
! Configure OSPF and advertise the networks in outside security domain. Redistribute
! the OSPF process of the inside and DMZ security domains (ospf 4) to ospf 5
router ospf 5
 network 10.100.1.0 255.255.255.0 area 0
 log-adj-changes
 redistribute ospf 4 subnets
 summary-address 10.102.0.0 255.255.0.0
!
timeout xlate 3:00:00
timeout conn 1:00:00 half-closed 0:10:00 udp 0:02:00 icmp 0:00:02
timeout sunrpc 0:10:00 h323 0:05:00 h225 1:00:00 mgcp 0:05:00
timeout mgcp-pat 0:05:00 sip 0:30:00 sip_media 0:02:00
timeout uauth 0:05:00 absolute
no snmp-server location
no snmp-server contact
snmp-server enable traps snmp authentication linkup linkdown coldstart
telnet timeout 5
ssh timeout 5
console timeout 0
```

The following are the outputs for the configuration shown in "OSPF Design Example 2."
Example 9-8 displays the **show route** command at FWSM.

Example 9-8 *The* **show route** *Command at FWSM*

```
FWSM# show route

O    172.17.1.1 255.255.255.255 [110/11] via 10.102.1.1, 0:15:12, dmz
O    172.16.1.1 255.255.255.255 [110/11] via 10.100.1.1, 0:15:27, outside
O    10.102.0.0 255.255.0.0 is a summary, 0:01:50, OSPF Unknown Type
C    10.102.1.0 255.255.255.0 is directly connected, dmz
C    10.101.1.0 255.255.255.0 is directly connected, inside
C    10.100.1.0 255.255.255.0 is directly connected, outside
O*E2 0.0.0.0 0.0.0.0 [110/1] via 10.100.1.1, 0:15:27, outside
```

Note that the highlighted portion of the default route (O*E2) is learned in the FWSM from
the outside security domain.

To display routes in a particular OSPF process in the FWSM, use the **show ospf** <*process-
id*> **database** command, as shown in Example 9-9.

Example 9-9 *Check the OSPF Database in FWSM*

```
FWSM# show ospf 4 database


        OSPF Router with ID (10.101.1.2) (Process ID 4)


               Router Link States (Area 0)

Link ID         ADV Router      Age       Seq#          Checksum Link count
10.109.1.1      10.109.1.1      947       0x800003b5 0xc2c4 1
10.101.1.2      10.101.1.2      941       0x80000003 0x93ca 2
10.102.1.1      10.102.1.1      798       0x800003b6 0xeda5 2

               Net Link States (Area 0)

Link ID         ADV Router      Age       Seq#          Checksum
10.101.1.1      10.109.1.1      942       0x800003ab 0x3f5b
10.102.1.1      10.102.1.1      941       0x800003a9 0x2b99

               Type-5 AS External Link States

Link ID         ADV Router      Age       Seq#          Checksum Tag
0.0.0.0         10.101.1.2      944       0x80000001 0xd864 4
172.16.1.1      10.101.1.2      944       0x80000001 0x55bd 0
10.100.1.0      10.101.1.2      954       0x80000001 0xa820 0
10.102.0.0      10.101.1.2      128       0x80000001 0x418f 0
FWSM# show ospf 5 database


        OSPF Router with ID (10.102.1.2) (Process ID 5)


               Router Link States (Area 0)

Link ID         ADV Router      Age       Seq#          Checksum Link count
172.16.1.1      172.16.1.1      960       0x80000007 0x3497 2
10.102.1.2      10.102.1.2      954       0x80000004 0x4814 1

               Net Link States (Area 0)

Link ID         ADV Router      Age       Seq#          Checksum
10.100.1.1      172.16.1.1      960       0x80000001 0xdb32

               Type-5 AS External Link States

Link ID         ADV Router      Age       Seq#          Checksum Tag
0.0.0.0         172.16.1.1      1542      0x80000001 0x7416    5
172.17.1.1      10.102.1.2      946       0x80000001 0x63c7    0
10.101.1.0      10.102.1.2      965       0x80000001 0x9432    0
10.102.0.0      10.102.1.2      134       0x80000001 0x9333    0
```

Example 9-10 shows a partial output of routes learned at the Layer 3 device in the outside security domain, using the **show ip route** command. In the command output, you will notice the inside routes appearing as external Type 2 routes.

Example 9-10   *The* **show ip route** *Command at the Next Hop Layer 3 Device at the Outside Security Domain*

```
      172.17.0.0/32 is subnetted, 1 subnets
O E2    172.17.1.1 [110/11] via 10.100.1.2, 00:16:41, Vlan90
      172.16.0.0/32 is subnetted, 1 subnets
C       172.16.1.1 is directly connected, Loopback100
      10.0.0.0/8 is variably subnetted, 3 subnets, 2 masks
O E2    10.102.0.0/16 [110/10] via 10.100.1.2, 00:03:10, Vlan90
O E2    10.101.1.0/24 [110/10] via 10.100.1.2, 00:16:47, Vlan90
C       10.100.1.0/24 is directly connected, Vlan90
```

To display the IP routes at the DMZ Layer 3 device, use the **show ip route** command, as shown in Example 9-11. The default route is learned via OSPF from the FWSM.

Example 9-11   *The* **show ip route** *Command at a Layer 3 Device in the DMZ Domain*

```
Gateway of last resort is 10.102.1.2 to network 0.0.0.0

      172.17.0.0/32 is subnetted, 1 subnets
C        172.17.1.1 is directly connected, Loopback201
      172.16.0.0/32 is subnetted, 1 subnets
O E2     172.16.1.1 [110/11] via 10.102.1.2, 00:08:22, Vlan92
      10.0.0.0/24 is subnetted, 3 subnets
C        10.102.1.0 is directly connected, Vlan92
O        10.101.1.0 [110/11] via 10.102.1.2, 00:08:22, Vlan92
O E2     10.100.1.0 [110/10] via 10.102.1.2, 00:08:22, Vlan92
O*E2 0.0.0.0/0 [110/1] via 10.102.1.2, 00:08:22, Vlan92
```

Example 9-12 shows a partial output of the IP routes at the Layer 3 device in the inside security domain. The default route is learned via the FWSM.

Example 9-12   *The* **show ip route** *Command at the Inside Security Domain*

```
Gateway of last resort is 10.101.1.2 to network 0.0.0.0
      172.17.0.0/32 is subnetted, 1 subnets
O        172.17.1.1 [110/12] via 10.101.1.2, 00:09:14, Vlan91
      172.16.0.0/32 is subnetted, 1 subnets
O E2     172.16.1.1 [110/11] via 10.101.1.2, 00:09:14, Vlan91
      10.0.0.0/24 is subnetted, 3 subnets
O        10.102.1.0 [110/11] via 10.101.1.2, 00:09:14, Vlan91
C        10.101.1.0 is directly connected, Vlan91
O E2     10.100.1.0 [110/10] via 10.101.1.2, 00:09:14, Vlan91
O*E2 0.0.0.0/0 [110/1] via 10.101.1.2, 00:09:14, Vlan91
```

Routing Information Protocol

Routing Information Protocol (RIP) is a distance vector protocol. This protocol uses a hop count to determine the best path to the destination. RIP uses UDP over port 512 and is used primarily in small networks. RIP has two versions: RIPv1 and RIPv2. Version 2 supports variable-length subnet masking (VLSM) and summarization. Some of the other important terminologies in RIP are the following:

- **Split Horizon:** This mechanism is used to prevent loops. The router will not advertise networks through an interface from which it has learned the route.

- **Split Horizon with Poison Reverse:** All the routes learned via the neighbor are set to a metric of infinity (16 hops), which prevents loops.

RIP in FWSM

FWSM does not have a full implementation of RIP. It does not send the RIP updates to the directly connected interfaces. FWSM uses RIP in two modes:

- **Passive RIP:** FWSM listens to the RIP update from the neighbor but does not send the RIP updates. This helps the FWSM to learn about networks that are not directly connected to it in a particular security domain.

- **Default Route Updates:** The FWSM sends a default route to the Layer 3 neighbors, which identifies the FWSM as the default route for the Layer 3 device.

Both options can be used together or separately.

NOTE   OSPF and RIP cannot be enabled simultaneously on the FWSM.

Configuration Example of RIP on FWSM

The FWSM has inside, outside, and DMZ security zones. RIP is enabled on the inside and on DMZ security zones, as illustrated in Figure 9-5. Passive and default information is enabled on the FWSM to learn about the subnets that are not directly connected and also to advertise the default routes. The configuration does not have MD5 enabled. It is a good practice to enable MD5 authentication. Example 9-13 shows the FWSM configuration for RIP.

Figure 9-5   *RIP Between Security Domains*

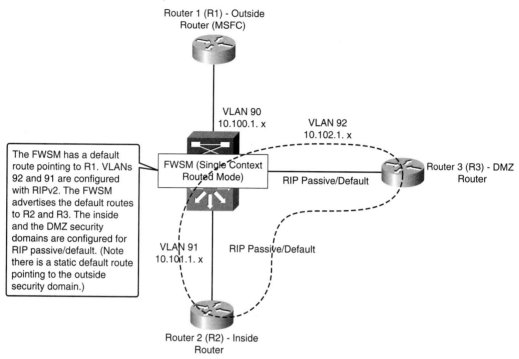

Router 1 (R1) - Outside
Router (MSFC)

VLAN 90
10.100.1. x

VLAN 92
10.102.1. x

The FWSM has a default route pointing to R1. VLANs 92 and 91 are configured with RIPv2. The FWSM advertises the default routes to R2 and R3. The inside and the DMZ security domains are configured for RIP passive/default. (Note there is a static default route pointing to the outside security domain.)

FWSM (Single Context Routed Mode)

RIP Passive/Default

Router 3 (R3) - DMZ Router

VLAN 91
10.101.1. x

RIP Passive/Default

RIP Passive/Default

Router 2 (R2) - Inside
Router

Example 9-13   *FWSM Configuration for RIP*

```
FWSM# show run
: Saved
:
FWSM Version 3.1(3)6
!
hostname FWSM
enable password 8Ry2YjIyt7RRXU24 encrypted
names
! Configure the outside interface
interface Vlan90
 nameif outside
 security-level 0
 ip address 10.100.1.2 255.255.255.0
! Configure the inside interface
interface Vlan91
 nameif inside
 security-level 100
 ip address 10.101.1.2 255.255.255.0
! Configure the dmz interface
interface Vlan92
```

continues

Example 9-13 *FWSM Configuration for RIP (Continued)*

```
 nameif dmz
 security-level 50
 ip address 10.102.1.2 255.255.255.0
 !
 passwd 2KFQnbNIdI.2KYOU encrypted
 ftp mode passive
 ! access list configuration will be based on the security policy. This example for
 ! access list will permit all traffic
 access-list 100 extended permit ip any any
 access-list 101 extended permit ip any any
 access-list 102 extended permit ip any any
 access-list 106 extended permit ip any any
 pager lines 24
 mtu outside 1500
 mtu inside 1500
 mtu dmz 1500
 no failover
 icmp permit any outside
 icmp permit any inside
 icmp permit any dmz
 no asdm history enable
 arp timeout 14400
 nat-control
 ! Configure NAT for the security domains
 nat (inside) 0 0.0.0.0 0.0.0.0
 nat (dmz) 0 0.0.0.0 0.0.0.0
 ! Apply the access list on the interface
 access-group 100 in interface outside
 access-group 100 out interface outside
 access-group 106 in interface inside
 access-group 101 out interface inside
 access-group 102 in interface dmz
 access-group 102 out interface dmz
 ! Configure RIP for the inside security domain. RIP will advertise the default route
 ! to inside security domain and learn routes from its Layer 3 next hop neighbor in
 ! the inside security domain
 rip inside passive version 2
 rip inside default version 2
 ! Configure RIP for the dmz security domain. RIP will advertise the default route
 ! to the dmz security domain and learn routes from its Layer 3 next hop neighbor in
 ! the dmz security domain
 rip dmz passive version 2
 rip dmz default version 2
 ! Default route points to the layer 3 next hop device at the outside security domain
 route outside 0.0.0.0 0.0.0.0 10.100.1.1 1
 timeout xlate 3:00:00
 timeout conn 1:00:00 half-closed 0:10:00 udp 0:02:00 icmp 0:00:02
 timeout sunrpc 0:10:00 h323 0:05:00 h225 1:00:00 mgcp 0:05:00
 timeout mgcp-pat 0:05:00 sip 0:30:00 sip_media 0:02:00
 timeout uauth 0:05:00 absolute
 no snmp-server location
 no snmp-server contact
```

Example 9-13   *FWSM Configuration for RIP (Continued)*

```
snmp-server enable traps snmp authentication linkup linkdown coldstart
telnet timeout 5
ssh timeout 5
console timeout 0
!
class-map inspection_default
 match default-inspection-traffic
!
policy-map global_policy
 class inspection_default
  inspect dns maximum-length 512
  inspect ftp
  inspect h323 h225
  inspect h323 ras
  inspect netbios
  inspect rsh
  inspect skinny
  inspect smtp
  inspect sqlnet
  inspect sunrpc
  inspect tftp
  inspect sip
  inspect xdmcp
!
service-policy global_policy global
prompt hostname context
Cryptochecksum:d82cb2b9d13d22c24c8208086ee48464
: end
```

The following are the outputs for the configuration shown in Example 9-13 for Figure 9-5. Example 9-14 displays the **show route** command on the FWSM.

Example 9-14   *The **show route** Command on the FWSM*

```
FWSM# show route
S     0.0.0.0 0.0.0.0 [1/0] via 10.100.1.1, outside
R     172.18.1.1 255.255.255.255 [120/1] via 10.101.1.1, inside
R     172.17.1.1 255.255.255.255 [120/1] via 10.102.1.1, dmz
C     10.100.1.0 255.255.255.0 is directly connected, outside
C     10.101.1.0 255.255.255.0 is directly connected, inside
C     10.102.1.0 255.255.255.0 is directly connected, dmz
```

The output of this **show route** command gives the static routes configured in the FWSM as **S**, networks learned from RIP neighbors as **R**, and directly connected routes at the FWSM as **C**.

Example 9-15 shows a partial output of the **show ip route** command at the Layer 3 device at the inside security domain.

Example 9-15   *The* **show ip route** *Command at the Inside Router*

```
Gateway of last resort is 10.101.1.2 to network 0.0.0.0

     172.18.0.0/32 is subnetted, 1 subnets
C       172.18.1.1 is directly connected, Loopback200
     10.0.0.0/24 is subnetted, 1 subnets
C       10.101.1.0 is directly connected, Vlan91
R*   0.0.0.0/0 [120/1] via 10.101.1.2, 00:00:09, Vlan91
```

The highlighted portion shows that the default route is learned from the FWSM via RIP.

Example 9-16 shows a partial output of **show ip route** command at the Layer 3 next hop device in the DMZ security zone.

Example 9-16   *The* **show ip route** *Command at the DMZ Router*

```
Gateway of last resort is 10.102.1.2 to network 0.0.0.0
     172.17.0.0/32 is subnetted, 1 subnets
C       172.17.1.1 is directly connected, Loopback201
     10.0.0.0/24 is subnetted, 1 subnets
C       10.102.1.0 is directly connected, Vlan92
R*   0.0.0.0/0 [120/1] via 10.102.1.2, 00:00:13, Vlan92
```

The highlighted portion shows that the default route is learned from the FWSM via RIP.

Border Gateway Protocol

Border Gateway Protocol (BGP) is a connection-oriented routing protocol. It uses TCP port 179. The connection is maintained by periodic keepalives. With BGP, the metrics and attributes give a granularity in path selection. BGP within the same autonomous system is called internal BGP (iBGP). All iBGP neighbors should have full meshed connectivity. In large BGP configurations, the concept of route reflectors and confederations help to build the hierarchy of connection for iBGP peers. External BGP (eBGP) peers are formed between two separate autonomous systems. The states in BGP message types are as follows:

- **Open Message:** Used to establish connections
- **Keepalives:** Periodically sent to maintain peer relationship
- **Update Messages:** Contains route information for paths and metric/attributes
- **Notification:** Informs the receiving routers for errors

BGP routing protocol is a widely used protocol. The Internet communication is based on this protocol. This section will not cover the details of BGP because the FWSM does not have a full implementation of BGP.

BGP in FWSM

The FWSM has a partial implementation of BGP. The FWSM can be configured for BGP in stub mode. In stub mode, static routes and connected routes are advertised by the FWSM. The FWSM does not process any updates from the neighbor. The main advantage of this feature is the support of routing protocols in multiple context mode. In multiple context mode, BGP stub configuration is enabled in the admin context. It handles redistribution of the static routes from each context.

The following are some of the limitations of BGP in FWSM:

- eBGP is not supported. iBGP is supported.
- Only one BGP autonomous system can be configured.
- Only one neighbor can be configured. This can be overcome by using route reflectors and making the FWSM as one of the neighbors.
- Redistribution between routing processes is not allowed.
- Updates are sent only to neighbors. Updates from BGP neighbors are not processed in the FWSM.
- Network address translations cannot be advertised as routes.
- Route map CLI is not supported in BGP stub.
- All the static routes and directly connected networks in the contexts sharing the interface will be available to the BGP routing process when the BGP neighbor is reachable through an interface that is shared across multiple contexts. Overlapping IP addresses of the context is not supported in this feature.
- BGP in FWSM does not support IPv6, VPN, and multicast Network Layer Reachability Information (NLRI).

NOTE   For this feature, FWSM is required to have a special license. The minimum FWSM code version required for this feature is 3.2.

BGP Topology with FWSM

Figure 9-6 depicts a scenario of multiple context routed mode. In this scenario, the FWSM also participates in the routing decision. The context for customer A has inside and outside interfaces. For these interfaces, there are respective static routes. VLANs allocated for customer A context are VLAN 500 and VLAN 600. VLAN 600 connects to the outside VLAN, and VLAN 500 connects to the inside VLAN. The default route for the outside route points to VLAN 600, and respective static routes are enabled for the non-directly connected subnets, toward the inside next hop Layer 3 address. These static routes are important and have to be mentioned in the network statement. Similarly, context for customer B is configured. The only difference is that the context for customer B has a DMZ zone. This example shows advertising routes of multiple security domains. The customer A and customer B contexts have a single shared outside interface.

Figure 9-6 *BGP Stub Configuration*

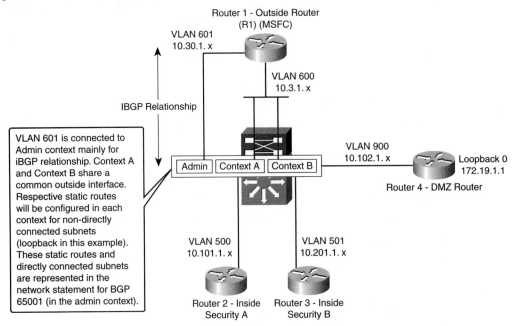

While configuring the BGP stub feature, admin context configuration is a must. For example:

```
admin-context admin
context admin
  allocate-interface Vlan601
  config-url disk:/admin.cfg
```

In the admin context, you need to define the interface for BGP neighbor peering (VLAN 601). If the BGP neighbor peering is in the inside security zone, VLAN 601 is defined as the inside interface. Similarly, if the BGP neighbor peering is in the outside security zone, the VLAN 601 is defined as the outside interface. In this scenario, the BGP peering is done in the outside security zone. Example 9-17 shows the Router 1 configuration.

Example 9-17 *Router 1 Configuration*

```
R1# show run | begin router bgp 65001
router bgp 65001
 no synchronization
 bgp router-id 10.30.1.1
 bgp log-neighbor-changes
 network 172.19.1.1 mask 255.255.255.255
```

Example 9-17 *Router 1 Configuration (Continued)*

```
   redistribute connected
   neighbor 10.30.1.2 remote-as 65001
   neighbor 10.30.1.2 update-source Vlan601
   no auto-summary

R1# show run interface vlan 600
   interface Vlan600
   ip address 10.3.1.1 255.255.255.0
   end

R1# show run interface vlan 601
   interface Vlan601
   ip address 10.30.1.1 255.255.255.0
   end
```

The Policy Feature Card configuration is as follows:

```
firewall multiple-vlan-interfaces
firewall module 9 vlan-group 1,9
firewall vlan-group 1  400-402,500,501,600,601,900
```

Example 9-18 shows the FWSM configuration (system context).

Example 9-18 *FWSM Configuration (System Context)*

```
FWSM# show run
: Saved
:
FWSM Version 3.2(1) <system>
!
resource acl-partition 12
hostname FWSM
enable password 8Ry2YjIyt7RRXU24 encrypted
!
interface Vlan400
!
interface Vlan401
!
interface Vlan500
!
interface Vlan501
!
interface Vlan600
!
interface Vlan601
!
interface Vlan900
!
passwd 2KFQnbNIdI.2KYOU encrypted
class default
  limit-resource All 0
  limit-resource IPSec 5
  limit-resource Mac-addresses 65535
```

continues

Example 9-18 *FWSM Configuration (System Context) (Continued)*

```
     limit-resource ASDM 5
     limit-resource SSH 5
     limit-resource Telnet 5
 !
ftp mode passive
pager lines 24
no failover
no asdm history enable
arp timeout 14400
console timeout 0
admin-context admin
context admin
  allocate-interface Vlan601
  config-url disk:/admin.cfg
 !
context customerA
  description This is the context for customer A
  allocate-interface Vlan500
  allocate-interface Vlan600
  config-url disk:/contexta.cfg
 !
context customerB
  description This is the context for customer B
  allocate-interface Vlan501
  allocate-interface Vlan600
  allocate-interface Vlan900
  config-url disk:/contextb.cfg
 !
prompt hostname context
Cryptochecksum:8f8d6fad72555ac6e1ca08f5c46a5584
 : end
```

Example 9-19 shows the contextA configuration in FWSM.

Example 9-19 *ContextA Configuration in FWSM*

```
FWSM/contexta# show run
 : Saved
 :
FWSM Version 3.2(1) <context>
 !
hostname contexta
enable password 8Ry2YjIyt7RRXU24 encrypted
names
 !
interface Vlan500
 nameif inside
 security-level 100
 ip address 10.101.1.2 255.255.255.0
 !
interface Vlan600
 nameif outside
 security-level 0
```

Example 9-19   *ContextA Configuration in FWSM (Continued)*

```
 ip address 10.3.1.3 255.255.255.0
 !
 passwd 2KFQnbNIdI.2KYOU encrypted
 access-list 100 extended permit ip any any
 access-list INTERNET extended permit ip any any
 access-list SECRULES extended permit ip any any
 pager lines 24
 mtu outside 1500
 mtu inside 1500
 icmp permit any outside
 icmp permit any inside
 no asdm history enable
 arp timeout 14400
 nat (inside) 1 0.0.0.0 0.0.0.0
 static (inside,outside) 10.14.1.1 10.14.1.1 netmask 255.255.255.255
 access-group SECRULES in interface outside
 access-group 100 out interface outside
 access-group INTERNET in interface inside
 route outside 0.0.0.0 0.0.0.0 10.3.1.1 1
 route inside 10.14.1.1 255.255.255.255 10.101.1.1 1
 timeout XLATE 3:00:00
 timeout conn 1:00:00 half-closed 0:10:00 udp 0:02:00 icmp 0:00:02
 timeout sunrpc 0:10:00 h323 0:05:00 h225 1:00:00 mgcp 0:05:00
 timeout mgcp-pat 0:05:00 sip 0:30:00 sip_media 0:02:00
 timeout sip-invite 0:03:00 sip-disconnect 0:02:00
 timeout uauth 0:05:00 absolute
 no snmp-server location
 no snmp-server contact
 telnet timeout 5
 ssh timeout 5
 !
 class-map inspection_default
  match default-inspection-traffic
 !
  policy-map global_policy
  class inspection_default
   inspect dns maximum-length 512
   inspect ftp
   inspect h323 h225
   inspect h323 ras
   inspect netbios
   inspect rsh
   inspect skinny
   inspect smtp
   inspect sqlnet
   inspect sunrpc
   inspect tftp
   inspect sip
   inspect xdmcp
 !
 service-policy global_policy global
 Cryptochecksum:0c942300184afdaa7409ded0cf673a26
 : end
```

Example 9-20 shows contextB configuration in FWSM.

Example 9-20 *ContextB Configuration in FWSM*

```
FWSM/contextb# show run
: Saved
:
FWSM Version 3.2(1) <context>
!
hostname contextb
enable password 8Ry2YjIyt7RRXU24 encrypted
names
!
interface Vlan501
 nameif inside
 security-level 100
 ip address 10.201.1.2 255.255.255.0
!
interface Vlan600
 nameif outside
 security-level 0
 ip address 10.3.1.4 255.255.255.0
!
interface Vlan900
 nameif dmz
 security-level 50
 ip address 10.50.1.2 255.255.255.0
!
passwd 2KFQnbNIdI.2KYOU encrypted
access-list 100 extended permit ip any any
access-list 101 extended permit ip any any
access-list INTERNET extended permit ip any any
access-list SECRULES extended permit ip any any
access-list dmz extended permit ip any any
pager lines 24
mtu inside 1500
mtu outside 1500
mtu dmz 1500
monitor-interface inside
icmp permit any inside
icmp permit any outside
icmp permit any dmz
no asdm history enable
arp timeout 14400
nat (inside) 1 0.0.0.0 0.0.0.0
nat (dmz) 1 0.0.0.0 0.0.0.0
static (inside,outside) 10.14.1.2 10.14.1.2 netmask 255.255.255.255
static (dmz,outside) 172.19.1.1 172.19.1.1 netmask 255.255.255.255
access-group INTERNET in interface inside
access-group 101 out interface inside
access-group SECRULES in interface outside
access-group 100 out interface outside
access-group dmz in interface dmz
access-group dmz out interface dmz
```

Example 9-20   *ContextB Configuration in FWSM (Continued)*

```
route inside 10.14.1.2 255.255.255.255 10.201.1.1 1
route outside 0.0.0.0 0.0.0.0 10.3.1.1 1
route outside 10.30.1.0 255.255.255.0 10.3.1.1 1
route dmz 172.19.1.1 255.255.255.255 10.50.1.1 1
timeout XLATE 3:00:00
timeout conn 1:00:00 half-closed 0:10:00 udp 0:02:00 icmp 0:00:02
timeout sunrpc 0:10:00 h323 0:05:00 h225 1:00:00 mgcp 0:05:00
timeout mgcp-pat 0:05:00 sip 0:30:00 sip_media 0:02:00
timeout sip-invite 0:03:00 sip-disconnect 0:02:00
timeout uauth 0:05:00 absolute
no snmp-server location
no snmp-server contact
snmp-server enable traps snmp authentication linkup linkdown coldstart
telnet timeout 5
ssh timeout 5
!
class-map inspection_default
 match default-inspection-traffic
!
 policy-map global_policy
 class inspection_default
  inspect dns maximum-length 512
  inspect ftp
  inspect h323 h225
  inspect h323 ras
  inspect netbios
  inspect rsh
  inspect skinny
  inspect smtp
  inspect sqlnet
  inspect sunrpc
  inspect tftp
  inspect sip
  inspect xdmcp
!
service-policy global_policy global
Cryptochecksum:db5a9366ff6a56fbdb5d00c90c09a81b
: end
```

Example 9-21 shows the configuration for the admin context. This configuration has the BGP stub configuration.

Example 9-21   *Admin Context Configuration in FWSM*

```
FWSM/admin# show run
: Saved
:
FWSM Version 3.2(1) <context>
!
hostname admin
enable password 8Ry2YjIyt7RRXU24 encrypted
```

continues

Example 9-21 *Admin Context Configuration in FWSM (Continued)*

```
names
!VLAN 601 is used to establish BGP peering in the outside security domain
interface Vlan601
 nameif outside
 security-level 0
 ip address 10.30.1.2 255.255.255.0
!
passwd 2KFQnbNIdI.2KYOU encrypted
same-security-traffic permit inter-interface
access-list INTERNET extended permit ip any any
access-list SECRULES extended permit ip any any
pager lines 24
mtu outside 1500
icmp permit any outside
no asdm history enable
arp timeout 14400
! The BGP configuration peers with the next hop layer 3 interface for VLAN 601. The
! IP address in each context is mentioned in BGP network configuration
router bgp 65001
 bgp router-id 10.30.1.2
 neighbor 10.30.1.1 remote-as 65001
 network 172.19.1.1 mask 255.255.255.255
 network 10.3.1.0 mask 255.255.255.0
 network 10.14.1.1 mask 255.255.255.255
 network 10.14.1.2 mask 255.255.255.255
 network 10.50.1.0 mask 255.255.255.0
 network 10.101.1.0 mask 255.255.255.0
 network 10.201.1.0 mask 255.255.255.0
!
timeout XLATE 3:00:00
timeout conn 1:00:00 half-closed 0:10:00 udp 0:02:00 icmp 0:00:02
timeout sunrpc 0:10:00 h323 0:05:00 h225 1:00:00 mgcp 0:05:00
timeout mgcp-pat 0:05:00 sip 0:30:00 sip_media 0:02:00
timeout sip-invite 0:03:00 sip-disconnect 0:02:00
timeout uauth 0:05:00 absolute
no snmp-server location
no snmp-server contact
snmp-server enable traps snmp authentication linkup linkdown coldstart
telnet timeout 5
ssh timeout 5
!
class-map inspection_default
 match default-inspection-traffic
!
policy-map global_policy
 class inspection_default
  inspect dns maximum-length 512
  inspect ftp
  inspect h323 h225
  inspect h323 ras
  inspect rsh
```

Example 9-21 *Admin Context Configuration in FWSM (Continued)*

```
  inspect smtp
  inspect sqlnet
  inspect skinny
  inspect sunrpc
  inspect xdmcp
  inspect sip
  inspect netbios
  inspect tftp
!
service-policy global_policy global
Cryptochecksum:8537b0ff443f5292982141c6e0a851bd
: end
```

In the admin context, you can verify the BGP peer relationship with the following command:

```
show ip bgp neighbor ip-address
```

Example 9-22 verifies the BGP peer relationship.

Example 9-22 *Verifying BGP Peer Relationship*

```
FWSM/admin# show ip bgp nei 10.30.1.1
BGP neighbor is 10.30.1.1,  remote AS 65001, internal link
  BGP version 4, remote router ID 10.30.1.1
  BGP state = Established, up for 01:00:45
  Last read 00:00:47, hold time is 180, keepalive interval is 60 seconds
  Neighbor capabilities:
    Route refresh: advertised and received(old & new)
    Address family IPv4 Unicast: advertised and received
  Message statistics:
    InQ depth is 0
    OutQ depth is 0
                       Sent        Rcvd
    Opens:         3           3
    Notifications: 0           0
    Updates:       35          0
    Keepalives:    636         633
    Route Refresh: 0           0
    Total:         674         642
  Default minimum time between advertisement runs is 5 seconds

 For address family: IPv4 Unicast
  neighbor version 1
  Index 0, Offset 0, Mask 0x0
                         Sent        Rcvd
  Prefix activity:       ----        ----
    Prefixes Current:    15          0
    Prefixes Total:      15          0
    Implicit Withdraw:   0           0
    Explicit Withdraw:   0           0
    Used as bestpath:    n/a         0
```

continues

Example 9-22 *Verifying BGP Peer Relationship (Continued)*

```
      Used as multipath:      n/a         0
  Number of NLRIs in the update sent: max 1, min 0

  Connections established 3; dropped 2
  Last reset 01:01:16, due to BGP protocol initialization
```

To display the status of all the BGP connections, enter the **show ip bgp summary** command, as shown in Example 9-23.

Example 9-23 *Summary of BGP Neighbors from FWSM*

```
FWSM/admin# show ip bgp summary
BGP router identifier 10.30.1.2, local AS number 65001

Neighbor         V     AS MsgRcvd MsgSent   TblVer  InQ OutQ Up/Down  State/PfxRcd
    10.30.1.1 4 65001 644       676      1       0    0    01:02:37 0
```

To verify the BGP connections in Router 1 (R1), enter the **show ip bgp summary** command, as shown in Example 9-24.

Example 9-24 *Summary of All Neighbors for BGP Process in Router R1*

```
R1# show ip bgp summary
BGP router identifier 10.30.1.1, local AS number 65001
BGP table version is 10, main routing table version 10
9 network entries using 1017 bytes of memory
10 path entries using 480 bytes of memory
3/2 BGP path/bestpath attribute entries using 300 bytes of memory
0 BGP route-map cache entries using 0 bytes of memory
0 BGP filter-list cache entries using 0 bytes of memory
BGP using 1797 total bytes of memory
BGP activity 18/9 prefixes, 20/10 paths, scan interval 60 secs

Neighbor         V     AS MsgRcvd MsgSent   TblVer  InQ OutQ Up/Down  State/PfxRcd
10.30.1.2        4 65001    677     649      10    0    0 01:03:07        7
```

To verify the routes learned in BGP at the next hop Layer 3 device, enter the **show ip bgp** command, as shown in Example 9-25.

Example 9-25 *Verify the Routes Learned in Layer 3 Next Hop Router*

```
R1# show ip bgp
BGP table version is 10, local router ID is 10.30.1.1
Status codes: s suppressed, d damped, h history, * valid, > best, i - internal,
              S Stale
Origin codes: i - IGP, e - EGP, ? - incomplete

   Network          Next Hop         Metric LocPrf Weight Path
*>i172.19.1.1/32    10.3.1.4           0      100    0     i
*>172.20.1.1/32     0.0.0.0            0           32768 ?
```

Example 9-25 *Verify the Routes Learned in Layer 3 Next Hop Router (Continued)*

```
  *  i10.3.1.0/24      10.3.1.3           0      100    0    i
  *>                   0.0.0.0            0      32768  ?
  *>i10.14.1.1/32      10.3.1.3           0      100    0    i
  *>i10.14.1.2/32      10.3.1.4           0      100    0    i
  *> 10.30.1.0/24      0.0.0.0            0      32768  ?
  *>i10.50.1.0/24      10.3.1.4           0      100    0    i
  *>i10.101.1.0/24     10.3.1.3           0      100    0    i
  *>i10.201.1.0/24     10.3.1.4           0      100    0    i
```

To verify the routes in the routing table of the next hop Layer 3 device, enter the **show ip route** command, as shown in Example 9-26.

Example 9-26 *To Verify the Routes in the Layer 3 Next Hop Router in the Outside Security Domain*

```
R1# show ip route
Codes: C - connected, S - static, R - RIP, M - mobile, B - BGP
       D - EIGRP, EX - EIGRP external, O - OSPF, IA - OSPF inter area
       N1 - OSPF NSSA external type 1, N2 - OSPF NSSA external type 2
       E1 - OSPF external type 1, E2 - OSPF external type 2, E - EGP
       i - IS-IS, su - IS-IS summary, L1 - IS-IS level-1, L2 - IS-IS level-2
       ia - IS-IS inter area, * - candidate default, U - per-user static route
       o - ODR, P - periodic downloaded static route

Gateway of last resort is not set

     172.19.0.0/32 is subnetted, 1 subnets
B       172.19.1.1 [200/0] via 10.3.1.4, 01:05:02
     172.20.0.0/32 is subnetted, 1 subnets
C       172.20.1.1 is directly connected, Loopback100
     10.0.0.0/8 is variably subnetted, 7 subnets, 2 masks
B       10.14.1.1/32 [200/0] via 10.3.1.3, 01:05:02
B       10.14.1.2/32 [200/0] via 10.3.1.4, 01:05:02
C       10.3.1.0/24 is directly connected, Vlan600
C       10.30.1.0/24 is directly connected, Vlan601
B       10.50.1.0/24 [200/0] via 10.3.1.4, 01:02:54
B       10.101.1.0/24 [200/0] via 10.3.1.3, 01:05:02
B       10.201.1.0/24 [200/0] via 10.3.1.4, 01:05:02
```

Summary

This chapter covers the basics of routing protocol supported in the FWSM with configuration examples. Static routes, OSPF, RIP, and BGP stub are the supported routing protocols in FWSM. EIGRP is supported in 4.X code version, and details of EIGRP are covered in Chapter 25, "Understanding FWSM 4.x Routing and Feature Enhancements."

CHAPTER 10

AAA Overview

In access control, the admin controls the user's access into the node, controls what the user can access in the node, and also monitors the actions made by the user in the node. Authentication, authorization, and accounting (AAA) is a framework through which you can achieve this control to access the node. It is important to understand each component of AAA and its uses. This type of access to the network/security nodes and access to the resources in the node gives a profile to the user. Each user can have different access rights. The user profile is maintained in an external database or the local database of a device. When controlling access to a large number of network/security devices, the common practice is to use an external database and have a backup single user profile in the local database. This backup single user profile is used for fallback purposes. Communication between FWSM and the external database server is achieved through security protocols, such as TACACS+ or RADIUS.

Understanding AAA Components

It is very important to understand the three AAA components and their functions.

Authentication in FWSM

Authentication allows the user to access the network node through password dialog. This password dialog for user access is also an encrypted session, depending on the type of security protocol chosen. Authentication can be done through a centralized server, or it can be done locally (based on the configuration of the local database).

The FWSM can authenticate management commands, network access, and virtual private network (VPN) management access. When a user accesses the FWSM, the user sends its username and password to the FWSM. The FWSM forwards this username and password to the external server and communicates to the external server using RADIUS or TACACS+. The choice of the security protocol used depends on the configuration at the FWSM.

In case of local authentication, the FWSM compares the username/password given by the user with the configured username and password in the FWSM. If the credentials match, the access is allowed. If not, access is denied.

For authentication of traffic between the security zones, the traffic has to match the authentication statement configured in the FWSM. Based on the match criteria, the traffic is sent to the external server for authentication, and then the user is allowed to access a different security zone.

Authorization in FWSM

Authorization works by identifying the set of attributes that the user is authorized to perform after getting access to the node through the authentication process. These attributes can be present locally in the FWSM or in a database server for the user profile. Authorization defines what a user can access in the node after the authentication is successful. The FWSM supports the authorization request for each user and caches the first 16 authorization requests per user.

If the user accesses the same service during the current authentication session, the FWSM does not resend the same request to the authorization server.

The server sends the user credentials, and the user is granted access to services as per the profile. For a local database, the FWSM checks the local configuration to verify the access rights for the user to access different services.

Accounting in FWSM

Accounting allows the network administrator to monitor the services the user's access at the FWSM, after being authenticated to the node. Security protocols such as TACACS+ or RADIUS are used.

In accounting, user traffic that passes through the FWSM can be tracked. A per-user accounting is possible if accounting is enabled. The following information is included in accounting:

- Traffic Internet Protocol (IP) address
- Duration of each session
- Session start and stop
- Username
- Service type

Accounting will have a record of user profiles having access and authorization rights to the device. This is an important component for auditing. Only after authentication is established can authorization or accounting work. Authorization and accounting need not be configured for authentication to work.

Comparing Security Protocols

The two prominent security protocols used in the industry are RADIUS and TACACS+. RADIUS is defined in RFC 2865 and TACACS+ is defined in RFC 1492.

RADIUS uses User Datagram Protocol (UDP), whereas TACACS+ uses Transmission Control Protocol (TCP). As you may know, TCP offers reliable connection, which is not offered in RADIUS. RADIUS offers some level of reliability but lacks the built-in reliability available in TCP used by TACACS+. Also note that RADIUS encrypts only passwords in the access-request packet from the client to the server, and the rest of the packet in RADIUS goes unencrypted.

TACACS+ encrypts the complete packet. The header field indicates whether the packet is encrypted. The unencrypted option in TACACS+ is used only for troubleshooting purposes. In a normal operation, the packet is completely encrypted. RADIUS combines the authentication and authorization in the access-accept packet sent by the RADIUS server. TACACS+ uses separate authentication and authorization. In this case, it is easy to decouple TACACS+. The administrator can use Kerberos for authentication and TACACS+ for authorization and accounting. TACACS+ provides multi-protocol support, which is not offered by RADIUS.

The FWSM provides RADIUS, TACACS+, Security Dynamics International (SDI, a solution provided by RSA SecurID), NT, Kerberos, Lightweight Directory Access Protocol (LDAP), and local database support. SDI, NT, Kerberos, and LDAP Server support are only for VPN-Management connection to the FWSM.

Table 10-1 summarizes the updated support of security protocols for AAA service offered by FWSM. Refer to the product documentation for FWSM on Cisco.com for new security protocol support based on newer code releases.

Table 10-1 *FWSM Security Protocol Support for AAA Service*

Authentication			
	VPN Users	**Firewall Sessions**	**Administrators**
Local	Yes	Yes	Yes
RADIUS	Yes	Yes	Yes
TACACS+	Yes	Yes	Yes
SDI	Yes	No	No
NT	Yes	No	No
Kerberos	Yes	No	No
LDAP	No	No	No
Authorization			
	VPN Users	**Firewall Sessions**	**Administrators**
Local	Yes	No	Yes
RADIUS	Yes	Yes	No
TACACS+	No	Yes	Yes
SDI	No	No	No
NT	No	No	No
Kerberos	No	No	No
LDAP	Yes	No	No
Accounting			
	VPN Connections	**Firewall Sessions**	**Administrators**
Local	No	No	No
RADIUS	Yes	Yes	No
TACACS+	Yes	Yes	Yes
SDI	No	No	No
NT	No	No	No
Kerberos	No	No	No
LDAP	No	No	No

VPN in FWSM is available only for Management connections.

Firewall authorization in RADIUS is available only in user access lists received in radius authentication response.

The term "local" means the FWSM can use the configuration locally for AAA. This is manually configured in the FWSM.

Local authorization is available in command authorization for privileged mode.

Understanding Two-Step Authentication

Two-step authentication, also called two-factor authentication, is a process in which a user must authenticate twice. The common way the two-step authentication works is that the user knows the PIN or password and has a token generator. The user uses the PIN on the token generator to generate a random sequence of numbers. This number sequence is the password, which is a component of the user password and token card. The authenticating system deciphers the random number sequence to get the password and allows the user access rights.

Two-step authentication is supported by SDI protocol. The FWSM obtains the server list when the first user authenticates to the configured server. This can be either a primary or a replica. The FWSM then assigns priorities to each server on the list, and subsequent server selection is derived at random from those assigned priorities.

Two-step authentication is more secure than the single authentication method. Two-step access authentication is common in the VPN world.

Understanding Fallback Support

Configuration practice dictates having fallback support for all AAA configurations on FWSM. The fallback support helps when the external server is not reachable. In this case, the user will not be able to access the FWSM or AAA functionality for other service types. With the fallback method, the last resort for the user to get access to the FWSM is at the local database of the FWSM. For external server redundancy, you can have more than one external server. More servers can be configured in the FWSM for redundancy and is referred to as a list of servers. Under normal circumstances, the FWSM contacts the first server configured. If that fails, it will sequentially contact other servers in the list. If the network is down, the FWSM will continue to contact the server list until the network comes up. If fallback is configured, during network downtime the FWSM will use the local profile for fallback to authenticate, provided the username and password for the access matches the configured username and password in the FWSM.

The local database supports fallback for authentication, authorization, VPN authentication, and VPN authorization.

Configuring Fallback Authentication

To configure fallback authentication in the FWSM, perform the following steps in the FWSM:

Step 1   Configure the username and password/enable password.

To configure the password for username cisco and user privilege level 15, enter the command

```
username cisco password jmINXNH6p1BxUppp encrypted privilege 15
```

To configure the enable password, enter the command

```
enable password  cisco
```

Step 2 Configure authentication with fallback.

```
! This command enables TACACS+ protocol
aaa-server TACACS protocol tacacs+
aaa-server TACACS max-failed-attempts 3
aaa-server TACACS deadtime 10
! This command configures the inside security domain for the server, IP
! address of the server and timeout value
aaa-server TACACS (inside) host 10.1.1.149 timeout 10
! This command enables local authentication for telnet access
aaa authentication telnet console TACACS LOCAL
! This command enables local authentication for console access
aaa authentication enable console TACACS LOCAL
```

Note that the LOCAL keyword is very important; it forces the FWSM to check the local database. If all servers in the server group cannot be reached, authentication will be done using the local database.

Step 3 Test the local authentication.

```
6504-E-2#session slot 3 processor 1
The default escape character is Ctrl-^, then x.
You can also type 'exit' at the remote prompt to end the session
Trying 127.0.0.31 ... Open


User Access Verification

Username: cisco
Password: *****
Type help or '?' for a list of available commands.
FWSM> en
Password: *****
FWSM#
```

The user accesses the FWSM using local configuration of username and password. This method can always be used as a backup method in case the network is down and the external TACACS+ server is not accessible.

Configuring Local Authorization

To configure local authorization in the FWSM, perform the following steps in the FWSM:

Step 1 Configure the username and password.

```
username NOCENG password h0TuW5XCVyAHLsUN encrypted privilege 5
username cisco1 password jmINXNH6p1BxUppp encrypted privilege 15
username cisco password 3USUcOPFUiMCO4Jk encrypted privilege 2
```

Before enabling authorization, ensure that you have a local user with privilege level of 15. If this is not configured, you can be locked out of the enable syntax in the firewall. In Step 1, three usernames and passwords are configured with different privilege modes.

Step 2 Configure the **enable** password.

```
enable password  cisco
```

Step 3 Enable privilege level.

```
privilege show level 5 command access-list
privilege show level 5 command arp
```

The user with privilege level 5 can have access only to **show access-list** and **show arp** commands. At privilege level 15, all the commands are available to the user. In lower privilege levels, only a few commands are available. If you want to restrict a user to a few commands, use a lower privilege level and allow only the commands that the user can access.

To configure authorization with fallback in the FWSM, enter the following commands in the FWSM:

```
! This command enables TACACS+ protocol
aaa-server TACACS protocol tacacs+
aaa-server TACACS max-failed-attempts 3
aaa-server TACACS deadtime 10
!This command configures the inside security domain for the server, IP address
! of the server and timeout value
aaa-server TACACS (inside) host 10.1.1.149 timeout 10
!This command enables local authentication for telnet access
aaa authentication telnet console TACACS LOCAL
! This command enables local authentication for console access
aaa authentication enable console TACACS LOCAL
! This command enables local authorization
aaa authorization command LOCAL
```

Example 10-1 shows how to test the local authorization.

Example 10-1 *Testing Local Authorization*

```
6504-E-2#session slot 3 processor 1
The default escape character is Ctrl-^, then x.
You can also type 'exit' at the remote prompt to end the session
Trying 127.0.0.31 ... Open


User Access Verification
```

continues

Example 10-1 *Testing Local Authorization (Continued)*

```
Username: NOCENG
Password: *****
Type help or '?' for a list of available commands.
FWSM> enable
Password: *****
FWSM# config t
Command authorization failed
FWSM# show run
Command authorization failed
FWSM# show access-list
access-list mode auto-commit
access-list cached ACL log flows: total 0, denied 0 (deny-flow-max 4096)
            alert-interval 300
access-list OUT; 2 elements
access-list OUT extended permit ip any any (hitcnt=176702)
access-list OUT extended permit icmp any any (hitcnt=0)
access-list IN; 2 elements
access-list IN extended permit ip any any (hitcnt=176702)
access-list IN extended permit icmp any any (hitcnt=0)
FWSM#
```

The **NOCENG** user accesses the FWSM. The user is allowed to access only the **show access-list** command and cannot access any other command.

For the VPN authentication and authorization, the fallback method is specified in the **authentication-server-group** command with a **LOCAL** keyword.

The local authorization in the FWSM is similar to the Cisco IOS configuration for local authorization. This is used when two user groups need to have fallback profiles and different access rights after authentication.

Understanding Cut-Through Proxy in FWSM

In cut-through proxy, the firewall requires the user to authenticate before passing any traffic through the FWSM. Figure 10-1 shows how the cut-through proxy works.

The high-level steps that describe cut-through proxy are as follows:

Step 1   A user from the outside security domain tries to access a web server in a more secured domain.

Step 2   The FWSM prompts user authentication.

Step 3   After the FWSM receives the information from the user, it passes this information to the access control server (ACS).

Step 4   The ACS verifies the credentials and gives access rights to the user.

Step 5   The FWSM allows the user to access the web server.

Figure 10-1   *Cut-Through Proxy*

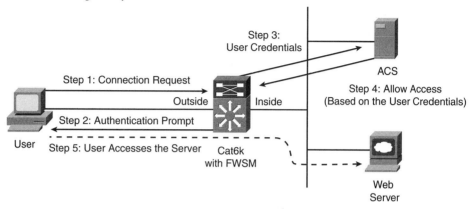

The cut-through proxy method significantly improves the performance in comparison to the traditional proxy server. In cut-through proxy, the firewall authenticates the user against TACACS+, RADIUS server, or the local database. After the authentication is complete, the traffic session flow is maintained between the source and destination. This is not the case with the traditional proxy server.

The cut-through proxy server concept is used in FWSM. The FWSM can authenticate the user at the application layer, and then authenticates against standard RADIUS, TACACS+, or the local database. After the FWSM authenticates the user, it shifts the session flow, and all traffic flows directly and quickly between the source and destination while maintaining session state information with any network access or any protocol. The first authentication prompt can be done through Hypertext Transfer Protocol (HTTP), Hypertext Transfer Protocol over Secure Socket Layer (HTTPS), Telnet, or File Transfer Protocol (FTP) only.

Using these methods, the FWSM generates a user authentication prompt for authenticating the user. For HTTP authentication, the FWSM checks the Port Address Translation (PAT) configuration when a connection for port 80 is seen. The FWSM immediately gives the authentication prompt to the user based on the PAT entry.

Example 10-2 shows a configuration example of Telnet-based proxy for inside users of the demilitarized zone (DMZ). The Telnet authentication will be applicable for all users, and the authorization and accounting will be available for users accessing servers in 10.2.2.0/ 24 network subnet.

Example 10-2 *Configuring Telnet-Based Proxy for DMZ Inside Users*

```
FWSM(config)# aaa-server  Outbound protocol tacacs+
FWSM(config-aaa-server-group)# exit
FWSM(config)# aaa-server  Outbound (dmz) host 10.2.2.151
FWSM(config-aaa-server-host)# key cisco
FWSM(config-aaa-server-host)# exit
! access-list is defined to match the traffic for cut-through proxy
FWSM(config)# access-list SERVER_1 extended permit tcp any 10.2.2.0 0.0.0.255 eq
telnet
! authenticates the traffic that matches the access-list
FWSM(config)# aaa authentication match SERVER 1 dmz Outbound
```

The commands in Example 10-3 authenticate all inside HTTP traffic.

Example 10-3 *Configuring Authentication for All Inside HTTP Traffic*

```
FWSM(config)# aaa-server AuthOutbound protocol tacacs+
FWSM(config-aaa-server-group)# exit
FWSM(config)# aaa-server AuthOutbound (inside) host 10.2.2.151
FWSM(config-aaa-server-host)# key cisco
FWSM(config-aaa-server-host)# exit
! access-list is defined to match the traffic for cut-through proxy
FWSM(config)# access-list OUT_WWW extended permit tcp any any eq www
! authenticates the traffic that matches the access-list
FWSM(config)# aaa authentication match OUT_WWW inside AuthOutbound
```

Configuring Custom Login Prompts

You can configure local prompts only for FTP and HTTP traffic. For Telnet, you cannot configure the user-defined prompt. Use the following steps to configure custom login prompts:

Step 1 To customize the login prompt:

```
FWSM(config)# auth-prompt prompt text
```

Step 2 When the user is accepted:

```
FWSM(config)# auth-prompt accept text
```

Step 3 When the user is rejected:

```
FWSM(config)# auth-prompt reject text
```

For example:

```
FWSM(config)# auth-prompt prompt Please enter your username and password
FWSM(config)# auth-prompt reject Authentication failed. Try again.
FWSM(config)# auth-prompt accept Authentication succeeded.
```

It's good to have custom login prompts to let the user know the result of the authentication process.

Using MAC Addresses to Exempt Traffic from Authentication and Authorization

Using this method, the FWSM can permit or deny authentication or authorization based on Media Access Control (MAC) addresses.

Follow the steps to configure MAC address for authentication and authorization:

Step 1   Configure the MAC list.

```
FWSM(config)# mac-list id {deny | permit} mac macmask
```

For example:

```
FWSM(config)# mac-list test permit 0cb0.c0ad.0180 ffff.ffff.ffff
```

Step 2   Attach the MAC list to the AAA statement.

```
FWSM(config)# aaa mac-exempt match id
```

For example:

```
FWSM(config)# aaa mac-exempt match test
```

The use of this feature is seen in IP phones, which cannot authenticate. For example, if you have an IP phone in a particular security zone that has authentication and authorization for cut-through proxy configured, you can use either the IP address to deny the list of subnets or you can use a MAC address–based filter for the specific phones or servers.

Summary

After reading this chapter, you will understand AAA components and the configuration of AAA in relation to the FWSM. Fallback support should be added when the AAA access solution for the FWSM is designed. You will know the difference between TACACS+ and RADIUS and the different security protocols supported in the FWSM. The concept of cut-through proxy is covered with configuration examples.

CHAPTER 11

Modular Policy

This chapter describes how to use and configure application inspection on the Firewall Services Module (FWSM) with modular policy. The FWSM mechanisms used for stateful application inspection enforce a secure use of services offered in the network.

This chapter covers the following topics:

- Components of modular policy
- Configuration of modular policy
- Understanding application engines

Modular policy is a three-step process: classification, policy map, and service policy.

In the first step, classification, the traffic is assessed and is divided into classes as per user configuration.

In the second step, policy map defines actions on the traffic defined in these classes. The traffic flow is based on the interface.

In the third step, service policy applies the policy map to the interface. This applies the configuration of the policy map to the traffic passing through the interface.

Using Modular Policy in FWSM

Modular policy is used in FWSM similar to IOS quality of service (QoS). The configuration of modular policy is a three-step process (see Figure 11-1):

Step 1 Classify traffic.

Step 2 Define actions to the classified traffic.

Step 3 Activate the policy.

Figure 11-1 *Description of Modular Policy*

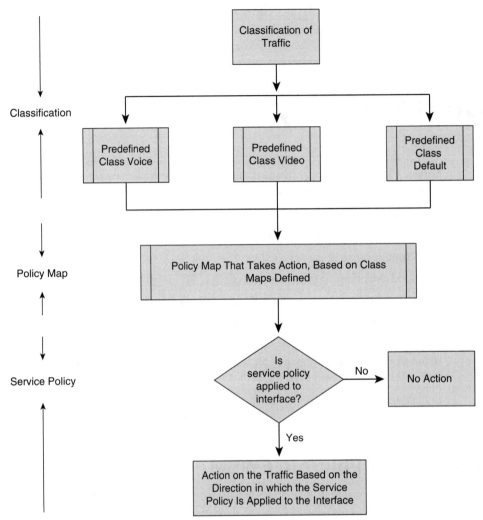

In the FWSM, you can use the same concept of modular policy for inspection of protocols and TCP timeout connections.

NOTE   What is TCP timeout?

TCP provides reliability to the communication from the acknowledgment that it receives from each end of the transmission. These acknowledgments can get lost traversing through the network. TCP sets a timeout when it sends data, and if no acknowledgment is received when the timeout expires, it retransmits the data.

Figure 11-2 *Components of Modular Policy in FWSM*

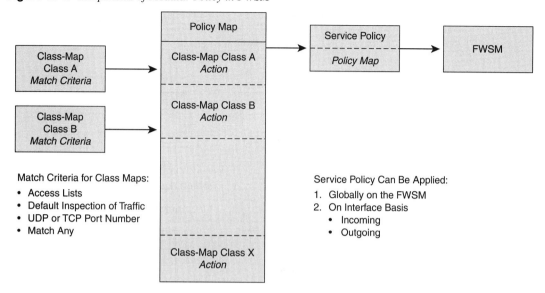

Understanding Classification of Traffic

The traffic can be classified into multiple classes (as configured). On these classes, you can perform specific actions. A class map identifies the traffic that needs a selective action. In the FWSM, by default 255 class maps are allowed in a single or in multiple context modes.

Creating class maps is a two-step process:

Step 1   Create a class map:

```
FWSM(config)# class-map class_map_name
```

Step 2   This step defines the traffic that is classified in a class map. This can be done using any of the following methods:

— **Access-list:** An access list is used to classify traffic in a class map. In the access list, you can specify the source and destination of the traffic that needs to be classified.

Syntax:

```
FWSM(config-cmap)# match access-list acl_ID
```

— **Default inspection traffic:** The traffic that is inspected by default can be classified in a class map. For more details about the default inspection traffic, refer to sections "Understanding Application Engines" and "Configuring Global Policy" in this chapter.

Syntax:

```
hostname(config-cmap)# match default-inspection-traffic
```

Table 11-1 *Protocols Inspected in Default Class*

Protocol	TCP/UDP	Port Numbers
Ctiqbe	TCP	2748
ftp	TCP	21
H323-h225	TCP	1720
http	TCP	80
Ils	TCP	389
Netbios	UDP	137–138
Rsh	TCP	514
Sip	TCP	5060
Skinny	TCP	2000
Sqlnet	TCP	1521
Xdmcp	UDP	177
Dns	UDP	53
Gtp	UDP	2123, 3386
H323-ras	UDP	1718–1719
Icmp	Icmp	
gcp	UDP	2427, 2727
Rpc	UDP	111
Rtsp	TCP	554
Sip	UDP	5060
Smtp	TCP	25
Tftp	UDP	69

— **Port numbers:** You can match traffic using TCP or UDP port numbers.

Syntax:

```
hostname(config-cmap)# match tcp eq 80
```

— **Using match any:** You can match all the traffic in one class map using this command:

Syntax:

```
hostname(config-cmap)# match any
```

Multiple classes can be defined and classified using any of these four methods.

Understanding Application Engines

The application engines are invoked using the **inspect** command. By default, inspection for certain applications is enabled in the global service profile and is applied to all interfaces.

NOTE   The application inspection in the FWSM ensures the secure use of applications and services through stateful inspection.

Application inspection can work with Network Address Translation (NAT) to help identify the location of embedded addressing information. This allows NAT to translate these embedded addresses and to update any checksum or other fields that are modified by the translation. The application engine also determines the port numbers of the secondary channels.

The sequence in which the application engine works is as follows:

1   After a TCP SYN arrives at the FWSM, a new connection is established.

2   If it is permitted, the Access Control List (ACL) is checked to permit the packet through the FWSM.

3   FWSM creates a new entry in the connection database (XLATE and CONN tables).

4   Inspection database is checked if the FWSM needs to do an application-level inspection.

5   If the inspection is needed, the inspection engine performs the required inspection and forwards the packet to the destination system.

6   The destination system responds to the initial request.

7   The FWSM receives the reply packet, looks up the connection in the connection database, and forwards the packet because it belongs to an established session.

The default configuration of the FWSM includes a set of application inspection entries, which help to determine the port number and identify if any special handling is required.

The use of NAT and Port Address Translation (PAT) needs assessment because some of the application engines do not support NAT or PAT, as the applications have fixed port assignments that cannot be changed.

Table 11-2 shows the application engine that is enabled by default, and its relationship with NAT and PAT.

Table 11-2 *Application Engine Details*

Application	Enabled by Default	No Impact on PAT	No Impact on NAT (1-1)
CTIQBE	No	Yes	Yes
DNS	Yes	Yes	Yes
FTP	Yes	Yes	Yes
GTP	No	Yes	Yes
H.323	Yes	Yes	Yes
HTTP	No	Yes	Yes
ICMP	No	Yes	Yes
ICMP ERROR	No	Yes	Yes
ILS (LDAP)	No	Yes	Yes
MGCP	No	Yes	Yes
NetBIOS Datagram Service/UDP	Yes	Yes	Yes
NetBIOS Name Service/UDP	Yes	No	No
NetBIOS over IP	Yes	No	No
PPTP	No	Yes	Yes
RSH	Yes	Yes	Yes
RTSP	No	No	No
SKINNY (SCCP)	Yes	Yes	Yes
SNMP	Yes	No	No
SMTP/ ESMTP	Yes	Yes	Yes
SQL*Net	Yes	Yes	Yes
Sun RPC	Yes	No	Yes
TFTP	Yes	Yes	Yes
XDCMP	Yes	No	No

While configuring PAT, the FWSM has a capability to perform inspection on the translated port numbers rather than the real port numbers.

It is important to have the knowledge of the application engine while configuring the policy map in the FWSM. The functionality of NAT or PAT on the application engine also should be considered while configuring the inspection engine, based on security policy. In most cases, unless a security policy requirement exists, inspection engines enabled by default can be used.

Defining Policy Maps

To take action on the classified traffic, a policy map is used with a service policy statement. Multiple class maps are defined in a policy map. In a policy map, you can have actions for each class map. In this way, through policy map, multiple actions can be defined for the traffic flow. The packet can match only one feature type, and the subsequent action by FWSM will be performed in a class map.

A packet can match one feature type of TCP connection or other feature type of application inspection. The action can be applied to both the class maps. Two separate class maps of different application inspections cannot be applied to the same policy map. A single policy is applied per interface. The same policy can be reused for multiple interfaces.

Configuring Global Policy

A policy map is applied globally and used in all the interfaces. When a policy map is applied to an individual interface, it takes precedence over the global policy map and will be applied only to the interface.

To configure a policy map, follow these steps:

Step 1   Configure the policy name.

For example:

```
FWSM(config)# policy-map TEST1
```

Step 2   Attach the classified traffic that needs action.

For example:

```
FWSM(config)# policy-map TEST1 <- Define the policy map
FWSM(config-pmap)# class TEST2 <- Define a class map
FWSM (config-pmap-c)# set connection conn-max 256<- Define action for
    this class TEST2
FWSM(config-pmap)# class-map inspection_default<- Define a second class
    map under the policy map 'default class'
FWSM (config-pmap-c)# match default-inspection-traffic<- Define action
    for 'default class'
```

You can have multiple class maps enabled on a policy map. In this command, **TCP max connection** is enabled for user-defined actions on the class map. Another class map defined is **default**, which matches the **default inspection engine** defined in FWSM. Keep in mind that the class map has to be defined prior to associating with a policy map.

Configuring Service Policy

After configuring classification of the traffic and action on the classified traffic, the activation of the policy map is done through **service-policy** commands. This command can be applied globally, which is applicable to all interfaces or to a single interface. The single interface takes more precedence than the global policy map.

Applying the **service-policy** command with the policy map is a single-step process. The service policy can be applied globally; the actions will be applicable to all the interfaces. When a service policy is applied at an interface level, the action is applicable to that particular interface.

Example of global policy (configured by default):

```
FWSM(config)# service-policy global_policy global
```

Example of an interface policy:

```
FWSM(config)# service-policy TEST1 interface ?
Current available interface(s):
  dmz       Name of interface Vlan92
  inside    Name of interface Vlan91
  outside   Name of interface Vlan90
FWSM(config)# service-policy TEST1 interface outside
```

Understanding Default Policy Map

FWSM has a default policy map. The default policy map classifies and inspects the traffic for the following applications:

```
inspect dns maximum-length 512
inspect ftp
inspect h323 h225
inspect h323 ras
inspect netbios
inspect rsh
inspect skinny
inspect smtp
inspect sqlnet
inspect sunrpc
inspect tftp
inspect sip
inspect xdmcp
```

The default policy enabled in the FWSM is called the *global policy*, and it is applied to all the interfaces unless you have a user-configured policy map configured and applied to an interface.

Using the **show running-config** commmand, the global policy can be seen as a default configuration:

```
policy-map global_policy
 class inspection_default
  inspect dns maximum-length 512
  inspect ftp
  inspect h323 h225
  inspect h323 ras
  inspect netbios
  inspect rsh
  inspect skinny
  inspect smtp
  inspect sqlnet
  inspect sunrpc
  inspect tftp
  inspect sip
  inspect xdmcp
 !
service-policy global_policy global
```

Sample Configuration of Modular Policy in FWSM

The configuration in Example 11-1 adds a new user-defined classification and action to the existing global policy. This user-defined classification is represented in class maps TEST1 and TEST2. In class map TEST2, the TCP port range from 1 to 65535 is matched. The class map TEST1 matches the UDP port equivalent for SNMP. These two class maps are applied to the global policy and separate actions are specified for each of the classes. The global service policy inspects traffic at all interfaces. This condition is true if no interface-based service policy is applied.

Example 11-1 *Modular Policy in FWSM*

```
! Define a class-map TEST2 to classify TCP traffic port range from
! 1- 65535
 class-map TEST2
 match port tcp range 1 65535
 ! In this configuration, define a class-map TEST1 to classify UDP traffic
 ! port for SNMP
class-map TEST1
 match port udp eq snmp-status
 ! Class for 'default inspect' is enabled
class-map inspection_default
 match default-inspection-traffic
 ! In this configuration, Global policy is defined by default
policy-map global_policy
 class inspection_default
  inspect dns maximum-length 512
  inspect ftp
  inspect h323 h225
  inspect h323 ras
  inspect netbios
  inspect rsh
  inspect skinny
```

continues

Example 11-1 *Modular Policy in FWSM (Continued)*

```
    inspect smtp
    inspect sqlnet
    inspect sunrpc
    inspect tftp
    inspect sip
    inspect xdmcp
! Define policy map and actions for class maps: In this configuration, user defined
! class-map is added to default policy-map
class TEST1
   set connection conn-max 100
   set connection timeout tcp 0:00:00
class TEST1
   inspect snmp
!
! Apply service policy to an interface or globally: In this configuration, the policy
! is applied to all the interfaces through global service policy
service-policy global_policy global
```

Modular policy configuration is a three-step process, as shown in Example 11-1. Following is a recap of the configuration steps:

Step 1 Define class map.

Step 2 Define policy map and define the actions for class maps in policy map.

Step 3 Apply service policy to an interface or globally.

These steps are shown in Figure 11-3.

Summary

This chapter captures the modular policy used in IOS with reference to the FWSM. In FWSM, application engines are associated in modular policy. User-defined functions can be added to the *default policy* enabled by default and applied to all interfaces. Interface policy-map will take precedence over global policy-map, when applied to the interface.

Figure 11-3 *Modular Policy Configuration in FWSM*

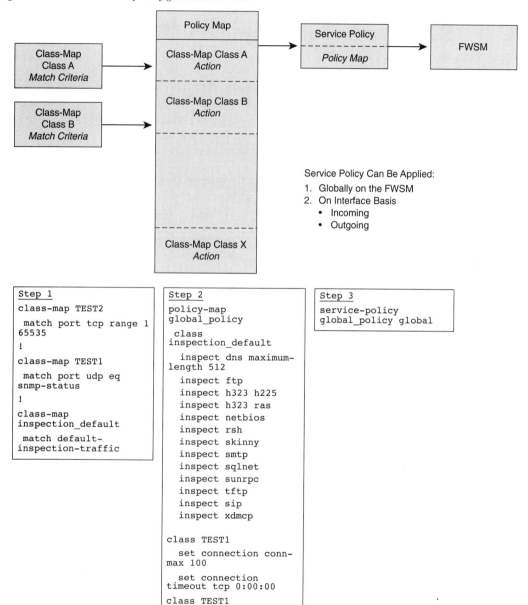

PART III

Advanced Configuration

CHAPTER 12

Understanding Failover in FWSM

This chapter covers the concept of failover, its configurations, and redundancy in a Firewall Services Module (FWSM). Planning failure scenarios is always a good practice when designing a network solution. Redundancy for disaster recovery should always be a part of the network. Likewise, redundancy is also needed for firewalls.

Creating Redundancy in the FWSM

The two types of modes for redundancy in FWSM are as follows:

- Active/Standby mode
- Active/Active mode

The sections that follow cover the two modes in detail.

Understanding Active/Standby Mode

The firewall has an active unit and a nonactive unit. The active unit is called a primary firewall and the nonactive unit is called a secondary firewall. These two FWSM modules are symmetric to each other. All the traffic passes through the primary module and does not pass through the secondary module. The two symmetric modules can be in the same chassis or in a redundant Catalyst 65xx chassis. It is always a good practice to place firewalls in two separate chassis for full redundancy. This is a classic failover mode supported in firewalls. In multiple context mode, using Active/Standby mode, a primary FWSM is used and does not take advantage of redundant secondary FWSM unit for normal operations. For example, in multiple context mode, the FWSM is configured with two contexts: 1a and 2a in the primary FWSM and 1b and 2b in the secondary FWSM, as illustrated in Figure 12-1. For contexts 1a and 2a, the traffic flows only from the primary FWSM. The secondary FWSM will be in a standby mode. This failover mode does not split the traffic between primary and secondary units.

Figure 12-1 *Understanding Active/Standby Mode*

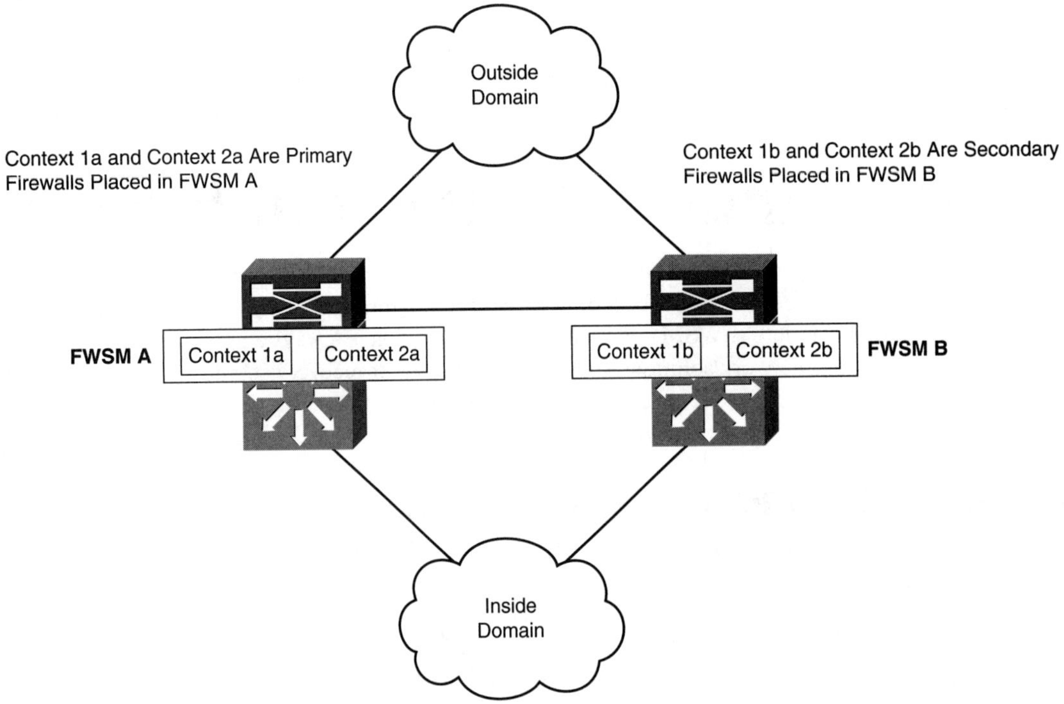

Context 1a and Context 2a Are Primary
Firewalls Placed in FWSM A

Context 1b and Context 2b Are Secondary
Firewalls Placed in FWSM B

FWSM A   Context 1a   Context 2a   Context 1b   Context 2b   **FWSM B**

Outside
Domain

Inside
Domain

Understanding Active/Active Mode

The Active/Active mode is applicable to the FWSM in multiple context mode and is
supported in 3.1 release and later. The FWSM module can split the traffic between different
contexts. The active context will be present in either the primary firewall or the secondary
firewall. In this way, both the FWSM units will be passing traffic for different contexts. For
example, in multiple context mode, two contexts are configured: 1a and 2a in FWSM 1 and
1b and 2b in FWSM 2, as illustrated in Figure 12-2. With multiple context mode, 1a is the
primary firewall and 1b is the secondary firewall for context 1. The traffic for context 1
flows from the FWSM 1. The context 2 will have 2a as a standby firewall and 2b as a
primary firewall. The traffic for context 2 flows from context 2b; that is, FWSM 2. In this
way, the traffic is split between the two FWSM units using multiple context mode, and each
FWSM will be a redundant pair for each other, based on the context.

Figure 12-2 *Understanding Active/Active Mode*

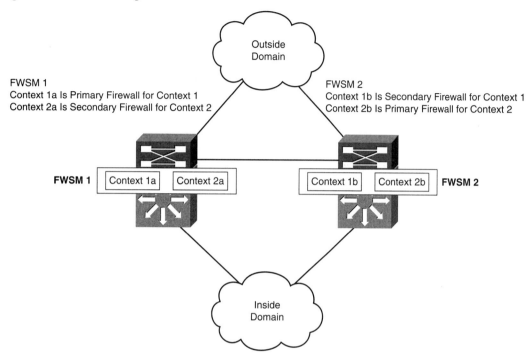

FWSM 1
Context 1a Is Primary Firewall for Context 1
Context 2a Is Secondary Firewall for Context 2

FWSM 2
Context 1b Is Secondary Firewall for Context 1
Context 2b Is Primary Firewall for Context 2

The IP address defined in the primary firewall is called the active IP address, and the IP address defined in the secondary firewall is called the standby IP address. The standby IP address must be in the same subnet as the active IP address. The requirement for the same IP subnet is to make failover work. There is no need for routing to identify the standby IP address subnet mask. The state link IP address and the MAC address do not change at failover. The secondary interfaces in the failover group that become active assume the MAC addresses and IP addresses of the primary interfaces in different security domains, after a failover. The interfaces for the failover function that is now in the standby state take over the standby MAC addresses and IP addresses.

In short, these sections cover two ways of enabling failover from a design perspective in an FWSM. The Active/Active mode can be used as a design advantage in multiple context mode. The traditional way of doing failover is still very prevalent for box-level redundancy.

Understanding Failover Link and State Link

Failover between two physical FWSMs is achieved through a failover link. Some of the important points for a failover link are as follows:

- Hellos and other messages for failover are exchanged between the primary and secondary FWSM units.

- The primary and the secondary FWSMs communicate to determine the operating status of each FWSM.

- When the primary unit fails, the failover takes place in the secondary unit. The state information of the active sessions is not copied to the secondary firewall.

- A VLAN interface needs to be configured in the FWSM. The VLAN must be configured in both the switches having FWSM modules and should carry the failover link information between the two switch chassis hosting the FWSMs.

The information exchanged through the failover link is as follows:

- **State of the unit:** Defines whether the unit is primary or secondary.

- **Hello message:** Keepalives for failover are sent via a failover link.

- **Network link status:** Describes the network link.

- **MAC address exchange:** Occurs during failover.

- **Configuration replication and synchronization:** Takes place from the primary to the secondary FWSM.

State link is needed for a stateful failover to function. Stateful failover for the FWSM enables the secondary firewall to continue processing and forwarding user sessions after a planned or unplanned outage. For this process, the entire state information is maintained between the primary and secondary FWSMs. State link maintains this communication, and it is configured with a failover link. The state link passes the state information of the active session from the primary FWSM to the secondary FWSM.

The state link is used to achieve stateful failover. It is required to have two separate VLANs for failover link and state link. In multiple context mode, both the failover and state links reside in the system context.

The stateful failover replicates the following types of traffic:

- TCP and User Datagram Protocol (UDP) connections

- Network Address Translation (NAT)

- Address Resolution Protocol (ARP) table

- Layer 2 bridge table (applicable for the firewall in transparent mode)

- GTP PDP connection database, where GTP is GPRS Tunneling Protocol and PDP is Packet Data Protocol

- Routing tables

- HTTP connection table (unless HTTP replication is enabled)

- User authentication (uauth) table

The common practice is to enable failover link and state link on any failover configuration. Always make sure the VLANs for both the links need to be separate. The physical connection between the two switch chassis for these VLANs should be separate from the regular traffic.

Requirements for Failover

The requirements and considerations needed to enable failover configuration in FWSM are as follows:

- System license requirements are needed for failover between two units.
- Both FWSMs should have the same software image.
- Both FWSMs should have the same interfaces, which is mandatory as a part of the configuration.
- It is a good practice to have the pair of FWSMs adjacent to all the Layer 2 interfaces. This will make the Layer 2 connections symmetric to both the FWSMs.
- To avoid loops in transparent mode, the failover configuration will need to allow BPDUs through the FWSM. This can be done using an EtherType access list.

Synchronizing the Primary and Secondary Firewalls

Configurations are synchronized from the active FWSM unit to the standby FWSM unit. The FWSM is configured with an initial set of commands for failover. The primary and secondary status for FWSM is defined in this initial set of commands (refer to Table 12-1 in the next section, "Monitoring Interfaces"). The FWSM becomes the primary firewall and its peer FWSM becomes the secondary or standby firewall, after enabling the initial set of failover commands. The standby FWSM will have failover commands, and the rest of the configurations are obtained from the primary FWSM. The secondary FWSM synchronizes with the primary FWSM. The synchronization can be triggered by the **write standby** command, which will copy the configuration from the primary FWSM to the secondary FWSM.

In multiple context mode, in a specific context in the primary FWSM, if **write memory** is executed, the primary FWSM copies the configuration to the secondary FWSM. The **write memory** must be executed per context level. Likewise, in the system context, if **write memory all** is executed, all the configurations from all the contexts are copied to the secondary FWSM. When using the **write memory all** command, it is not necessary to access each context for copying the configurations to the secondary FWSM.

Monitoring Interfaces

The FWSM determines the health of the primary and secondary firewalls by monitoring the failover link. When a unit does not receive hello messages on the failover link, the unit sends an ARP request to all interfaces, including the failover interface. Interfaces in different security domains can also be monitored in the FWSM. In multiple context mode, use the **monitor** command to monitor interfaces in different contexts. The maximum number of monitored interfaces on the FWSM is 250, divided among all contexts. The FWSM exchanges hellos after the failover configuration is completed between the primary and secondary firewalls on the monitored interfaces. If these hellos are not received within 15 seconds (default), the FWSM runs the following four tests before declaring the interface failure as a reason for the failover. This testing stage is a 30-second process that has four components:

- **Link Up/Down test:** If the Link Up/Down test indicates that the interface is operational, FWSM performs the network activity test.

- **Network activity test:** The unit counts all received packets for up to five seconds. If a packet is received anytime during this interval, the interface is considered operational and testing stops.

- **ARP test:** A reading of the ARP cache is done. Based on entry, the unit sends ARP requests to these machines (done sequentially one at a time from the list), attempting to stimulate network traffic. After each request, the unit counts all received traffic for up to five seconds. If the traffic is received, the interface is operational. If no traffic is received, an ARP request is sent to the next machine. If at the end of the list no traffic is received, the broadcast ping test begins.

- **Broadcast ping test:** This test consists of a broadcast ping request. The unit then counts all received packets for up to five seconds. If traffic is received, the interface is considered operational and the testing stops.

If all network tests fail for an interface but are successful on the unit, the interface is still considered to be failed. The monitoring interface threshold is 50 percent. If this is met, a failover occurs. If the other unit interface also fails all the network tests, both interfaces go into an *unknown state*. Interfaces in the unknown state will not be considered for the failover limit.

Rapid link failure detection (RaLFD) is a feature introduced in the 2.3 code release. RaLFD is an enhancement for interface monitoring that allows it to bypass interface test mode. This is achieved by having the switch's supervisor engine issue specific serial control protocol (SCP) messages to the FWSM. An SCP message is the communication of the supervisor (RP/SP) to other line cards. The FWSM running 2.3 code release is capable of understanding autostate messages sent by the supervisor engine. For the supervisor, the SCP messages are sent from the 12.2.18SXF5 release and the supervisor engine can notify the FWSM of the last physical port, leaving a particular VLAN. The combination of supervisor and FWSM codes are needed to enable the RaLFD feature.

TIP	The monitoring interface threshold can be changed using the following CLI command:

```
failover interface-policy num [percent]
```
You can use a percentage or a number as a threshold to trigger failover.

It is very important to understand the concept of monitoring the interfaces while designing redundancy. The change in thresholds in monitoring should be tested in a staged environment before tweaking the values in the production environment.

Configuring Poll Intervals

The FWSM monitors the unit and interface health for failover through *hellos*. The hello timer can be tweaked, both for unit and for interface. Decreasing the timer allows the failure detection to be faster.

The poll interval can be configured using the CLI commands for FWSM, using the following command:

```
failover poll 15
```

To change the interface polling time, issue the following command in global configuration mode:

```
failover polltime interface seconds
```

The default poll interface for failover is 15 seconds and is used for both unit and interface health monitoring.

Design Principle for Monitoring Interfaces

To enable a complete failover solution, you need a **monitor** command on all the interfaces, in all contexts. The **monitor** command in FWSM in multiple context mode needs to follow the network symmetry. There are also scenarios where monitoring of all interfaces may cause failover issues, if the FWSM failover concept is not symmetric to the network.

In certain deployments of multiple context mode, the interfaces across all the contexts in the primary and secondary FWSMs situated in two separate chassis will not be symmetric.

In Figure 12-3, Department A is in context A and Department B is in context B. With failover configured with interface monitoring in both contexts, when Switch B's connection to Cat6k1 goes to a down/down state and the FWSM failover threshold is reached, the FWSM switches over to the secondary FWSM. However, Switch A for Department A will lose the connectivity to the FWSM. When you plan redundancy for the FWSM, the Layer 2 symmetry is very important. In this case, the FWSM failover is configured, and the context interfaces are not monitored. Because all interfaces are not monitored, this is not a recommended design. This type of failover will also not support a complete failure scenario.

If the EtherChannel trunks between the switches are destined to carry the failover link and state VLANs, it is desirable to have at least two Gigabit Ethernet interfaces in the channel/trunk mode.

Figure 12-3 *Design Principle for Monitoring Interfaces*

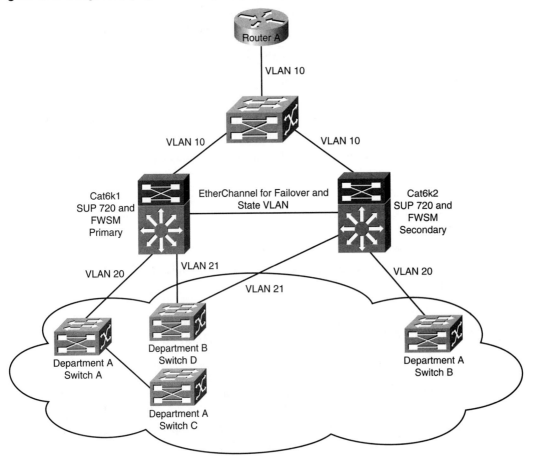

Configuring Single Context FWSM Failover

The spanning tree root and Hot Standby Router Protocol (HSRP) primary should be in the same switch as the active FWSM. In a single context mode, the failover mode is Active/Standby, where one of the physical firewalls will be the primary FWSM and the peer firewall will be the secondary FWSM. The traffic passes through the primary FWSM when no failure takes place, and in case of failover, the traffic passes through the secondary FWSM.

In the network in Figure 12-4, the static route from the switch has a next hop defined as the interface of the primary FWSM for the subnets in the inside security zone. The FWSM has a default route with a next hop to the outside VLAN 9 HSRP VIP address. The FWSM also points to the route for the subnets, which constitutes the inside security domain to the VLAN 10 VIP HSRP address. The inside interface of the FWSM is in VLAN 10.

Table 12-1 lists the first configuration that needs to be enabled for the failover. The configuration enables the primary and secondary FWSMs to communicate. In Figure 12-4, VLAN 30 represents failover link, and VLAN 31 represents the state link. When the FWSM is configured with **failover lan unit primary,** it becomes a primary FWSM, and when the peer FWSM is configured with **failover lan unit secondary,** it becomes the secondary FWSM. Before configuring any other interfaces for failover, the commands in Table 12-1 must be enabled on both the FWSMs.

Table 12-1   *Active/Standby Failover Configuration*

Primary FWSM	Secondary FWSM
| ```
interface Vlan30
 description LAN Failover Interface
!
interface Vlan31
 description STATE Failover Interface
!
failover
! Configures FWSM as primary unit
failover lan unit primary
! define the failover VLAN as VLAN 30
failover lan interface fover Vlan30
failover replication http
! define the state link as VLAN 31
failover link flink Vlan31
! define IP addresses for the primary and
!standby FWSMs for VLAN 30

failover interface ip fover 192.168.1.1
255.255.255.0 standby 192.168.1.2

!define IP addresses for the primary and
!standby for VLAN 31
failover interface ip flink 192.168.2.1
255.255.255.0 standby 192.168.2.2
``` | ```
interface Vlan30
 description LAN Failover Interface
!
interface Vlan31
 description STATE Failover Interface
!
failover
!Configures FWSM as secondary unit
failover lan unit secondary
! define the failover VLAN as VLAN 30
failover lan interface fover Vlan30
failover replication http
! define the state link as VLAN 31
failover link flink Vlan31
! define IP addresses for the primary and
!standby FWSMs for VLAN 30. The
!configuration is similar to the primary
!unit
failover interface ip fover 192.168.1.1
255.255.255.0 standby 192.168.1.2
! define IP addresses for the primary and
!standby for VLAN 31. The configuration is
!similar to the primary unit
failover interface ip flink 192.168.2.1
255.255.255.0 standby 192.168.2.2
``` |

Figure 12-4 *Single Context FWSM Failover*

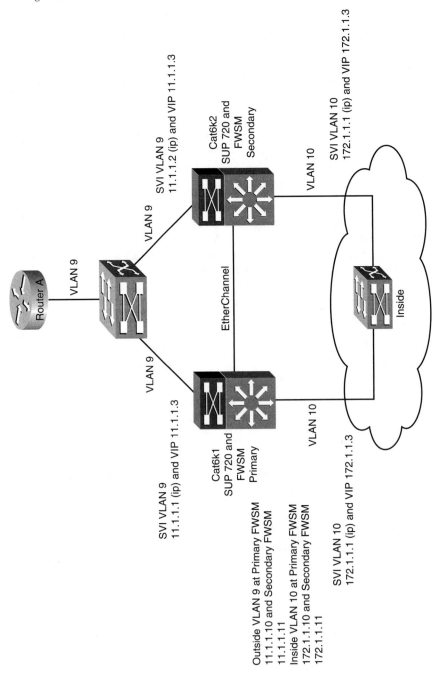

Example 12-1 shows the configuration for the primary FWSM in the topology shown in Figure 12-4.

Example 12-1 *Primary FWSM Configuration*

```
FWSM# show run
: Saved
:
FWSM Version 3.1(4)
!
hostname FWSM
enable password 8Ry2YjIyt7RRXU24 encrypted
names
! configure the outside interface of the FWSM. The primary IP address of the
! FWSM and standby address should be configured in the primary FWSM
interface Vlan9
 nameif outside
 security-level 0
 ip address 11.1.1.10 255.255.255.0 standby 11.1.1.11
! configure the inside interface of the FWSM. The primary IP address of the
! FWSM and standby active address should be configured in the primary FWSM
 interface Vlan10
 nameif inside
 security-level 100
 ip address 172.1.1.10 255.255.255.0 standby 172.1.1.11
 !
interface Vlan30
 description LAN Failover Interface
 !
interface Vlan31
 description STATE Failover Interface
 !
passwd 2KFQnbNIdI.2KYOU encrypted
ftp mode passive
! the access-list in production script will be based on the security policy
access-list ANY extended permit ip any any
pager lines 24
logging enable
logging buffered debugging
mtu outside 1500
mtu inside 1500
failover
failover lan unit primary
failover lan interface fover Vlan30
failover replication http
failover link flink Vlan31
failover interface ip fover 192.168.1.1 255.255.255.0 standby 192.168.1.2
failover interface ip flink 192.168.2.1 255.255.255.0 standby 192.168.2.2
monitor-interface outside
monitor-interface inside
icmp permit any outside
icmp permit any inside
no asdm history enable
arp timeout 12400
```

continues

Example 12-1 *Primary FWSM Configuration (Continued)*

```
nat-control
nat (inside) 0 0.0.0.0 0.0.0.0
access-group ANY in interface outside
access-group ANY out interface outside
access-group ANY in interface inside
access-group ANY out interface inside
! default route pointing to the VLAN 9 HSRP IP address
route outside 0.0.0.0 0.0.0.0 11.1.1.3 1
! route pointing to the inside subnets
route inside 172.1.0.0 255.255.0.0 172.1.1.3 1
timeout xlate 3:00:00
timeout conn 1:00:00 half-closed 0:10:00 udp 0:02:00 icmp 0:00:02
timeout sunrpc 0:10:00 h323 0:05:00 h225 1:00:00 mgcp 0:05:00
timeout mgcp-pat 0:05:00 sip 0:30:00 sip_media 0:02:00
timeout uauth 0:05:00 absolute
no snmp-server location
no snmp-server contact
snmp-server enable traps snmp authentication linkup linkdown coldstart
telnet timeout 5
ssh timeout 5
console timeout 0
!
class-map inspection_default
 match default-inspection-traffic
!
policy-map global_policy
 class inspection_default
  inspect dns maximum-length 512
  inspect ftp
  inspect h323 h225
  inspect h323 ras
  inspect netbios
  inspect rsh
  inspect skinny
  inspect smtp
  inspect sqlnet
  inspect sunrpc
  inspect tftp
  inspect sip
  inspect xdmcp
!
service-policy global_policy global
prompt hostname context
Cryptochecksum:96ff2a1f536fb43e19ac477ad4e19288
: end
FWSM#
```

Now focus your attention on the secondary FWSM for the topology shown in Figure 12-4.

The secondary FWSM has only configuration statements based on Table 12-1. After the primary FWSM is configured, the **write standby** command will enable all configurations to the secondary FWSM.

When you use **write standby** in the primary FWSM, the output for **show run** for the secondary FWSM is as shown in Example 12-2.

Example 12-2 *Secondary FWSM Configuration*

```
FWSM# show run
: Saved
:
FWSM Version 3.1(4)
!
hostname FWSM
enable password 8Ry2YjIyt7RRXU24 encrypted
names
!
interface Vlan9
 nameif outside
 security-level 0
 ip address 11.1.1.10 255.255.255.0 standby 11.1.1.11
!
interface Vlan10
 nameif inside
 security-level 100
 ip address 172.1.1.10 255.255.255.0 standby 172.1.1.11
!
interface Vlan30
 description LAN Failover Interface
!
interface Vlan31
 description STATE Failover Interface
!
passwd 2KFQnbNIdI.2KYOU encrypted
ftp mode passive
access-list ANY extended permit ip any any
pager lines 24
logging enable
logging buffered debugging
mtu outside 1500
mtu inside 1500
failover
failover lan unit secondary
failover lan interface fover Vlan30
failover replication http
failover link flink Vlan31
failover interface ip fover 192.168.1.1 255.255.255.0 standby 192.168.1.2
failover interface ip flink 192.168.2.1 255.255.255.0 standby 192.168.2.2
monitor-interface outside
monitor-interface inside
icmp permit any outside
icmp permit any inside
no asdm history enable
```

continues

Example 12-2 *Secondary FWSM Configuration (Continued)*

```
arp timeout 12400
nat-control
nat (inside) 0 0.0.0.0 0.0.0.0
access-group ANY in interface outside
access-group ANY out interface outside
access-group ANY in interface inside
access-group ANY out interface inside
route outside 0.0.0.0 0.0.0.0 11.1.1.3 1
route inside 172.1.0.0 255.255.0.0 172.1.1.3 1
timeout xlate 3:00:00
timeout conn 1:00:00 half-closed 0:10:00 udp 0:02:00 icmp 0:00:02
timeout sunrpc 0:10:00 h323 0:05:00 h225 1:00:00 mgcp 0:05:00
timeout mgcp-pat 0:05:00 sip 0:30:00 sip_media 0:02:00
timeout uauth 0:05:00 absolute
no snmp-server location
no snmp-server contact
snmp-server enable traps snmp authentication linkup linkdown coldstart
telnet timeout 5
ssh timeout 5
console timeout 0
!
class-map inspection_default
 match default-inspection-traffic
!
policy-map global_policy
 class inspection_default
  inspect dns maximum-length 512
  inspect ftp
  inspect h323 h225
  inspect h323 ras
  inspect netbios
  inspect rsh
  inspect skinny
  inspect smtp
  inspect sqlnet
  inspect sunrpc
  inspect tftp
  inspect sip
  inspect xdmcp
!
service-policy global_policy global
prompt hostname context
Cryptochecksum:a2b6c039b58765399846d7fb5da541b1
: end
```

The output in Example 12-3 confirms the configuration of failover for both the primary and secondary FWSMs in the topology, shown in Figure 12-4.

Example 12-3 *Verifying Failover for the Primary and Secondary FWSM Configurations*

```
! output from the Primary FWSM
FWSM# show failover
Failover On
Failover unit Primary
Failover LAN Interface: fover Vlan 30 (up)
Unit Poll frequency 1 seconds, holdtime 15 seconds
Interface Poll frequency 15 seconds
Interface Policy 50%
Monitored Interfaces 2 of 250 maximum
failover replication http
Config sync: active
Version: Ours 3.1(4), Mate 3.1(4)
Last Failover at: 15:22:04 UTC Apr 11 2007
        This host: Primary - Active
                Active time: 566984 (sec)
                    Interface outside (11.1.1.10): Normal
                    Interface inside (172.1.1.10): Normal
        Other host: Secondary - Standby Ready
                Active time: 25624 (sec)
                    Interface outside (11.1.1.11): Normal
                    Interface inside (172.1.1.11): Normal

Stateful Failover Logical Update Statistics
        Link : flink Vlan 31 (up)
        Stateful Obj    xmit        xerr        rcv         rerr
        General         73676       0           73670       0
        sys cmd         73670       0           73670       0
        up time         0           0           0           0
        RPC services    0           0           0           0
        TCP conn        0           0           0           0
        UDP conn        0           0           0           0
        ARP tbl         6           0           0           0
        Xlate_Timeout   0           0           0           0

        Logical Update Queue Information
                        Cur     Max     Total
        Recv Q:         0       2       640613
        Xmit Q:         0       0       73676
! output from the secondary FWSM
FWSM# show failover
Failover On
Failover unit Secondary
Failover LAN Interface: fover Vlan 30 (up)
Unit Poll frequency 1 seconds, holdtime 15 seconds
Interface Poll frequency 15 seconds
Interface Policy 50%
Monitored Interfaces 2 of 250 maximum
failover replication http
Config sync: active
```

continues

Example 12-3 *Verifying Failover for the Primary and Secondary FWSM Configurations (Continued)*

```
Version: Ours 3.1(4), Mate 3.1(4)
Last Failover at: 21:42:27 UTC Apr 2 2007
        This host: Secondary - Standby Ready
                Active time: 25624 (sec)
                    Interface outside (11.1.1.11): Normal
                    Interface inside (172.1.1.11): Normal
        Other host: Primary - Active
                Active time: 567017 (sec)
                    Interface outside (11.1.1.10): Normal
                    Interface inside (172.1.1.10): Normal

Stateful Failover Logical Update Statistics
        Link : flink Vlan 31 (up)
        Stateful Obj    xmit        xerr        rcv         rerr
        General         73674       0           73680       0
        sys cmd         73674       0           73674       0
        up time         0           0           0           0
        RPC services    0           0           0           0
        TCP conn        0           0           0           0
        UDP conn        0           0           0           0
        ARP tbl         0           0           6           0
        Xlate_Timeout   0           0           0           0

        Logical Update Queue Information
                        Cur     Max     Total
        Recv Q:         0       2       640662
        Xmit Q:         0       0       73674
```

The single context FWSM failover is configured in Active/Standby mode. The commands in Table 12-1 are very important to define the functionality of the two FWSMs as primary and secondary.

Configuring Multiple Context FWSM Failover

This section for multiple context mode goes through Active/Active mode of configuring FWSM. The two FWSMs are present in two different chassis. The spanning tree of the VLAN representing the active firewall context should be represented in the same switch. The HSRP VIP for the VLAN should also be represented in the same switch. If the HSRP Spanning Tree Protocol (STP) root follows the placement of primary context, this will reduce the traffic that passes between the two chassis. In this way, the traffic that enters the switch has active context FWSM and leaves through the same switch. The route statements will be similar to the description in single context mode covered in the previous section. The only difference is that the routes will be mentioned based on the context of the firewall.

Figure 12-5 shows an example of Active/Active context using failover groups. Here, both the FWSMs are actively passing traffic for the respective contexts.

Figure 12-5 *Network Topology for Multiple Context FWSM Failover*

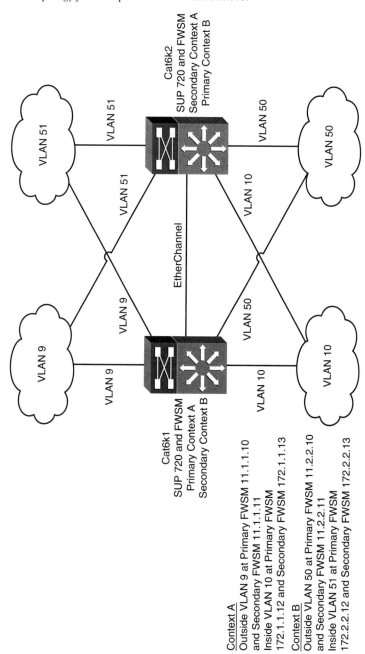

NOTE   The configuration for failover for routed mode or transparent mode is the same except for the way the VLANs are defined in the transparent mode. The failover configuration must allow BPDUs through the FWSM, which can be done using an EtherType access list.

Example 12-4 shows the multiple context failover configuration for the primary FWSM. Refer to the topology shown in Figure 12-5.

Example 12-4 *Primary FWSM System Configuration*

```
FWSM# show run
: Saved
:
FWSM Version 3.1(4) <system>
!
resource acl-partition 12
hostname FWSM
enable password 8Ry2YjIyt7RRXU24 encrypted
!
interface Vlan9
!
interface Vlan10
! VLAN 30 represents a failover link
interface Vlan30
description LAN Failover Interface
! VLAN 31 represents State link
interface Vlan31
description STATE Failover Interface
!
interface Vlan50
!
interface Vlan51
!
passwd 2KFQnbNIdI.2KYOU encrypted
class default
limit-resource IPSec 5
limit-resource Mac-addresses 65535
limit-resource ASDM 5
limit-resource SSH 5
limit-resource Telnet 5
limit-resource All 0!ftp mode passive
pager lines 24
! Configure failover
failover
! configure unit as a primary FWSM
failover lan unit primary
! VLAN 30 is configured as a failover link and VLAN 31 as a state link
failover lan interface fover Vlan30
failover replication http
```

Example 12-4   *Primary FWSM System Configuration (Continued)*

```
failover link flink Vlan31
! configure IP addresses for the interfaces for failover and state link.
! These VLANS should be trunked in the switch between the two chassis
failover interface ip fover 192.168.1.1 255.255.255.0 standby 192.168.1.2
failover interface ip flink 192.168.2.1 255.255.255.0 standby 192.168.2.2
! Active/Active mode introduces the concept of failover group. Each failover group
! has properties attached per context or attached to multiples contexts. In this
! case,there are two contexts.
! The failover group 1 is active in the primary unit and the failover group 2
!  is active in the secondary unit
failover group 1
preempt
replication http
failover group 2
secondary
preempt
replication http
no asdm history enable
arp timeout 12400
console timeout 0

admin-context admin
context admin
allocate-interface Vlan10
allocate-interface Vlan9
config-url disk:/admin.cfg
!
! contexta is attached to failover group 1
context contexta
allocate-interface Vlan10
allocate-interface Vlan9
config-url disk:/contexta.cfg
join-failover-group 1
!
! contextb is attached to failover group 2
context contextb
allocate-interface Vlan50
allocate-interface Vlan51
config-url disk:/contextb.cfg
join-failover-group 2
!
prompt hostname context
Cryptochecksum:3499722301e9febd9f25ced03d4bec32
: end
```

It is necessary to configure the secondary FWSM to identify the failover link and state link,
as demonstrated in Example 12-5. The secondary FWSM obtains the context configurations
from the primary FWSM when failover is enabled. The **preempt** command in the failover
group configurations cause the failover groups to become active on their designated unit

after the configurations have been synchronized and the preempt delay has passed. Make sure these VLANs are defined in the switch and allowed in the trunk.

Example 12-5 *Configuring the System Context of the Secondary FWSM*

```
failover
failover lan unit secondary
failover lan interface fover Vlan30
failover replication http
failover link flink Vlan31
failover interface ip fover 192.168.1.1 255.255.255.0 standby 192.168.1.2
failover interface ip flink 192.168.2.1 255.255.255.0 standby 192.168.2.2
```

Example 12-6 gives a snapshot of the commands needed to configure context A in the primary FWSM, from the **show running-config** output.

Example 12-6 *Active Context A Configuration (Primary FWSM)*

```
interface Vlan9
nameif outside
security-level 0
ip address 11.1.1.12 255.255.255.0 standby 11.1.1.13
!
interface Vlan10
nameif inside
security-level 100
ip address 172.1.1.12 255.255.255.0 standby 172.1.1.13
!
access-list 100 extended permit ip any any
pager lines 24
mtu outside 1500
mtu inside 1500
monitor-interface outside
monitor-interface inside
icmp permit any outside
icmp permit any inside
global (outside) 1 11.1.1.0 netmask 255.255.255.0
nat (inside) 1 0.0.0.0 0.0.0.0
access-group 100 in interface outside
access-group 100 out interface outside
access-group 100 in interface inside
access-group 100 out interface inside
route outside 0.0.0.0 0.0.0.0 11.1.1.3 1
```

Example 12-7 gives a snapshot of the commands needed to configure context B in the secondary FWSM, from the **show running-config** command output.

Example 12-7 *Active Context B Configuration (Secondary FWSM)*

```
interface Vlan50
 nameif inside
 security-level 100
 ip address 172.2.2.10 255.255.255.0 standby 172.2.2.11
```

Example 12-7 *Active Context B Configuration (Secondary FWSM) (Continued)*

```
!
interface Vlan51
 nameif outside
 security-level 0
 ip address 11.2.2.10 255.255.255.0 standby 11.2.2.11
!
passwd 2KFQnbNIdI.2KYOU encrypted
access-list 100 extended permit ip any any
access-list 101 extended permit ip any any
pager lines 24
mtu inside 1500
mtu outside 1500
monitor-interface inside
monitor-interface outside
icmp permit any inside
icmp permit any outside
no asdm history enable
arp timeout 12400
global (outside) 1 11.2.2.0 netmask 255.255.255.0
nat (inside) 1 0.0.0.0 0.0.0.0
access-group 101 in interface inside
access-group 101 out interface inside
access-group 101 in interface outside
access-group 101 out interface outside
route outside 0.0.0.0 0.0.0.0 11.2.2.3 1
```

Use the **show failover** command to verify the failover in each context. The "Configuring Multiple Context FWSM Failover" section shows Active/Active context configuration. The 3.x code supports Active/Active features. The example shows configurations of failover groups and how they are attached to each context. The failover group gives distinct failover characteristics to each context. This helps achieve Active/Active configurations for multiple context mode and use both the FWSM units.

Summary

After reading this chapter, you should know the following key topics:

- The redundancy concept in FWSM—Active/Active and Active/Standby
- Understanding state link and failover link in a FWSM
- Requirements needed to enable redundancy in the FWSM
- Understanding redundancy parameters of a FWSM, such as poll interval and monitoring
- Configuration of Active/Standby and Active/Active modes of failover in FWSM

CHAPTER 13

Understanding Application Protocol Inspection

Application protocol inspection provides three primary functions:

- It validates control traffic flows and/or verifies for RFC compliance.
- It monitors sessions for embedded IP addressing in the data portion of the packet.
- It examines session information for secondary channels.

Validation of control traffic flows may occur with protocols, such as Extended Simple Mail Transfer Protocol (ESMTP), where you want to allow only specific commands, such as DATA, HELO, QUIT, and so on. An example of RFC compliance verification is when the inspection engine is monitoring port 80 for HTTP traffic and another protocol (that is, Telnet) is attempting to use port 80 as well. Because the Telnet traffic does not comply with HTTP (RFC 2621), it will be dropped.

A session with embedded IP addressing would be NetBIOS over TCP (NBT) or Domain Name Services (DNS). The challenge occurs when these types of protocols are used in conjunction with Network Address Translation (NAT). The FWSM might need to change embedded IP addresses for the application to work properly.

An application that opens a secondary channel or multiple secondary channels is H.323. Up to six UPD sessions may be dynamically allocated during a connection, and the FWSM needs to be aware of these connections to open the specific ports for communication.

If you have some previous experience with the Private Internet Exchange (PIX), you probably remember the **fixup** command. This was replaced by the **inspect** command. Neither term really describes the function it performs alone, but together they provide a much better definition; "fixup" the applications to work properly, and "inspect" traffic flows for appropriate conformance, but you are stuck with the **inspect** command.

This process of inspection examines session information for secondary connections and illicit activity, and when NAT is configured, it translates IP addresses embedded in the data portion of the packet. Application inspection may be the most significant differentiator between a typical router using Access Control Lists (ACL) and a firewall that has the capability to understand and control the communication within protocols.

Inspecting Hypertext Transfer Protocol

Hypertext Transfer Protocol (HTTP) is a communication protocol used for the exchange of information (typically web pages) on the Internet or an intranet.

The HTTP inspection engine can provide application inspection and control for the following:

- **Content protection and attack prevention:** Enforces HTTP-specific parameters, such as URL, Header, Cookie length, and so on, detection.

- **Worm mitigation:** Filters on HTTP encoding mechanisms, content type, non-ASCII characters, and so on.

- **Application access control:** Inspects and filters tunneled applications such as adware, spyware, remote PC control, and so on.

Figure 13-1 shows an example of a client on the outside attempting to telnet to a device on the inside. This may be a unique case to find someone obfuscating Telnet traffic inside port 80, but it provides a good understanding of how the inspection engine functions.

The Firewall Services Module (FWSM) is preconfigured to allow port 23 from the outside client to the host on the inside. HTTP inspection has been configured to monitor port 23, provide a "strict" inspection, drop any traffic that is not HTTP, and then log the appropriate information. This means that any traffic destined to port 23 that does not meet the requirements of "standard" HTTP traffic (RFC 2616) will be dropped and logged.

To accomplish this task, an **http-map** must be added using the following commands in configuration mode:

```
http-map HTTP-MAP
  strict-http action drop log
```

A **class-map** also must be created specifying the type of traffic to inspect. This example uses a simple port map specifying TCP port 23, but other ports as well as an access list can be defined.

```
class-map HTTP-CLASS
  match port tcp eq telnet
```

Finally, the class map needs to be applied to the policy used for inspection. In this case, it is the default global policy map:

```
policy-map global_policy
 class inspection_default
  inspect dns maximum-length 512
  inspect ftp
  inspect h323 h225
  inspect h323 ras
  inspect netbios
  inspect rsh
  inspect skinny
  inspect smtp
  inspect sqlnet
  inspect sunrpc
  inspect tftp
```

```
inspect sip
inspect xdmcp
class HTTP-CLASS
inspect http HTTP-MAP
```

Figure 13-1 *HTTP Inspection Example*

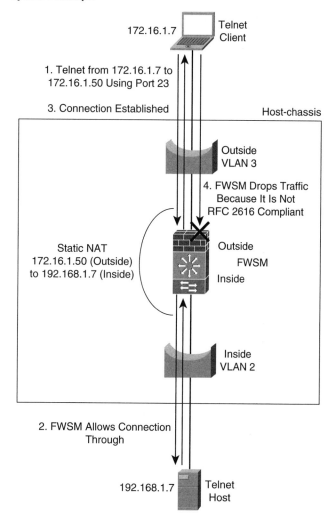

When the client attempts to access the host on the inside, the connection is established initially but subsequent packets are denied (dropped) because Telnet traffic does not meet the specific requirements of RFC 2616. Because the violation action will be logged, the following output is generated:

```
%FWSM-6-302013: Built inbound TCP connection 1456730330626822579 for
outside:172.16.1.7/48698 (172.16.1.7/48698) to inside:172.16.1.50/23 (192.168.1.50/
  23)
%FWSM-5-415010:16 HTTP protocol violation detected - Drop -  HTTP Protocol not
detected from 172.16.1.7 to 172.16.1.50
```

HTTP is the predominant protocol for the exchange of information on the Internet; consequently, it is one of the most exploited. Being able to inspect HTTP traffic for compliance will protect against a myriad of exploits and attacks, consequently helping you better secure your valuable resources.

Inspecting File Transfer Protocol

File Transfer Protocol (FTP) is a communication mechanism used to transfer data from one device to another using a command and control connection for the communication-specific commands and a data connection for the exchange of bulk information. FTP operates in active and passive modes.

Using active mode, the client establishes a TCP connection to the host on port 21 (command and control), and the host connects to the client on a negotiated destination TCP port (data) sourcing from TCP port 20.

With passive mode, the client establishes a TCP connection to the host on port 21 (command and control) and opens a second TCP connection to the host to a negotiated port.

Figure 13-2 shows a client on the "inside" connecting to an FTP server on the "outside." This configuration will not allow the client to "get" any files from the FTP server, because we have restricted the "get" function with the policy map, but it will allow other functions.

As in the first example, create an *ftp map* as follows, and deny the "get" function. This function is part of the "command and control" TCP connection.

```
ftp-map FTP-MAP
  request-command deny get
```

Add the class map to match FTP traffic:

```
class-map FTP-CLASS
  match port tcp eq ftp
```

If the default **inspect ftp** configuration is not removed, FTP traffic will not "hit" the class map. Remove it with the following commands:

```
policy-map global_policy
  class inspection_default
  no inspect ftp
```

Figure 13-2 *FTP Inspection Example*

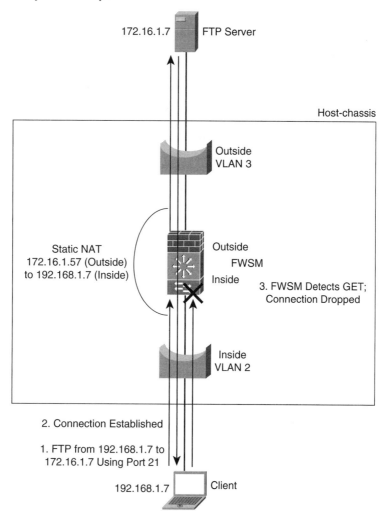

The final step is to apply the class and map to the policy used for inspection. In this case, it is the default global policy map:

```
policy-map global_policy
 class inspection_default
  inspect dns maximum-length 512
  inspect h323 h225
  inspect h323 ras
  inspect netbios
  inspect rsh
  inspect skinny
  inspect smtp
  inspect sqlnet
```

```
  inspect sunrpc
  inspect tftp
  inspect sip
  inspect xdmcp
class HTTP-CLASS
  inspect http HTTP-MAP
class FTP-CLASS
  inspect ftp strict FTP-MAP
```

The FWSM log message shows the initial TCP connection established from the client IP/ephemeral port to the FTP server/TCP port 21.

```
%FWSM-6-302013: Built outbound TCP connection 145673097487192049 for
  inside:192.168.1.7/50048 (172.16.1.57/50048) to outside:172.16.1.7/21 (172.16.1.7/
  21)
```

When the client attempts to get a file, a data channel is established. The following log message also indicates that the FTP session between the client and server is using passive FTP:

```
%FWSM-6-302013: Built outbound TCP connection 145673097487192049 for
  inside:192.168.1.7/44770 (172.16.1.57/44770) to outside:172.16.1.7/57360
  (172.16.1.7/57360)
```

The FWSM FTP inspection engine recognizes the "get" command and terminates the control session with a TCP reset.

```
%FWSM-6-303003: FTP get command denied - failed strict inspection, terminating
  connection from inside:192.168.1.7/50048 to outside:172.16.1.7/21
%FWSM-6-302014: Teardown TCP connection 145673097487192049 for inside:192.168.1.7/
  50048 to outside:172.16.1.7/21 duration 0:00:14 bytes 1553 TCP Reset
```

The client has now lost the connection to the FTP server.

You should also be aware that application inspection may break certain applications. This could occur because of poor application coding, nonstandard conformance of the application, applying the inspection process to traffic flows (ports) that do not match the application (as in the HTTP inspection example), and so on.

For detailed information on configuration parameters, refer to the FWSM documentation at Cisco.com.

Because FTP is a protocol that uses both a command and control connection and a dynamic data connection, it would be impossible to control very tightly using just a traditional ACL. The FTP inspection engine not only helps ensure that appropriate communication channels are opened, it also controls which commands are allowed.

Working with Supported Applications

Many applications are supported with specific inspection engines. Based on how those applications behave or how they have been written, you might need to alter the actions of the inspection engines or potentially disable a particular inspection engine if those applications do not function properly.

Table 13-1 provides a list of supported applications (courtesy of the Cisco Firewall Services Module documentation on Cisco.com). Table 13-1 provides a reference, but for detailed information refer to the FWSM technical documentation on Cisco.com.

Table 13-1   *Application Inspection Engines and Their Defaults for Version 3.2*

Application	Enabled by Default?	PAT?	NAT (1-1)?	Configure Port?	Default Port	Standards	Comments
Computer Telephony Interface Quick Buffer Encoding (CTIQBE)	No	Yes	Yes	Yes	TCP/2748	—	—
Domain Name Service (DNS)[1]	Yes	Yes	Yes	No	UDP/53	RFC 1123	Only forward NAT. No pointer (PTR) records are changed. Default maximum packet length is 512 bytes.
FTP	Yes	Yes	Yes	Yes	TCP/21	RFC 959	Default FTP inspection does not enforce compliance with RFC standards. To do so, configure the **inspect ftp** command with the strict keyword.

continues

Table 13-1 *Application Inspection Engines and Their Defaults for Version 3.2 (Continued)*

Application	Enabled by Default?	PAT?	NAT (1-1)?	Configure Port?	Default Port	Standards	Comments
General Packet Radio Service (GPRS) Tunneling Protocol (GTP)	No	Yes	Yes	Yes	UDP/ 3386 UDP/ 2123	—	Requires a special license.
H.323	Yes	Yes	Yes	Yes	TCP/1720 UDP/ 1718 UDP (RAS) 1718-1719	ITU-T H.323, H.245, H225.0, Q.931, Q.932	By default, both Registration, Admission, and Status (RAS) and H.225 inspection are enabled.
HTTP	No	Yes	Yes	Yes	TCP/80	RFC 2616	Beware of maximum transmission unit (MTU) limitations when stripping ActiveX and Java.[2]
Internet Control Message Protocol (ICMP)	No	Yes	Yes	No	—	—	—
ICMP ERROR	No	Yes	Yes	No	—	—	—
Internet Locator Service (ILS) Lightweight Directory Access Protocol (LDAP)	No	Yes	Yes	Yes	—	—	—

Table 13-1 *Application Inspection Engines and Their Defaults for Version 3.2 (Continued)*

Application	Enabled by Default?	PAT?	NAT (1-1)?	Configure Port?	Default Port	Standards	Comments
Media Gateway Control Protocol (MGCP)	No	Yes	Yes	Yes	2427, 2727	RFC 2705bis-05	—
Network Basic Input/Output System (NetBIOS) Datagram Service / User Datagram Protocol (UDP)	Yes	Yes	Yes	No	UDP/138	—	—
NetBIOS Name Service / UDP	Yes	No	No	No	UDP/137	—	No Windows Internet Naming Service (WINS) support.
NetBIOS over IP[3]	Yes	No	No	No	—	—	—
Point-to-Point Tunneling Protocol (PPTP)	No	Yes	Yes	Yes	1723	RFC 2637	—
Remote shell protocol (rsh)	Yes	Yes	Yes	Yes	TCP/514	Berkeley UNIX	—
Real-time Streaming Protocol (RTSP)	No	Yes	No	Yes	TCP/554	RFC 2326, RFC 2327, RFC 1889	No handling for HTTP cloaking.
Session Initiation Protocol (SIP)	Yes	Yes	Yes	Yes	TCP/5060 UDP/5060	RFC 2543	—

continues

Table 13-1 *Application Inspection Engines and Their Defaults for Version 3.2 (Continued)*

Application	Enabled by Default?	PAT?	NAT (1-1)?	Configure Port?	Default Port	Standards	Comments
Skinny Call Control Protocol (SCCP)	Yes	Yes	Yes	Yes	TCP/2000	—	Does not handle TFTP uploaded Cisco IP Phone configurations under certain circumstances.
Simple Network Management Protocol (SNMP)	Yes	No	No	Yes	UDP/161, 162	RFC 1155, 1157, 1212, 1213, 1215	v.2 RFC 1902-1908; v.3 RFC 2570-2580.
Simple Mail Transfer Protocol (SMTP)/ Extended Simple Mail Transfer Protocol (ESMTP)	Yes	Yes	Yes	Yes	TCP/25	RFC 821, 1123	By default, SMTP inspection is enabled rather than ESMTP inspection.
SQL*Net	Yes	Yes	Yes	Yes	TCP/1521 (v.1)	—	V.1 and v.2.
Sun remote-procedure call (RPC)	Yes	No	Yes	No	UDP/111 TCP/111	—	Payload not Network Address Translated (NATed).
Trivial File Transfer Protocol (TFTP)	Yes	Yes	Yes	Yes	TCP/69 UDP/69	RFC 1350	—
X Display Manager Control Protocol (XDCMP)	Yes	No	No	No	UDP/177	—	—

[1] No NAT support is available for name resolution through WINS.

[2] If the MTU is too small to allow the Java or ActiveX tag to be included in one packet, stripping may not occur.

[3] NetBIOS is supported by performing NAT of the packets for NetBIOS Name Service UDP port 137 and NetBIOS Datagram Service UDP port 138.

A significant number of inspection engines are available, each with unique parameters. Review the appropriate documentation on Cisco.com for the specific version you are using.

Configuring ARP

Address Resolution Protocol (ARP) is a mechanism to find a device's hardware or MAC address from the IP address of the device. When these devices are on the same subnet (excluding proxy-ARP) and need to communicate using IP, each of them must know what the other's MAC address is. With this information, the devices now have the capability to communicate.

From a security perspective, malicious attackers can exploit the ARP by sending an unsolicited ARP or gratuitous ARP to devices within the same subnet, indicating that they are the owners of a particular MAC address. When the unsuspecting host sends traffic to another device or default gateway (router), that traffic is redirected to the attacker. The attacker can then redirect that traffic to the destination device and very stealthfully conduct a man-in-the-middle attack, as shown in Figure 13-3.

Figure 13-3 *Man-in-the-Middle Attack*

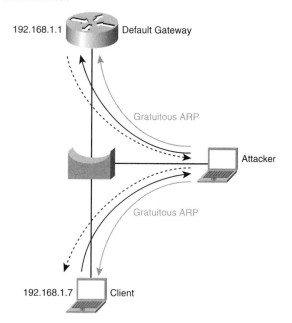

ARP is critical to the operation of an IP network and unfortunately opens additional opportunities for attackers to circumvent security devices. The following sections will provide a better understanding of how to control ARP, and consequently protect your valuable network resources.

Inspecting ARP

With the FWSM configured in transparent mode, it has the capability to match the source interface, MAC address, and IP address of IP packets. This process helps mitigate a man-in-the-middle attack as described in Figure 13-3. Because the traffic flow from the source has a unique IP/MAC pair, the FWSM recognizes the mismatch and has the capability to drop the traffic.

Figure 13-4 illustrates that when an attacker attempts to send a gratuitous ARP request to the FWSM, the FWSM denies the update because of a MAC/IP address mismatch.

Figure 13-4 *ARP Inspection*

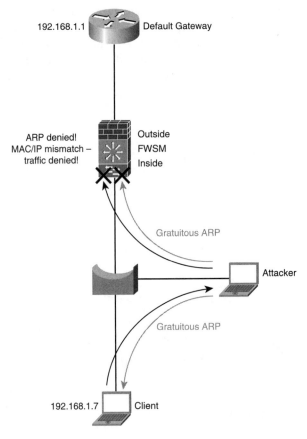

ARP inspection is a feature that improves the security posture of your network by helping to mitigate a man-in-the-middle attack caused by ARP cache poisoning.

Configuring Parameters for ARP

Two options need to be configured for ARP inspection to provide the greatest security capability:

- Configuring MAC entries
- Adding static IP to MAC mappings

Configuring MAC Entries

The first option is to configure how specific MAC entries are learned for a particular interface. By default, when MAC entries are learned, they are entered into the mac-address-table of the FWSM and associated with the interface in which it was learned. If the FWSM does not have the MAC in the mac-address-table, it will either send an ARP request if the subnet is directly connected or will send an ICMP to the destination to determine the appropriate return interface and then populate the mac-address-table accordingly.

To disable the automatic MAC learning capability, use the following command with the appropriate interface selected, in configuration mode:

```
mac-learn inside disable
mac-learn outside disable
```

Individual MAC addresses must be populated manually in the FWSM using the following command:

```
mac-address-table static outside 00d0.0622.6400
mac-address-table static inside 000b.cd4e.6424
```

You can already see the downside to this! Each entry must be added, and when a device's MAC address changes (because of a network interface card [NIC] replacement), so do the entries in the FWSM. The benefit is that you have much better control over the devices in the network.

Adding Static Entries

The second option is to configure ARP inspection and add static entries.

If the FWSM does not have an entry in the local ARP table, it will flood the packet out of all interfaces and when a response is received, it will create an entry in the ARP table. To stop the FWSM from flooding the ARP, use the following commands in configuration mode:

```
arp-inspection inside enable no-flood
arp-inspection outside enable flood
```

In this example, both the inside and outside interfaces have ARP flooding disabled.

At this point in the configuration, no traffic will be allowed to pass through the FWSM until static ARP entries are added. This is performed using the following commands in configuration mode:

```
arp inside 192.168.1.7 000b.cd4e.6424
arp outside 192.168.1.1 00d0.0622.6400
```

If you have MAC address learning disabled and ARP inspection set to no-flood, you might not be able to easily find the MAC/IP address pair. This might have to be accomplished by connecting directly to the host or to another host off the same interface of the FWSM to determine the MAC/IP relationship.

From either Microsoft Windows, Linux, Solaris, MAC, and so on, you can use the following command to display the ARP entries:

```
arp -ia
? (192.168.1.1) at 00:D0:06:22:64:00 [ether] on eth1
```

This example is from a Linux command prompt.

If the MAC entry does not exist in mac-address-table, it will be silently dropped and traffic will not be forwarded. This may cause you hours of troubleshooting fun!

When a static ARP entry has not been configured, the following entry will be logged:

```
%FWSM-3-322003: ARP inspection check failed for arp request received from host
000b.cd4e.6424 on interface inside. This host is advertising MAC Address
000b.cd4e.6424 for IP Address 192.168.1.7, which is not bound to any MAC Address
```

When a mismatch of the MAC/IP pair occurs, the following message will be logged:

```
%FWSM-3-322002: ARP inspection check failed for arp request received from host
000b.cd4e.6424 on interface inside. This host is advertising MAC Address
000b.cd4e.6424 for IP Address 192.168.1.7, which is statically bound to MAC Address
0bad.c0ff.ee00
```

As you can see, a significant amount of configuration is required to take full advantage of ARP inspection. Although it does provide a significant security advantage, be aware of the administrative overhead to manage such a configuration.

The implementation of security mechanisms is directly proportional to the complexity of the security design. Maintaining a configuration of a large number of MAC/IP addresses can be an overwhelming task. Use this feature where the additional security is necessary and does not overburden the administrative aspect.

Summary

Application protocol inspection is a very powerful tool that supports many applications and will help you maintain the security of your network by ensuring protocol conformance, controlling specific commands, and so on. The use of ARP inspection and static MAC/IP mappings assists in preventing man-in-the-middle attacks by protecting ARP entries on the FWSM. As always, be sure of the impact of implementing new features on production networks to minimize network outages.

References

Cisco documentation:

RFC 792—*Internet Control Message Protocol (ICMP)*
RFC 821, 1123—*Simple Mail Transfer Protocol (SMTP)*
RFC 959—*File Transfer Protocol (FTP)*
RFC 1123—*Domain Name System (DNS)*
RFC 1155, 1157, 1212, 1213, 1215—*Simple Network Management Protocol (SNMP)*
RFC 1350—*Trivial File Transfer Protocol (TFTP)*
RFC 2326, RFC 2327, RFC 1889—*Real-time Streaming Protocol (RTSP)*
RFC 2543—*Session Initiation Protocol (SIP)*
RFC 2637—*Point-to-Point Tunneling Protocol (PPTP)*
RFC 3435—*Media Gateway Control Protocol (MGCP)*
ITU-T International Telecommunications Union—H.323

CHAPTER 14

Filtering

With the tremendous amount of "inappropriate" content on the Internet, organizations may need to have the capability to determine where users can surf. This will help minimize the organizations' liability, which may incur from users viewing "inappropriate" material, and it will also help to increase user productivity by limiting access to certain locations. This is accomplished by redirecting HTTP/Secure HTTP(S) and FTP traffic to an external device that will either permit or deny the connection.

ActiveX controls and Java software products improve the user experience by adding animation to web pages (stock tickers), integrating the use of audio and video players, as well as adding command buttons, and so on. As with any silver lining, it does have a cloud. There is always a risk that the ActiveX control or Java applets could be used for illegitimate purposes. Applications such as spyware, pop-ups, keystroke loggers, viruses, and so on can be contained in the ActiveX control or Java applications. This may be a manageable risk for some organizations, but it may not be for others. The Firewall Service Module (FWSM) has the capability of removing ActiveX objects and/or Java applets contained within HTTP traffic.

Working with URLs and FTP

The third-party applications that are supported today are Websense Enterprise and Secure Computing SmartFilter (previously N2H2, which was acquired by Secure Computing in October, 2003). Deploying either of these "off-box" solutions requires a server running the application software.

These applications help to enforce Internet access policies by categorizing Internet sites and providing the capability to permit or deny access to these locations. Access can be controlled for the entire organization to individual users.

Table 14-1 explains the basic capability of each solution. Be aware that features and functionality change; consult the vendors for the latest information.

Table 14-1 *Product Capabilities*

Product	Filtering Services
Websense Enterprise	HTTP, HTTPS, and FTP
Secure Computing SmartFilter	HTTP, FTP, and long URL[1]

[1]More than 1159 characters

URL and FTP filtering is done from a more secure to a less secure interface, and up to four filtering servers are supported per context. Filtering servers cannot be mixed within a context. The addition of a filter server incurs some delay. To provide the most optimal user experience, the filter server should be placed very close to the FWSM.

Figure 14-1 shows the FWSM configured with three interfaces: an inside, an outside, and one with the filter server. The client resides on the inside, with the WWW server located on the outside (Internet) and the filter server located on the associated interface.

In the following example, the FWSM is configured in routed mode with a Websense server connected on the Filter interface with an IP address of 172.20.1.7.

Configure the filter server (from configuration mode):

```
FWSM(config)# url-server (Filter) vendor websense host 172.20.1.7 timeout 10
   protocol TCP version 4
```

If you are using Secure Computing SmartFilter (N2H2), specify the vendor as **smartfilter**. You also have the capability to configure the port number, protocol, and timeout values (default is 30 seconds). In this example, the time value has been set to the minimum time of 10 seconds and the version set to 4 to support caching.

Content buffering minimizes the delay in the user experience. When a user attempts to establish a connection with a server on the Internet, the FWSM will forward the request to the Internet server and simultaneously send a request to the filter server. In the event that the server on the Internet responds before the filter server, the traffic would be dropped unless a buffer has been configured.

```
url-block block 32
```

This configuration is using a block size of 32, but may need some tweaking in your specific environment. You can monitor the block size using the **show url-block block statistics** command, as shown in Example 14-1.

Figure 14-1 *URL and FTP Filtering*

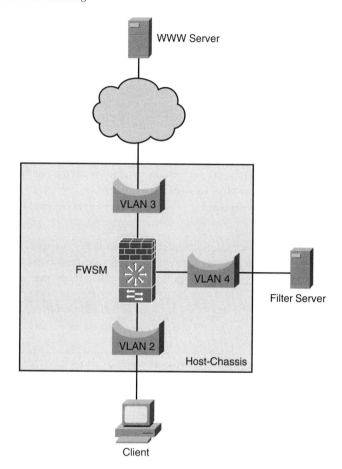

Example 14-1 *Monitoring the Block Size*

```
FWSM(config)# show url-block block statistics
URL Pending Packet Buffer Stats with max block  32
-------------------------------------------------------
Cumulative number of packets held:             572
Maximum number of packets held (per URL):       82
Current number of packets held (global):        17
Packets dropped due to
        exceeding url-block buffer limit:        0
        HTTP server retransmission:              0
Number of packets released back to client:       0
```

| NOTE | Two additional features exist for configuration of **url-block** parameters, but these are available only with Websense.
| | |

The **url-block url-mempool** command specifies the amount of memory allocated to buffer pending requests. The per URL size should be smaller than the memory pool size; otherwise, you will receive an error message when attempting to add the command.

```
url-block url-mempool memory-pool-size
```

The **url-block url-size** command allows you to increase the maximum single URL size up to 4K:

```
url-block url-size block-size
```

The memory allocated from the previous commands is used from the FWSM complex and has no effect on access control lists (ACL) memory.

To expedite the process of filtering, and to improve the user experience, URL-caching allows the FWSM to cache request from clients to specific servers. The **dst** parameter can be used if all clients share the same policy; if they do not, the **src_dst** option should be chosen.

```
FWSM(config)# url-cache {dst | src_dst} size
```

| NOTE | If URL-caching is performed, the FWSM does not send a request to the filter server. Consequently, the filter server will not maintain any historical information about the request. |

In this example, all users share the same policy. Consequently, the dst option would be used. The maximum amount of memory (128KB) has been allocated.

```
FWSM(config)# url-cache dst 128
```

To view the filtering statistics information collected by the FWSM, use the **show url-server statistics** command, as shown in Example 14-2. This is a very good troubleshooting tool to verify the status of the filter server and the number of requests performed.

Example 14-2 *Displaying Filtering Statistics Information*

```
FWSM(config)# show url-server statistics
Global Statistics:
- - - - - - - - - - - - - - - - -
URLs total/allowed/denied        537/456/81
URLs allowed by cache/server     0/456
URLs denied by cache/server      0/81
HTTPs total/allowed/denied       0/0/0
HTTPs allowed by cache/server    0/0
```

Example 14-2   *Displaying Filtering Statistics Information (Continued)*

```
HTTPs denied by cache/server         0/0
FTPs total/allowed/denied            0/0/0
FTPs allowed by cache/server         0/0
FTPs denied by cache/server          0/0
Requests dropped                     0
Server timeouts/retries              0/1
Processed rate average 60s/300s      0/0 requests/second
Denied rate average 60s/300s         0/0 requests/second
Dropped rate average 60s/300s        0/0 requests/second
Server Statistics:
- - - - - - - - - - - - - - - - - -
172.20.1.7                           UP
  Vendor                             websense
  Port                               15868
  Requests total/allowed/denied      456/456/0
  Server timeouts/retries            0/1
  Responses received                 456
  Response time average 60s/300s  0/0 seconds/request
URL Packets Sent and Received Stats:
- - - - - - - - - - - - - - - - - - - - - - - - - - - - - -
Message                 Sent    Received
STATUS_REQUEST          13030   7877
LOOKUP_REQUEST          539     538
LOG_REQUEST             0       NA
Errors:
- - - - - - - -
RFC noncompliant GET method     0
URL buffer update failure       0
```

The final portion of the filter example is for HTTP configuration, the port number, source IP address and mask, destination IP address and mask, the capability to make exemptions for the previous parameters, the option to allow the traffic in the event that the filter server is unavailable and the proxy-block feature will not forward requests to a proxy server. All these options are configured under a single command, **filter url**:

```
FWSM(config)# filter url [http | port[-port] | except} local_ip local_mask foreign_ip
    foreign_mask] [allow] [cgi-truncate] [longurl-deny] [longurl-truncate] [proxy-
    block]
```

With the following command, HTTP traffic originating from the 192.168.1.0/24 network destined to anywhere will be redirected to the filter server. The allow option will permit traffic through the FWSM when the filter server is unavailable (obviously it must pass the ACL associated with the interface). The proxy-block feature precludes users from accessing a proxy server. If the length of the URL is longer than the maximum length allowed, the longurl-truncate option will cause only the IP address or hostname to be sent to the filter server. The longurl-deny will drop requests that have a URL longer than the maximum length allowed, and the cgi-truncate will truncate the request to only the script name and location.

```
filter url http 192.168.1.0 255.255.255.0 0.0.0.0 0.0.0.0 allow proxy-block longurl-
    truncate
```

If you need to provide devices within your network access to specific resources without being filtered, an exception can be added using the following command:

```
filter url except 192.168.1.23 255.255.255.255 0 0
```

In this case, the exception option is used to allow the device at 192.168.1.23 to bypass the filter server.

HTTPS and FTP have very similar command-line options. These include port numbers, the source IP address and mask, the destination IP address and mask, and finally the allow option, which will permit the traffic in the event the filter server(s) are unavailable. The interactive-block option prevents users from connecting to FTP servers using interactive mode.

HTTP configuration:

```
FWSM(config)# filter https {port[-port] | except} localIP local_mask foreign_IP
    foreign_mask [allow]
```

FTP configuration:

```
FSM(config)# filter ftp {port[-port] | except} localIP local_mask foreign_IP
    foreign_mask [allow] [interact-block]
```

From the users' perspective, they would not have any idea that a filter server was being used within the network until they attempt to access a location that is being denied by the filter server policy. The following example shows what happens when a user attempts to access a site being protected by a Websense filter server.

Figure 14-2 shows what a user would experience in the event an attempt was made to access a restricted location.

A log message is also generated from the FWSM, indicating that access to the specific URL has been denied. The FWSM will also send a TCP reset and tear down the connection.

```
%FWSM-6-302013: Built outbound TCP connection 145673024472748016 for
    Inside:192.168.1.23/1127 (192.168.1.23/1127) to Outside:10.147.82.82/80
    (10.147.82.82/80)
%FWSM-5-304002: Access denied URL http://www.find-me-a-job-because-i-didnot-read-
    the-fwsm-book.com/ SRC 192.168.1.23 DEST 10.147.82.82 on interface Inside
%FWSM-6-302014: Teardown TCP connection 145673024472748016 for Inside:192.168.1.23/
    1127 to Outside:10.147.82.82/80 duration 0:00:01 bytes 5577 TCP Reset
```

Controlling client HTTP(S) and/or FTP access to "authorized" locations will not only help to reduce the amount of "inappropriate" or "unauthorized" content that is downloaded, it will also help to minimize the potential risk of malware, because many "illicit" sites contain that type of material. Many configuration options provide flexibility in filtering appropriate content and locations.

Figure 14-2 *Filtering by Websense*

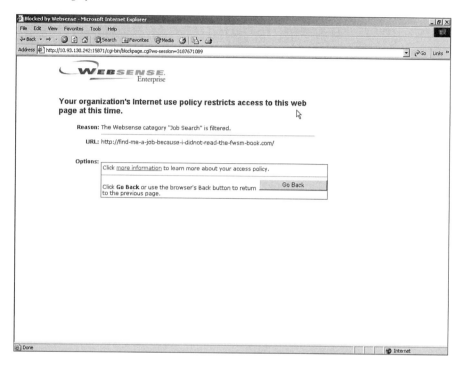

Configuring ActiveX and Java

ActiveX controls and Java applets are similar in functionality, but the ActiveX control has additional capabilities because it can run with the same privileges as the user running the application. With either of these applications, a potential risk for malicious use always exists. Because the FWSM has the capability of removing ActiveX objects and/or Java applets contained within HTTP traffic, you have options.

Filtering ActiveX replaces the object and applet tags with comments. The filter **activex** command also comments out Java files, images, and objects that are embedded within object tags.

NOTE   Packets that are fragmented cannot be blocked.

If you plan to use ActiveX or Java filtering, HTTP inspection must be enabled, or you will wonder why the filtering is not working. If the default global policy is used, the following commands need to be added:

```
policy-map global_policy
  class inspection_default
  inspect http
```

ActiveX and Java are configured using the following command set:

```
filter {activex | java} {port[-port] | except} local_ip local_mask foreign_ip
  foreign_mask
```

In this example, ActiveX is being filtered from 192.168.1.23 to any destination:

```
filter activex 80 192.168.1.23 255.255.255.255 0.0.0.0 0.0.0.0
```

A log message will be generated by the FWSM indicating that ActiveX content was filtered.

```
%FWSM-5-500001: ActiveX content modified src 192.168.1.23 dest 10.29.201.21 on
  interface Outside
```

ActiveX control and Java have the potential to be used for malicious intent. Fortunately, the FWSM has the capability to filter both types of content. Filtering will obviously break applications that need ActiveX or Java to operate properly. Use the **except** option as in URL filtering to allow this behavior from specific address(es).

Summary

Filtering URL/FTP locations through the use of a third-party filter server can be very helpful in controlling what resources or categories of resources you want clients to access, consequently reducing illicit content and increasing productivity. ActiveX control and Java filtering can be accomplished using the FWSM exclusively, by replacing objects or applet tags with comments. Filtering will help to minimize the impact of malware on client devices, thereby making your organization more successful.

References

Microsoft Developer Network—ActiveX control
http://msdn.microsoft.com/en-us/library/aa751968(VS.85).aspx
Sun Developer Network—Java
http://java.sun.com/

CHAPTER 15

Managing and Monitoring the FWSM

You can choose from several options when managing or monitoring the Firewall Services Module (FWSM). Having a good understanding of the capabilities of each solution and how to use them to your best interest will make your job much easier.

Although alternatives to the command-line interface (CLI) exist, and it certainly may be more difficult to use, it is highly recommended to have a good understanding of how to manage, monitor, and troubleshoot the FWSM using the CLI. Because the CLI is the least common denominator, if you get access to the host-chassis, you can still configure the FWSM.

Using Telnet

Telnet is an application that uses TCP/IP and allows a client virtual terminal access to a host. Because Telnet was one of the first applications, security was not an integral component.

Consequently, passwords are exchanged in the clear between the client and the host (in this case the FWSM). Telnet should be used only when encrypted and authenticated (see the section, "Securing Access," later in this chapter). Figure 15-1 shows a packet capture of a Telnet session to the FWSM, with both login and enable passwords displayed in the clear.

If you must use Telnet for management, be as restrictive as possible by allowing only the specific devices used for management, because this will reduce the possibility of unauthorized access.

In this example, only the device at 192.168.1.23 is allowed to access the FWSM via the Inside interface.

```
telnet 192.168.1.23 255.255.255.255 Inside
```

Figure 15-1 *Password Capture of Telnet Session*

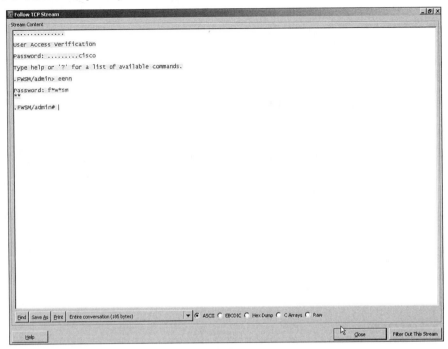

The only other option for configuring Telnet parameters is the timeout feature. This will drop an idle session after the timeout specified—for example, 10 minutes, as shown here:

```
telnet timeout 10
```

When using Telnet as a means of management, other items should be considered:

- You cannot Telnet to the outside (or lowest level) interface directly.

- Telnet to the FWSM is permitted from the telnet ip_address mask interface command, regardless of any access lists applied to the interface.

- Having multiple Telnet connections to a single context may cause sessions to hang when <--- More ---> is displayed. The output <--- More ---> is shown when there are more lines of output than allowed by the pager command, 24 lines by default. To minimize this risk, use the no pager command from configuration mode.

- 100 Telnet sessions are allowed per FWSM, with 5 sessions per context. The number of sessions can be modified using resource classes as described in Chapter 5, "Understanding Contexts."

Telnet is an application on just about every operating system with an IP stack. Given its ubiquity and ease of setup, you may be tempted to use it as a management mechanism, but always consider a more secure method, such as secure shell, to minimize your risk of compromise.

Using Secure Shell

To achieve data integrity and confidentiality while managing or monitoring the FWSM from a command-line application, secure shell version 2 (SSHv2) is the method of choice. SSH also allows connections to be established to the outside interface. Use caution when enabling SSH support on the outside interface. If this is done, minimize the impact of a Denial-of-Service (DoS) attack by specifying individual IP address used for management.

NOTE   Because of the vulnerabilities associated with SSHv1, only SSHv2 should be used.

To enable SSH support, execute the following commands (in multi-context mode and perform them in each context that requires SSH access):

Step 1   Generate crypto keys:

```
FWSM(config)# crypto key generate rsa modulus 1024
INFO: The name for the keys will be: <Default-RSA-Key>
Keypair generation process begin. Please wait...
[OK]
```

NOTE   The modulus of 1024 was chosen in this example and should be considered the minimum value. When it comes to modulus size, bigger is better.

Step 2   Configure support for SSHv2 only, using the following command:

```
FWSM(config)# ssh version 2
```

Step 3   Specify the idle timeout period (optional):

```
FWSM(config)# ssh timeout 10
```

Step 4   Identify the device(s) that will be used to manage the FWSM and indicate the interface. This should be as restrictive as possible:

```
FWSM(config)# ssh 10.1.1.7 255.255.255.255 Outside
```

Step 5   Do not forget to write the configuration:

```
FWSM(config)# write memory
```

When connecting to the FWSM via SSH, the username should be pix unless you have authentication configured. The following is a sample command issued from a command prompt from a Linux client:

```
[root@localhost /]# ssh pix@10.1.1.1
pix@10.1.1.1's password:
Type help or '?' for a list of available commands.
FWSM/CustB>
```

The required password is the "login" password.

After entering enable mode, issue the **show ssh sessions** command to view the SSH session statistics:

```
FWSM/CustB# show ssh sessions
SID Client IP      Version Mode Encryption Hmac    State            Username
0   10.1.1.7       2.0      IN  aes128-cbc md5     SessionStarted   pix
                            OUT aes128-cbc md5     SessionStarted   pix
```

Did you notice that the connection is using SSHv2? This is what you want.

If a Rivest, Shamir, and Adelman (RSA) key pair has not been defined and an SSH connection is attempted, the following message will be logged by the FWSM:

```
%FWSM-6-302013: Built inbound TCP connection 0 for Outside:10.1.1.7/35586 (10.1.1.7/
   35586) to Outside:10.1.1.1/22 (10.1.1.1/22)
%FWSM-3-315004: Fail to establish SSH session because RSA host key retrieval failed.
%FWSM-6-315011: SSH session from 10.1.1.7 on interface Outside for user ""
   disconnected by SSH server, reason: "Internal error" (0x00)
```

When deploying SSHv2, the following items also need to be considered:

- SSH to the FWSM is permitted from the **ssh** *ip_address mask interface* command, regardless of any access lists applied to the interface.

- Having multiple SSH connections to a single context may cause sessions to hang when <--- More ---> is displayed. The output <--- More ---> is shown when there are more lines of output than allowed by the pager command, 24 lines by default. To minimize this risk, use the no pager command from configuration mode.

- 100 SSH sessions are allowed per FWSM, with 5 sessions per context. The number of sessions can be modified using resource classes as described in Chapter 5.

SSHv2 is by far the best CLI alternative to managing the FWSM and should always be used over Telnet if any concern exists about malicious individuals capturing traffic either in the communication path or performing a man-in-the-middle attack. Knowing how to navigate the FWSM using the CLI is highly recommended and may be a life saver, or at least a job saver, some day.

Using Adaptive Security Device Manager

Adaptive Security Device Manager (ASDM) is a web-based management tool that is very easy to use, intuitive, and best of all—it's free! With ASDM, you can configure, monitor, and troubleshoot, all using a graphical user interface (GUI).

ASDM is a tremendously valuable tool for managing and monitoring an individual FWSM. ASDM provides a secure connection using Hypertext Transfer Protocol Security (HTTPS) and allows for management to the outside interface. Multiple contexts can be managed from a single session to the "admin" context, or individual contexts can be managed from the context specified.

Configuring the FWSM Using ASDM

In the CLI sections, "Using Telnet" and "Using Secure Shell," you were encouraged to have an understanding of the CLI. To get the web-based interface operational, you will need to start with CLI access.

To begin using ASDM, configure the FWSM as follows:

Step 1   Configure an interface for management; in multiple-context mode, use the admin context. See Chapter 6, "Configuring and Securing the 6500/7600 Chassis," for a quick refresher.

Step 2   Enable HTTPS services on the FWSM:

```
FWSM/admin# http server enable
```

Step 3   Identify the device(s) that will be used to manage the FWSM and indicate the interface. This should be as restrictive as possible to minimize the potential access of malicious users.

```
http 192.168.1.23 255.255.255.255 Inside
```

Managing the FWSM from the Client

The FWSM acts as the host (web server), and the device used to manage the FWSM is obviously the client. The client application is the user interface into the FWSM that provides the GUI for management, monitoring, and troubleshooting.

To manage the FWSM from the client, follow these steps:

Step 1   Verify that the client requirements (including Java) are met via Cisco Connection Online (CCO).

Step 2   Open a browser and enter the following: https://ipaddress_of_FWSM.

Step 3 Accept the certificate. If you are extremely security conscious, you may already have a Certificate Authority (CA) server. In that case, you should enroll the FWSM. Additional information can be found on CCO.

Step 4 When prompted with a username and password, use only the "enable" password and leave the username blank, unless you have authentication, authorization, and accounting (AAA) enabled.

Step 5 There are two options to choose from: Install ASDM as a Local Application or Run ASDM Applet. No capability differences exist between the two, but installing the local ASDM application will improve performance. If you decide to install the application, just follow the prompts.

Step 6 With ASDM up and running, it is just point and click!

The real-time log viewer collects and displays logging events in a graphical format and is very helpful in monitoring the FWSM, as shown in Figure 15-2. This feature will not only display real-time events, but it provides an explanation, recommended action, and details for each event.

Figure 15-2 *ASDM Logging*

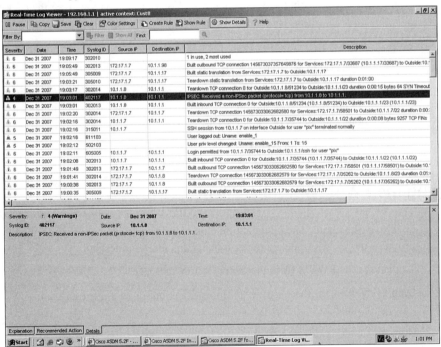

You might be thinking, "This is way too easy. You should have shown me sooner!" Don't forget how to configure, monitor, and troubleshoot the old-fashioned way, via command line. You can get a refresher from Chapters 6 through 11. There may be times when you do not have access to ASDM and need to fix a problem. You might have wished you spent more time on the console. Additionally, not all commands are supported using ASDM. A few features must be configured from the CLI. For complete details, refer to the release notes on CCO. CLI configuration can be accomplished using Telnet, SSH, or using ASDM by selecting Tools, Command Line Interface. For a list of current configuration commands ignored by ASDM, select Options, Show Commands Ignored by ASDM on Device.

ASDM is an extremely valuable tool for managing a single FWSM. You can view real-time system resource statistics, traffic status, event logging, packet capture, and so on, besides being able to make configuration changes. Considering this is a zero cost item, it should be a management tool that you take full advantage of.

Securing Access

To use Telnet in a secure manner, or other management tools from a location outside the FWSM, an encrypted tunnel can be established from a client running the Cisco Virtual Private Network (VPN) client software or to the VPN termination device, such as an Adaptive Security Appliance (ASA)/Private Internet Exchange (PIX), Internetwork Operating System (IOS) router, or VPN concentrator. The connection provides encryption and authentication using Internet Protocol Security (IPsec). The FWSM supports five IPsec connections per context with a maximum of ten connections per FWSM, and transparent mode will not support clients running the Cisco VPN client software.

Figure 15-3 and the following excerpt from the FWSM provide an example of how to create a VPN connection from a client running the VPN software.

When configuring a VPN connection, the split-tunneling feature enables only specific traffic destined for the "secure" network (the network behind the VPN termination device) to be encrypted; all traffic to other locations is passed in the clear (unencrypted). If split tunneling is used, the potential exists that an attacker could gain access to the client device via an unencrypted connection and traverse the encrypted tunnel, consequently obtaining access to the secure network.

NOTE	Split tunneling is not recommended because a host could potentially be compromised and give an attacker access to the FWSM.

Figure 15-3 *Secure Access*

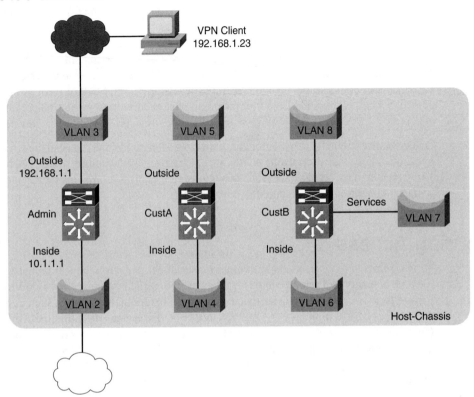

Figure 15-3 illustrates a VPN client with the IP address of 192.168.1.23 connecting to the outside interface with the IP address of 192.168.1.1 on the Admin context of the FWSM. The following two sections, "Configuring the FWSM for VPN Termination" and "Configuring the VPN Client," provide configuration examples of how to build a VPN tunnel for network management.

This configuration was completed using FWSM code version 3.2(3) and VPN Client software version 5.0.02.0090.

Configuring the FWSM for VPN Termination

The FWSM acts as the VPN termination device for client access. IP address pools are configured on the FWSM that provides the VPN client a "virtual" IP address. This address is essentially the new source IP address for applications residing on the client. Traffic between the FWSM and the client is encrypted with Data Encryption Standard (DES) or

3DES using Secure Hash Algorithm (SHA) or Message Digest 5 (MD5), Hash Message Authentication Codes (HMAC).

Step 1 Create a pool of addresses for the VPN client. This example uses the IP address space assigned to the inside interface.

```
ip local pool IP-POOL 10.1.1.253-10.1.1.254
```

Step 2 Configure a transform set; use 3DES for better security.

```
crypto ipsec transform-set 3DES esp-3des esp-sha-hmac
```

NOTE   DES is an encryption method using a 56-bit key, which has been found to be vulnerable to brute-force attacks. 3DES uses three 56-bit keys for a key length of 168 bits, which provides significantly better security.

Step 3 Using a dynamic crypto map, the client can have any IP address that is reachable via the outside interface.

```
crypto dynamic-map DYN-MAP 10 set transform-set 3DES
```

Step 4 Apply the dynamic map to the crypto map that will be assigned to the outside interface.

```
crypto map CR-MAP 10 ipsec-isakmp dynamic DYN-MAP
```

Step 5 Apply the crypto map to the outside interface.

```
crypto map CR-MAP interface Outside
```

Step 6 This example uses shared key authentication.

```
isakmp policy 10 authentication pre-share
```

Step 7 3DES is used for Internet Security Association and Key Management Protocol (ISAKMP).

```
isakmp policy 10 encryption 3des
```

Step 8 SHA offers better security than MD5, because SHA produces a 160-bit message digest and MD5 produces a 128-bit message digest.

```
isakmp policy 10 hash sha
```

Step 9 Use group 2 to support the VPN client.

```
isakmp policy 10 group 2
```

Step 10 This is the default ISAKMP lifetime value.

```
isakmp policy 10 lifetime 86400
```

Step 11   Apply ISAKMP to the outside interface.

```
isakmp enable Outside
```

Step 12   Using the default DefaultRAGroup, associate the pool of address space
from Step 1 and use the FWSM as the authentication server.

```
tunnel-group DefaultRAGroup general-attribute
address-pool IP-POOL
authentication-server-group (Outside) LOCAL
```

Step 13   Apply the preshared key to the tunnel group.

```
tunnel-group DefaultRAGroup ipsec-attributes
pre-shared-key cisco123
```

Step 14   Allow Telnet from the pool of address space, first address.

```
telnet 10.1.1.253 255.255.255.255 Inside
```

Step 15   Allow Telnet from the pool of address space, second address.

```
telnet 10.1.1.254 255.255.255.255 Inside
```

Step 16   If you are testing this in the lab, you must have an outside route or the
FWSM will be unable to communicate back to the client.

```
route Outside 0.0.0.0 0.0.0.0 192.168.1.254 1
```

Step 17   Enable management access to the inside interface.

```
management-access Inside
```

Step 18   Create a username and password.

```
username Admin password fwsm123
```

Now that the FWSM has been configured with an address pool, the encryption method is
built, management access has been allowed from the pool, and a user has been configured,
the VPN client can be set up.

Configuring the VPN Client

The client is the origination point for the VPN tunnel and also the device that will be used
to manage the FWSM. This process is significantly easier than configuring the VPN
termination on the FWSM, so you are almost finished.

Some of the most important aspects to establishing a VPN tunnel are to make absolutely
sure that encryption algorithms match, names and passwords match, and that the IP address
is correct.

Configure the client using the following procedure:

Step 1   Start the VPN client software and add a new entry.

Step 2   Under the authentication tab (see Figure 15-4), provide a name in Connection Entry, add the IP address corresponding to the outside interface of the FWSM, select Group Authentication using the name of DefaultRAGroup from Step 12 in the FWSM configuration example, and then apply the password to the group. In this case it is "cisco123."

Figure 15-4 *VPN Client Authentication Tab*

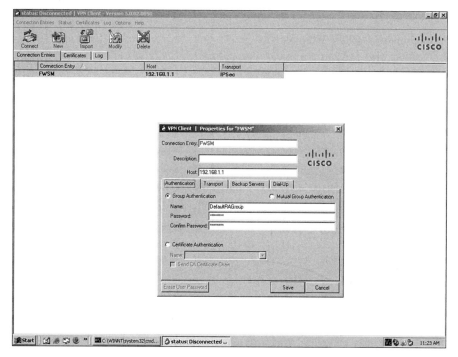

Step 3   Save the configuration and select Connect.

Step 4   When prompted, use the username and password defined in Step 18 from the FWSM configuration example.

NOTE   The use of UDP transport tunneling mode is supported.

If it worked, you are ready to manage the FWSM; if not, you will have an opportunity to hone your skills at troubleshooting, which will be a very valuable experience. If you have it working, you may consider making some changes to the encryption algorithm or password to see how the FWSM behaves. This may save you some time troubleshooting in the future when it doesn't work.

With the number of crypto commands that have been deprecated, this is where the fun begins! Snippets from the following **debug** and **show** commands will show what the output is supposed to look like.

Using the **debug crypto isakmp** command, you can begin troubleshooting the key exchange.

From the output in Example 15-1, check that the Internet Key Exchange (IKE) Security Association (SA) proposals are acceptable (IKE SA Proposal # 1, Transform # 9 acceptable Matches global IKE entry # 1), and that the appropriate group and usernames are shown (Group = DefaultRAGroup).

Example 15-1 *Debugging ISAKMP*

```
FWSM/admin# debug crypto isakmp
FWSM/admin# terminal monitor
Jan 03 2008 17:51:09: %FWSM-6-302015: Built inbound UDP connection 0 for
  Outside:192.168.1.23/3314 (192.168.1.23/3314) to Outside:192.168.1.1/500
  (192.168.1.1/500)
Jan 03 2008 17:51:09: %FWSM-7-713236: IP = 192.168.1.23, IKE_DECODE RECEIVED Message
  (msgid=0) with payloads : HDR + SA (1) + KE (4) + NONCE (10) + ID (5) + VENDOR
  (13) + VENDOR (13) + VENDOR (13) + NONE (0) total length : 814
Jan 03 2008 17:51:09: %FWSM-7-713906: IP = 192.168.1.23, Connection landed on
  tunnel_group DefaultRAGroup
Jan 03 2008 17:51:09: %FWSM-7-715028: Group = DefaultRAGroup, IP = 192.168.1.23, IKE
  SA Proposal # 1, Transform # 9 acceptable  Matches global IKE entry # 1
Jan 03 2008 17:51:13: %FWSM-7-715001: Group = DefaultRAGroup, IP = 192.168.1.23,
  process_attr(): Enter!
Jan 03 2008 17:51:13: %FWSM-6-113012: AAA user authentication Successful : local
  database : user = Admin
Jan 03 2008 17:51:13: %FWSM-6-113009: AAA retrieved default group policy
  (DfltGrpPolicy) for user = Admin
Jan 03 2008 17:51:13: %FWSM-6-113008: AAA transaction status ACCEPT : user = Admin
```

Some of the critical aspects to the next section are user authentication (AAA user authentication Successful : local database : user = Admin) and that the client receives an IP address from the pool (Group = DefaultRAGroup, Username = Admin, IP = 192.168.1.23, Assigned private IP address 10.1.1.253 to remote user). In the output in Example 15-2, notice that the client received the address of 10.1.1.253.

Example 15-2 *Debugging IPsec*

```
FWSM/admin# debug crypto ipsec
FWSM/admin# term mon
Jan 03 2008 18:00:10: %FWSM-7-715028: Group = DefaultRAGroup, IP = 192.168.1.23, IKE
  SA Proposal # 1, Transform # 9 acceptable  Matches global IKE entry # 1
Jan 03 2008 18:00:16: %FWSM-6-113012: AAA user authentication Successful : local
  database : user = Admin
Jan 03 2008 18:00:16: %FWSM-6-113009: AAA retrieved default group policy
  (DfltGrpPolicy) for user = Admin
Jan 03 2008 18:00:16: %FWSM-6-113008: AAA transaction status ACCEPT : user = Admin
```

Example 15-2 *Debugging IPsec (Continued)*

```
Jan 03 2008 18:00:16: %FWSM-6-713228: Group = DefaultRAGroup, Username = Admin, IP
  = 192.168.1.23, Assigned private IP address 10.1.1.253 to remote user
Jan 03 2008 18:00:16: %FWSM-3-713119: Group = DefaultRAGroup, Username = Admin, IP
  = 192.168.1.23, PHASE 1 COMPLETED
Jan 03 2008 18:00:16: %FWSM-7-713066: Group = DefaultRAGroup, Username = Admin, IP
  = 192.168.1.23, IKE Remote Peer configured for crypto map: DYN-MAP
```

The following are a couple other handy commands.

This command shows the status of the ISAKMP SA:

```
FWSM/admin# show crypto isakmp sa
```

This command shows the status of the IPsec SA:

```
FWSM/admin# show crypto ipsec sa
```

As you have seen from the two previous sections, configuring VPN access can be a significant amount of work, especially if you made a configuration mistake and needed to spend some time troubleshooting. Hopefully you spent some time troubleshooting, because this experience will pay dividends in the future!

Working with Simple Network Management Protocol

The FWSM has the capability to either poll Management Information Base (MIB) information or to send Simple Network Management Protocol (SNMP) traps (notifications) in the event a specific condition is met. Because the FWSM is a "security" device, there is not an option to use the write capabilities of SNMP. To enable support for SNMP, follow this example:

Step 1   Enable the SNMP service.

```
FWSM(config)# snmp-server enable
```

Step 2   Specify the address of the network management server and assign parameters:

```
FWSM(config)# snmp-server host Inside 192.168.1.23 community Secret_Key
  version 2c
```

This example indicates that the network management server is located on the inside interface with an IP address of 192.168.1.23. Because the Poll or Trap options were not specified, the default is to allow both functions. The community string was set to Secret_Key, and of the two versions supported (v1 and v2c), v2c was chosen. Last, the User Datagram Protocol (UDP) port was left at the default value of 162.

At this point, the network management server has the capability to view MIB information on the FWSM.

NOTE	SNMP requests are handled by the FWSM complex and require CPU resources. The FWSM can be overwhelmed by performing a "MIB-walk" (collecting each MIB); this may drive utilization through the roof!

Step 3 To configure the FWSM to send traps, perform the following:

```
FWSM(config)# snmp-server enable traps snmp linkdown
```

You can choose from several parameters. This example will send a trap when a link goes down.

Step 4 Configure the logging level:

```
FWSM(config)# logging history warnings
```

The previous command logs warning messages and lower.

SNMP can provide a tremendous amount of information regarding the condition of the FWSM, violations, and so on. Remember to use SNMP polling judiciously and avoid MIB-walks to minimize the processing impact on the FWSM. Additional information on SNMP can be found using the MIB locator at ftp://ftp-sj.cisco.com/pub/mibs/supportlists/fwsm/fwsm-supportlist.html.

Examining Syslog

System log, or syslog, is a means by which event information can be collected. This information can be used for troubleshooting or stored for auditing, network analysis, and so on. Unfortunately, syslog messages are sent without being encrypted and may provide valuable information to an unscrupulous individual, so use caution when sending these messages. It is especially important to send syslog messages out a secure interface. Although the FWSM allows you to send messages out the outside interface, this is not recommended. When operating the multi-context mode, each context generates syslog messages unique to the context.

Syslog messages are categorized according to severity levels. Eight severity levels range from the most significant (level 0) to the least significant (level 7), as defined in Table 15-1.

Table 15-1   *Syslog Levels*

Code	Severity	Description
0	Emergencies	The system is unstable.
1	Alerts	Action must be taken immediately.
2	Critical	Critical conditions.
3	Errors	Error conditions.

Table 15-1   *Syslog Levels (Continued)*

Code	Severity	Description
4	Warnings	Warning conditions.
5	Notifications	Normal but significant condition.
6	Informational	Informational message.
7	Debugging	Debug messages.

The FWSM provides several mechanisms to export syslog messages, including a syslog server, the local display (that is, a monitor), a mail server, ASDM, to local flash memory or to a File Transfer Protocol (FTP) server. When configuring the FWSM to send syslog messages, the severity level specified is inclusive of that level and all the lower levels. For example, if you select "critical," the events sent will be "critical," "alerts," and "emergencies."

Sending this information to these devices requires an understanding of the following limitations:

- **Syslog server:** The number of messages logged is limited only to the disk space allocated for storage of syslog messages on the server itself. If you are using UDP as a transport mechanism, messages could potentially be dropped. Spoofed messages could also be sent to the syslog server, appearing as though they originated from the FWSM. Depending on the number of messages sent to the syslog server, categorizing, searching, or finding valuable information in a timely fashion is almost impossible to do manually.

- **Local display:** If any significant amount of traffic to the FWSM exists, you will probably be overwhelmed with log messages. Additionally, you have to be watching the events or they may be lost.

- **Mail server:** Here is an easy way to conduct a DoS service attack on your mail server. If you plan to use this feature, select only the most significant events to send.

- **ASDM:** Do not bother using the command line to enable this feature. Because you need ASDM to view the messages, use the ASDM graphical user interface (GUI).

- **Local flash:** Given the size of the memory space on the local flash, the number of messages stored will be very limited. Using the filtering capabilities gives you much better control over which messages will be saved, significantly reducing the number of messages stored.

- **FTP server:** An FTP server can be used to automatically store syslog messages when the local buffer is full.

The following list provides an example of how to configure the FWSM to send syslog messages to a syslog server located on the inside with an IP address of 192.168.1.23:

Step 1 Specify the interface and IP address of the syslog server.

```
FWSM/admin(config)# logging host Inside 192.168.1.23
```

Step 2 Set the trap logging level (refer to Table 15-1).

```
FWSM/admin(config)# logging trap warnings
```

Step 3 Turn on logging.

```
logging enable
```

Step 4 Optionally, turn on timestamps.

```
FWSM/admin(config)# logging timestamp
```

To view the logging parameters, use the following command:

```
FWSM/admin(config)# show logging
Syslog logging: enabled
    Facility: 20
    Timestamp logging: enabled
    Standby logging: disabled
    Deny Conn when Queue Full: disabled
    Console logging: disabled
    Monitor logging: disabled
    Buffer logging: disabled
    Trap logging: level warnings, facility 20, 186 messages logged
        Logging to Inside 192.168.1.23
    History logging: disabled
    Device ID: disabled
    Mail logging: disabled
    ASDM logging: disabled
```

System log messages provide valuable information for troubleshooting, auditing, network analysis, and so on. Be aware that too much of a good thing (an overabundance of messages) may be difficult to sort through unless you have a device that can automate the process and provide you with the most valuable information, such as the Monitoring Analysis and Response System (MARS).

Working with Cisco Security Manager

Cisco Security Manager (CSManager) is an enterprise class management package for central administration of networks with thousands of devices, including multiple types of security devices, such as the FWSM, ASA, PIX, and IOS routers running the security feature image, Intrusion Prevention System (IPS) sensors, and Catalyst security modules.

The primary functions of the CSManager include the following:

- **Policy-based management:** This allows you to create policies that are shared among multiple devices.
- **Policy hierarchy:** This is a logical structure for the organization policy management.
- **Device overrides:** These provide the capability for individual devices to have unique configuration parameters.
    - **Role-based access control:** Allows the capability to control user access and permission to specific devices.
    - **Workflow:** Offers an approval process for the implementation of configuration changes.
    - **FlexConfig:** Enables you to create specific CLI commands for device management.
    - **Device-manager x-launch:** A mechanism in which other management interfaces are launched—for example, ASDM.
    - **Flexible device deployment:** Provides device deployment to the specific device, a configuration file, or using a call-home feature.
    - **MARS links:** Provides a mechanism to exchange information with MARS.

Three main security services are included in CSManager: firewall management, VPN management, and IPS management.

Firewall management provides a device agnostic GUI that manages the FWSM, ASA, PIX, Integrated Service Router (ISR), and Catalyst switches. Policy inheritance and reusable objects allow for sharing, enforcement, and scalability. Analysis and optimization tools also help minimize configuration errors.

The VPN management component consists of a VPN wizard that provides a simple user interface for the configuration of site-to-site and remote access VPN topologies, VPN discovery, which will automatically discover an existing VPN deployment, and a VPN monitoring component that monitors that performance and status of the VPN connections.

IPS management also includes a device agnostic graphical interface for the management of IPS appliances (4200 series), the Advanced Inspection and Prevention Security Services Module (AIP-SSM), Intrusion Detection System Module 2 (IDSM-2), Advanced Integration Module (AIM), and IOS Intrusion Prevention System (IPS) software. The IPS management component also has the capability to automatically update IPS devices with current signatures and maintain licensing. Last, the IPS management component incorporates an event and anomaly detector that allows you to drill down into the event for specific signature information.

CSManager gives you the ability to manage firewalls, VPNs, and IPS devices from one central location. Devices can be configured individually, in groups, or globally. Consequently, one change on the CSManager console can result in a change in many devices. This significantly reduces time spent administering devices (especially if a threat exists) and provides a consistent configuration template.

Monitoring Analysis and Response System

The Monitoring Analysis and Response System (MARS) is an appliance-based threat-mitigation solution that provides the primary functions of rapid threat identification and mitigation, data correlation, and offers topology awareness.

MARS has the capability to rapidly identify events through a receive process (push) and/or it can gather information (pulls) from firewalls, such as the FWSM, IDS devices, switches, routers, and so on. The collection of Netflow and traffic analysis information also assists in enhancing threat detection through behavior analysis.

Data correlation is one of the most valuable functions of the MARS. It has the capability to compare information from multiple sources and determine whether those events would be considered a threat.

The MARS correlates information based on predefined or a user-defined set of inspection rules. Sets of sessions that match these inspection rules are called incidents, and MARS handles this information in three phases, as follows:

Phase 1—Events are normalized:

1 Events are received on the MARS either through the push or pull process.

2 Those events are parsed.

3 Normalization of the events occur.

4 Sessions (set of events) are correlated across NAT boundaries.

5 The rule engine performs an analysis of the information.

Phase 2—Rules are applied:

6 The target host is determined to be vulnerable based on assessed information.

Phase 3—Analysis and mitigation:

7 Events are checked for false positives.

8 Events are finally checked against traffic profiling and anomaly detection information.

MARS also builds a topology map of the network infrastructure. It is aware of switches, routers, routing information, and Network Address Translation (NAT).

Last, MARS has the capability to suggest mitigation solutions through the use of disabling ports, ACLs, shunning, and so on.

To aid in the process of network operations, the MARS solution has the capability of collecting information from many types of devices, analyzing that information, and providing a solution to mitigate the threat.

Summary

The FWSM has several alternatives from which to choose regarding management and monitoring. Both Telnet and SSH offer a command-line interface, but using SSH provides an encrypted session and allows you to manage the FWSM from the outside interface. ASDM is a free graphical interface that provides configuration, monitoring, and troubleshooting functionality. SNMP and syslog provide information that aids in auditing, troubleshooting, capacity planning, and so on. For large-scale deployments, CSManager offers a centralized management platform for firewalls, VPNs, and IPS. MARS adds a centralized solution to minimize the impact of threats. Having a good understanding of the capabilities of each management/monitoring solution will significantly increase your success in operating your network.

References

RFC 854—*Telnet Protocol Specification*
RFC 1155, 1157, 1212, 1213, 1215—*Simple Network Management Protocol (SNMP)*
RFC 1901—*Introduction to Community-Based SNMPv2*
RFC 4254—*Secure Shell (SSH) Connection Protocol*

CHAPTER 16

Multicast

This chapter covers FWSM support for multicast technology. It discusses only the basics of multicast and emphasizes the support of multicast in FWSM. The following are some of the discussion points covered in detail:

- Designs in FWSM to make multicast pass through the firewall
- Features of multicast supported in FWSM
- Configuration examples

NOTE   Before moving on, you should have a good understanding of multicast technology. For more specific details, you can refer to the book, *Developing IP Multicast Networks* (ISBN 157870079).

What is multicast? Multicast defines a communication between a single source and multiple receivers through a single stream. In unicast flow, a separate flow is maintained from a source to a destination. For ten receivers to receive a flow from a single source, the network will have ten flows. In multicast stream, this can be achieved in a single flow. For example, one multicast stream from the source can be received by "n" number of receivers in the local-area network (LAN). In multicast stream, the flow will replicate only when there are multiple egress interfaces for the receiver. The local Layer 3 device having multiple egress interfaces to the receivers does the replication of the flow. In multicast, a conservation of bandwidth exists for one-to-many types of communication. The sections that follow offer snapshot concepts of multicast technology.

Protocol Independent Multicast

The multicast tree allows the multicast communication to be established between the source and the receiver. The multicast tree is built using protocol independent multicast (PIM). The communication to build the tree is not dependent on any protocol. It uses the routing protocol in the network to build the tree. Through this multicast tree, one-to-many or many-to-many communication is established.

The following are the four modes of PIM:

- **PIM Dense mode:** The multicast source sends the traffic to the receiver through the flooding of traffic in a multicast domain. The traffic is pruned at areas of network where there are no receivers. PIM Dense mode is not a scalable solution. There is no concept of rendezvous point (RP) in PIM Dense mode. PIM Dense mode standards are defined in RFC 3973.

  The receivers for a particular multicast group will send an Internet Group Management Protocol (IGMP) request to receive the traffic from a particular group. The IGMP request is Layer 2 based. The first hop Layer 3 router maintains the state for all the receivers in the LAN segment and communicates this state using PIM to other Layer 3 devices that have multicast and PIM enabled. During transmission, the source sends the packet to the first hop Layer 3 device, which in turn forwards the packet to the receivers through flooding. This state in every router for multicast forwarding is called a *source tree*. Source tree is referred to as (S,G) state. The "S" is the IPv4 address of the source and "G" is the multicast group.

- **PIM Sparse mode:** The communication from the multicast source to the receiver takes place through an explicit multicast tree called the *shared tree*. The shared tree is centered at an RP. The group entry in the shared tree is created per multicast source. PIM sparse mode standards are defined in RFC 4601.

  When the source sends an *IGMP join message* to the first hop Layer 3 device, the first hop Layer 3 device sends a unicast registry packet to the RP. The first hop Layer 3 device has unicast reachability to the RP through a PIM-enabled interface. The RP then sends a unicast registry *stop message* back to the Layer 3 first hop device (in case the state exists for the receivers for a particular group at the RP). The multicast traffic flows to the RP. The RP has the state for the receivers that need to join the multicast group and forwards the traffic to the receivers for the particular group. This flow of multicast traffic is through the shared tree. Shared tree is referred to as a (*,G) state. The "*" is any unicast source and "G" is the multicast group.

  After the initial traffic flow is established between the source and the destination (the first hop Layer 3 device for the receivers), the destination Layer 3 device calculates the reverse path forwarding (RPF) to the source. If the RPF path to the source is learned better from another PIM-enabled interface other than the RPF interface for the RP, a new path is calculated to the source. The destination Layer 3 device sends the RP prune bit to the RP, and the shared tree (*,G) gets RP pruned. The traffic then starts flowing from the source tree (S,G).

- **PIM Bidirectional:** PIM builds an explicit bidirectional shared tree. The source tree is not built. By relying on one tree, it reduces the latency component of building two multicast trees, and the memory is conserved.

- **Source Specific Multicast (SSM):** In SSM, the multicast data forwarding is based on the Source IP address and the Group address. The Source and Group (S,G) multicast flow can be uniquely understood as a channel. SSM always builds a source tree between the receivers and the source. Because the source is known, an explicit (S,G) join message is issued for the source tree. This removes the need for shared trees and RPs in SSM. SSM needs IGMP version 3 enabled in the network.

Understanding Rendezvous Point

The RP is a central point that sees the communication between the source and the receiver. The receivers send IGMP Join messages to the first hop Layer 3 device, called the *designated router*. The designated router will send the packet to the RP. The RP should be configured on the Layer 3 device and also be reachable from the Layer 3 device through a PIM enabled interface. The RP will maintain the state for the respective groups.

Refer to PIM Sparse mode to understand the functionality of the RP in a multicast tree. This RP information in a network should be advertised to the other Layer 3 routers, referred to as downstream routers. The RP information can be advertised to the entire downstream Layer 3 devices through different methodologies:

- **Static RP:** All the downstream routers will have RP configuration enabled in the router.

- **Auto-RP:** The RP information is not configured in the downstream routers. This information is sent from the central RP distribution agent. The groups that function in Auto-RP (in PIM Dense mode) are 224.0.1.39 and 224.0.1.40. These two groups are needed for the propagation of RP information. Auto-RP supports Active/Standby RP redundancy. This is Cisco propriety.

- **BSR:** The Bootstrap Router (BSR) mechanism is available in PIM version 2. The RP information is not configured in the downstream routers. Devices are configured as candidate BSRs by enabling the **ip pim bsr-candidate** command. These devices announce themselves to other routers using the 224.0.0.13 group address. Because a message sent to this address is forwarded hop-by-hop throughout the network, all the routers learn about the candidate BSRs and select one of them as an RP. The RP is selected based on the highest priority in the BSR configuration. BSR supports Active/Standby RP redundancy.

- **Anycast RP:** Anycast RP is an implementation strategy that provides load sharing and redundancy in PIM Sparse mode networks. Multicast Source Discovery Protocol (MSDP) is the key protocol, which makes the Anycast RP redundancy possible. Using Anycast RP, Active/Active RP redundancy is achieved. In Active/Active RP redundancy, both the RPs can function as redundant RPs for sources and receivers at the same time.

PIM Interface Modes

The PIM interface mode defines the functionality of the interface in PIM protocol. There are three interface configuration modes for PIM:

- **PIM Dense mode:** Interface functions in PIM Dense mode specification. Refer to the PIM Dense mode section in this chapter for functionality details.

- **PIM Sparse mode:** Interface functions in PIM Sparse mode specification. You will need to configure the RP for multicast delivery. Refer to the PIM Sparse mode section in this chapter for functionality details.

- **PIM Sparse-Dense mode:** PIM Sparse-Dense mode is essential for the Auto-RP to function. The 12.2.x Mainline and later IOS codes introduce the **Auto-RP Listener** command. Enabling this command in all downstream routers makes **auto-rp** function in PIM Sparse mode.

IGMP Protocol

IGMP messages are used to allow hosts to communicate to the first hop Layer 3 router on a Layer 2 network, to receive multicast traffic.

There are three types of IGMP versions: IGMPv1, IGMPv2, and IGMPv3.

- **IGMP Version 1:** The two messages for IGMP version 1 (IGMPv1) are membership *Queries* and *Reports*. Queries are sent by the router to *All-Hosts* 224.0.0.1 address. This is done to solicit a multicast group address for active members. Reports are sent by hosts wanting to receive traffic for a specific multicast group. Membership reports are sent with time-to-live (TTL) 1. The TTL 1 confines the message to the first hop Layer 3 device.

- **IGMP Version 2:** The two new messages added to IGMP version 2 (IGMPv2) are *Group Specific query* and *Leave Group message*. A Group Specific query allows the router to query only membership in a single group, instead of all groups. This is to find out if any member has left the group. This is an optimized solution compared to version 1. You need to know the difference between the Query used in version 1 and the Group Specific query used in version 2. The Query (version 1) uses the multicast to send queries to *All-Hosts* (224.0.0.1) address, whereas a Group Specific query(version 2) sends the queries to a specific Group "G". The Leave Group message allows end systems to tell the router that they are leaving the group, which reduces the leave latency for the group on the segment when the member leaving is the last member of the group.

- **IGMP Version 3:** IGMP version 3 (IGMPv3) adds Group records, each containing a list of multicast sources to INCLUDE or EXCLUDE. In INCLUDE mode, the receiver announces membership to a host group and provides a list of IP addresses from which it wants to receive traffic. This list of IP addresses constitutes an

INCLUDE List. In EXCLUDE mode, the receiver announces membership to a host group and provides a list of IP addresses from which it does not want to receive traffic. This constitutes the EXCLUDE List. This provides granular control to avoid rogue sources in the network. This IGMP group is needed for the functionality of SSM mode. Refer to the SSM section in this chapter for more details.

Of the three modes of IGMP versions, the most common version used is IGMP version 2.

Multicast Stub Configuration

Multicast stub configuration does not participate in the PIM neighbor relationship; the device just passes the IGMP messages. In a Layer 3 network world, this type of stub configuration is common in routers connecting to satellite links. In this case, the IGMP messages pass through the satellite unidirectional link using an IGMP helper address configuration or an IGMP unidirectional link configuration in the IOS.

The FWSM can also be configured in stub mode. In stub configuration, the FWSM will not participate in the PIM neighbor relationship. The FWSM acts as an *IGMP proxy agent* and forwards the host *Join* and *Leave* messages from the stub area interface to an upstream interface.

Multicast Traffic Across Firewalls

As more applications adapt to make the optimized use of bandwidth, dependence of these applications on multicast is becoming more prevalent. Therefore, there is an increasing requirement for multicast to traverse from one security domain to the other security domain. The placement of firewalls at the Internet's edge might require multicast to traverse across the firewall, based on the security environment. In an enterprise data center, the placement of a firewall for security domain segregation has made it very critical for multicast to traverse across the firewalls. With the increased dependency on multicast for application delivery, support for multicast on the firewall is increasingly critical in the data center. The FWSM placed in the data center therefore must support multicast traffic. The support depends on the code version the FWSM is running. The older versions do not support multicast natively.

FWSM 1.x and 2.x Code Releases

FWSM 1.x and 2.x code releases do not support multicast natively. Multicast support in a transparent firewall is facilitated using Access Control Lists (ACL). FWSM support for multicast traffic in 1.x and 2.x code releases can be designed using the following options:

- FWSM in routed mode does not support native multicast. The generic routing encapsulation (GRE) solution is used to encapsulate multicast traffic through FWSMs. In this solution, the multicast traffic is not inspected by the FWSM because it is encapsulated with GRE.

- In transparent mode, multicast traffic is bridged across the FWSMs. The access list must be configured to pass the multicast traffic through the firewall.

FWSM 3.x Code Release

Multicast is handled natively in single context routed mode and the transparent FWSM forwards multicast traffic through hardware shortcuts. In the 3.x code release, multicast replication is handled natively on the network processors of the FWSM.

The following are some of the multicast features supported in the 3.x code release or later:

- In single context routed mode, PIM routing, Bi-directional PIM, and IGMP v1/v2 are supported.

- Topologies with PIM neighbors are supported.

- Destination Network Address Translation (NAT) is supported with multicast streams (as well as source NAT).

- All packet replications are handled by the FWSM directly.

Table 16-1 shows the different multicast features and the support in the 3.x code release for FWSM.

Table 16-1 *Multicast Feature Matrix for FWSM 3.x Code Release*

Features	Syntax
igmp join-group	Configure igmp join-group: FWSM(config-if)# **igmp join-group** *group-address*
static join-group	Configure the static join-group: FWSM(config-if)# **igmp static-group** *group-address*
Controlling multicast through access list	Step 1: Define access list. • Standard access list: FWSM(config)# **access-list** *name* **standard** [permit I deny] *ip_addr mask* • To create an extended access list, enter the following command: FWSM(config)# **access-list** *name* **extended** [permit I deny] **protocol** *src_ip_addr src_mask dest_ip_addr dest_mask* Step 2: Apply the access list to an interface by entering the following command: FWSM(config-if)# **igmp access-group** *acl*

Table 16-1   *Multicast Feature Matrix for FWSM 3.x Code Release (Continued)*

Features	Syntax
IGMP Limit IGMP states per interface	To limit IGMP states per interface: FWSM(config-if)# **igmp limit** *number*
IGMP query interval	The PIM designated router is responsible for sending query messages. This query interval can be changed from 125 seconds to a user-defined value by using the following command: FWSM(config-if)# **igmp query-interval** *seconds*
IGMP query response time	To change the IGMP query response time from 10 seconds to a user-defined value, use the following command: FWSM(config-if)# **igmp query-max-response-time** *seconds*
IGMP version	After **multicast-routing** is enabled, IGMP version 2 is enabled by default on the interfaces. To change the IGMP version, the command is FWSM(config-if)# **igmp version** {1	2}
Stub multicast routing (supported in earlier codes)	Stub multicast configuration: Forward the host *join* and *leave* messages. Enable the following command for stub multicast configuration to the interface, attached to the stub area: FWSM(config-if)# **igmp forward interface** *if_name*
Static mroutes	For static multicast route , enter the following command: FWSM(config)# **mroute** src_ip src_mask (input_if_name	rpf_neighbor} [distance]

continues

Table 16-1 *Multicast Feature Matrix for FWSM 3.x Code Release (Continued)*

Features	Syntax
PIM	To configure PIM on an interface level: After **multicast-routing** is enabled, PIM is enabled on the interface level.
RP address	To enable static multicast IP address, the command is FWSM(config)# **pim rp-address** *ip_address* [acl] [bidir]
PIM DR priority	To change the FWSM designated router priority from 1, the command is FWSM(config-if)# **pim dr-priority** *num*
PIM accept-register	To configure the accept-register message filter: FWSM(config)# **pim accept-register** {list acl | route-map *map-name*} Accept-register messages are unicast messages sent to the RP.
PIM Hello interval/ Join prune interval	To change the PIM hello message interval from a default of 30 seconds: FWSM(config-if)# **pim hello-interval** *seconds* To change the prune message from a default of 60 seconds, the command is FWSM(config-if)# **pim join-prune-interval** *seconds*

There are different ways to support multicast traffic across the FWSM:

1 For the 3.x code release or later, use the FWSM in the single context routed mode. The FWSM can participate as a PIM router. It can also have an RP configuration. The RP configuration is really not recommended from a design perspective because troubleshooting and operational complexity increases.

2 GRE passes the multicast traffic through the tunnel. This is used as a solution quite often. The FWSM does not need a special configuration for configuring multicast. However, special configuration is needed in the FWSM to allow GRE packets to pass through the FWSM. The routing at the Layer 3 device that sources and terminates the GRE needs to be configured, to verify if the multicast traffic takes a correct RPF interface toward the source, receivers, and the RP. GRE can be used for multiple context routed mode. In this method, the FWSM does not inspect the multicast packet encapsulated in the GRE header.

3   In transparent firewalls through ACLs, the firewall passes the traffic in single context and multiple context modes. In the 3.1 code version or later, the performance has been optimized for this configuration.

4   When policy-based routing (PBR) is configured on Layer 3 first hop devices to the FWSM, the PBR will divert the traffic from the FWSM. Configuring multiple context modes for the multicast pass-through with PBR will need careful study of multicast congruency. Sometimes this might become a complex scenario to understand and troubleshoot.

5   The FWSM can be configured as a stub network to pass the IGMP query to the upstream interface for the firewall. The FWSM does not participate in the PIM messages.

FWSM with the 3.x code version or later supports multicast in different modes. This facilitates better integration of the firewall in different parts of the network.

Configuration Methods

This section covers the common configuration methods to pass the multicast traffic through the FWSM. The following are three common ways of configuring:

- Multicast through firewall in single context routed mode
- Multicast through firewall via GRE
- Multicast through transparent firewall in multiple context mode

Method 1: Configuration Example for Multicast Through Firewall in Single Context Routed Mode

To understand method 1, refer to Figure 16-1, which illustrates a configuration example of multicast through single context routed mode.

Figure 16-1 *Configuration Example of Multicast Through Single Context Routed Mode in FWSM*

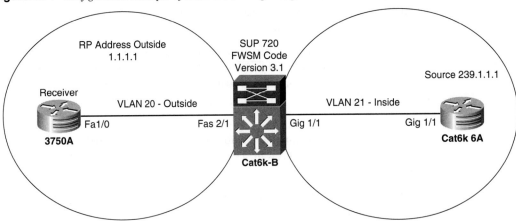

Example 16-1 shows the configuration of multicast through FWSM using the 3.1 code release. The FWSM mode is in single context routed mode. The RP's IP address in this example is 1.1.1.1 and is on the outside interface of the FWSM. The receiver is on the outside interface and the source is on the inside interface of the FWSM. This example replicates the data center environment, where the source is on the inside interface connecting the data center and the receivers, and RP is at the outside interface of the data center. The RP can also be on the inside interface of the data center, and the FWSM can also participate as an RP. This may require detailed discussion between the security and networking teams to resolve potential operational issues.

Example 16-1 *Configuration Example of Multicast Through Single Context Routed Mode in FWSM (Code Version 3.1)*

```
FWSM# show run
FWSM Version 3.1(3)6
!
hostname FWSM
enable password 8Ry2YjIyt7RRXU24 encrypted
! Step1: Enable multicast routing on the FWSM
multicast-routing
names
!
interface Vlan20
 nameif outside
 security-level 0
 ip address 10.1.11.1 255.255.255.0
!
interface Vlan21
 nameif inside
 security-level 100
 ip address 10.1.1.1 255.255.255.0
```

Example 16-1   *Configuration Example of Multicast Through Single Context Routed Mode in FWSM (Code Version 3.1) (Continued)*

```
!
! Step2: This command configures RP's IP address defined in the network
pim rp-address 1.1.1.1
ftp mode passive
access-list 101 extended permit ip any any
access-list 101 extended permit igmp any any
pager lines 24
mtu outside 1500
mtu inside 1500
no failover
icmp permit any outside
icmp permit any inside
no asdm history enable
arp timeout 14400
nat (inside) 0 0.0.0.0 0.0.0.0
static (inside,outside) 10.1.1.0 10.1.1.0 netmask 255.255.255.0
access-group 101 in interface outside
access-group 101 out interface outside
access-group 101 in interface inside
access-group 101 out interface inside
! The default route takes care of reachability to RP's IP address 1.1.1.1 at the
! outside security domain
route outside 0.0.0.0 0.0.0.0 10.1.11.2 1
```

The **show mroute** command verifies the multicast state on the FWSM:

Verify (*,G),(S,G) state, RP information, and the flags. Explanation of multicast flags is beyond the scope of this book.

```
FWSM# show mroute 239.1.1.1
Multicast Routing Table
Flags: D - Dense, S - Sparse, B - Bidir Group, s - SSM Group,
       C - Connected, L - Local, I - Received Source Specific Host Report,
       P - Pruned, R - RP-bit set, F - Register flag, T - SPT-bit set,
       J - Join SPT
Timers: Uptime/Expires
Interface state: Interface, State
(*, 239.1.1.1), 1d21h/never, RP 1.1.1.1, flags: SPC
  Incoming interface: outside
  RPF nbr: 10.1.11.2
  Outgoing interface list:
(10.1.1.2, 239.1.1.1), 00:12:36/00:03:23, flags: ST
  Incoming interface: inside
  RPF nbr: 10.1.1.2
  Outgoing interface list:
    outside, Forward, 00:00:28/00:03:12  Outgoing interface list:
    outside, Forward, 00:00:13/00:03:16
```

NOTE   After enabling *multicast-routing*, PIM and IGMP are enabled by default on the interface. No explicit command is needed to enable PIM or IGMP.

If the RP is defined at the inside security domain, a *static* translation is required for the RP's IP address. Remember, a static translation is required when a less-secured domain accesses a more-secured domain.

Method 2: Configuration Example for Multicast Through Firewall via GRE

To understand method 2, refer to Figure 16-2, which illustrates a configuration example for multicast through firewall via GRE.

Figure 16-2 *Configuration Example for Multicast Through Firewall via GRE*

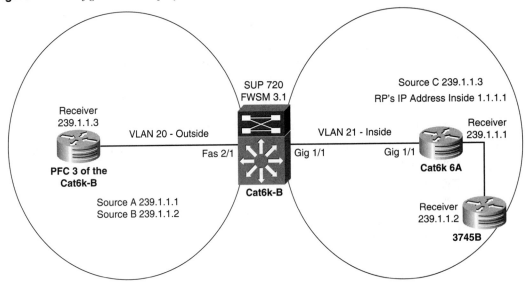

This is another method for multicast to traverse through the FWSM. The pass-through of GRE traffic will need careful configuration on the routing part for congruency and RPF checks for multicast reachability. The FWSM has to be configured for reachability of unicast routing flow, between the two security zones. FWSM should have ACL configuration to allow GRE packets to traverse the FWSM. Example 16-2 shows the configuration to achieve multicast through FWSM via GRE.

PFC3bofcat6kB: This is the next hop device connected to the FWSM and has the configuration of the GRE tunnel and the receiver at the outside security domain.

Example 16-2 *Configuration Example for Multicast Through Firewall via GRE*

```
PFC3bofcat6kB#show run
hostname PFC3bofcat6kB
! Enable multicast on the router
ip multicast-routing
! For testing, you can use igmp join-group to have the loopback 200 act as a receiver
! for 239.1.1.3. Note that the traffic will be process switched for 239.1.1.3. PIM
! sparse mode should be enabled on the interface.
interface Loopback200
 ip address 10.1.50.1 255.255.255.255
 ip pim sparse-mode
 ip igmp join-group 239.1.1.3
! Enable GRE tunnel with destination of the first Layer 3 router at the inside
! interface of the FWSM. Enable pim sparse-mode. VLAN 20 is the SVI interface which
! is also defined at the FWSM's outside VLAN. You need to define the SVI interface on
! the switch.
interface Tunnel0
 ip address 10.1.40.2 255.255.255.252
 ip pim sparse-mode
 tunnel source Vlan20
 tunnel destination 10.1.1.2
!
interface Vlan20
 ip address 10.1.11.2 255.255.255.0
!Routing for the multicast source and the RP will need to pass through the tunnel
ip route 1.0.0.0 255.0.0.0 Tunnel0
ip route 10.1.1.0 255.255.255.0 10.1.11.1
ip route 10.1.3.0 255.255.255.0 Tunnel0
! RP's IP address for the multicast domain is 1.1.1.1. This IP address for the RP
! is defined at the inside security domain.
!
ip pim rp-address 1.1.1.1
```

Firewall at Cat6kB (FWSM configuration): For passing GRE, ACL configuration is needed. No special multicast configuration is needed at the FWSM.

```
FWSM# show run
: Saved
:
FWSM Version 3.1(3)6
!
hostname FWSM
enable password 8Ry2YjIyt7RRXU24 encrypted
names
!
interface Vlan20
 nameif outside
 security-level 0
 ip address 10.1.11.1 255.255.255.0
!
interface Vlan21
 nameif inside
 security-level 100
```

continues

Example 16-2 *Configuration Example for Multicast Through Firewall via GRE (Continued)*

```
 ip address 10.1.1.1 255.255.255.0
ftp mode passive
! Access list will allow GRE. In production networks, a more specific access list
! for allowing GRE is needed. GRE uses protocol 47
access-list 101 extended permit ip any any
access-list 101 extended permit igmp any any
pager lines 24
mtu outside 1500
mtu inside 1500
no failover
mroute 10.1.1.2 255.255.255.255 inside
icmp permit any outside
icmp permit any inside
no asdm history enable
arp timeout 14400
nat (inside) 0 0.0.0.0 0.0.0.0
static (inside,outside) 10.1.40.0 10.1.40.0 netmask 255.255.255.0
! Access list is applied on the interfaces
access-group 101 in interface outside
access-group 101 out interface outside
access-group 101 in interface inside
access-group 101 out interface inside
route outside 0.0.0.0 0.0.0.0 10.1.11.2 1
```

Cat6k6a: This is the next hop Layer 3 device for the FWSM at the inside security domain and is also configured as an RP.

```
cat6k6a# show run
! Enable multicast routing
ip multicast-routing
! igmp_join-group defines another receiver at the inside security domain 239.1.1.1
! and also Loopback 0 is configured with the IP address for the RP. PIM sparse mode
! should be enabled on the interface.
interface Loopback0
 ip address 1.1.1.1 255.255.255.255
 ip pim sparse-mode
 ip igmp join-group 239.1.1.1
! Enable GRE tunnel with destination of the first Layer 3 router at the outside
! interface of the FWSM. PIM sparse mode should be enabled on the interface.
! Vlan 21 is the SVI interface defined at the inside VLAN of the FWSM.
interface Tunnel0
 ip address 10.1.40.1 255.255.255.252
 ip pim sparse-mode
 tunnel source Vlan21
 tunnel destination 10.1.11.2
 !
interface FastEthernet2/1
 ip address 10.1.3.2 255.255.255.252
 ip pim sparse-mode
 !
interface Vlan21
 ip address 10.1.1.2 255.255.255.0
! Configuration to reach the receiver at the outside security domain through the
! tunnel
```

Example 16-2   *Configuration Example for Multicast Through Firewall via GRE (Continued)*

```
ip route 0.0.0.0 0.0.0.0 10.1.1.1
ip route 10.1.50.1 255.255.255.255 Tunnel0
! Configure the RP's IP address
ip pim rp-address 1.1.1.1
cat6k6a#
```

E-R3745-B: Router configured with a receiver at the inside security domain

```
E-R3745-B# show run
hostname E-R3745-B
! Enable multicast routing
ip multicast-routing
! For testing, you can use igmp join-group to have the FastEthernet 1/0 act as a
! receiver for 239.1.1.2. Note that the traffic will be process switched. PIM sparse
! mode should be enabled on the interface.
interface FastEthernet1/0
 ip address 10.1.3.1 255.255.255.252
 ip pim sparse-mode
 ip igmp join-group 239.1.1.2
 duplex auto
 speed auto
!
ip route 0.0.0.0 0.0.0.0 10.1.3.2
! Configure RP's IP address
ip pim rp-address 1.1.1.1
E-R3745-B#
```

Method 3: Configuration Example for Multicast Through Transparent Firewall in Multiple Context Mode

To understand method 3, refer to Figure 16-3, which illustrates a configuration example of multicast through a transparent firewall in multiple context mode.

Figure 16-3 *Configuration Example of Multicast Through Transparent Firewall in Multiple Context Mode*

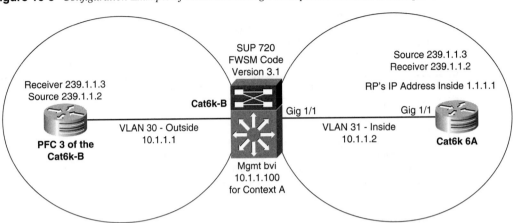

In this example, the FWSM is in multiple context mode. The contexts of the FWSM are configured for transparent mode. In multiple context mode, the support for multicast is achieved through transparent firewall. The RP is in the inside security zone. The FWSM is running code version 3.1. The FWSM does not need any configuration, except ACL entries. In the 3.1 code version or later, the performance is optimized for this configuration.

Example 16-3 shows the support of multicast in multiple context mode using transparent firewall.

Example 16-3 *Configuration of Multicast Through Transparent Firewall in Multiple Context Mode*

```
! System configuration of FWSM is in multiple context mode. This does not need any
! specific configuration to pass multicast traffic through the FWSM
FWSM# show run
: Saved
:
FWSM Version 3.1(3)6 <system>
!
resource acl-partition 12
hostname FWSM
enable password 8Ry2YjIyt7RRXU24 encrypted
!
interface Vlan30
!
interface Vlan31
!
passwd 2KFQnbNIdI.2KYOU encrypted
class default
  limit-resource IPSec 5
  limit-resource Mac-addresses 65535
  limit-resource ASDM 5
  limit-resource SSH 5
```

Example 16-3 *Configuration of Multicast Through Transparent Firewall in Multiple Context Mode (Continued)*

```
    limit-resource Telnet 5
    limit-resource All 0
  !
  ftp mode passive
  pager lines 24
  no failover
  no asdm history enable
  arp timeout 14400
  console timeout 0
  admin-context admin
  context admin
    config-url disk:/admin.cfg
  !
  context A
    allocate-interface Vlan30
    allocate-interface Vlan31
    config-url disk:/A.cfg
  !
  prompt hostname context
  Cryptochecksum:1415c3d58fb402ff51afc7ce292f874f
  : end
  FWSM#
```

Context A configuration:

```
  ! To Access context A
  FWSM# changeto context A
  FWSM/A# show run
  ! Firewall is in transparent mode
  firewall transparent
  hostname A
  enable password 8Ry2YjIyt7RRXU24 encrypted
  names
  !
  interface Vlan30
   nameif outside
   bridge-group 1
   security-level 0
  !
  interface Vlan31
   nameif inside
   bridge-group 1
   security-level 100
  ! For management purposes, have an IP address assigned to the BVI
  interface BVI1
   ip address 10.1.1.100 255.255.255.0
  !
  passwd 2KFQnbNIdI.2KYOU encrypted
  ! Access list in this example is not specific, you can use multicast source and
  ! destination specific access list defined, to be more specific
  access-list 100 extended permit ip any any
  access-list 100 extended permit udp any any
  access-list 101 ethertype permit bpdu
```

continues

Example 16-3 *Configuration of Multicast Through Transparent Firewall in Multiple Context Mode (Continued)*

```
mtu outside 1500
mtu inside 1500
monitor-interface outside
monitor-interface inside
no asdm history enable
arp timeout 14400
access-group 101 in interface outside
access-group 100 in interface outside
access-group 100 out interface outside
access-group 101 in interface inside
access-group 100 in interface inside
access-group 100 out interface inside
route outside 0.0.0.0 0.0.0.0 10.1.1.1 1
telnet 10.1.1.2 255.255.255.255 inside
telnet timeout 5
ssh timeout 5
!
class-map inspection_default
 match default-inspection-traffic
!
policy-map global_policy
 class inspection_default
  inspect dns maximum-length 512
  inspect ftp
  inspect h323 h225
  inspect h323 ras
  inspect rsh
  inspect smtp
  inspect sqlnet
  inspect skinny
  inspect sunrpc
  inspect xdmcp
  inspect sip
  inspect netbios
  inspect tftp
!
service-policy global_policy global
Cryptochecksum:ac2c109d3861e051064dbaa9f777dfd7
: end
```

PFC3bofcat6kB: Router at the outside security domain

```
PFC3bofcat6kB# show run
firewall multiple-vlan-interfaces
firewall module 4 vlan-group 2
firewall vlan-group 2  30-34
ip subnet-zero
!
! Enable multicast on the router
ip multicast-routing
!
vlan 10,20-24,30-31,34
! For testing, you can use igmp join-group to have the Loopback 200 act as a receiver
! for 239.1.1.3. Note that the traffic will be process switched. PIM sparse mode
```

Example 16-3 *Configuration of Multicast Through Transparent Firewall in Multiple Context Mode (Continued)*

```
! should be enabled on the interface.
interface Loopback200
 ip address 10.1.50.1 255.255.255.255
 ip pim sparse-mode
 ip igmp join-group 239.1.1.3
! Connects to the FWSM outside interface and has pim sparse mode enabled
 interface Vlan30
 ip address 10.1.1.1 255.255.255.0
 ip pim sparse-mode
! Configure the RP's IP address. RP propagation method is static
ip pim rp-address 1.1.1.1
PFC3bofcat6kB#
```

cat6k6a: Router at the inside security domain of the FWSM

```
cat6k6a#show run
hostname cat6k6a
! Enable multicast routing
ip multicast-routing
!
! Configure IP address for the RP (1.1.1.1), located at the inside security domain
interface Loopback0
 ip address 1.1.1.1 255.255.255.255
 ip pim sparse-mode
!
interface GigabitEthernet1/1
 switchport
 switchport access vlan 31
 no ip address
!
interface FastEthernet2/1
 ip address 10.1.3.2 255.255.255.252
 ip pim sparse-mode
! Enable PIM on all the interfaces to maintain congruency
interface Vlan31
 ip address 10.1.1.2 255.255.255.0
 ip pim sparse-mode
! Configure RP's IP address
ip pim rp-address 1.1.1.1
cat6k6a#
```

In multiple context mode, transparent firewall is the best way to make the multicast packet
pass through the FWSM. No special configuration is required in the FWSM. ACL is
configured to allow multicast traffic to pass through the FWSM. In this example, the
configuration in Layer 3 routers is simple. The transparent mode fits in an environment
where a need exists for multiple context mode and multicast support.

Summary

This chapter covers the essential elements of multicast technology. Most of the features for multicast technology are supported in the FWSM 3.x code release. This chapter gives design options available to the reader. Multicast is supported in the single context routed mode, and FWSM takes part in the multicast state distribution tree. For multiple context mode, transparent firewall is an option, where the FWSM inspects the packet flow for the multicast stream.

CHAPTER 17

Asymmetric Routing

This chapter provides an overview of asymmetric routing prevalent in the enterprise network. You will learn how the placement of a firewall in a network breaks an asymmetric flow. This chapter also includes designs for symmetric routing with firewalls and covers the FWSM feature that supports asymmetric routing.

In asymmetric routing, the packet traverses from a source to a destination in one path and takes a different path when it returns to the source. Asymmetric routing is not a problem by itself, but will cause issues when Network Address Translation (NAT) or firewalls are used. For example, in firewalls, state information is built when the packets flow from a higher security domain to a lower security domain. The firewall will be an exit point from one security domain to the other. If the return path passes through another firewall, the packet will not be allowed to traverse the firewall from the lower to higher security domain because the firewall in the return path will not have any state information. The state information exists in the first firewall.

Asymmetric Routing Without a Firewall

Figure 17-1 shows asymmetric routing without firewalls in the path from a source to a destination. The source is in 10.1.1.0 subnet, with a source IP address 10.1.1.100. The destination for the packet flow is 11.1.1.100. The **Flow 1** depicts the flow from source to the destination. The host 11.1.1.100 receives the communication and transmits it back to the source 10.1.1.100 (in 10.1.1.0 subnet). In the return path, R1 routes the packet to R3. Note that the packet should have been forwarded to R2 to take the same path of **Flow 1** (in Figure 17-1). From R3 the packet flows to Cat6k2 and then to R4. Even though the path from the source to destination is different from the return path of the packet, the flow is completed without any issue. In a routing environment, the component of latency needs to be reviewed for different paths.

Figure 17-1 *Asymmetric Routing Without a Firewall*

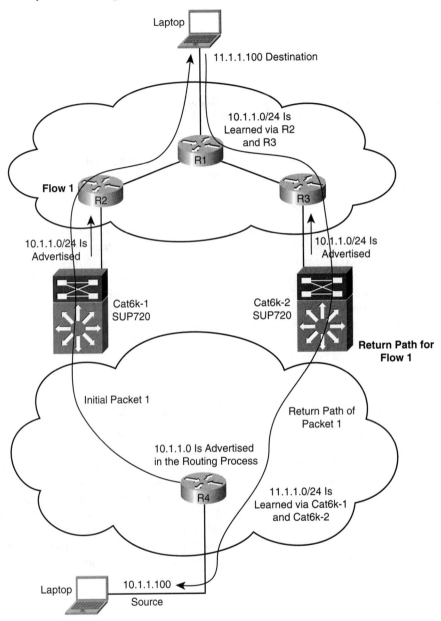

Laptop

11.1.1.100 Destination

10.1.1.0/24 Is
Learned via R2
and R3

R1

Flow 1
R2

R3

10.1.1.0/24 Is
Advertised

10.1.1.0/24 Is
Advertised

Cat6k-1
SUP720

Cat6k-2
SUP720

**Return Path for
Flow 1**

Initial Packet 1

Return Path of
Packet 1

10.1.1.0 Is Advertised
in the Routing Process

R4

11.1.1.0/24 Is
Learned via Cat6k-1
and Cat6k-2

Laptop   10.1.1.100
Source

Asymmetric Traffic Flow in a Firewall Environment

In Figure 17-2, there are two FWSMs (for firewalls) added in both the Catalyst 6500 chassis. The asymmetric traffic flow is from 10.1.1.0 subnet to host 11.1.1.100.

Figure 17-2   *FWSM and Asymmetric Routing*

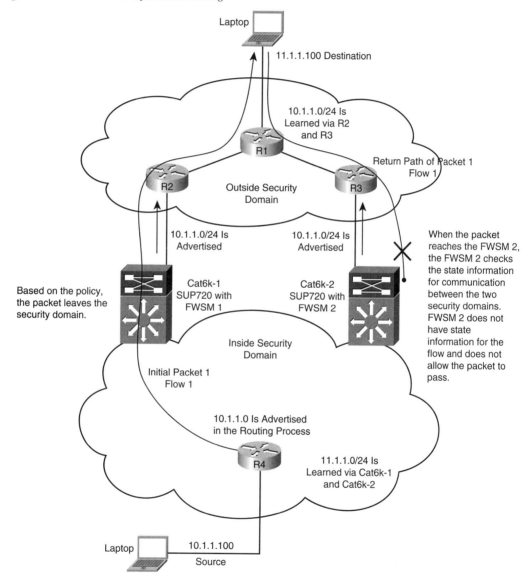

The source for the flow is in the inside security domain, and the destination is in the outside security domain. The **Flow 1** depicts the flow of the packet from source to destination. The FWSM 1 forms a state translation when the packets traverse the firewall. The flow is from a higher security domain (inside) to a lower security domain (outside). The host 11.1.1.100 receives the communication and transmits back to the source 10.1.1.100 (in 10.1.1.0 subnet). In the return path, the R1 routes the packet to R3. Note that the packet should have been forwarded to R2 to pass through FWSM 1. The packet flows from R3 to FWSM 2. FWSM 2 looks for state translation entry for this flow and because no state translation entry exists, the packet is dropped.

This example shows how asymmetric routing can cause problems in a firewall environment when a packet traverses from one security domain to another security domain. The next section covers options to overcome asymmetric routing in a firewall environment.

Avoiding Asymmetric Routing Through Firewalls

The next section covers options for a symmetric traffic flow in a firewall environment with and without redundancy.

Option 1: Symmetric Routing Through Firewalls

Make sure the routing flows through the desired symmetric architecture as shown in Figure 17-3.

Figure 17-3   *Symmetric Routing Through Firewalls Without Redundancy*

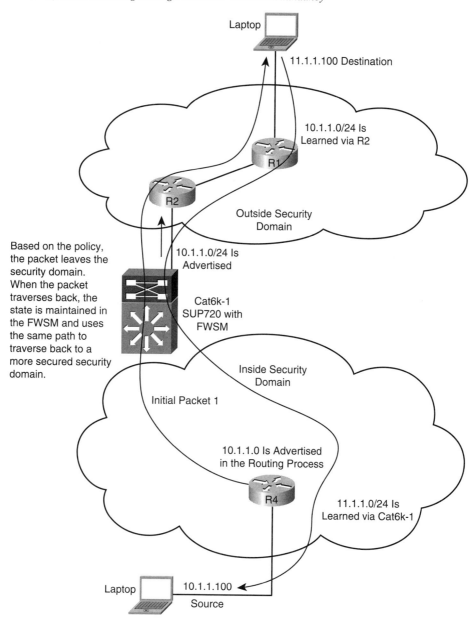

In this example, the packet traverses through the Cat6k-1 and the FWSM. Based on the security policies, the state is maintained in the FWSM. When the packet originates from the source 10.1.1.100, it flows through the FWSM1, builds a state table, and then flows to the destination 11.1.1.100. On the return path, the packet traverses through the same path because the route for subnet 10.1.1.0 at R1 is learned only via R2. The packet reaches the Cat6k-1 and the FWSM.

The state is maintained for the packet flow in the FWSM1 and the packet is allowed to traverse through FWSM1 to reach R4.

The next section covers the redundancy component added to Figure 17-3.

Option 2: Firewall Redundancy and Routing Redundancy Symmetry

Figure 17-4 shows the failover capability of the firewall and the routing decision to follow the failover state of the firewall. This design has redundancy for the FWSM and Layer 3 portion of the network in each security domain. This is achieved by using the Layer 3 devices to point to the virtual IP address (VIP) of the active interface for a particular security domain. The FWSM points to the VIP address of the Hot Standby Router Protocol (HSRP) for the respective VLANs. In this case, the FWSM can also take advantage of the redundant Layer 3 devices in the network. The FWSM is configured in routed mode. Layer 3 redundancy will prevent multiple failures in the Layer 3 domain. For more information on achieving this type of redundancy, refer to Chapter 12, "Understanding Failover in FWSM."

Figure 17-4   *FWSM Redundancy and Routing Symmetry to Avoid Asymmetric Routing*

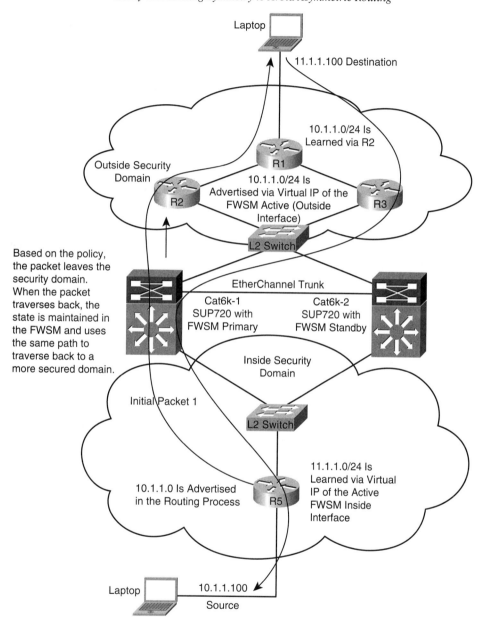

Supporting Asymmetric Routing in FWSM

The FWSM supports asymmetric traffic flow from the 3.x code version and later. The previous section covers the problems caused by routing while introducing firewalls in asymmetric routing and gives a solution with and without redundancy to avoid these problems in the network. The solution aligns the firewalls with the Layer 3 network to *avoid* asymmetric routing issues. Asymmetric routing problems can occur when traffic flows between multiple security domains and these security domains are represented in a multiple context firewall. In this case, the flow of traffic for all security domains will be achieved by using symmetric firewall redundancy, congruent with the routing architecture. FWSM redundancy can be designed using Active/Standby and Active/Active modes.

The concept of asymmetric routing can be applied to single or multiple context mode. Asymmetric routing (ASR) feature support is available in 3.1 code version and later to support asymmetric routing. Based on the 3.1 code, the FWSM can have a maximum of 32 groups of ASR. The ASR support is also available in transparent and routed firewalls.

In this section, you will learn to support asymmetric routing using the following failover modes:

- Active/Standby mode
- Active/Active mode

Asymmetric Routing Support in Active/Standby Mode

For the network topology shown in Figure 17-5, the configuration for the outside interface of security context A and security context B will have ASR group 1 (it will belong in the same ASR group) enabled. The packet arrives at the outside interface of context B. Because the ASR group is the same for the two outside interfaces of contexts A and B, the packet will get redirected to context A's outside interface from context B's outside interface. The packet then flows through context A to reach the destination.

Active/Active FWSM configuration is leveraged in an environment that has routing redundancy. This design increases the redundancy and availability of resources for the traffic flow.

Figure 17-5 *FWSM and Asymmetric Routing Support Between Two Contexts*

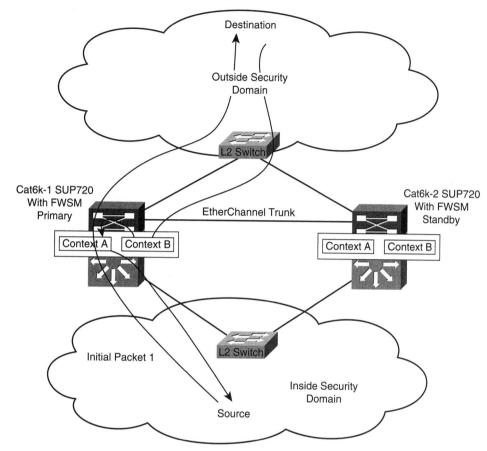

Asymmetric Routing Support in Active/Active Mode

In Active/Active mode, the two FWSM units in failover state are active. This is achieved using multiple context mode. The active firewalls for the respective contexts are distributed between the two FWSM units in failover mode.

Consider a scenario where a packet flows through a single security rule set. When a need exists to have two desired paths, a redundant path can be designed using Active/Active redundancy and the ASR feature in the FWSM. The same rule set is applied in both contexts. ASR group is enabled in the interfaces of the two contexts. The firewall is configured to be in transparent mode.

For the network topology shown in Figure 17-6, the FWSMs are in Active/Active failover configuration.

Figure 17-6 *FWSM and Asymmetric Routing Support Between Two Contexts in Active/Active Failover Mode*

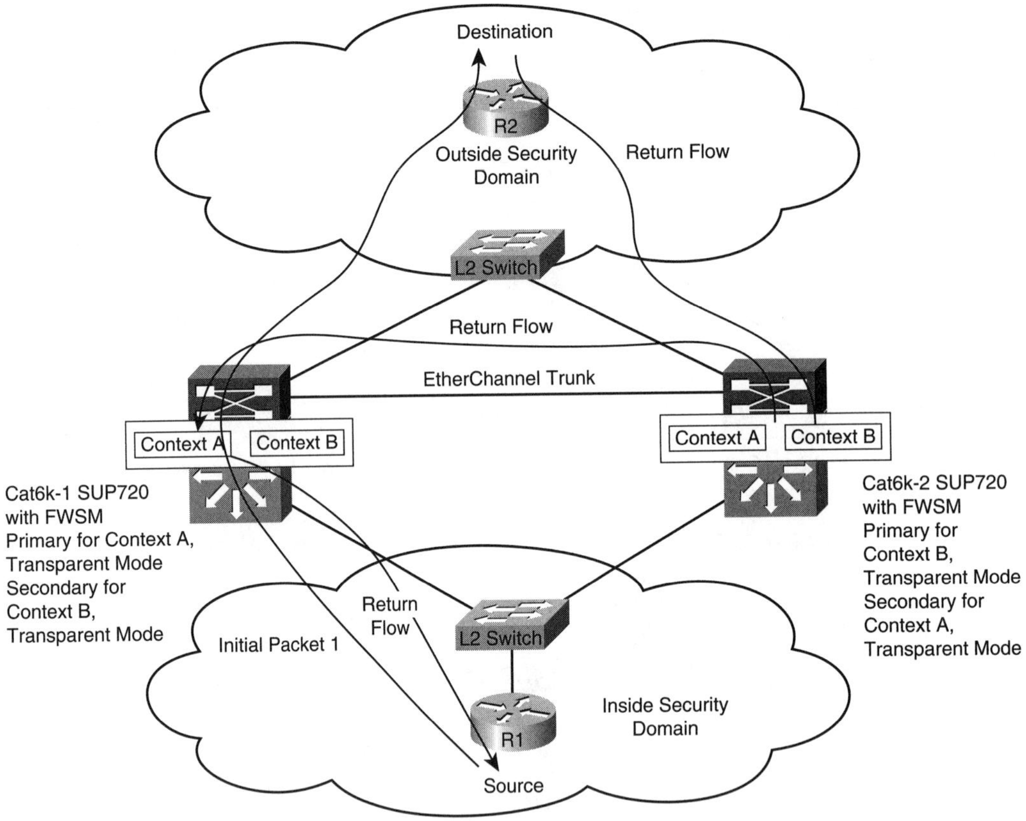

The firewalls in both contexts are in transparent mode, and the security policies in both the contexts are the same. From the Layer 3 next hop in each security domain, there are two equal paths for routing adjacencies across the firewall through the two contexts. The traffic from the inside to outside security domain can flow through either context A or context B because the ASR feature is enabled on the interfaces of each security domain of both contexts. The dependence on state information is removed because of the ASR feature.

In this example, the packet from the inside to the outside security domain flows through Cat6k-1 context A. In the return path, the packet flows to context B in the Cat6k-2. The outside interfaces of the two contexts are in the same ASR group. After the packet arrives in context B, the outside interface of context B finds the session information in the outside interface of context A (because they are configured with the same ASR group), which is in the standby state on the unit. It then forwards the return traffic to the unit where context A is active.

Asymmetric routing concepts can also be extended to the single context mode. In this case, the packet leaves the FWSM interface in a security domain, and the return path will be in an interface of a different security domain. Note that both the interfaces will be in the same ASR group. The interfaces in the same ASR group will pass the packet from one interface to the other. However, in multiple context mode, the interfaces in the same security domain share the same ASR group.

In general, avoid asymmetric routing in a firewall design solution. The ASR feature is purely to protect issues such as link failovers. Note that even though state is shared between the Active and Standby firewalls periodically, it is possible to have race conditions, which could cause connections to be dropped.

Active/Active failover with ASR is a design advantage for parallel paths across firewalls with the same security rule sets. Care should be taken for Active/Active redundancy and the Layer 3 network symmetry. This depends on each environment, and limitations may arise based on individual scenarios.

Configuring ASR in FWSM

The command to enable the ASR feature introduced in the 3.1 code release for the FWSM is

```
asr-group number
```

This command-line interface (CLI) should be attached to the interface configuration, for example:

```
interface vlan 9
    nameif outside
    security-level 0
    ip address 11.1.1.10 255.255.255.0 standby 11.1.1.11
    asr-group 1
```

Example 17-1 represents the FWSM in multiple context routed mode. ASR groups are configured to allow the FWSM to pass the traffic.

The spanning tree root for a VLAN is represented by the switch with an active firewall context, and HSRP Primary for the VLAN is represented in the same switch.

Figure 17-7 gives an example of Active/Active context using failover groups. The outside interfaces of both context A and context B are configured for ASR routing with **asr-group 1**.

Figure 17-7 *FWSM and Asymmetric Routing Support in Multiple Context Routed Mode*

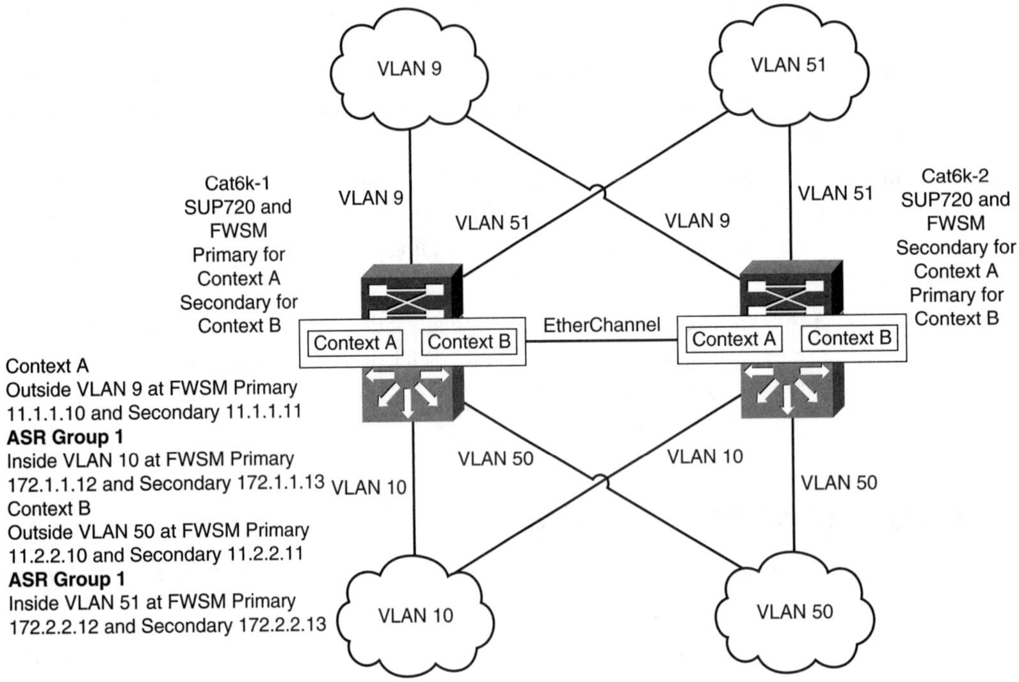

Next is the snapshot configuration of FWSMs in multiple context mode with ASR group.

Example 17-1 *FWSM and Asymmetric Routing Support in Multiple Context Routed Mode*

```
! (Cat 6k1) FWSM primary for contexta
FWSM/contexta# show run
: Saved
:
FWSM Version 3.1(4) <context>
!
hostname contexta
enable password 8Ry2YjIyt7RRXU24 encrypted
names
!
interface Vlan9
 nameif outside
 security-level 0
 ip address 11.1.1.12 255.255.255.0 standby 11.1.1.13
 asr-group 1
! ASR group 1 is configured for the interface in the outside security domain
interface Vlan10
 nameif inside
 security-level 100
 ip address 172.1.1.12 255.255.255.0 standby 172.1.1.13
```

Example 17-1 *FWSM and Asymmetric Routing Support in Multiple Context Routed Mode (Continued)*

```
!
passwd 2KFQnbNIdI.2KYOU encrypted
access-list 100 extended permit ip any any
pager lines 24
mtu outside 1500
mtu inside 1500
monitor-interface outside
monitor-interface inside
icmp permit any outside
icmp permit any inside
no asdm history enable
arp timeout 14400
global (outside) 1 11.1.1.0 netmask 255.255.255.0
nat (inside) 1 0.0.0.0 0.0.0.0
access-group 100 in interface outside
access-group 100 out interface outside
access-group 100 in interface inside
access-group 100 out interface inside
route outside 0.0.0.0 0.0.0.0 11.1.1.3 1
timeout xlate 3:00:00
timeout conn 1:00:00 half-closed 0:10:00 udp 0:02:00 icmp 0:00:02
timeout sunrpc 0:10:00 h323 0:05:00 h225 1:00:00 mgcp 0:05:00
timeout mgcp-pat 0:05:00 sip 0:30:00 sip_media 0:02:00
timeout uauth 0:05:00 absolute
no snmp-server location
no snmp-server contact
telnet timeout 5
ssh timeout 5
!
class-map inspection_default
 match default-inspection-traffic
!
 policy-map global_policy
 class inspection_default
  inspect dns maximum-length 512
  inspect ftp
  inspect h323 h225
  inspect h323 ras
  inspect netbios
  inspect rsh
  inspect skinny
  inspect smtp
  inspect sqlnet
  inspect sunrpc
  inspect tftp
  inspect sip
  inspect xdmcp
!
service-policy global_policy global
Cryptochecksum:2873ca18580fb555ea47c15d0ac94a08
: end
```

continues

Example 17-1 *FWSM and Asymmetric Routing Support in Multiple Context Routed Mode (Continued)*

```
FWSM/contexta#
! (Cat 6k2) FWSM primary for contextb
FWSM/contextb# show run
: Saved
:
FWSM Version 3.1(4) <context>
!
hostname contextb
enable password 8Ry2YjIyt7RRXU24 encrypted
names
!
interface Vlan50
 nameif inside
 security-level 100
 ip address 172.2.2.10 255.255.255.0 standby 172.2.2.11
!
interface Vlan51
 nameif outside
 security-level 0
 ip address 11.2.2.10 255.255.255.0 standby 11.2.2.11
 asr-group 1
! ASR group 1 is configured for the interface in the outside security domain
passwd 2KFQnbNIdI.2KYOU encrypted
access-list 100 extended permit ip any any
access-list 101 extended permit ip any any
pager lines 24
mtu inside 1500
mtu outside 1500
monitor-interface inside
monitor-interface outside
icmp permit any inside
icmp permit any outside
no asdm history enable
arp timeout 14400
global (outside) 1 11.2.2.0 netmask 255.255.255.0
nat (inside) 1 0.0.0.0 0.0.0.0
access-group 101 in interface inside
access-group 101 out interface inside
access-group 101 in interface outside
access-group 101 out interface outside
route outside 0.0.0.0 0.0.0.0 11.2.2.3 1
timeout xlate 3:00:00
timeout conn 1:00:00 half-closed 0:10:00 udp 0:02:00 icmp 0:00:02
timeout sunrpc 0:10:00 h323 0:05:00 h225 1:00:00 mgcp 0:05:00
timeout mgcp-pat 0:05:00 sip 0:30:00 sip_media 0:02:00
timeout uauth 0:05:00 absolute
no snmp-server location
no snmp-server contact
telnet timeout 5
ssh timeout 5
!
class-map inspection_default
```

Example 17-1   *FWSM and Asymmetric Routing Support in Multiple Context Routed Mode (Continued)*

```
  match default-inspection-traffic
 !
 policy-map global_policy
  class inspection_default
   inspect dns maximum-length 512
   inspect ftp
   inspect h323 h225
   inspect h323 ras
   inspect netbios
   inspect rsh
   inspect skinny
   inspect smtp
   inspect sqlnet
   inspect sunrpc
   inspect tftp
   inspect sip
   inspect xdmcp
 !
 service-policy global_policy global
 Cryptochecksum:b59531047507cf7e9ee7effb2cce9a21
 : end
```

Summary

Asymmetric routing is the traversal of a packet from a source to a destination in one path, and follows a different path when the packet returns to the source. Asymmetric routing is seen in the Layer 3 environment and does not cause a problem by itself. Asymmetric routing with firewalls causes issues. After reading this chapter, the reader will know to overcome asymmetric routing issues in a network with FWSM. It is a good practice to follow the design options for symmetric routing. The reader will also know to enable the ASR feature to support asymmetric routing for the FWSM with the 3.1 code version or later.

CHAPTER 18

Firewall Load Balancing

Firewall load balancing is commonly seen in data centers or Internet architecture of e-commerce networks, where there is a high volume of traffic traversing the firewall infrastructure. With firewall load balancing, multiple firewalls can be referenced by a single IP address defined in a load balancer. The load balancer can distribute the traffic load among firewalls, or multiple virtual IP addresses (VIP) in a load balancer can reference firewalls for different traffic profiles, to give alignment between VIP and traffic profiles. The redundancy properties can be separated per traffic profiles attached to a VIP. This concept helps define a firewall cluster, which is a group of firewalls, aligned with load-balancing policies.

Reasons for Load Balancing Firewalls

The inherent reasons to load balance the firewalls are as follows:

- **Increase volume of traffic**: In any network, a secured domain can have an increase burst in traffic. The traffic burst is destined to a single security domain, in which case the other security domain's traffic passing through the firewall should not be starved. If traffic volume in firewall designs is a concern, firewall load balancing should be considered as a solution.

- **Improve scalability**: This is commonly seen in shared firewall architecture. A shared firewall infrastructure will have virtual firewalls for multiple entities. When different security domains represent different entities, the growth and services offered by the firewall architecture cannot be determined in the initial deployment. The growth is based on estimation and probability. It is important to forecast the services offered and the flow of traffic through the firewall. This forecasted number should be compared with the traffic throughput that the firewall can handle. If the requirement forecasted is greater than the current throughput of the firewall, firewall load balancing should be considered as an option.

- **Create symmetry with available network bandwidth**: This scenario is usually seen in the data center environment, where a 10 Gbps traffic requirement exists at the Layer 2 and Layer 3 levels. A data center normally has high bandwidth links as compared to the rest of the network. This bandwidth is used for server-to-server communication. If firewalls are placed in the data center, the firewalls need to support high-bandwidth traffic to avoid a traffic bottleneck. When firewalls are deployed in the data center, the firewall architecture will need to support high-bandwidth applications or environments of grid computing. In this case, firewall load balancing is a good option to explore to increase the throughput of the firewall architecture in the data center environment.

- **Provide independent traffic flow**: This requirement is seen in networks where critical applications will need flow redundancy. The redundancy parameters should be kept in mind while designing the firewall load-balancing solution.

NOTE   Redundancy has to be considered for each of the design requirements. The firewall has its own redundancy methods. The method chosen for load balancing should have redundancy considered in the design.

Several valid requirements exist for firewall load balancing. The next section covers the design requirements, which are important to define the type of load balancing needed for FWSM and its components.

Design Requirements for Firewall Load Balancing

Some of the design criteria to be considered for firewall load balancing are as follows:

- **Business need for firewall load-balancing solution**: Based on the reasons shown in the previous section, you need to define and determine the need for a firewall load-balancing solution and then design or deploy it.

- **Application requirements**: It is important to understand the application requirements to select a load-balancing solution. The two key types of application requirements are server location and traffic flow. For firewall load balancing the location of the server based on security domain needs to be determined.

- **Server location**: The server location in the security domain has to be determined for the alignment of security and load-balancing policies. This determines the type of load balancing and the security policies to be used in the design.

- **Traffic flow**: The current estimated traffic flow and the forecasted flow for future should be assessed in the design phase. The difference (if only) between the current supported traffic and the forecasted flow should be taken as a design parameter for load balancing. Some of the load-balancing components chosen, based on the traffic flow, are firewall, load balancer, and network device.

CAUTION	If you base your design on other principles, make sure the security requirements are not compromised. The firewall load-balancing design should be in symmetry with the network.

- **Security requirements**: Understanding the security requirements is necessary while designing the load-balancing architecture. With firewall load balancing, the security rules will be granular and symmetric to the traffic flowing through the load-balancing architecture.

- **Network requirements**: This is an important requirement. The Firewall Services Module (FWSM) is integrated into a network device. It is very important to understand and design the routing requirements based on how the different security domains communicate with each other, and verify the changes needed in the next hop reachable device to align the network, firewall, and load balancer.

Firewall Load-Balancing Solutions

The three firewall load-balancing solutions discussed in the next section are firewall load balancing with PBR, CSM, and ACE.

Firewall Load Balancing with Policy-Based Routing

The traditional routing forwards the packet based on the destination IP address in the routing table. With policy-based routing (PBR), packets are forwarded based on the source IP address. This provides the flexibility to forward packets based on the source IP address to the next hop destination. This concept is used in firewall load balancing. The next section shows the use of PBR in firewall load balancing.

In Figure 18-1, the throughput of FWSM is doubled from 5.1 Gbps to 10.2 Gbps for multiple traffic flows. The traffic for a single session cannot be greater than 1 Gbps. The FWSM Gigabit Ethernet channel (6 Gbps in total) connection to the back plane of the switch restricts the flow of a single session to 1 Gbps. The load-balancing solution offers max-throughput of 10.2 Gbps or more for multiple sessions. Refer to Chapter 2, "Overview of the Firewall Services Module," for details on FWSM architecture.

Figure 18-1 *High-Level Explanation of Load Balancing Using PBR*

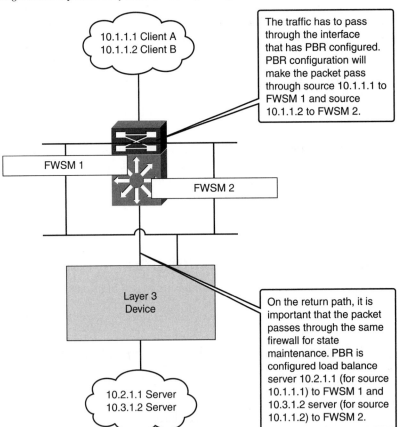

Based on routing, the packet passes through the interface where the policy map is applied to the PBR to reach the destination servers. In the policy map, a route map is used to send the traffic to the destination of the respective FWSM modules (outside interface), based on the source (client) IP address.

The packet passes through the FWSM based on the PBR and hits the server for the respective clients. Communication from the server flows symmetrically to the same FWSM through which the packet had already passed. This is to maintain state information. PBR is used in the Layer 3 hop to make the respective server source IP address flow through the same FWSM through which the previous flow had passed. The two FWSMs are in single-context routed mode.

In this solution, for each of the FWSM 1 and FWSM 2 (as defined in Figure 18-2), failover pairs are necessary for redundancy. Redundancy is not covered in Figure 18-2. In this scenario, the next hop of the PBR should be the virtual IP (VIP) address of the primary FWSM pair. Example 18-1 shows a high-level explanation of firewall load balancing (FLB) using PBR.

Example 18-1   *High-Level Explanation of FLB Using PBR*

```
access-list 1 permit host 10.1.1.1
!ip address that needs to be matched - HOST A
access-list 2 permit host 10.1.1.2
!ip address that needs to be matched - HOST B
!
interface VLAN 10
 ip policy route-map FW-LB
!
route-map FW-LB permit 10
 match ip address 1
set ip next-hop 10.10.10.1
!Next hop of the FW1 interface, to which the traffic is sent
route-map equal-access permit 20
 match ip address 2
set ip next-hop 10.10.10.2
! Next hop of the FW2 interface, to which the traffic is sent
```

If the match takes place on an access list, the traffic that matches the access list is sent to the next hop address of the respective firewalls. In Example 18-1, if the traffic match does not happen at the access list, there is an *implicit deny* as per the principle of access list.

Firewall Load Balancing with Content Switch Module

This is an inline module in the 7600 or 6500 devices. Content switch module (CSM) is a load-balancing product from Cisco. Its architecture can support 165,000 connections per second and 1 million concurrent connections. When you're designing the solution with a CSM, interfaces defined in the FWSM should have the next hop address defined at the CSM. The common subnet between the firewall and the CSM should not be defined in the multilayer switch feature card (MSFC) of the switch. The switch should not have any instance of the switched virtual interface (SVI) for this subnet. This is needed for the CSM to be the next hop of the FWSM. The max-throughput of a single CSM is 4 Gbps. By using a CSM for load balancing the FWSM, you will be underutilizing the max-throughput of the FWSM; that is, 5.1 Gbps. This load-balancing solution cannot be used for increasing the throughput of the firewall infrastructure.

In the CSM, the interface facing the user segment is known as the client side, and the interface facing the FWSM is known as the server side. It is important to understand these two terminologies while configuring the CSM for load balancing with FWSM.

Configuring the CSM

A CSM can be configured in three ways:

- **CSM in Routed mode**: The client traffic entering the Catalyst 6500 through the MSFC passes through the CSM. Based on the interesting traffic list defined, the CSM makes a load-balancing decision. The traffic will then be forwarded to the server farm based on this decision. The forwarding is done via routing. The client and server VLANs will be in different subnets.

- **CSM in Transparent mode**: In this mode, CSM is similar to a bridge. The transparent mode in CSM is similar to FWSM in a Layer 2 (transparent) mode. The same subnet space will be available in the client and the server VLANs on the CSM.

- **CSM in One-Arm mode**: In this mode, the CSM is on a "stick." When the CSM is used in a one-arm configuration, the single VLAN can be either a client or a server VLAN. After the traffic gets load balanced, the traffic can be sent directly to the client from the server (bypassing the CSM), or if the NAT functionality is enabled when the traffic leaves the CSM toward the server, the return path from the server to the client will be via the CSM.

CSM Firewall Load Balancing: Scenario 1

In this example, as shown in Figure 18-2, the CSM1 load balances the flow from the outside to the inside direction. The CSM1 can have multiple server-side VLANs (if in routed mode). The server-side IP address for CSM1 is the IP address of the firewall. The return path of the packet will pass through the CSM2. The policies in CSM1 and CSM2 will have a symmetry, and this symmetry will make the packets pass through the same firewall that was used for incoming and outgoing packets. In this way, the state information of the firewall is maintained for a packet flow.

Figure 18-2 *High-Level Explanation of Firewall Load Balancing Using CSM*

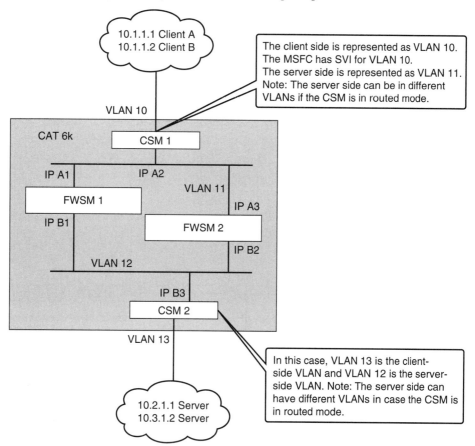

CSM Firewall Load Balancing: Scenario 2

In this example, as shown in Figure 18-3, high availability/redundancy is also integrated into the firewall load balancing design. The figure has a primary block and a secondary block. The primary block passes the traffic in the normal operation. The next hop IP address from the FWSM will be pointed to the **alias** virtual address of the CSM. Note that the next hop IP address from the CSM will be the primary FWSM interface. The rest will be the same as scenario 1 of the CSM design.

The two design options are in routed mode for CSM. The design options will change when CSM or FWSM mode changes to transparent mode.

Figure 18-3 *High-Level Explanation of Load Balancing Using CSM with Redundancy*

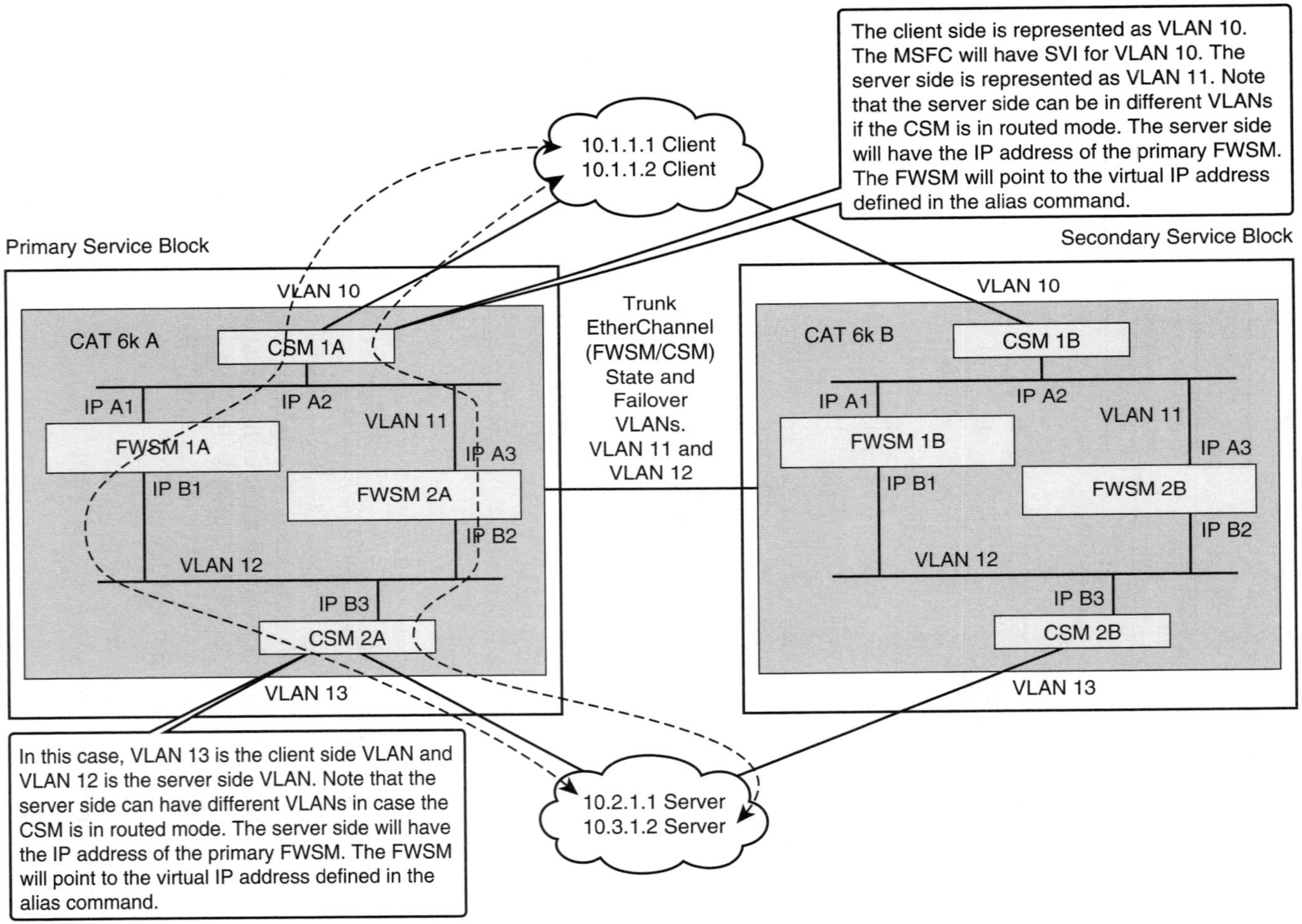
The client side is represented as VLAN 10. The MSFC will have SVI for VLAN 10. The server side is represented as VLAN 11. Note that the server side can be in different VLANs if the CSM is in routed mode. The server side will have the IP address of the primary FWSM. The FWSM will point to the virtual IP address defined in the alias command.
10.1.1.1 Client
10.1.1.2 Client
Primary Service Block
Secondary Service Block
VLAN 10
CAT 6k A
CSM 1A
IP A1
IP A2
VLAN 11
FWSM 1A
IP A3
IP B1
FWSM 2A
IP B2
VLAN 12
IP B3
CSM 2A
VLAN 13
Trunk
EtherChannel
(FWSM/CSM)
State and
Failover
VLANs.
VLAN 11 and
VLAN 12
VLAN 10
CAT 6k B
CSM 1B
IP A1
IP A2
VLAN 11
FWSM 1B
IP A3
IP B1
FWSM 2B
IP B2
VLAN 12
IP B3
CSM 2B
VLAN 13
In this case, VLAN 13 is the client side VLAN and VLAN 12 is the server side VLAN. Note that the server side can have different VLANs in case the CSM is in routed mode. The server side will have the IP address of the primary FWSM. The FWSM will point to the virtual IP address defined in the alias command.
10.2.1.1 Server
10.3.1.2 Server

NOTE IP A1, A2, A3, B1, B2, and B3 represents the forwarding path of the next hop for IP packets.

Snapshot Configuration for CSM Supporting Firewall Load Balancing

Configuring a load-balancing policy in a CSM is explained in three steps. This example does not give the complete firewall load-balancing solution using CSM. However, it gives a sample of a single policy that will be a part of multiple policies for the firewall load-balancing solution using CSM to work.

Step 1 The client and server VLANs are configured at the Catalyst 6500. For the client VLAN only, an SVI on the Catalyst 6500 is defined.

```
6504-E-1(config)# vlan 50
6504-E-1(config-vlan)# name client-vlan
6504-E-1(config-vlan)# vlan 10
6504-E-1(config-vlan)# name server-vlan
6504-E-1(config-vlan)# interface vlan 50
6504-E-1(config-if)# ip address 172.20.1.1 255.255.255.0
```

Step 2 Perform a **show module** to verify where the CSM module is located and configure the CSM.

```
6504-E-1# show module
Mod Ports Card Type                                      Model             Serial No.
--- ----- -------------------------------- --------------- ----------
  1   2 Supervisor Engine 720 (Active)     WS-SUP720-BASE  SAD0741006K
  2   4 SLB Application Processor Complex WS-X6066-SLB-APC SAD090800TL
  3   6 Firewall Module                    WS-SVC-FWM-1    SAD091201KC
  4   6 Firewall Module                    WS-SVC-FWM-1    SAD090608J8
Mod MAC addresses                       Hw   Fw    Sw             Status
--- -------------------------------- ---- --- ----------- ------
  1 000d.6535.cfc4 to 000d.6535.cfc7 2.6  8.1(3) 12.2(18)SXF5 Ok
  2 0012.80d4.cfb8 to 0012.80d4.cfbf 1.7         3.1(3)C7(1) Ok
  3 0012.7ff6.c4f4 to 0012.7ff6.c4fb 3.0  7.2(1) 3.1(3)6     Ok
  4 0003.3236.0842 to 0003.3236.0849 3.0  7.2(1) 3.1(3)6     Ok
Mod Sub-Module              Model         Serial      Hw   Status
---- ---------------------- ------------- ----------- --- ------
  1 Policy Feature Card 3  WS-F6K-PFC3A  SAD0721045G 1.4  Ok
  1 MSFC3 Daughterboard    WS-SUP720     SAD074006H1 1.9  Ok
Mod Online Diag Status
---- ------------------
  1 Pass
  2 Pass
  ! To access the CSM in module 2
6504-E-1(config)# module csm 2
6504-E-1(config-module-csm)#
```

Step 3 Configure the CSM with load balancing. Probe the address of the FWSM using Internet Control Message Protocol (ICMP). The NAT principle will depend on the design.

```
vlan 50 client
  ip address 172.20.1.2 255.255.255.0
  gateway 172.20.1.1
!
 vlan 10 server
  ip address 10.1.1.1 255.255.255.0
! VLAN 10 is in the outside interface of the FWSM
 probe LB icmp
! probe to ping the Firewall interfaces
serverfarm LB
  no nat server
  no nat client
  predictor hash address source 255.255.255.255

! Predictor hash selects a server using a hash value, based on the source
IP address
  real 10.1.1.2
! FW1 ip address
    inservice
  real 10.1.1.3
! FW2 ip address
    inservice
  probe LB
!
 vserver 2LB
  virtual 10.0.0.0 any
! 10.0.0.0 matches the interesting traffic to be load balanced
  vlan 10
! client vlan
  serverfarm LB
! server farm for load balancing
  persistent rebalance
  inservice
```

The FWSM will not have any new configuration except to point to the next hop of the CSM.

NOTE	The configuration depicts the outside security domain's traffic to the inside security domain. For the inside security domain to access the outside security domain, a separate set of policies is needed in the CSM. This is beyond the scope of this example.

Firewall Load Balancing Using the Application Control Engine

The application control engine (ACE) is the new load balancer from Cisco. The ACE can offer a max-throughput of 16 Gbps and 350,000 connections per second. It is another load balancer that you can use for greater throughput to load balance a firewall. ACE also supports virtualization similar to the FWSM. Instead of using the outside load balancer or the inside load balancer, you can use ACE as a single load balancer for outside and inside load balancers through virtualization. This is achieved using virtual contexts on the ACE. For a single ACE used in an outside security domain and inside security domain as a load balancer with virtualization, the combined packet flow of the outside load balancer and the inside load balancer should be less than 16 Gbps. If two separate ACE blades are used, there can be a maximum of 16 Gbps traffic load balanced (for 8 Gbps or 16 Gbps traffic, equivalent throughput needs to be achieved via multiple FWSMs).

ACE Design for Firewall Load Balancing

The dual ACE solution will be able to provide a 10 Gbps throughput for firewall load balancing, and the multiple FWSMs have to match this throughput. Figure 18-4 shows a high-level design of firewall load balancing using ACE.

Figure 18-4 *High-Level Explanation of Firewall Load Balancing Using ACE*

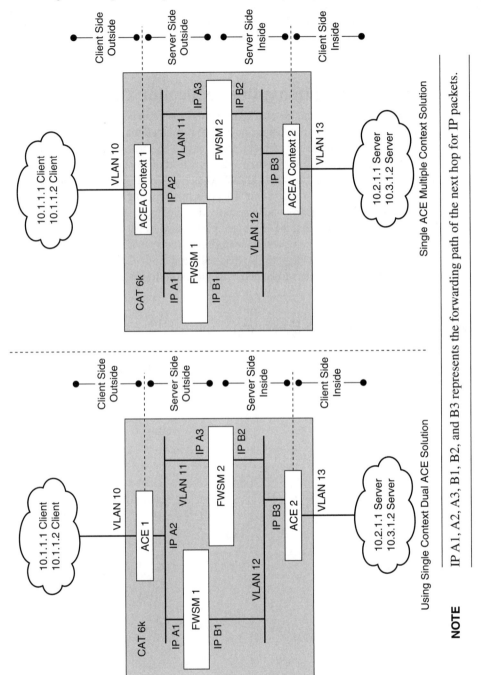

Figure 18-5 *Firewall Load Balancing Using ACE with Redundancy*

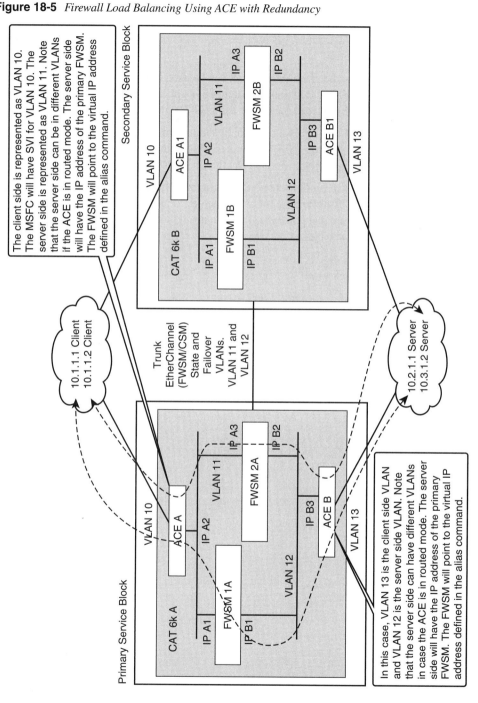

The client side is represented as VLAN 10. The MSFC will have SVI for VLAN 10. The server side is represented as VLAN 11. Note that the server side can be in different VLANs if the ACE is in routed mode. The server side will have the IP address of the primary FWSM. The FWSM will point to the virtual IP address defined in the alias command.

In this case, VLAN 13 is the client side VLAN and VLAN 12 is the server side VLAN. Note that the server side can have different VLANs in case the ACE is in routed mode. The server side will have the IP address of the primary FWSM. The FWSM will point to the virtual IP address defined in the alias command.

NOTE   IP A1, A2, A3, B1, B2, and B3 represents the forwarding path of the next hop for IP packets.

By using multiple context design in a single ACE, the max-throughput of 8 Gbps can be achieved using ACE (for unidirectional traffic). The ACE A is split into two contexts: context 1 and context 2. Context 1 is used as an outside load balancer and context 2 is used as an inside load balancer.

The ACE module, together with the FWSM, can be used in Layer 2 or Layer 3 mode. The configuration concept of ACE in transparent mode is similar to FWSM in transparent mode. Figure 18-5 shows firewall load balancing using ACE with redundancy.

The redundancy in ACE for firewall load balancing is similar to the design concept of firewall load balancing using CSM, which is explained in detail in the "Firewall Load Balancing with Content Switch Module" section in this chapter.

In Figure 18-6, two ACE modules have two pairs for redundancy in the secondary switch. The same design for lesser throughput can be achieved using a single ACE module with multiple contexts, where one context will be the inside load balancer and the other context will be the outside load balancer.

Figure 18-6 *Firewall Load Balancing Using a Single ACE with Virtual Contexts for Redundancy*

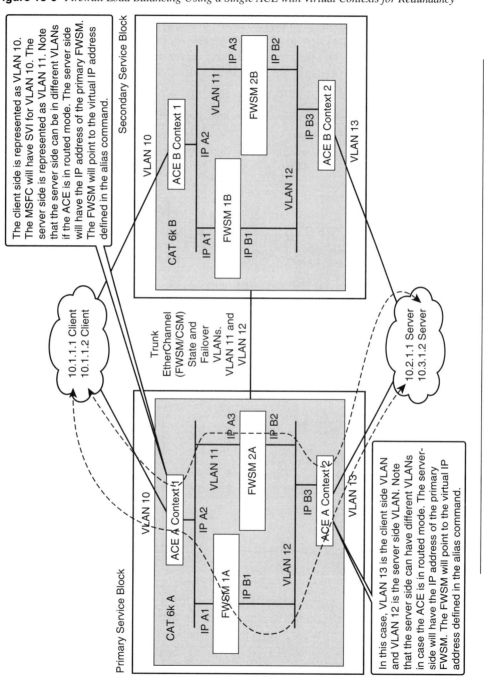

NOTE   IP A1, A2, A3, B1, B2, and B3 represents the forwarding path of the next hop for IP packets.

Firewall Load Balancing Configuration Example

Figure 18-7 gives an example of load balancing through policy-based routing. The traffic sourced from 172.16.1.1 client to 10.2.100.1 server will pass through FWSM1, using OUT2IN policy. The return path from 10.2.100.1 server will be load balanced from IN2OUT policy and will pass through FWSM1 back to 172.16.1.1 client. This defines a complete session flow.

Figure 18-7 *High-Level Explanation of Firewall Load Balancing Using PBR*

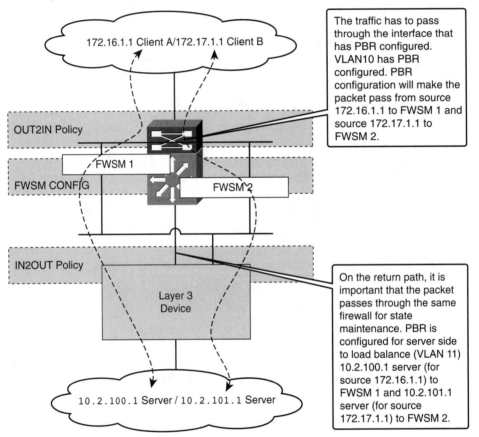

In the same way, packets from 172.17.1.1 client to 10.2.101.1 server will pass through FWSM2, using OUT2IN policy. The return path from 10.2.101.1 server to 172.17.1.1 client will be load balanced to FWSM2 using IN2OUT policy. This defines another complete session flow.

The configuration has three main functional blocks:

- **OUT2IN policy:** Defines load-balancing configuration at the outside of the FWSM
- **Firewall configuration:** Gives the details of the FWSM configuration
- **IN2OUT policy:** Defines the load-balancing configuration at the inside of the FWSM

OUT2IN Policy Configuration

The OUT2IN policy configuration references the outside security domain. The incoming VLAN for packets has the PBR configured as shown:

Step 1   Policy routing OUT2IN configuration.

```
route-map LB permit 10
 match ip address 1
 set ip next-hop 10.1.1.2
 ! This will be a virtual IP address of the FWSM, if redundancy is built
 ! in the load balancing design
route-map LB permit 20
 match ip address 2
 set ip next-hop 10.1.1.3
 ! This will be a virtual IP address of the FWSM, if redundancy is built

 ! in the load balancing design
```

Step 2   Configure access list to permit the source traffic that needs to be load balanced.

```
access-list 1 permit 172.16.1.1
access-list 2 permit 172.17.1.1
```

Step 3   Apply the policy to interface.

```
interface Vlan10
 ip address 10.1.1.1 255.255.255.0
 ip policy route-map LB
```

Firewall Configuration

This section covers the basic firewall configuration, which allows packets to pass through the FWSM. No special configuration is needed in the FWSM for configuring a load-balancing solution.

Step 1   MSFC configuration for FWSM. This covers the configuration of VLANs present in the FWSM:

```
firewall multiple-vlan-interfaces
firewall module 3 vlan-group 3
```

```
firewall module 4 vlan-group 3
firewall vlan-group 3  10,11
```

Make sure VLAN 10 and VLAN 11 are configured in the switch data base. VLAN 11 does not have a SVI interface on the switch.

Step 2   FWSM1 configuration.

The FWSM is in routed mode. Static translation is needed for the packets to access higher security domain from the lower security domain. This firewall configuration does not have redundancy. Out of the two flows tested, static translation is defined in FWSM1 configuration for only one destination directed from the load-balancing policy. Note the highlighted portion in the configuration for the defined static translation.

```
FWSM-A# show run
: Saved
:
FWSM Version 3.1(3)6
!
hostname FWSM-A
enable password 8Ry2YjIyt7RRXU24 encrypted
names
!
interface Vlan10
 nameif outside
 security-level 0
 ip address 10.1.1.2 255.255.255.0
!
interface Vlan11
 nameif inside
 security-level 100
 ip address 10.2.1.2 255.255.255.0
!
passwd 2KFQnbNIdI.2KYOU encrypted
ftp mode passive
access-list ANY extended permit ip any any
access-list 100 extended permit ip any any
pager lines 24
logging console debugging
logging monitor debugging
mtu outside 1500
mtu inside 1500
no failover
icmp permit any outside
icmp permit any inside
no asdm history enable
```

```
arp timeout 14400
nat (inside) 0 0.0.0.0 0.0.0.0
static (inside,outside) 10.2.100.1 10.2.100.1 netmask 255.255.255.255
access-group 100 in interface outside
access-group ANY out interface outside
access-group 100 in interface inside
access-group ANY out interface inside
route outside 0.0.0.0 0.0.0.0 10.1.1.1 1
route inside 10.2.100.0 255.255.255.0 10.2.1.1 1
timeout xlate 3:00:00
timeout conn 1:00:00 half-closed 0:10:00 udp 0:02:00 icmp 0:00:02
timeout sunrpc 0:10:00 h323 0:05:00 h225 1:00:00 mgcp 0:05:00
timeout mgcp-pat 0:05:00 sip 0:30:00 sip_media 0:02:00
timeout uauth 0:05:00 absolute
no snmp-server location
no snmp-server contact
snmp-server enable traps snmp authentication linkup linkdown coldstart
telnet timeout 5
ssh timeout 5
console timeout 0
!
class-map inspection_default
 match default-inspection-traffic
!
policy-map global_policy
 class inspection_default
  inspect dns maximum-length 512
  inspect ftp
  inspect h323 h225
  inspect h323 ras
  inspect netbios
  inspect rsh
  inspect skinny
  inspect smtp
  inspect sqlnet
  inspect sunrpc
  inspect tftp
  inspect sip
  inspect xdmcp
!
service-policy global_policy global
prompt hostname context
Cryptochecksum:e0d91ecd0a1f6fdde721353f7e78b007
: end
```

Step 3 FWSM2 configuration.

The FWSM is in routed mode. This firewall configuration does not have redundancy. Out of the two flows tested, static translation is defined in FWSM2 configuration for only one destination directed from the load-balancing policy. Note the highlighted portion in the configuration for the defined static translation.

```
FWSM-B# show run
: Saved
:
FWSM Version 3.1(3)6
!
hostname FWSM-B
enable password 8Ry2YjIyt7RRXU24 encrypted
names
!
interface Vlan10
 nameif outside
 security-level 0
 ip address 10.1.1.3 255.255.255.0
!
interface Vlan11
 nameif inside
 security-level 100
 ip address 10.2.1.3 255.255.255.0
!
passwd 2KFQnbNIdI.2KYOU encrypted
ftp mode passive
access-list 100 extended permit ip any any
access-list ANY extended permit ip any any
pager lines 24
mtu outside 1500
mtu inside 1500
no failover
icmp permit any outside
icmp permit any inside
no asdm history enable
arp timeout 14400
nat (inside) 0 0.0.0.0 0.0.0.0
static (inside,outside) 10.2.101.1 10.2.101.1 netmask 255.255.255.255
access-group ANY in interface outside
access-group ANY out interface outside
access-group ANY in interface inside
access-group ANY out interface inside
route outside 0.0.0.0 0.0.0.0 10.1.1.1 1
```

```
route inside 10.2.101.1 255.255.255.255 10.2.1.1 1
timeout xlate 3:00:00
timeout conn 1:00:00 half-closed 0:10:00 udp 0:02:00 icmp 0:00:02
timeout sunrpc 0:10:00 h323 0:05:00 h225 1:00:00 mgcp 0:05:00
timeout mgcp-pat 0:05:00 sip 0:30:00 sip_media 0:02:00
timeout uauth 0:05:00 absolute
no snmp-server location
no snmp-server contact
snmp-server enable traps snmp authentication linkup linkdown coldstart
telnet timeout 5
ssh timeout 5
console timeout 0
!
class-map inspection_default
 match default-inspection-traffic
!
prompt hostname context
Cryptochecksum:27f05c00bf7d45e025f370c75f3d961b
: end
```

IN2OUT Policy Configuration

IN2OUT policy is configured on the Layer 3 device in Figure 18-7. VLAN 11 is the Layer 3 VLAN for the inside interfaces on both the FWSMs. The FWSMs are two separate units and are not in failover mode. The load-balancing technology will decide on the firewall to which the packet has to be forwarded. It is therefore very important to synchronize the inbound and outbound load-balancing policies to maintain the state of a flow through the firewall.

Step 1   Policy routing IN2OUT configuration.

```
route-map LB permit 10
 match ip address 1
 set ip next-hop 10.2.1.2
 ! This will be a virtual IP address of the FWSM, if redundancy is
 ! built in the load balancing design
 !
route-map LB permit 20
 match ip address 2
 set ip next-hop 10.2.1.3
 ! This will be a virtual IP address of the FWSM, if redundancy is

 ! built in the load balancing design
```

The access list matches the source traffic to the policies defined for load balancing.

Step 2   Access list configuration.

This is to match the source traffic to the route-map for firewall load balancing:

```
access-list 1 permit 10.2.100.1
access-list 2 permit 10.2.101.1
```

Step 3   Apply PBR to the interface.

```
interface Vlan11
ip address 10.2.1.1 255.255.255.0
 ip policy route-map LB
```

The configuration example shows a three-step process. The load-balancing method chosen is with PBR. If the steps are followed in the same order, the components that include OUT2IN policy, firewall configuration, and IN2OUT policy will be the same for any load-balancer product, such as CSM or ACE. The changes will be in the command-line configurations for OUT2IN or IN2OUT policy. The configuration steps might include subpolicies for OUT2IN and IN2OUT policies based on the load-balancer product line chosen. The subpolicies will define a policy for a given direction of traffic passing through the load balancer.

Summary

In firewall load balancing, it is very important to understand the requirements for load balancing. The firewall and load balancer are the two important components of the firewall load-balancing solution. After reading this chapter, you must be able to compare the various solutions for firewall load balancing. It is also important to estimate and forecast the throughput and traffic profiling, prior to designing a firewall load-balancing solution.

CHAPTER 19

IP Version 6

IP version 6 (IPv6) has come to prominence because of the extensive use of the Internet. The current address, IPv4, is predominantly deployed and extensively used throughout the world. When IPv4 was designed, Internet usage and growth to this extent was not predicted. The main feature of IPv6 that is driving adoption today is the larger address space: addresses in IPv6 are 128 bits long compared to 32 bits in IPv4.

The 32 bits in IPv4 have 2^{32}(4,294,967,296) unique IP addresses. In IPv6, the address space has 128 bits. The total number of unique IP addresses for IPv6 is 2^{128}; that is, 340,282,366,920,938,463,463,374,607,431,770,000,000 addresses.

For a device to be IPv6 compatible, the machine needs to have an IPv6 stack. Nowadays, end host machines are manufactured with dual stacks, one for IPv4 and the other for IPv6.

Cisco routers can run IPv6. When devices have compatibility for IPv6, it is important for the firewalls to also have compatibility. The Firewall Services Module (FWSM) has a dual stack and can be configured with IPv6 and IPv4 addresses. The use of a private IP address for IPv4 has helped in conservation of IP address space. However, there is an inherent difficulty of applications going through Network Address Translation (NAT) for IPv4. IPv6 is very promising and is the future of networking. The need and demand for IPv6 in the world of networks can happen anytime. Consumers using the Internet via mobile phones will need more IP address space. A short-term solution of NAT and Dynamic Host Control Protocol (DHCP) leasing can be considered as workarounds. As new products in the consumer market increase, so will the need of IP address space, for which there will be a slow migration and adoption of IPv6.

Understanding IPv6 Packet Header

IPv6 consists of 128-bit addresses. There are 8 octets of 16 bits each, separated by ":". In IPv4, 4 octets are separated by ".". IPv6 specifications are defined in RFC 2460. Figure 19-1 illustrates the header of an IPv6 packet.

Figure 19-1 *IPv6 Packet*

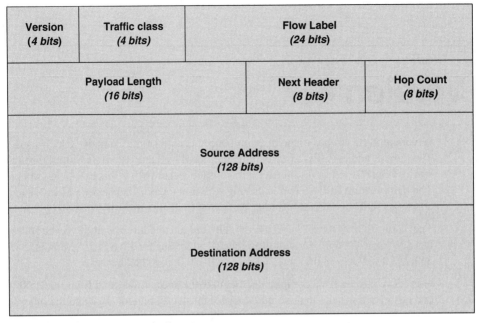

Table 19-1 *IPv6 Header Field Description*

Header Fields	Description
Version	4-bit Internet Protocol version number = 6.
Traffic Class	8-bit traffic class field. This is similar to IPv4 TOS bit.
Flow Label	A 24-bit field is used to identify the flow of IPv6 packets. The flow in IPv4 is identified by the IP source address and IP destination address. In IPv6, the flow can be identified using the Flow Label field. The routers can identify the flow without looking deeper into the packet.
Payload	A 16-bit field gives the payload of the entire packet (except that headers and extension are not considered part of the packet payload).
Next Header	An 8-bit field identifies the header of the IP protocol. This field can be related to the protocol number for IPv4.
Hop Count	The hop count gives the number of hops a packet has traveled. The packet decrements for every hop. This is similar to time-to-live (TTL) in IPv4.
Source Address	The source address is a 128-bit identifier of the source address of the packet.
Destination Address	The destination address is a 128-bit identifier of the destination address of the packet.

Examining IPv6 Address Types

IPv6 addressing architecture is defined in RFC 3513. The three types of IPv6 addresses in the RFC are the following:

- **Unicast:** Communication is between a single source and a single receiver.
- **Multicast:** Communication is between a single source and multiple receivers.
- **Anycast:** Communication is between a single source and a group of receivers, where the destined traffic is forwarded to the nearest receiver (in the group) from the source.

The predefined scopes contained in one single IPv6 address are as follows:

- **Link-local scope:** The host attached is in a single Layer 2 domain. The address has a reference to the local domain.
- **Unique-local scope:** This addressing is used for the host to communicate to other hosts within an administrative domain. This can be referred to as a private IP address for IPv4.
- **Global scope:** The address is routable via the Internet and has a global significance.

The global unicast address structure has three components:

- **Global Routing prefix:** Internet Assigned Numbers Authority (IANA) assigns address space to the service provider. The service provider can assign this address space to its respective customers as subsets.
- **Subnet ID:** The subnet ID identifies the structure of the organization's network.
- **Interface ID:** This is the lower 64 bits that identify interface nodes.

The 128-bit IPv6 address is represented in hexadecimal format. For example: x:x:x:x:x:x:x:x, where x is a 16-bit hexadecimal field and the last 64 bits are used for the interface ID.

The IPv6 address, 2001:100:4:1:0:0:10:1/64, can be written as 2001:100:4:1::10:1/64.

0:0:0:0:0:0:0:0 can be compressed as ::. By this all zeros can be eliminated.

This gives a quick snapshot of IPv6 addressing. For more detailed insights for IPv6, refer to RFC 3513.

Neighbor Discovery Protocol

IPv6 Neighbor Discovery Protocol (NDP) provides functionality features for router and host operations in the same link. The NDP process in IPv6 functions similar to the following protocols used in IPv4:

- IP Maximum Transmission Unit Discovery (IPMTUD)
- Internet Control Message Protocol (ICMP) Router Discovery (RFC 1256)

- Address Resolution Protocol (ARP) and Proxy ARP
- ICMP redirect
- Address resolution and next hop detection

The following messages are used in NDP:

- **Router Solicitation (RS):** A multicast message sent by a node to all the routers, to send a Router Advertisement immediately, instead of waiting for the next scheduled advertisement.

- **Router Advertisement (RA):** Sent periodically or in response to a solicitation. Routers advertise their presence, as well as provide information necessary for a node's identity.

- **Neighbor Solicitation (NS):** Enables a node to determine the link layer address of a neighbor. This also helps the node to detect duplicate IP addresses that exist on the link.

- **Neighbor Advertisement (NA):** Sent in response to NS, or an unsolicited response is sent if a node's link layer address changes. The information sent in the Neighbor Advertisement is the link layer address of the node.

- **Redirect:** Sent by routers to redirect traffic to a better first hop node on the link.

- **Inverse Neighbor Discovery:** Neighbor Discovery Protocol for IPv6 takes care of the same functionality as ARP does for IPv4. The same reasoning of Inverse ARP in IPv4 resulted in Inverse Neighbor Discovery Protocol for IPv6. The details of this extension are specified in RFC 3122. The two messages defined for Inverse neighbor discovery are the following:

  — Inverse neighbor solicitation (INS)

  — Inverse neighbor advertisement (INA)

NDP is also used to detect duplicate IPv6 addresses. NDP uses ICMPv6 for this purpose.

For more information on NDP, refer to the book, *Deploying IPv6 Networks* (ISBN number 1-58705-210-5).

IPv6 in FWSM

FWSM has dual stacks. It can be configured for IPv4 and IPv6 simultaneously on the same interface. Some of the limitations for the support of IPv6 while configuring FWSM are as follows:

- Anycast addresses are not supported on FWSM.
- Shared VLAN support is not available in IPv6.

The FWSM configured with IPv6 has lesser throughput compared to IPv4 because the IPv6 features and packet forwarding are software based in the FWSM.

Configuring Multiple Features of IPv6 in FWSM

This section covers various features of IPv6 on the FWSM.

Interface Configuration

You can configure IPv6 on an interface in multiple ways:

- **Autoconfig address:** By issuing this command, auto configuration is enabled on the interface for the IPv6 address. It receives the IPv6 address from RA messages. A link local address based on the extended unique identifier (EUI) interface ID is automatically generated by issuing the following command.

  For example:

  ```
  FWSMB(config-if)# ipv6 address autoconfig
  ```

  After issuing this command, enter a **show ipv6 interface** command to verify the interface configured:

  ```
  FWSM-B(config-if)# show ipv6 interface
  outside is up, line protocol is up
    IPv6 is enabled, link-local address is fe80::208:7cff:feed:2700
    No global unicast address is configured
    Joined group address(es):
      ff02::1
      ff02::2
      ff02::1:ffed:2700
    ICMP error messages limited to one every 100 milliseconds
    ICMP redirects are enabled
    ND DAD is enabled, number of DAD attempts: 1
    ND reachable time is 30000 milliseconds
    ND advertised reachable time is 0 milliseconds
    ND advertised retransmit interval is 1000 milliseconds
    ND router advertisements are sent every 200 seconds
    ND router advertisements live for 1800 seconds
    Hosts use stateless autoconfig for addresses.
  ```

- **User defined link-local address:** You can create a link local address based on the interface MAC address in the EUI format.

  The syntax is

  ```
  FWSM(config-if)# ipv6 address ipv6-address link-local
  ```

  For example:

  ```
  FWSM-B(config-if)# ipv6 address fe80::212:bbff:fe87:1 link-local
  ```

To verify the IPv6 address configuration, use the **show ipv6 interface** command:

```
FWSM-B(config-if)# show ipv6 interface
outside is up, line protocol is up
  IPv6 is enabled, link-local address is fe80::212:bbff:fe87:1
  No global unicast address is configured
  Joined group address(es):
    ff02::1
    ff02::2
    ff02::1:ff87:1
  ICMP error messages limited to one every 100 milliseconds
  ICMP redirects are enabled
  ND DAD is enabled, number of DAD attempts: 1
  ND reachable time is 30000 milliseconds
  ND advertised reachable time is 0 milliseconds
  ND advertised retransmit interval is 1000 milliseconds
  ND router advertisements are sent every 200 seconds
  ND router advertisements live for 1800 seconds
  Hosts use stateless autoconfig for addresses.
```

NOTE   For auto-configuration of the IPv6 address, configure the **ipv6 enable** command in the interface. When the complete IPv6 address is entered, the **ipv6 enable** command is not necessary. The IPv6 is enabled by default while configuring the interface address in the FWSM.

- Assign a site-local or global address to the interface:

```
FWSM(config-if)# ipv6 address ipv6-address [eui-64]
```

For example:

```
FWSM-A# show run interface vlan 10
!
interface Vlan10
 nameif outside
 security-level 0
 ip address 10.1.1.2 255.255.255.0
 ipv6 address 2001:500:10:1::2/64
 ipv6 nd suppress-ra
```

To verify the configuration:

```
FWSM-A# show ipv6 interface
outside is up, line protocol is up
  IPv6 is enabled, link-local address is fe80::211:bbff:fe87:dd80
  Global unicast address(es):
    2001:500:10:1::2, subnet is 2001:500:10:1::/64
  Joined group address(es):
    ff02::1
    ff02::2
    ff02::1:ff00:2
```

```
      ff02::1:ff87:dd80
    ICMP error messages limited to one every 100 milliseconds
    ICMP redirects are enabled
    ND DAD is enabled, number of DAD attempts: 1
    ND reachable time is 30000 milliseconds
    Hosts use stateless autoconfig for addresses.
  inside is up, line protocol is up
    IPv6 is enabled, link-local address is fe80::211:bbff:fe87:dd80
    Global unicast address(es):
      2001:400:10:1::2, subnet is 2001:400:10:1::/64
    Joined group address(es):
      ff02::1
      ff02::2
      ff02::1:ff00:2
      ff02::1:ff87:dd80
    ICMP error messages limited to one every 100 milliseconds
    ICMP redirects are enabled
    ND DAD is enabled, number of DAD attempts: 1
    ND reachable time is 30000 milliseconds
    Hosts use stateless autoconfig for addresses.
```

Router Advertisement

In Router Advertisement (RA), advertisements can be suppressed on an interface. By default, the RA messages are allowed on the interface.

The command syntax is

```
FWSM(config-if)# ipv6 nd suppress-ra
```

Duplicate Address Detection

The FWSM interface configured as IPv6 can detect duplicate IP addresses. The command syntax for this is as follows:

```
FWSM(config-if)# ipv6 nd dad attempts value
```

The range of this value is from 0–600. In the FWSM, the default value is 1.

Timer for Duplicate Address Detection

The timer for duplicate address detection on an IPv6-enabled interface in FWSM is 1000 milliseconds. This value can be changed using the following command:

```
FWSM(config-if)# ipv6 nd ns-interval value
```

Configuring Access Lists

The syntax for the access list is similar to IPv4:

```
FWSM(config)# ipv6 access-list id [line num] {permit | deny} protocol source
[src_port] destination [dst_port]
```

For ICMP traffic, the access list needs to have ICMP specified. The details of the fields used in IPv6 are as follows:

- **id:** The name of the access list. This is similar to the IPv4 access list. This field is referenced in the IP access group command.

- **line num:** When adding an entry to an access list, this field specifies the order in which the entry should appear.

- **permit | deny:** Determines whether the specified traffic is blocked or allowed to traverse.

- **icmp:** Indicates that the access list entry applies to ICMP traffic.

- **protocol:** Specifies the traffic being controlled by the access list entry. This can be the name (IP, TCP, or UDP) or number (1–254) of an IP protocol. Alternatively, you can specify a protocol object group using **object-group grp_id**.

- **source and destination:** Specifies the source or destination addresses of the traffic.

- **src_port and dst_port:** Specifies the source and destination port (or service) argument.

- **icmp_type:** Specifies the ICMP message type filtered by the access rule.

To apply the access list to an interface, **access-group** needs to be configured on an interface level (similar to the access-group in IPv4).

```
FWSM(config)# access-group access_list_name {in | out} interface if_name
```

Configuring Static Routes

FWSM supports only static routes to route traffic in IPv6. The command to configure a static route is

```
FWSM(config)# ipv6 route if_name destination next_hop_ipv6_addr [admin_distance]
```

To enable default IPv6 route, the command is

```
FWSM(config)# ipv6 route interface_name ::/0 next_hop_ipv6_addr
```

Configuring IPv6 Timers in FWSM

Table 19-2 describes the various timers that can be configured in IPv6 while configuring FWSM.

Table 19-2   *The Features and Syntax for IPv6 Support in FWSM*

Features	Description	Syntax
Neighbor solicitation message interval	This is to configure the time interval between IPv6 neighbor solicitation messages. The value argument ranges from 1000 to 3,600,000 milliseconds. The default value is 1000 milliseconds. This command is used when an interface is configured to send more than one duplicate address detection attempt.	**ipv6 nd ns-interval** *value*
Neighbor reachable timer	This timer helps in detecting unavailable IPv6 neighbors. The unavailability of a neighbor is learned via the RA messages. The range for this timer is from 0 to 3,600,000 milliseconds. The default is 0.	**ipv6 nd reachable-time** *value*
RA lifetime interval	Router lifetime value specifies how long the nodes on the local link should consider FWSM as the default router on the link. Values range from 0 to 9000 seconds. The default is 1800 seconds.	**ipv6 nd ra-lifetime** *seconds*
RA transmission interval	A time interval to transmit RA advertisements. Timer value ranges from 3 to 1800 seconds. The default value is 200 seconds.	**ipv6 nd ra-interval [msec]** *value*

Configuring IPv6 in FWSM

In Figure 19-2, the FWSM is configured for IPv4 and IPv6. The FWSM is configured in single context routed mode. The outside interface is VLAN 10 and the inside interface is VLAN 11.

In the policy feature card (PFC), IPv4 and IPv6 static routes are defined for networks at the inside security zone of the FWSM, pointing to VLAN 10 at the outside interface address of the FWSM. The static route for IPv4 will point to the IPv4 address and the static route for IPv6 will point to the IPv6 address.

From the Layer 3 device (see Figure 19-2) at the inside security zone, a default route will point to the FWSM inside interface at VLAN 11, which is the inside interface address of the FWSM.

In the FWSM, router advertisements are suppressed, and the IPv6 address is enabled for global routing.

Figure 19-2 *IPv6 Configuration in FWSM*

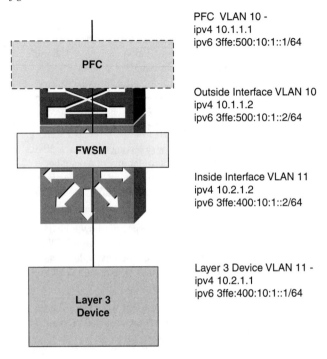

PFC VLAN 10 -
ipv4 10.1.1.1
ipv6 3ffe:500:10:1::1/64

Outside Interface VLAN 10
ipv4 10.1.1.2
ipv6 3ffe:500:10:1::2/64

Inside Interface VLAN 11
ipv4 10.2.1.2
ipv6 3ffe:400:10:1::2/64

Layer 3 Device VLAN 11 -
ipv4 10.2.1.1
ipv6 3ffe:400:10:1::1/64

Configuring PFC (Layer 3 Device) on the Outside Security Domain

Follow these steps to configure the PFC:

Step 1 Enable IPv6.

```
ipv6 unicast-routing
ipv6 cef
ipv6 multicast-routing
```

Step 2 Configure the interface that connects to the outside interface of the FWSM.

```
interface Vlan10
ip address 10.1.1.1 255.255.255.0
ipv6 address 3FFE:500:10:1::1/64
```

Step 3 Configure a static route for IPv6.

```
ipv6 route 3FFE:400::/32 3ffe:500:10:1::2/64
```

Note that the inside IPv6 address is 3FFE:400::/32 and the FWSM outside interface address is 3FFE:500:10:1::2.

Configuring FWSM

The FWSM has both IPv4 and IPv6 configured in the inside and outside security interfaces. Example 19-1 shows the FWSM configuration.

Example 19-1 *FWSM Configuration*

```
FWSM# show run
: Saved
:
FWSM Version 3.1(3)6
!
hostname FWSM
enable password 8Ry2YjIyt7RRXU24 encrypted
names
! configure the interface with IPv6 address and suppress RA message
interface Vlan10
 nameif outside
 security-level 0
 ip address 10.1.1.2 255.255.255.0
 ipv6 address 3ffe:500:10:1::2/64
 ipv6 nd suppress-ra
 ! configure the interface with IPv6 address and suppress RA message
interface Vlan11
 nameif inside
 security-level 100
 ip address 10.2.1.2 255.255.255.0
 ipv6 address 3ffe:400:10:1::2/64
 ipv6 nd suppress-ra
!
passwd 2KFQnbNIdI.2KYOU encrypted
ftp mode passive
access-list 100 extended permit ip any any
pager lines 24
mtu outside 1500
mtu inside 1500
! default route for ipv6 packets
ipv6 route outside ::/0 3ffe:500:10:1::1
! IPv6 access list permitting any IP traffic
ipv6 access-list OUTSIDE permit ip any any
! IPv6 access list permitting any IP traffic
ipv6 access-list INSIDE permit ip any any
no failover
icmp permit any outside
icmp permit any inside
no asdm history enable
arp timeout 14400
nat (inside) 0 0.0.0.0 0.0.0.0
access-group 100 in interface outside
access-group 100 out interface outside
! apply the access list to the outside interface
access-group OUTSIDE in interface outside
access-group OUTSIDE out interface outside
access-group 100 in interface inside
```

continues

Example 19-1 *FWSM Configuration (Continued)*

```
access-group 100 out interface inside
! apply the access list to the inside interface
access-group INSIDE in interface inside
access-group INSIDE out interface inside
timeout xlate 3:00:00
timeout conn 1:00:00 half-closed 0:10:00 udp 0:02:00 icmp 0:00:02
timeout sunrpc 0:10:00 h323 0:05:00 h225 1:00:00 mgcp 0:05:00
timeout mgcp-pat 0:05:00 sip 0:30:00 sip_media 0:02:00
timeout uauth 0:05:00 absolute
no snmp-server location
no snmp-server contact
telnet timeout 5
ssh timeout 5
console timeout 0
!
class-map inspection_default
 match default-inspection-traffic
class-map default
!
policy-map global_policy
 class inspection_default
  inspect dns maximum-length 512
  inspect ftp
  inspect h323 h225
  inspect h323 ras
  inspect netbios
  inspect rsh
  inspect skinny
  inspect smtp
  inspect sqlnet
  inspect sunrpc
  inspect tftp
  inspect sip
  inspect xdmcp
!
service-policy global_policy global
prompt hostname context
Cryptochecksum:c3ab955ce0510b8c52ddbde38fc4f2b8
: end
```

Configuring a Layer 3 Device on the Inside Security Domain

To configure a Layer 3 device, first configure the VLAN 11 interface at the first hop Layer 3 device at the inside security domain:

```
interface Vlan11
 ip address 10.2.1.1 255.255.255.0
 ipv6 address 3FFE:400:10:1::1/64
```

Next, configure the default route:

```
ipv6 route ::/0 3FFE:400:10:1::2
```

Verify the Functionality of FWSM

Example 19-2 shows **ping** from the inside to the outside security domain.

Example 19-2   *Ping from Inside to Outside Security Domain*

```
Layer3device# ping ipv6 3FFE:500:10:1::1
Type escape sequence to abort.
Sending 5, 100-byte ICMP Echos to 3FFE:500:10:1::1, timeout is 2 seconds:
!!!!!
Success rate is 100 percent (5/5), round-trip min/avg/max = 0/0/0 ms
```

The ping test passes through the FWSM and tests the connectivity from the inside to the outside security domain. Example 19-3 shows **ping** from the outside to the inside security domain.

Example 19-3   *Ping from Outside to Inside Security Domain*

```
6504-E-1# ping ipv6 3FFE:400:10:1::1
Type escape sequence to abort.
Sending 5, 100-byte ICMP Echos to 3FFE:400:10:1::1, timeout is 2 seconds:
!!!!!
Success rate is 100 percent (5/5), round-trip min/avg/max = 0/0/0 ms
```

The ping test passes through the FWSM and tests the connectivity from the outside to the inside security domain. Example 19-4 shows a snapshot of the **show capture** command enabled on the FWSM.

Example 19-4   *Snapshot of* **show capture** *Command Enabled on the FWSM*

```
FWSM# show capture test
10 packets captured
    1: 23:53:01.623426 802.1Q vlan#11 P0 3ffe:400:10:1::1 > 3ffe:500:10:1::1: icmp6:
       echo request
    2: 23:53:01.624006 802.1Q vlan#11 P0 3ffe:500:10:1::1 > 3ffe:400:10:1::1: icmp6:
       echo reply
    3: 23:53:01.624509 802.1Q vlan#11 P0 3ffe:400:10:1::1 > 3ffe:500:10:1::1: icmp6:
       echo request
    4: 23:53:01.624708 802.1Q vlan#11 P0 3ffe:500:10:1::1 > 3ffe:400:10:1::1: icmp6:
       echo reply
    5: 23:53:01.624998 802.1Q vlan#11 P0 3ffe:400:10:1::1 > 3ffe:500:10:1::1: icmp6:
       echo request
    6: 23:53:01.625181 802.1Q vlan#11 P0 3ffe:500:10:1::1 > 3ffe:400:10:1::1: icmp6:
       echo reply
    7: 23:53:01.625471 802.1Q vlan#11 P0 3ffe:400:10:1::1 > 3ffe:500:10:1::1: icmp6:
       echo request
    8: 23:53:01.625654 802.1Q vlan#11 P0 3ffe:500:10:1::1 > 3ffe:400:10:1::1: icmp6:
       echo reply
    9: 23:53:01.625928 802.1Q vlan#11 P0 3ffe:400:10:1::1 > 3ffe:500:10:1::1: icmp6:
       echo request
   10: 23:53:01.626112 802.1Q vlan#11 P0 3ffe:500:10:1::1 > 3ffe:400:10:1::1: icmp6:
       echo reply
10 packets shown
```

Working with the **show** Command for IPv6 in FWSM

To view the IPv6 routes, enter the **show ipv6 route** command as shown in Example 19-5.

Example 19-5 *Displaying IPv6 Routes*

```
FWSM# show ipv6 route
IPv6 Routing Table - 7 entries
Codes: C - Connected, L - Local, S - Static, R - RIP, B - BGP
       U - Per-user Static route
       I1 - ISIS L1, I2 - ISIS L2, IA - ISIS interarea
       O - OSPF intra, OI - OSPF inter, OE1 - OSPF ext 1, OE2 - OSPF ext 2
L    3ffe:400:10:1::2/128 [0/0]
      via ::, inside
C    3ffe:400:10:1::/64 [0/0]
      via ::, inside
L    3ffe:500:10:1::2/128 [0/0]
      via ::, outside
C    3ffe:500:10:1::/64 [0/0]
      via ::, outside
L    fe80::/10 [0/0]
      via ::, outside
      via ::, inside
L    ff00::/8 [0/0]
      via ::, outside
      via ::, inside
S    ::/0 [0/0]
      via 3ffe:500:10:1::1, outside
```

To view the IPv6 interfaces, enter the **show ipv6 interface** command as shown in
Example 19-6.

Example 19-6 *Displaying IPv6 Interfaces*

```
FWSM# show ipv6 interface
outside is up, line protocol is up
  IPv6 is enabled, link-local address is fe80::211:bbff:fe87:dd80
  Global unicast address(es):
    3ffe:500:10:1::2, subnet is 3ffe:500:10:1::/64
  Joined group address(es):
    ff02::1
    ff02::2
    ff02::1:ff00:2
    ff02::1:ff87:dd80
  ICMP error messages limited to one every 100 milliseconds
  ICMP redirects are enabled
  ND DAD is enabled, number of DAD attempts: 1
  ND reachable time is 30000 milliseconds
  Hosts use stateless autoconfig for addresses.
inside is up, line protocol is up
  IPv6 is enabled, link-local address is fe80::211:bbff:fe87:dd80
  Global unicast address(es):
    3ffe:400:10:1::2, subnet is 3ffe:400:10:1::/64
  Joined group address(es):
```

Example 19-6 *Displaying IPv6 Interfaces (Continued)*

```
      ff02::1
      ff02::2
      ff02::1:ff00:2
      ff02::1:ff87:dd80
 ICMP error messages limited to one every 100 milliseconds
 ICMP redirects are enabled
 ND DAD is enabled, number of DAD attempts: 1
 ND reachable time is 30000 milliseconds
 Hosts use stateless autoconfig for addresses.
```

To display IPv6 neighbors, enter the **show ipv6 neighbor** command as shown in Example 19-7.

Example 19-7 *Displaying IPv6 Neighbors*

```
FWSM# show ipv6 neighbor
IPv6 Address                              Age Link-layer Addr State Interface
fe80::213:5fff:fe1f:9040                    3 0013.5f1f.9040  STALE inside
fe80::213:5fff:fe1f:9000                    1 0013.5f1f.9000  STALE outside
3ffe:400:10:1::1                           13 0013.5f1f.9040  STALE inside
3ffe:500:10:1::1                           13 0013.5f1f.9000  STALE outside
```

To check the type of IPv6 traffic that passed through the FWSM, enter the **show ipv6 traffic** command, as shown in Example 19-8.

Example 19-8 *Displaying IPv6 Traffic*

```
FWSM# show ipv6 traffic
IPv6 statistics:
  Rcvd:  49 total, 49 local destination
         0 source-routed, 0 truncated
         0 format errors, 0 hop count exceeded
         0 bad header, 0 unknown option, 0 bad source
         0 unknown protocol, 0 not a router
         0 fragments, 0 total reassembled
         0 reassembly timeouts, 0 reassembly failures
         0 unirpf errors
  Sent:  22 generated, 0 forwarded
         0 fragmented into 0 fragments, 0 failed
         0 encapsulation failed, 0 no route, 0 too big
  Mcast: 37 received, 12 sent
ICMP statistics:
  Rcvd: 49 input, 0 checksum errors, 0 too short
        0 unknown info type, 0 unknown error type
        unreach: 0 routing, 0 admin, 0 neighbor, 0 address, 0 port
        parameter: 0 error, 0 header, 0 option
        0 hopcount expired, 0 reassembly timeout, 0 too big
        0 echo request, 0 echo reply
        0 group query, 0 group report, 0 group reduce
        0 router solicit, 13 router advert, 0 redirects
        8 neighbor solicit, 8 neighbor advert
```

continues

Example 19-8 *Displaying IPv6 Traffic (Continued)*

```
    Sent: 19 output, 0 rate-limited
            unreach: 0 routing, 0 admin, 0 neighbor, 0 address, 0 port
            parameter: 0 error, 0 header, 0 option
            0 hopcount expired, 0 reassembly timeout, 0 too big
            0 echo request, 0 echo reply
            0 group query, 0 group report, 0 group reduce
            0 router solicit, 0 router advert, 0 redirects
            10 neighbor solicit, 12 neighbor advert
UDP statistics:
  Rcvd: 0 input, 0 checksum errors, 0 length errors
            0 no port, 0 dropped
  Sent: 0 output
TCP statistics:
  Rcvd: 0 input, 0 checksum errors
  Sent: 0 output, 0 retransmitted
```

To display the IPv6 routers seen on the FWSM, enter the **show ipv6 routers** command as shown in Example 19-9.

Example 19-9 *Displaying IPv6 Routers*

```
FWSM# show ipv6 routers
Router fe80::213:5fff:fe1f:9000 on outside, last update 2 min
  Hops 64, Lifetime 1800 sec, AddrFlag=0, OtherFlag=0, MTU=1500
  Reachable time 0 msec, Retransmit time 0 msec
  Prefix 3ffe:500:10:1::/64 onlink autoconfig
    Valid lifetime 2592000, preferred lifetime 604800
Router fe80::213:5fff:fe1f:9040 on inside, last update 0 min
  Hops 64, Lifetime 1800 sec, AddrFlag=0, OtherFlag=0, MTU=1500
  Reachable time 0 msec, Retransmit time 0 msec
  Prefix 3ffe:400:10:1::/64 onlink autoconfig
    Valid lifetime 2592000, preferred lifetime 604800
```

To verify the IPv6 access list hit count, enter the **show ipv6 access-list** command as shown in Example 19-10.

Example 19-10   *Verifying IPv6 Access Lists*

```
FWSM-A# show ipv6 access-list
ipv6 access-list OUTSIDE; 1 elements
ipv6 access-list OUTSIDE line 1 permit ip any any (hitcnt=16) 0x0
ipv6 access-list INSIDE; 1 elements
ipv6 access-list INSIDE line 1 permit ip any any (hitcnt=16) 0x0
```

Summary

This chapter covers the basics of IPv6 and the FWSM support for IPv6. The main change brought by IPv6 is a much larger address space that allows greater flexibility in assigning addresses. The FWSM has dual stacks, which means IPv4 and IPv6 configurations can coexist. In FWSM, the IPv6 features and forwarding are software based. After reading this chapter, you will know how to configure IPv6 in FWSM.

CHAPTER 20

Preventing Network Attacks

Whether the motivation for a network attack is for monetary gain, revenge, or simply a challenge, it can potentially result in the same outcome if you are not prepared—Denial of Service (DoS). Having a security infrastructure that is well thought out will certainly minimize the impact of an attack.

The FWSM plays a critical role in an overall network security solution, but other devices also should be incorporated within the infrastructure; these include network intrusion prevention systems (IPS), host-based intrusion prevention systems (HIPS), VPN concentrators, screening routers, switches, and so on. The best defense is one that takes a holistic approach to security and leverages the full capabilities of all devices.

Protecting Networks

Take an in-depth look at the resources you are trying to protect, and consider, from the attackers' perspective, how they may try to circumvent the security devices you currently have in place.

To get a better idea of how to protect your network, consider these questions:

- What do I need to protect and where are those resources located?
- Would attacks predominately be from the outside, inside, or both?
- Besides a firewall, what other devices can I take advantage of?
- If I were going to attack this network, where would I start?
- If the resource(s) is unavailable, what impact will it have? Monetary, because of a loss of sales or customers? Bad press?
- Consider that it might not be a deliberate attack; it could simply be a high volume of traffic or flash crowd. Is the infrastructure able to support the load?
- Is what you are attempting to secure worth the effort?

When you are able to answer these questions, you will be able to establish a strategy for protecting your assets.

Network attacks could come in just about any form from just about any source or sources. The first step in minimizing attacks is to reduce the exposure of the resources in the first place. This is accomplished using very restrictive access control lists (ACL) on the Firewall Service Module (FWSM) that allow only traffic that is absolutely necessary. That means after you have completed testing/troubleshooting or opening a connection on a "temporary" basis, do not just leave it because it works. Take the steps necessary to do the job right. This will take more work in the long run but will be well worth it if an attack is avoided.

Many attackers spend a great deal of time and energy in determining how to circumvent security mechanisms and have developed some very creative solutions. There are some brilliant minds on the "dark side," so do not underestimate their capabilities.

TIP   The best way to defend against hackers is to think like one. Hackers try many new ways to break in to a network. Thus, it is imperative to keep securing your network using many approaches and tools.

If you are unfortunate enough to find yourself the recipient of an attack or perceived attack, start gathering information! Use syslogs, Netflow, sniffer traces, and similar tools to determine the following:

- What is being attacked and what is the IP address and port number?
- Is this attack targeted at a specific service or application?
- What are the source address(es) and port numbers of the attacker(s), and from what interface is the attack originating?
- Filter out the noise from the real threat. Many times attackers will try to hide their real intentions with noise, potentially targeting DoS attacks at different resources to obfuscate an attack on the real target device. If it is obvious that an attack is directed to a few services, you might be overlooking the real threat!
- You might not be able to stop them all, so keep your résumé up to date!

Finally, if you are not familiar with how to use your network monitoring and analysis tools, now is not the time to start. Refer to the last bullet item.

When considering a strategy for protecting your network, change your viewpoint from protector to attacker. It also helps to have other trusted security professionals review your security architecture and perform penetration testing. Sometimes, a different set of eyes may reveal obvious and not so obvious deficiencies. Be sure to have a thorough understanding of the tools needed to troubleshoot attacks, and have a plan in place as to what steps you will take to thwart the attack. There is absolutely no substitute for practice and preparation.

Shunning Attackers

After you have determined the source of the attack and that it is truly the attacker and not an attacker spoofing a legitimate source, the **shun** command is a handy option that will block any current or future connections based on the source IP address or the source IP address and port to the destination IP address and port number.

Use caution when implementing the **shun** command, because you may cause a DoS to valid traffic.

In multiple-context mode, the **shun** command can be configured in the admin context or in the specific context that is affected.

Figure 20-1 illustrates an attacker on the outside attacking a server on the services network.

Figure 20-1 *Shunning*

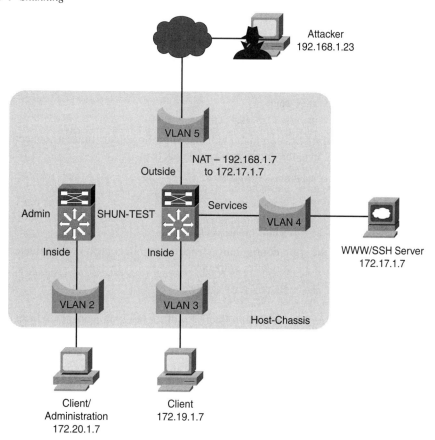

In this example, it has been determined that an attack is coming from a device on the outside with an IP address of 192.168.1.23 to a web server on the services interface. From the admin context, the following command would be issued to deny traffic from 192.168.1.23 (any port) to the translated destination address of 192.168.1.7 (172.17.1.7) on port 80 (www) associated with the virtual local-area network (VLAN) 5 interface.

```
FWSM/admin# shun 192.168.1.23 192.168.1.7 0 80 vlan 5
```

Notice also that the **shun** command can be issued without being in configuration mode.

This same function can also be accomplished by issuing the **shun** command from the affected context (SHUN-TEST).

When the **shun** command has been added, the FWSM generates a log message (401002) and denies additional connections matching the previous **shun** command.

```
FWSM/SHUN-TEST
%FWSM-4-401002: Shun added: 192.168.1.23 192.168.1.7 0 80
%FWSM-4-401004: Shunned packet: 192.168.1.23 ==> 192.168.1.7 on interface Outside
```

To view the information collected from issuing the **shun** option, use the following command: **show shun** and **show shun statistics**.

The **show shun** command shows the currently configured shuns.

```
FWSM/SHUN-TEST# show shun

shun (Outside) 192.168.1.23 192.168.1.7 0 80 0
```

The **show shun statistics** command will also show how many times a connection has been shunned and how long the command has been active:

```
FWSM/SHUN-TEST# show shun statistics
NP Identity Ifc=OFF, cnt=0
Inside=OFF, cnt=0
Services=OFF, cnt=0
Outside=ON, cnt=20
Shun 192.168.1.23 cnt=1367, time=(0:12:55)
```

You can remove the **shun** configuration from the admin context or the affected context by issuing the following commands, respectively:

```
FWSM/admin# no shun 192.168.1.23 vlan 5
FWSM/SHUN-TEST# no shun 192.168.1.23
```

The use of shunning can be a very effective tool for mitigating an attack from a single or a limited number of sources. As the number of attack devices grows to hundreds, thousands, or more, as in a Distributed Denial of Service (DDoS) attack, this is not an effective method. One significant feature of shunning is the ability to apply a shun from the admin context, which allows you to mitigate attacks to multiple contexts from a single management device. Also, use extreme caution that you do not affect legitimate traffic flows.

Spoofing

Spoofing occurs when an attacker modifies the source IP address in the IP packet to match someone else's. Many devices that perform a routing function "traditionally" look at the destination address and not the source address of the traffic. This can lead to a situation where someone connected to one interface of the FWSM can send traffic to a device on another interface and potentially impersonate a legitimate source, as shown in Figure 20-2.

Figure 20-2 *Spoofing*

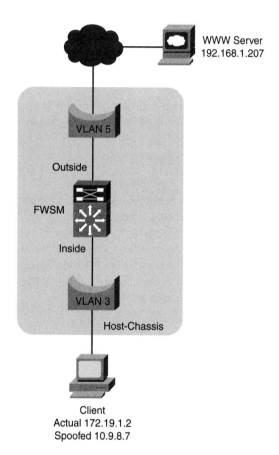

This example shows how a client can masquerade as another client. Although a connection can never be established, because the FWSM does not have a route to the source address, illegitimate traffic may be allowed to traverse the FWSM and wreak havoc on other networks.

This problem can be remedied very easily by verifying that the source of the IP traffic is truly coming from the appropriate interface. This works in routed mode only. When traffic enters an interface, the use of the **ip verify reverse-path** command will check the local routing table to determine whether a route to the source of the traffic exists. If no route exists, traffic is dropped. If the traffic entering the FWSM is part of an established session, there is no need to perform a Reverse Path Forwarding (RPF) check.

In this example, **ip verify reverse-path** is configured using the following command in configuration mode to verify traffic entering the inside interface:

```
FWSM(config)# ip verify reverse-path interface Inside
```

When the same spoofing attack is attempted and **ip verify reverse-path** has been configured, the assault has been denied, as shown by the log message generated by the FWSM:

```
%FWSM-1-106021: Deny tcp reverse path check from 10.9.8.7 to 192.168.1.207 on
    interface Inside
```

To view the statistical information collected by the FWSM that shows, by interface, the number of packets dropped because of an RPF check, use the **show ip verify statistics** command as demonstrated here:

```
FWSM# show ip verify statistics
interface Inside: 487 unicast rpf drops
interface Outside: 0 unicast rpf drops
```

Spoofing is a common method used by hackers to circumvent security mechanisms by masquerading as a legitimate device. You might be thinking, "Whats the big deal? It's not like they can establish a session." Although a session cannot be established there have been atomic attacks, which are contained within a single packet—for example, "SQL Slammer." It may require only one packet to traverse the FWSM illegitimately to cause a major disaster. Leveraging all the security mechanisms that you have at your disposal will significantly reduce a security compromise or DoS.

Understanding Connection Limits and Timeouts

The FWSM maintains information about all connections attempting to be established and all established sessions. When a client tries to make a TCP or UDP connection to a server through the FWSM, the FWSM tracks the state of the session.

TCP session establishment requires that the client send an initial packet to the server with the Synchronize Sequence Number (SYN) flag set in the IP header and an Initial Sequence Number (ISN). The server responds with the SYN and acknowledgment (ACK) flags set (SYN-ACK), the clients ISN incremented by 1 as the acknowledgment number, and the server also adds its own ISN. Finally, the client responds to the server with the server's ISN incremented by 1 as the acknowledgment number, the previous sequence number, and with the ACK flag set in the TCP header, consequently completing the three-way handshake. Anything short of the three-way handshake completion is called an embryonic connection.

UDP is a connectionless protocol, meaning there are no sequence numbers to acknowledge; as a result, there isn't a three-way handshake. Although state information is not built in to the protocol, the FWSM will track the source and destination IP addresses, source and destination port numbers, and so on, to create state information for connection tracking.

Connection limits and timeouts are used as follows:

- Connection limits specify the total number of sessions or connections that can be established.

- Timeouts specify the amount of time the FWSM will consider a connection active. When the timer expires, the connection will be dropped.

Configuring Connection Limits

Controlling the number of connections allowed to a particular host or service can be configured by using either static NAT or through the use of the modular policy framework configuration.

As described in Chapter 11, "Modular Policy," modular policy framework is a method used to classify traffic and perform actions based on that specific traffic. In this section, the modular policy framework will be used to control connection limits.

Static NAT has the capability to control the maximum number of TCP and User Data Protocol (UDP) connections and the number of TCP embryonic connections per host. Additionally, sequence randomization is supported.

To configure a NAT connection limit to allow only 2000 total TCP connections, 200 embryonic connections, and 50 UDP connections, use the following command:

```
static (Services,Outside) 192.168.1.7 172.17.1.7 netmask 255.255.255.255 tcp 2000
    200 udp 50
```

When the maximum number of TCP connections is exceeded, the FWSM generates the following log message:

```
%FWSM-3-201002: Too many tcp connections on xlate 192.168.1.7! 2000/2000
```

The alternative to using a static NAT statement is to use a policy map. The following example uses Figure 20-1. In this case, Secure Shell (SSH) traffic from the outside to the translated address of 192.168.1.7 will allow only 30 connections and timeout idle connections after 5 minutes.

To configure the FWSM to provide access as previously described, perform the following steps:

Step 1   Create an access list that defines the traffic you want to control:

```
access-list Services-ACL extended permit tcp any host 192.168.1.7 eq ssh
```

Step 2   Add a class map that references the newly created access list:

```
class-map Services-Class
 match access-list Services-ACL
```

Step 3   Apply the class map to a policy map:

In this particular example, the policy map used is the default **global_policy**. The maximum number of connections is configured for 30 with a 5-minute idle timeout:

```
policy-map global_policy
 class Services-Class
  set connection conn-max 30
  set connection timeout tcp 0:05:00 reset
```

Just as in the previous example, when the maximum number of TCP connections is exceeded, the FWSM generates the following log message:

```
%FWSM-3-201002: Too many tcp connections on xlate 192.168.1.7! 30/30
```

Limiting the number of connections allowed to a host will minimize the risk of a DoS attack on that device. You have the capability to control the number of connections using NAT and the **static** command, or by using the modular policy framework.

Configuring Timeouts

Two mechanisms control connection limits and timeouts: global configuration parameters and modular policy framework. Modular policy framework discussed in the previous section provides a very granular approach to how connection limits and timeouts are controlled. The other option is to use global timeout parameters. These are specific to a particular protocol and can be configured using the **timeout** command in configuration mode.

The following idle time parameters are configured using the **timeout** command:

- **conn:** Sets the idle timeout when the TCP connection will be closed.
- **h225:** Configures the idle timeout when the H.255 signaling connection will be closed.
- **h323:** Sets the idle timeout when the H.323 control connection will be closed.
- **half-closed:** Sets the idle timeout when the TCP half-closed connection will be freed.
- **icmp:** Configures the idle timeout for ICMP connections.
- **mgcp:** Sets the idle timeout when an MGCP media connection will be closed.
- **mgcp-pat:** Configures the time when the MGCP PAT translation will be removed.
- **sip:** Sets the idle timeout when the SIP control connection will be closed.

- **sip-disconnect:** Configures the idle timeout for when a SIP control connection is to be deleted.

- **sip-invite:** Sets the idle timeout when pinholes for provisional responses will be closed.

- **sip_media:** Configures the idle timeout when a SIP media connection will be closed.

- **sunrpc:** Configures the idle timeout for a SUN RPC slot to be deleted.

- **uauth:** Sets the timeout for which authentication cache information is maintained.

- **udp:** Configures the time for which general UDP connections will be closed.

- **xlate:** Sets the idle timeout when dynamic addresses are returned to pool.

If the timeout parameters are too aggressive, this will generally cause problems for TCP-based applications because the connection will be dropped without notification—for example, if the TCP timeout is configured for the minimum value of 5 minutes using the following command in configuration mode:

```
timeout conn 0:05:00
```

Using the **show conn** command to display the status of current connections (only pertinent information is shown), the idle time shows that the connection has been idle for 4 minutes and 17 seconds:

```
FWSM# show conn
TCP out 192.168.1.23:2378 in 172.17.1.7:22 idle 0:04:17 Bytes 11852 FLAGS - UBOI
```

In 43 more seconds the FWSM will drop the connection without sending a reset to either device and log the following message:

```
%FWSM-6-302014: Teardown TCP connection 145673076012355558 for
Outside:192.168.1.23/2378 to Services:192.168.1.7/22 duration 0:07:36 bytes 11852
Conn-timeout
```

The application will no longer be available because the FWSM will not allow the connection to be established without the initial SYN packet. Keep this in mind when you troubleshoot applications across the FWSM.

The timeout configuration is applied globally when the **timeout** command is used. For more granular control of timeout parameters, use the modular policy framework. By default, specific values are applied to individual parameters. The default values may cause long-lasting TCP connections to time out and the applications to fail. Use caution when making changes to these parameters.

Summary

Preventing network attacks should not be a function of a single device such as a firewall, but a combination of components working together to provide a holistic approach to network security. As you consider how to defend your valuable resources, approach this problem from the attacker's viewpoint as well. Having a trusted security professional review your security policy, perform penetration testing, and examine device configuration is also very beneficial. Several tools are available on the FWSM to thwart attacks, such as shunning, connection limits, timeouts, and so on. Having a good understanding of IP protocols, types of network attacks, the capabilities of your security devices, and how to use management and monitoring tools will help you immensely in maintaining a secure infrastructure.

References

RFC 792—Internet Control Message Protocol (ICMP)

RFC 2543—Session Initiation Protocol (SIP)

RFC 2637—Point-to-Point Tunneling Protocol (PPTP)

RFC 3435—Media Gateway Control Protocol (MGCP)

ITU-T International Telecommunications Union—H.323

CHAPTER 21

Troubleshooting the FWSM

This chapter introduces the logic of troubleshooting the FWSM. You need a basic knowledge of the network and security components to troubleshoot the FWSM. You will learn about the tools and commands needed for troubleshooting.

Understanding Troubleshooting Logic

Follow these steps to understand the basic troubleshooting logic:

Step 1 Understand the problem.

Step 2 Learn the symptoms and gather information.

Step 3 Understand the impact of the problem (technical and business impact).

Step 4 For the initial troubleshooting, identify areas where you need to focus. For example, narrow down the area where further analysis is required.

Step 5 If the root cause of the problem is identified

— Verify whether a solution exists for the problem.

— If there is no solution for the root cause, verify whether a workaround exists that will mitigate the root cause.

Step 6 Whether a solution for the root cause is implemented or mitigation methods are implemented, verify through a test procedure whether the problem is seen again.

Assessing Issues Logically

It is important for the troubleshooter to understand the issue and picture the logical design where the FWSM is a part.

Follow these steps to identify and understand the problem:

Step 1 Define the problem: It is very important to get the definition from the technical side and user impact.

(a) Define the problem.

(b) Identify one stream with source and destination.

(c) Verify whether all the packets are flowing through the FWSM, whether any one particular flow is impacted, or whether a few applications are impacted.

(d) Understand the security segregation for the flow (note whether the direction of the flow is from a lower to a higher security zone or from a higher to a lower security zone).

(e) Verify whether the FWSM has Network Address Translation (NAT) configured for the flow. Check the mode of the FWSM (routed or transparent mode/single or multiple context).

Step 2 Draw the logical design: It is important to trace the flow of IP packets having issues with the logical design available.

(a) Plot the source and destination of the stream identified in the diagram (this will depend on steps 1b and 1c).

(b) Verify whether all or a particular traffic is impacted.

(c) Check whether FWSM and the switch are communicating to each other before taking a deep dive into troubleshooting.

— Verify whether the ping from the inside next hop interface to the FWSM inside interface is successful.

— Verify whether the ping from the inside next hop interface to the outside next hop interface is successful. Repeat the same steps from the outside next hop interface or any of the demilitarized zone (DMZ) interfaces.

(d) Capture all your command outputs and configurations.

(e) Make sure you are able to ping the source and destination from the FWSM.

Step 3   Do a quick review of the configuration: It is important to review the configuration based on standards for configuring the sample design.

(a) Using the capture in Step 2d, review the configuration based on standards.

Topics to review are based on the flow of traffic from different security zones.

Verify whether

— NAT is configured (if applicable).

— Static translation is configured (if applicable).

— Access list is configured and the traffic hit is seen in the access list.

— The routing in the FWSM points to the correct interface (this can be verified in Step 2c).

— Verify whether other standard configurations, such as interface configuration, NAT, access-list configuration, routing statements, and other configurations, such as auth-proxy and authentication, authorization, and accounting (AAA), are configured properly.

(b) Based on capture details, if the root cause is identified:

— Work on the solution plan.

— If the solution plan is not available, work on the mitigation plan and possible options.

Step 4   Apply the planned change and verify whether the problem is fixed. After verification, it is important to conduct other standard tests to confirm the solution or workaround, and also verify whether it has problems on other traffic patterns passing through the firewall.

Troubleshooting in general is an art gained from experience. You need a good technical understanding and problem-solving skills. The following section gives a logical view to resolving problems with the FWSM and its flow.

Connectivity Test of a Flow at the FWSM

Follow the next steps to troubleshoot the basic connectivity to the FWSM:

Step 1   Make sure the ping is successful from the inside next hop of the FWSM to the inside interface, and follow the same from other security zones.

Step 2   Make sure from the FWSM that you are able to ping all the next hop addresses of the physical interfaces on the FWSM and of the static routes.

Step 3   Based on the security policy, ping from the next hop of the inside interface to the next hop of the outside interface in the FWSM. This will depend on the security policy used.

NOTE   It is common for Internet Control Message Protocol (ICMP) not to be allowed through the FWSM. In this case, you can make a source and destination specific access list to allow ICMP to pass through the FWSM. After the testing, this access list should be removed.

Troubleshooting Flow Issues

It is good practice to ensure that the connectivity check is done before troubleshooting the flow issues to have a general baseline to work. Figure 21-1 shows a logical flow chart on how to troubleshoot the FWSM.

Figure 21-1 *Logical Flowchart to Troubleshoot the FWSM*

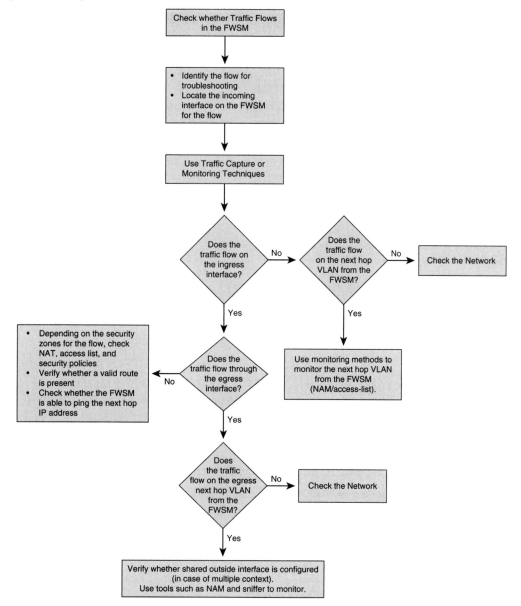

Figure 21-2 shows an example of a sniffer capture that can be analyzed for flow or TCP timeout issues.

Figure 21-2 *Sniffer Capture for a Packet Flow*

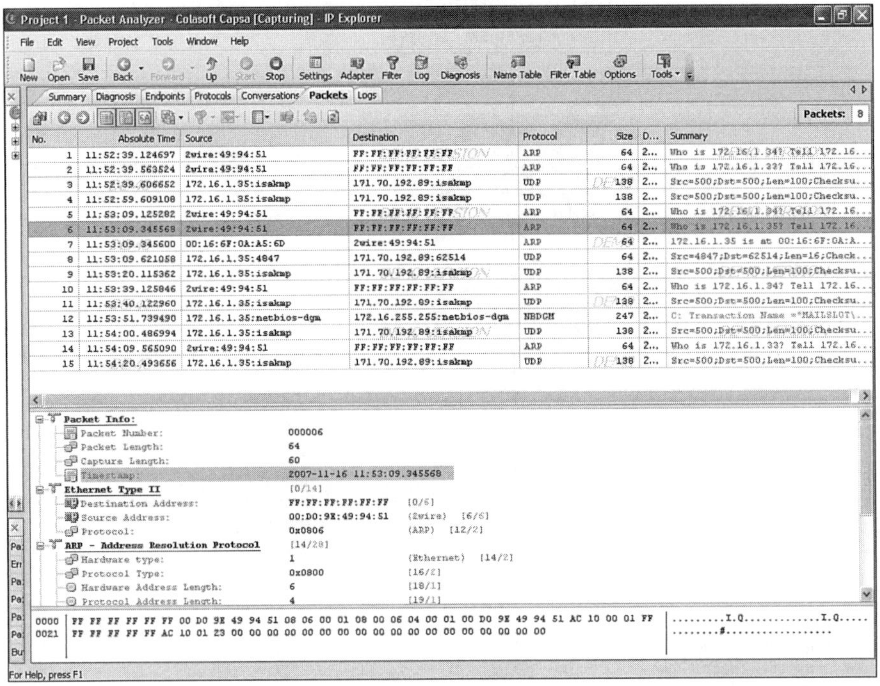

If you see no problems in the flow, the best way to troubleshoot TCP timeout issues is using sniffers at the source, destination, entry, and exit of the FWSM. A network analysis module (NAM) can be used on the entry and exit of the FWSM to monitor the packet flow. From the logs, verify the TCP timeouts in the FWSM. Retransmission and timeout for TCP sessions need to be monitored.

The following are some of the features that will help in troubleshooting a flow:

- Enable **logging** on the FWSM, in case traffic is not received.

- Do a **debug** command with the source and destination defined in an access list.

- Timestamps are disabled by default. To enable timestamps:

  ```
  fwsm(config)# logging timestamp
  ```

- Device IDs can be customized as hostname, ip address, interface name, context name, or custom string up to 16 characters.

  ```
  fwsm(config)# logging device-id {context-name | hostname | ipaddress
  interface_name | string text}
  ```

- Log on to syslog server(s) and capture relevant logging data.

- Review your logs frequently.

FAQs for Troubleshooting

When you are troubleshooting, chances are you will have questions. This section includes many common questions.

How Do You Verify Whether the Traffic Is Forwarded to a Particular Interface in the FWSM?

To verify whether the traffic is forwarded to a particular interface in the FWSM, use the **show access-list** command, as shown in Example 21-1.

Example 21-1 **show access-list** *Output Verifies Traffic Forwarding Information*

```
FWSM# show access-list
access-list mode auto-commit
access-list cached ACL log flows: total 0, denied 0 (deny-flow-max 4096)
          alert-interval 300
access-list 100; 1 elements
access-list 100 line 1 extended permit ip any any (hitcnt=5490768) 0xff4a2cd3
access-list 101; 1 elements
access-list 101 line 1 extended permit ip any any (hitcnt=2745364) 0xc222f093
access-list 102; 1 elements
access-list 102 line 1 extended permit ip any any (hitcnt=40) 0x22b2361f
access-list 106; 1 elements
access-list 106 line 1 extended permit ip any any (hitcnt=2745414) 0x3d27e738
access-list IPONLY; 2 elements
access-list IPONLY line 1 standard permit host 10.100.1.1 (hitcnt=0) 0x0
access-list IPONLY line 2 standard permit host 10.101.1.1 (hitcnt=0) 0x0
```

Notice the hit count for the access list. If the packet hit count is not increasing, verify the access list entry or use the **capture** command to note whether the packet is seen in the FWSM.

The **capture** command is very useful for troubleshooting connectivity related issues. Using the **capture** command, the FWSM is capable of tracking all IP traffic that flows across it. This command can be used to view the IP traffic that is destined to the FWSM, including all the management traffic.

Example 21-2 shows capture of traffic from source **any** to destination **any** on the inside interface. The name given to this capture sequence is 'captureA'.

Example 21-2 *To Configure and Display a Traffic Capture Command*

```
FWSM(config)# access-list 199 permit ip any any
FWSM(config)# capture captureA access-list 199 interface inside
FWSM# show capture captureA
3 packets captured
1: 19:28:04.3720029694 802.1Q vlan#91 P6 10.101.1.1 > 224.0.0.5:  ip-proto-89,
  length 56
2: 19:28:09.3720033854 802.1Q vlan#91 P6 10.101.1.1.520 > 224.0.0.9.520:  udp 24
```

continues

Example 21-2 *To Configure and Display a Traffic Capture Command (Continued)*

```
    3: 19:28:14.3720039694 802.1Q vlan#91 P6 10.101.1.1 > 224.0.0.5:  ip-proto-89,
       length 56
    3 packets shown
FWSM# show capture captureA
10 packets captured
    1: 19:28:04.3720029694 802.1Q vlan#91 P6 10.101.1.1 > 224.0.0.5:  ip-proto-89,
       length 56
    2: 19:28:09.3720033854 802.1Q vlan#91 P6 10.101.1.1.520 > 224.0.0.9.520:  udp 24
    3: 19:28:14.3720039694 802.1Q vlan#91 P6 10.101.1.1 > 224.0.0.5:  ip-proto-89,
       length 56
    4: 19:28:24.3720049694 802.1Q vlan#91 P6 10.101.1.1 > 224.0.0.5:  ip-proto-89,
       length 56
    5: 19:28:34.3720059694 802.1Q vlan#91 P6 10.101.1.1 > 224.0.0.5:  ip-proto-89,
       length 56
    6: 19:28:35.3720060744 802.1Q vlan#91 P6 10.101.1.1.520 > 224.0.0.9.520:  udp 24
    7: 19:28:44.3720069704 802.1Q vlan#91 P6 10.101.1.1 > 224.0.0.5:  ip-proto-89,
       length 56
    8: 19:28:54.3720079704 802.1Q vlan#91 P6 10.101.1.1 > 224.0.0.5:  ip-proto-89,
       length 56
    9: 19:29:01.3720086264 802.1Q vlan#91 P6 10.101.1.1.520 > 224.0.0.9.520:  udp 24
    10: 19:29:04.3720089704 802.1Q vlan#91 P6 10.101.1.1 > 224.0.0.5:  ip-proto-89,
       length 56
10 packets shown
```

The **capture** command is extremely helpful in troubleshooting connectivity issues or IP flows. It is recommended that you use a more specific access list with source and destination during troubleshooting.

Use the **capture** command to view the packets passing through the FWSM. To view the flow of packets on the network side, use an access list with the specific source and destination IP addresses applied at the next hop VLAN of the FWSM. Verify that you can view the hit count. This is a quick way to view the traversal of packets in the network side from the switch to the FWSM. Another way of monitoring the flow and the parameters of the flow is using NAM or sniffers.

Flow of packets on the application specified integrated circuit (ASIC) level on the fabric is beyond the scope of this book. It is recommended that you get Cisco product support engineers involved for ASIC-level troubleshooting.

How Do I Verify ACL Resource Limits?

This section gives the command to check the ACL resource limit on the FWSM. This is to verify and plan the application of new rules. The details on resource management are covered in Chapter 5, "Understanding Contexts." Example 21-3 uses the **show** command to see ACL statistics.

Example 21-3 **show** *Command to See the ACL Statistics*

```
FWSM# show np 3 acl stats
- - - - - - - - - - - - - - - - - - - - - - - - - - -
     ACL Tree Statistics
- - - - - - - - - - - - - - - - - - - - - - - - - - -
Rule count       :     116
Bit nodes (PSCB's):     49
Leaf nodes       :      50
Total nodes      :      99 (max 184320)
Leaf chains      :      45
Total stored rules:    158
Max rules in leaf :      8
Node depth       :       8
- - - - - - - - - - - - - - - - - - - - - - - - - - -
```

How Do I Verify the Connectivity and Packet Flow Through the Firewall?

The two useful commands that you can use for troubleshooting are **debug** and **ping**:

- **debug:** Debug commands are a very useful troubleshooting tool. You should use debug commands very carefully during the troubleshooting process because these commands are assigned high priority in the CPU process and can render the system unusable. Recommended practice dictates using debug commands only if the problem is narrowed to a specific issue and if more information is required.

- **ping:** To ping across the FWSM, it is important to enable the necessary two-way access lists on the source and destination of the traffic.

What Is Network Analysis Module?

Network Analysis Module (NAM) is a troubleshooting tool to understand the traffic flow in the VLAN. The flow capture of packets through VLANs and the VLAN interfaces in FWSM are analyzed using this tool. Follow these steps to set up a NAM to monitor the flow through a VLAN:

Step 1   Configure the switch port or trunk to send statistical data to the NAM. This can be done using Switched Port Analyzer (SPAN), VLAN Access-Control Lists (VACL), and NetFlow.

Step 2   In the NAM, you can configure monitoring parameters, such as statistics, host conversation, and application response time.

Step 3   Based on the data source configured, set up the alarms/traps. This can also be done to send proactive notifications.

Follow these steps to use a NAM for troubleshooting issues:

Step 1 After you identify the source and destination that fails to communicate via the FWSM, use the monitor tab/host option to check the packets in the external VLAN.

Step 2 In the host option, make sure the VLAN connecting the FWSM is selected as the data source, and the host is selected for the flow. Select the Capture tab and view the flow.

Figure 21-3 shows a screen capture using NAM to monitor a conversation on a particular VLAN.

Figure 21-3 *NAM Screen Capture for Conversation on a VLAN*

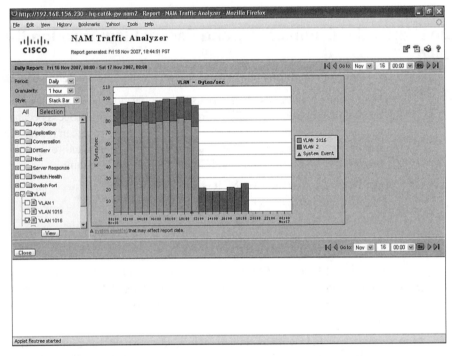

Figure 21-4 shows a screen capture with a server response for that particular flow.

Figure 21-4 *NAM Screen Capture for Conversation and Server Response*

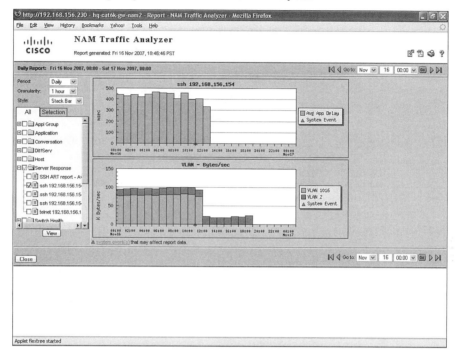

The response from the server to destination client is monitored on the VLAN connecting to the FWSM. Based on the response, you can monitor a packet flow between the source and destination on a particular VLAN connecting to the FWSM, as shown in Figure 21-5.

Figure 21-5 *NAM Screen Capture for Packet Decoder for a Particular Conversation*

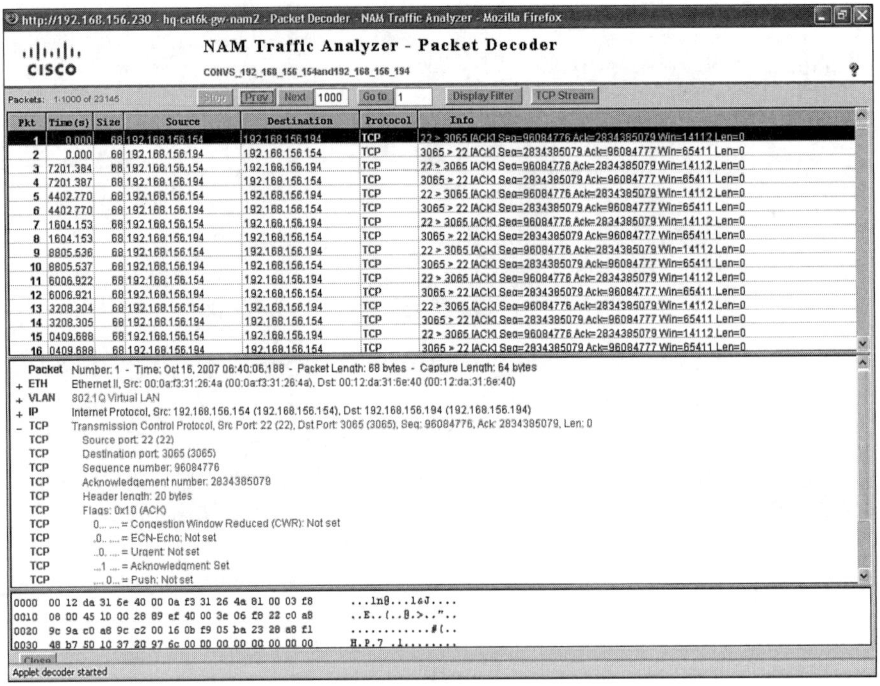

What Are Some Useful Management and Monitoring Tools?

The CSM and Cisco ASDM are useful management and monitoring tools used for troubleshooting:

- **Cisco Security Manager (CSM):** This tool is used for management of FWSM and also has features that help in troubleshooting the FWSM. This provides several monitoring and diagnostic features to get information regarding the services running on the device and a snapshot of the overall health of the system.

- **Cisco Adaptive Security Device Manager (ASDM):** Provides security management and monitoring through a web-based management interface. This tool gives detailed information for the following:

  — Device status information, including blocks free and used, current memory utilization, and CPU utilization.

  — Real-time session and performance monitoring, including information about

    — Data for connections

    — Address translations

— AAA transactions on a per-second basis

— CPU and memory usage details

— UDP and TCP connections per second

— Real-time syslog viewer

— Traffic throughput

Connection graphs show complete information about your network connections and activities. ASDM provides 16 graphs to display potentially malicious activity and provide real-time monitoring of bandwidth usage for each interface on the security appliance.

How Do I Recover Passwords?

Password recovery is common in any device. In the FWSM, the password recovery for the maintenance partition can be reset to default values. To reset the password to default values, use the following command:

```
FWSM# clear mp-passwd
```

Lockout situations can happen because of AAA settings. To reset the passwords and portions of AAA configuration to the default values, use the following steps in the maintenance partition:

Step 1   Check the current application boot partition using this command:

```
Router# show boot device [mod_num]
```

The output shows the boot partition for the module as cf:4 or cf:5. You can later specify the output for the boot partition for which the password can be reset.

Step 2   To boot the FWSM in the maintenance partition, use this command:

```
Router# hw-module module mod_num reset cf:1
```

Step 3   To session into the FWSM, use this command:

```
Router# session slot mod_num processor 1
```

Step 4   Log in to the maintenance partition as root and enter the password, as follows:

```
Login: root
Password: password
```

The default password is **cisco**.

Step 5 To clear the AAA authentication console and AAA authorization command, use the following command:

```
root@localhost# clear passwd cf:{4 | 5}
```

Specify the boot partition for which you want to clear passwords. By default, the FWSM boots from cf:4.

Step 6 Follow the screen prompts, as shown:

```
Do you wish to erase the passwords? [yn] y
The following lines will be removed from the configuration:
        enable password 8Ry2YjIyt7RRXU24 encrypted
        passwd 2KFQnbNIdI.2KYOU encrypted
Do you want to remove the commands listed above from the configuration?
[yn] y
Passwords and aaa commands have been erased.
```

Summary

Troubleshooting is an art. There is no defined way to troubleshoot an issue; it involves a clear and systemic approach to resolve a problem. Knowing the tools, commands, technical working of FWSM, and design knowledge helps the troubleshooter to be more effective in this process. Based on the time availability, you can use the shotgun approach to fix a problem. This approach is to fix the problem without following a systemic troubleshooting method that is accomplished only with experience. In many cases, it is successful. If time permits, it is always good to follow the systemic troubleshooting process.

Design Guidelines and Configuration Examples

CHAPTER 22

Designing a Network Infrastructure

Designing a network infrastructure is one of those topics that is subject to opinion. Previous experience, comfort level with different technologies, and feature likes and dislikes will all play a part in the outcome of a design. Although many solutions may exist, the ultimate goal is a reliable, manageable, cost-effective infrastructure that meets or exceeds the requirements of the project.

A very important aspect of designing, not only with the Firewall Services Module (FWSM) but with all networking components, is to understand the features and capabilities of the hardware and software.

One of the keys to success is to "keep it simple." This makes it easier to understand, configure, maintain, and troubleshoot.

For network design, consider the following three-step process as you plan and implement the design:

Step 1   Determine design considerations.

Step 2   Determine deployment options.

Step 3   Determine where or how to logically place the FWSM.

Determining Design Considerations

In the process of a network design, the first step is to determine exactly what you are attempting to accomplish and document that information. Yes, this should go without mentioning, but most people miss the documentation part. Why is the documentation so important? It sets expectations for all parties involved and minimizes any negative impact in your direction. This gives you documentation to refer to when "scope creep" becomes an issue, and it provides you with ammunition against the "You said it would support that!" comment.

A security policy is imperative for security designs. This will define the constraints that need to be adhered to. If you do not already have a security policy, you need one now! Creating security policies is beyond the scope of this book; however, for additional information, see the *Cisco Network Security Policy: Best Practices White Paper*, Document ID: 13601.

Documenting the Process

Documenting the process is one of the most important aspects of creating a network design because it provides a record of the requirements, the scope of the project, and so on. This document should be very clearly written to avoid ambiguity and will provide a foundation for the entire plan.

The project documentation should contain information such as the following:

- **What is the end goal?:** A general mission/project statement needs to define what you are attempting to accomplish. This could be something like "Protecting the Internet facing web server."

- **What resources need to be secured?:** Define the exact devices and IP addresses.

- **What are the applications?:** List all the IP TCP/UDP port numbers.

- **Is application inspection required?:** Refer to Chapter 14, "Filtering," for supported application inspection engines.

- **Is multicast needed to support this application?:** If multicast is necessary, configuring the FWSM in transparent mode may be beneficial.

- **Are other protocols needed?:** Hopefully not, but in the rare case when they are, it would be necessary to configure the FWSM in transparent mode. Recall also that non-IP protocols will not be inspected.

- **Who is allowed to have access?:** Are there specific devices that can be defined by IP address?

- **Will the FWSM need to authenticate access?:** If the FWSM needs to perform authentication, do you have the appropriate devices to perform this task? Refer to Chapter 10, "AAA Configuration," for additional information.

- **What are the bandwidth/performance requirements?:** Is a single FWSM capable of supporting the application, or will multiple FWSMs be required?

- **Are multiple contexts necessary or useful?:** Multiple contexts are very useful if you need a combination of routed and transparent firewalls or you have multiple customers with different security policies.

- **Is a secondary firewall needed for failover?:** If high availability is required, having a secondary FWSM is imperative. See Chapter 13, "Understanding Application Protocol Inspection," for details.

- **Who is managing the FWSM or context?:** If you have multiple customers, multiple contexts will allow them to manage their own FWSM instance.

- **Does this project fall under the constraints of the security policy?:** If not, you need to have the security policy changed or change the scope of the project. Good luck!

This is not an all-inclusive list, but it is a good baseline.

Creating a document outlining the aspects of the design will provide everyone involved with a central record from which to receive information. Having this type of document with well-defined criteria will certainly help minimize scope creep, unnecessary changes, and so on.

Determining Deployment Options

After collecting and compiling the information from Step 1, Step 2 is to determine the deployment options:

- **Should the FWSM be in single-context mode?:** If a single organization maintains control over the FWSM and logical separation of multiple firewalls is not required, the answer could be yes. Another benefit of single-context mode is a greater rule limit. Refer to Chapter 2, "Overview of the Firewall Services Module," for details.

  Native multicast and routing protocols are also supported in single-context routed mode. See Chapter 16, "Multicast," and Chapter 17, "Asymmetric Routing," for additional details.

- **Should the FWSM be in multi-context mode?:** If there are multiple organizations, or separation of applications/services are required, multi-context mode may be a good solution. Remember that in multi-context mode the rule limit is reduced. Refer to Chapter 2 for details.

  There is also a license cost if you need more than two contexts.

- **Should the FWSM be configured in routed mode?:** Routed mode is a great solution if a need exists for multiple interfaces. For example, you may require inside, outside, and DMZ interfaces, which are possible only in routed mode.

  If you are using multi-context mode, the only routing protocol that supports multiple contexts is Border Gateway Protocol (BGP) stub. For deployment considerations, see Chapter 17.

- **Should the FWSM be configured in transparent mode?:** Transparent mode supports only two interfaces, but up to eight bridge groups are allowed per context.

  No IP readdressing is required.

  Routing protocols (except IS-IS) can transparently pass through the FWSM.

- **What about high availability?:** Consider using multiple chassis with multiple firewalls and inter-chassis failover. See Chapter 13 for details.

- **How are access lists created?:** Based on the information gathered for who needs access, you can use a couple of options. The best option is to create a very limited rule-set to allow only specific traffic through. Then use noise-level detection (users complaining about not being able to access the service) and modify the access list accordingly.

The other option is to open the rule-set wider than necessary, monitor access to the resource, and then shrink the access list to specific traffic. This can be dangerous because interruptions in service make it difficult to troubleshoot, and many times the access lists are not restrictive enough to keep out unwanted guests.

You can choose from several deployment options, and some of these may be mutually exclusive. For example, you might be required to operate in transparent mode but need multiple interfaces. Applying the design considerations to the deployment options is the difficult part—and why you get paid the "big bucks." Thorough knowledge of the FWSM and the capabilities and limitations will significantly improve your success.

Determining Placement

Step 3 is where or how to logically place the FWSM. Given the flexibility in the configuration of the host-chassis and the FWSM, you can choose from many deployment options.

- **Single-context routed-mode inside/outside:** This option allows the FWSM to participate in the routing process and has the capability to support multiple interfaces.

    From a security perspective, having another process running creates additional vulnerabilities. Moving the routing process to the multilayer switch feature card (MSFC) or other router improves the security of the FWSM. Figure 22-1 illustrates how the FWSM can be placed in regard to the routing process on the host-chassis, either on the inside or the outside.

Figure 22-1 *Single-Context Routed-Mode Inside/Outside*

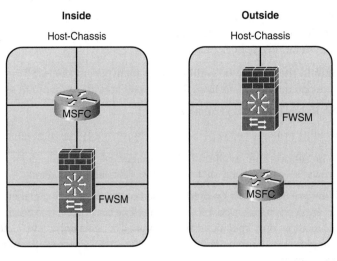

- **Single-context transparent-mode inside/outside:** This option limits the number of interfaces to two, but does not require IP address changes and allows the capability to pass routing information. Figure 22-2 illustrates how the routing process on the host-chassis can be used with the FWSM, with the FWSM placed on either the inside or the outside.

Figure 22-2 *Single-Context Transparent-Mode Inside/Outside*

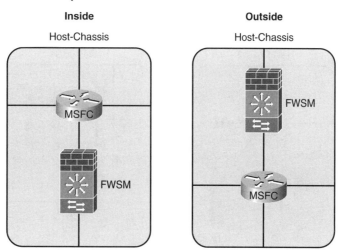

- **Multiple-context routed-mode inside/outside:** This option allows the routed context to have multiple interfaces, but remember that in multi-context mode, static routing and BGP stub are the only supported routing protocols. Refer to Chapter 9, "Configuring Routing Protocols," for additional information. Figure 22-3 illustrates how multiple contexts can be used in conjunction with the routing process of the host-chassis.

Figure 22-3 *Multiple-Context Routed-Mode Inside/Outside*

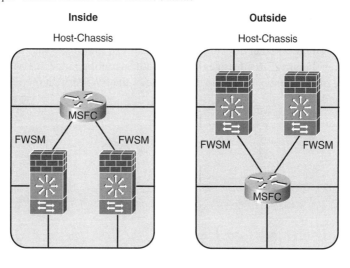

- **Multi-context transparent-mode inside/outside:** This option provides the capability to pass routing protocols between Layer 3 devices and does not require IP address changes. Figure 22-4 illustrates how the FWSM can support multiple contexts in transparent mode, either being placed on the inside or the outside of the routing process on the host-chassis.

Figure 22-4 *Multi-Context Transparent-Mode Inside/Outside*

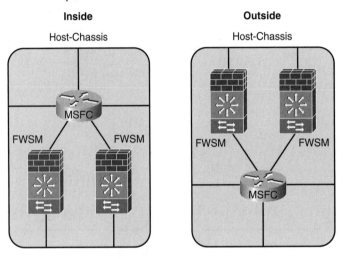

- **FWSM-sandwich in routed-mode:** This functionality significantly leverages the investment in the host-chassis by creating multiple virtual routing instances. Figure 22-5 illustrates how virtualized routing processes on the host-chassis can be placed on the inside and the outside of the FWSM with the FWSM in routed-mode.

- **FWSM-sandwich in transparent-mode:** This functionality significantly leverages the investment in the host-chassis by creating multiple virtual routing instances. Transparent mode allows the capability to establish routing adjacencies between virtual routing instances. This configuration now uses routing information to determine whether any link failures occur and minimizes any impact of Spanning Tree. Figure 22-6 illustrates how virtualized routing processes on the host-chassis can be placed on the inside and the outside of the FWSM with the FWSM in transparent-mode.

Figure 22-5 *Multiple-Context Transparent-Mode Inside/Outside*

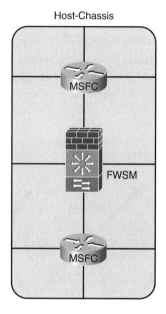

Figure 22-6 *Multiple-Context Transparent-Mode Inside/Outside*

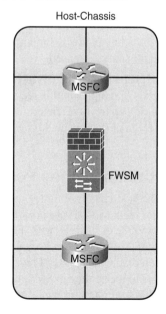

- **Shared interfaces in routed-mode:** Due to packet classification, the only configuration of shared interfaces that should be used is a shared outside deployment model. A shared inside deployment model could be used but requires static NAT translations for the destination addresses, which can be used only in limited situations.

  Sharing the inside interface or multiple interfaces should be avoided. Figure 22-7 illustrates deployment methods of which a single shared interface—for example, the outside—would be the only recommended approach.

Figure 22-7 *Shared Interfaces Routed-Mode*

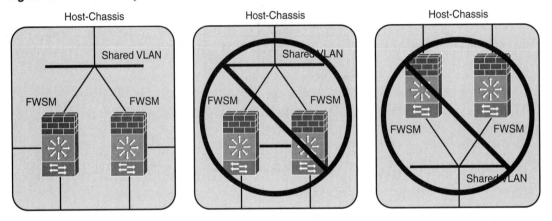

- **FWSM only:** The FWSM can be used without any interaction from the MSFC, as shown in Figure 22-7. Although this is supported, you are paying for valuable hardware (MSFC) that is not being used.

Many options exist for the placement of the FWSM in regard to the routing process or processes on the host-chassis. Examples in this section demonstrate how flexible the placement can actually be; it's up to you to determine what the appropriate deployment model will look like to meet your documented project requirements.

Working with FWSM and the Enterprise Perimeter

Because the FWSM and the host-chassis are integrated devices, greater care must be taken when placing any interfaces on untrusted networks. If either the FWSM or host-chassis are compromised, the results will be disastrous, with the potential for compromised devices, the loss of information, denial-of-service, and so on. If you find yourself in this situation, you might have wished you read Chapter 20, "Preventing Network Attacks." The recommended placement is to locate the FWSM interfaces on the untrusted networks and not those of the MSFC. This configuration would be the outside model referred to in Figures 22-1, 22-2, 22-3, and 22-4. Because the FWSM is a true security device, it has a better capability of fending off malicious attacks than the routing process of the host-chassis. It also provides better protection against inadvertent mistakes—for example, placing an FWSM interface in the wrong VLAN—that may occur during configuration changes because of the fail-closed nature of a firewall in contrast to the fail-open nature of a router.

Also, be sure when configuring the VLAN interface that connects to the untrusted network that it has been "hard-set" for that specific VLAN and will not trunk! This prevents the possibility of bypassing the FWSM on a separate VLAN. Follow the practices for securing the host-chassis outlined in Chapter 6, "Configuring and Securing the 6500/7600 Chassis."

When considering the placement of the FWSM in regard to the routing process of the host-chassis, the FWSM should always be closest to the most untrusted network(s). If the FWSM is placed in a location without a trusted network connection, consider not using any routing process on the host-chassis to minimize the potential compromise of the host-chassis.

FWSM in the Datacenter

With the number of new applications that are being developed, the requirement to keep them secure and the expectation that they are always available can be difficult to accomplish. Having the flexibility to support these applications while providing uptime is paramount to providing services to your customers.

The primary considerations for deploying an FWSM in the datacenter are throughput, flexibility, availability, and support for virtualization.

Throughput

Throughput requirements continue to grow as new applications are added and as additional devices require those resources. Up to four FWSMs can be installed in the host-chassis to maximize throughput. Remember from Chapter 2 that the connection from the FWSM to the host-chassis is a 6-gigabit EtherChannel. This means that a single flow can reach a maximum of only 1 Gbps because of the way in which flows are distributed across the EtherChannel.

Flexibility

Having the flexibility to operate the FWSM in multiple-context mode allows the capability to quickly add contexts to support new applications. Applications associated with particular contexts can also be given additional resources. Refer to the section titled "Understanding Resource Management" in Chapter 5.

Configuring contexts in transparent mode allows you to support dynamic routing protocols for Layer 3 failover and will also easily support multicast or non-IP traffic if the requirement arises.

Availability

High availability using a redundant FWSM in multiple host-chassis allows access to the datacenter resources in the event of a FWSM or host-chassis failure.

Using the FWSM to provide firewall services to applications within the datacenter is one of the most common implementations of the FWSM. Given the performance capability, the high availability using redundant FWSMs, the small footprint and low power requirements, the flexibility of deployment using routed-mode or transparent-mode, and the capability to virtualize contexts makes the FWSM an excellent choice for datacenter deployments.

Supporting Virtualized Networks

Many organizations have realized the benefits of traffic separation or network virtualization through the use of multiprotocol label switching (MPLS), multiple virtual routing and forwarding (multi-VRF), multitopology routing (MTR), virtual private LAN services (VPLS), and so on. These technologies leverage a single physical infrastructure while providing a logical mechanism for traffic separation. Rather than installing a unique physical firewall per virtual network, you can configure the FWSM to support multiple contexts using a combination of routed or transparent mode. Because this can be accomplished in a single chassis, configuration changes do not require physical rewiring.

The host-chassis can support multiple routing instances (contexts) and bridging contexts (VLANs). Consider the host-chassis as a whiteboard, and you have the ability to connect routing, bridging, or firewall instances in many configurations. Using a routing context between FWSM instances allows you to overcome the limitation of cascading contexts, which is not a supported configuration.

Figure 22-8 illustrates the capabilities of virtualizing the FWSM, LANs, and routing processes on the host-chassis. Although this probably wouldn't be a configuration you would want to manage, it does show the tremendous flexibility of the solution. Example 22-1 shows the configuration associated with the illustration in Figure 22-8.

Figure 22-8 *Example of Multiple Routing and Firewall Instances*

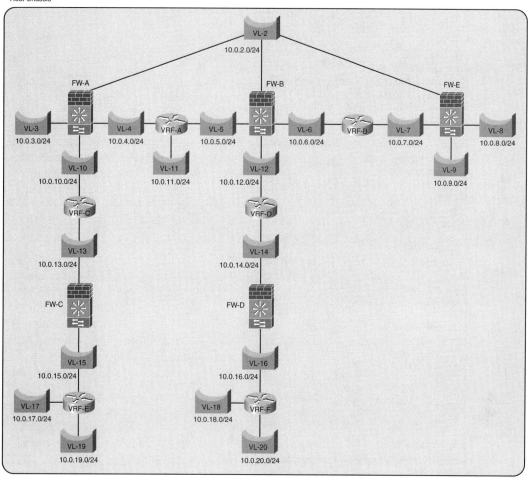

Example 22-1 *Configuring Multiple Routing and Firewall Instances*

```
! Host-chassis:
host-chassis#show run
Building configuration...
Current configuration : 8794 bytes
!
upgrade fpd auto
version 12.2
service timestamps debug uptime
service timestamps log uptime
no service password-encryption
```

continues

Example 22-1 *Configuring Multiple Routing and Firewall Instances (Continued)*

```
service counters max age 5
!
hostname host-chassis
!
!
no aaa new-model
firewall multiple-vlan-interfaces
firewall module 9 vlan-group 9
firewall vlan-group 9  2-16
ip subnet-zero
!
!
!
ip vrf VRF-A
 rd 1:1
!
ip vrf VRF-B
 rd 1:2
!
ip vrf VRF-C
 rd 1:3
!
ip vrf VRF-D
 rd 1:4
!
ip vrf VRF-E
 rd 1:5
!
ip vrf VRF-F
 rd 1:6
!
vlan 2-20
!
!
interface Vlan1
 no ip address
 shutdown
!
interface Vlan4
 ip vrf forwarding VRF-A
 ip address 10.0.4.1 255.255.255.0
!
interface Vlan5
 ip vrf forwarding VRF-A
 ip address 10.0.5.1 255.255.255.0
!
interface Vlan6
 ip vrf forwarding VRF-B
 ip address 10.0.6.1 255.255.255.0
!
interface Vlan7
 ip vrf forwarding VRF-B
```

Example 22-1 *Configuring Multiple Routing and Firewall Instances (Continued)*

```
  ip address 10.0.7.1 255.255.255.0
 !
 interface Vlan10
  ip vrf forwarding VRF-C
  ip address 10.0.10.1 255.255.255.0
 !
 interface Vlan11
  ip vrf forwarding VRF-A
  ip address 10.0.11.1 255.255.255.0
 !
 interface Vlan12
  ip vrf forwarding VRF-D
  ip address 10.0.12.1 255.255.255.0
 !
 interface Vlan13
  mac-address 0000.0000.0013
  ip vrf forwarding VRF-C
  ip address 10.0.13.1 255.255.255.0
 !
 interface Vlan14
  mac-address 0000.0000.0014
  ip vrf forwarding VRF-D
  ip address 10.0.14.1 255.255.255.0
 !
 interface Vlan15
  mac-address 0000.0000.0015
  ip vrf forwarding VRF-E
  ip address 10.0.13.2 255.255.255.0
 !
 interface Vlan16
  mac-address 0000.0000.0016
  ip vrf forwarding VRF-F
  ip address 10.0.14.2 255.255.255.0
 !
 interface Vlan17
  ip vrf forwarding VRF-E
  ip address 10.0.17.1 255.255.255.0
 !
 interface Vlan18
  ip vrf forwarding VRF-F
  ip address 10.0.18.1 255.255.255.0
 !
 interface Vlan19
  ip vrf forwarding VRF-E
  ip address 10.0.19.1 255.255.255.0
 !
 interface Vlan20
  ip vrf forwarding VRF-F
  ip address 10.0.20.1 255.255.255.0
 !
 ip classless
 ip route vrf VRF-A 10.0.6.0 255.255.255.0 Vlan5 10.0.5.2
```

continues

Example 22-1   *Configuring Multiple Routing and Firewall Instances (Continued)*

```
ip route vrf VRF-A 10.0.7.0 255.255.255.0 Vlan5 10.0.5.2
ip route vrf VRF-A 10.0.8.0 255.255.255.0 Vlan5 10.0.5.2
ip route vrf VRF-A 10.0.9.0 255.255.255.0 Vlan5 10.0.5.2
ip route vrf VRF-A 10.0.10.0 255.255.255.0 Vlan4 10.0.4.2
ip route vrf VRF-A 10.0.12.0 255.255.255.0 Vlan5 10.0.5.2
ip route vrf VRF-A 10.0.13.0 255.255.255.0 Vlan4 10.0.4.2
ip route vrf VRF-A 10.0.14.0 255.255.255.0 Vlan5 10.0.5.2
ip route vrf VRF-A 10.0.15.0 255.255.255.0 Vlan4 10.0.4.2
ip route vrf VRF-A 10.0.16.0 255.255.255.0 Vlan5 10.0.5.2
ip route vrf VRF-A 10.0.17.0 255.255.255.0 Vlan4 10.0.4.2
ip route vrf VRF-A 10.0.18.0 255.255.255.0 Vlan5 10.0.5.2
ip route vrf VRF-A 10.0.19.0 255.255.255.0 Vlan4 10.0.4.2
ip route vrf VRF-A 10.0.20.0 255.255.255.0 Vlan5 10.0.5.2
ip route vrf VRF-B 10.0.3.0 255.255.255.0 Vlan6 10.0.6.2
ip route vrf VRF-B 10.0.4.0 255.255.255.0 Vlan6 10.0.6.2
ip route vrf VRF-B 10.0.5.0 255.255.255.0 Vlan6 10.0.6.2
ip route vrf VRF-B 10.0.8.0 255.255.255.0 Vlan7 10.0.7.2
ip route vrf VRF-B 10.0.9.0 255.255.255.0 Vlan7 10.0.7.2
ip route vrf VRF-B 10.0.10.0 255.255.255.0 Vlan6 10.0.6.2
ip route vrf VRF-B 10.0.12.0 255.255.255.0 Vlan6 10.0.6.2
ip route vrf VRF-B 10.0.13.0 255.255.255.0 Vlan6 10.0.6.2
ip route vrf VRF-B 10.0.14.0 255.255.255.0 Vlan6 10.0.6.2
ip route vrf VRF-B 10.0.17.0 255.255.255.0 Vlan6 10.0.6.2
ip route vrf VRF-B 10.0.18.0 255.255.255.0 Vlan6 10.0.6.2
ip route vrf VRF-B 10.0.19.0 255.255.255.0 Vlan6 10.0.6.2
ip route vrf VRF-B 10.0.20.0 255.255.255.0 Vlan6 10.0.6.2
ip route vrf VRF-C 0.0.0.0 0.0.0.0 Vlan10 10.0.10.2
ip route vrf VRF-C 10.0.15.0 255.255.255.0 Vlan13 10.0.13.2
ip route vrf VRF-C 10.0.17.0 255.255.255.0 Vlan13 10.0.13.2
ip route vrf VRF-C 10.0.19.0 255.255.255.0 Vlan13 10.0.13.2
ip route vrf VRF-D 0.0.0.0 0.0.0.0 Vlan12 10.0.12.2
ip route vrf VRF-D 10.0.16.0 255.255.255.0 Vlan14 10.0.14.2
ip route vrf VRF-D 10.0.18.0 255.255.255.0 Vlan14 10.0.14.2
ip route vrf VRF-D 10.0.20.0 255.255.255.0 Vlan14 10.0.14.2
ip route vrf VRF-E 0.0.0.0 0.0.0.0 Vlan15 10.0.13.1
ip route vrf VRF-F 0.0.0.0 0.0.0.0 Vlan16 10.0.14.1
!
End
! FWSM System Context:
FWSM# show run
: Saved
:
FWSM Version 3.2(1) <system>
!
resource acl-partition 12
hostname FWSM
enable password 8Ry2YjIyt7RRXU24 encrypted
!
interface Vlan2
!
interface Vlan3
!
```

Example 22-1 *Configuring Multiple Routing and Firewall Instances (Continued)*

```
interface Vlan4
!
interface Vlan5
!
interface Vlan6
!
interface Vlan7
!
interface Vlan8
!
interface Vlan9
!
interface Vlan10
!
interface Vlan12
!
interface Vlan13
!
interface Vlan14
!
interface Vlan15
!
interface Vlan16
!
interface Vlan17
!
interface Vlan18
!
interface Vlan19
!
interface Vlan20
!
passwd 2KFQnbNIdI.2KYOU encrypted
class default
  limit-resource All 0
  limit-resource IPSec 5
  limit-resource Mac-addresses 65535
  limit-resource ASDM 5
  limit-resource SSH 5
  limit-resource Telnet 5
!
ftp mode passive
pager lines 24
no failover
no asdm history enable
arp timeout 14400
console timeout 0
admin-context admin
context admin
  config-url disk:/admin.cfg
!
context FW-A
```

continues

Example 22-1 *Configuring Multiple Routing and Firewall Instances (Continued)*

```
    allocate-interface Vlan10
    allocate-interface Vlan2
    allocate-interface Vlan3
    allocate-interface Vlan4
    config-url disk:/FW-A.cfg
!

context FW-C
  allocate-interface Vlan13
  allocate-interface Vlan15
  config-url disk:/FW-C.cfg
!
context FW-B
  allocate-interface Vlan12
  allocate-interface Vlan2
  allocate-interface Vlan5
  allocate-interface Vlan6
  config-url disk:/FW-B.cfg
!
context FW-E
  allocate-interface Vlan2
  allocate-interface Vlan7
  allocate-interface Vlan8
  allocate-interface Vlan9
  config-url disk:/FW-E.cfg
!
context FW-D
  allocate-interface Vlan14
  allocate-interface Vlan16
  config-url disk:/FW-D.cfg
!
prompt hostname context
Cryptochecksum:9d12e90dcabcb9f485ec54d372a45d78
: end
! FWSM FW-A Context:
FWSM/FW-A# show run
: Saved
:
FWSM Version 3.2(1) <context>
!
hostname FW-A
enable password 8Ry2YjIyt7RRXU24 encrypted
names
!
interface Vlan2
 nameif outside
 security-level 0
 ip address 10.0.2.2 255.255.255.0
!
interface Vlan3
 nameif DMZ-3
 security-level 50
```

Example 22-1 *Configuring Multiple Routing and Firewall Instances (Continued)*

```
 ip address 10.0.3.2 255.255.255.0
 !
interface Vlan4
 nameif DMZ-4
 security-level 60
 ip address 10.0.4.2 255.255.255.0
 !
interface Vlan10
 nameif inside
 security-level 100
 ip address 10.0.10.2 255.255.255.0
 !
passwd 2KFQnbNIdI.2KYOU encrypted
access-list ANY extended permit ip any any
pager lines 24
mtu outside 1500
mtu DMZ-3 1500
mtu DMZ-4 1500
mtu inside 1500
icmp permit any outside
icmp permit any DMZ-3
icmp permit any DMZ-4
icmp permit any inside
no asdm history enable
arp timeout 14400
access-group ANY in interface outside
access-group ANY in interface DMZ-3
access-group ANY in interface DMZ-4
access-group ANY in interface inside
route outside 0.0.0.0 0.0.0.0 10.0.1.1 1
route DMZ-4 10.0.5.0 255.255.255.0 10.0.4.1 1
route DMZ-4 10.0.6.0 255.255.255.0 10.0.4.1 1
route DMZ-4 10.0.7.0 255.255.255.0 10.0.4.1 1
route DMZ-4 10.0.8.0 255.255.255.0 10.0.4.1 1
route DMZ-4 10.0.9.0 255.255.255.0 10.0.4.1 1
route DMZ-4 10.0.12.0 255.255.255.0 10.0.4.1 1
route DMZ-4 10.0.14.0 255.255.255.0 10.0.4.1 1
route DMZ-4 10.0.16.0 255.255.255.0 10.0.4.1 1
route DMZ-4 10.0.18.0 255.255.255.0 10.0.4.1 1
route DMZ-4 10.0.20.0 255.255.255.0 10.0.4.1 1
route inside 10.0.13.0 255.255.255.0 10.0.10.1 1
route inside 10.0.15.0 255.255.255.0 10.0.10.1 1
route inside 10.0.17.0 255.255.255.0 10.0.10.1 1
route inside 10.0.19.0 255.255.255.0 10.0.10.1 1
timeout xlate 3:00:00
timeout conn 1:00:00 half-closed 0:10:00 udp 0:02:00 icmp 0:00:02
timeout sunrpc 0:10:00 h323 0:05:00 h225 1:00:00 mgcp 0:05:00
timeout mgcp-pat 0:05:00 sip 0:30:00 sip_media 0:02:00
timeout sip-invite 0:03:00 sip-disconnect 0:02:00
timeout uauth 0:05:00 absolute
no snmp-server location
no snmp-server contact
```

continues

Example 22-1 *Configuring Multiple Routing and Firewall Instances (Continued)*

```
telnet timeout 5
ssh timeout 5
!
class-map inspection_default
 match default-inspection-traffic
 !
 !
policy-map global_policy
 class inspection_default
  inspect dns maximum-length 512
  inspect ftp
  inspect h323 h225
  inspect h323 ras
  inspect netbios
  inspect rsh
  inspect skinny
  inspect smtp
  inspect sqlnet
  inspect sunrpc
  inspect tftp
  inspect sip
  inspect xdmcp
 !
service-policy global_policy global
Cryptochecksum:6763fabd0efe5404b8b8273be9784a24
: end
! FWSM FW-B Context:
FWSM/FW-B# show run
: Saved
:
FWSM Version 3.2(1) <context>
!
hostname FW-B
enable password 8Ry2YjIyt7RRXU24 encrypted
names
!
interface Vlan5
 nameif DMZ-5
 security-level 50
 ip address 10.0.5.2 255.255.255.0
 !
interface Vlan6
 nameif DMZ-6
 security-level 60
 ip address 10.0.6.2 255.255.255.0
 !
interface Vlan12
 nameif inside
 security-level 100
 ip address 10.0.12.2 255.255.255.0
 !
```

Example 22-1 *Configuring Multiple Routing and Firewall Instances (Continued)*

```
interface Vlan2
 nameif outside
 security-level 0
 ip address 10.0.2.3 255.255.255.0
 !
passwd 2KFQnbNIdI.2KYOU encrypted
access-list ANY extended permit ip any any
pager lines 24
mtu outside 1500
mtu DMZ-5 1500
mtu DMZ-6 1500
mtu inside 1500
icmp permit any outside
icmp permit any DMZ-5
icmp permit any DMZ-6
icmp permit any inside
no asdm history enable
arp timeout 14400
access-group ANY in interface outside
access-group ANY in interface DMZ-5
access-group ANY in interface DMZ-6
access-group ANY in interface inside
route outside 0.0.0.0 0.0.0.0 10.0.2.1 1
route DMZ-5 10.0.13.0 255.255.255.0 10.0.5.1 1
route DMZ-5 10.0.15.0 255.255.255.0 10.0.5.1 1
route DMZ-5 10.0.17.0 255.255.255.0 10.0.5.1 1
route DMZ-5 10.0.19.0 255.255.255.0 10.0.5.1 1
route DMZ-5 10.0.3.0 255.255.255.0 10.0.5.1 1
route DMZ-5 10.0.4.0 255.255.255.0 10.0.5.1 1
route DMZ-6 10.0.7.0 255.255.255.0 10.0.6.1 1
route DMZ-6 10.0.9.0 255.255.255.0 10.0.6.1 1
route DMZ-6 10.0.8.0 255.255.255.0 10.0.6.1 1
route inside 10.0.20.0 255.255.255.0 10.0.12.1 1
route inside 10.0.14.0 255.255.255.0 10.0.12.1 1
route inside 10.0.16.0 255.255.255.0 10.0.12.1 1
route inside 10.0.18.0 255.255.255.0 10.0.12.1 1
timeout xlate 3:00:00
timeout conn 1:00:00 half-closed 0:10:00 udp 0:02:00 icmp 0:00:02
timeout sunrpc 0:10:00 h323 0:05:00 h225 1:00:00 mgcp 0:05:00
timeout mgcp-pat 0:05:00 sip 0:30:00 sip_media 0:02:00
timeout sip-invite 0:03:00 sip-disconnect 0:02:00
timeout uauth 0:05:00 absolute
no snmp-server location
no snmp-server contact
telnet timeout 5
ssh timeout 5
!
class-map inspection_default
 match default-inspection-traffic
!
!
policy-map global_policy
```

continues

Example 22-1 *Configuring Multiple Routing and Firewall Instances (Continued)*

```
 class inspection_default
  inspect dns maximum-length 512
  inspect ftp
  inspect h323 h225
  inspect h323 ras
  inspect netbios
  inspect rsh
  inspect skinny
  inspect smtp
  inspect sqlnet
  inspect sunrpc
  inspect tftp
  inspect sip
  inspect xdmcp
!
service-policy global_policy global
Cryptochecksum:afe8275e09e0db6c9a32360f07f24906
: end
! FWSM FW-C Context:
FWSM/FW-C# show run
: Saved
:
FWSM Version 3.2(1) <context>
!
firewall transparent
hostname FW-C
enable password 8Ry2YjIyt7RRXU24 encrypted
names
!
interface Vlan13
 nameif outside
 bridge-group 4
 security-level 0
!
interface Vlan15
 nameif inside
 bridge-group 4
 security-level 100
!
interface BVI4
 ip address 10.0.15.254 255.255.255.0
 !
passwd 2KFQnbNIdI.2KYOU encrypted
access-list ANY extended permit ip any any
pager lines 24
mtu outside 1500
mtu inside 1500
icmp permit any outside
icmp permit any inside
no asdm history enable
arp timeout 14400
```

Example 22-1   *Configuring Multiple Routing and Firewall Instances (Continued)*

```
access-group ANY in interface outside
access-group ANY in interface inside
timeout xlate 3:00:00
timeout conn 1:00:00 half-closed 0:10:00 udp 0:02:00 icmp 0:00:02
timeout sunrpc 0:10:00 h323 0:05:00 h225 1:00:00 mgcp 0:05:00
timeout mgcp-pat 0:05:00 sip 0:30:00 sip_media 0:02:00
timeout sip-invite 0:03:00 sip-disconnect 0:02:00
timeout uauth 0:05:00 absolute
no snmp-server location
no snmp-server contact
snmp-server enable traps snmp authentication linkup linkdown coldstart
telnet timeout 5
ssh timeout 5
!
class-map inspection_default
 match default-inspection-traffic
!
!
policy-map global_policy
 class inspection_default
  inspect dns maximum-length 512
  inspect ftp
  inspect h323 h225
  inspect h323 ras
  inspect rsh
  inspect smtp
  inspect sqlnet
  inspect skinny
  inspect sunrpc
  inspect xdmcp
  inspect sip
  inspect netbios
  inspect tftp
!
service-policy global_policy global
Cryptochecksum:ad8df9ac0505628a9aa584a69a67d0b1
: end
! FWSM FW-D Context:
FWSM/FW-D# show run
: Saved
:
FWSM Version 3.2(1) <context>
!
firewall transparent
hostname FW-D
enable password 8Ry2YjIyt7RRXU24 encrypted
names
!
interface Vlan14
 nameif outside
 bridge-group 5
```

continues

Example 22-1 *Configuring Multiple Routing and Firewall Instances (Continued)*

```
 security-level 0
!
interface Vlan16
 nameif inside
 bridge-group 5
 security-level 100
!
interface BVI5
 ip address 10.0.14.254 255.255.255.0
!
passwd 2KFQnbNIdI.2KYOU encrypted
access-list ANY extended permit ip any any
pager lines 24
mtu outside 1500
mtu inside 1500
icmp permit any outside
icmp permit any inside
no asdm history enable
arp timeout 14400
access-group ANY in interface outside
access-group ANY in interface inside
timeout xlate 3:00:00
timeout conn 1:00:00 half-closed 0:10:00 udp 0:02:00 icmp 0:00:02
timeout sunrpc 0:10:00 h323 0:05:00 h225 1:00:00 mgcp 0:05:00
timeout mgcp-pat 0:05:00 sip 0:30:00 sip_media 0:02:00
timeout sip-invite 0:03:00 sip-disconnect 0:02:00
timeout uauth 0:05:00 absolute
no snmp-server location
no snmp-server contact
snmp-server enable traps snmp authentication linkup linkdown coldstart
telnet timeout 5
ssh timeout 5
!
class-map inspection_default
 match default-inspection-traffic
!
!
policy-map global_policy
 class inspection_default
  inspect dns maximum-length 512
  inspect ftp
  inspect h323 h225
  inspect h323 ras
  inspect rsh
  inspect smtp
  inspect sqlnet
  inspect skinny
  inspect sunrpc
  inspect xdmcp
  inspect sip
  inspect netbios
  inspect tftp
```

Example 22-1 *Configuring Multiple Routing and Firewall Instances (Continued)*

```
!
service-policy global_policy global
Cryptochecksum:98134172a007d34d6be74182a558854a
: end
! FWSM FW-E Context:
FWSM/FW-E# show run
: Saved
:
FWSM Version 3.2(1) <context>
!
hostname FW-E
enable password 8Ry2YjIyt7RRXU24 encrypted
names
!
interface Vlan7
 nameif DMZ-7
 security-level 50
 ip address 10.0.7.2 255.255.255.0
!
interface Vlan8
 nameif DMZ-8
 security-level 60
 ip address 10.0.8.2 255.255.255.0
!
interface Vlan9
 nameif inside
 security-level 100
 ip address 10.0.9.2 255.255.255.0
!
interface Vlan2
 nameif outside
 security-level 0
 ip address 10.0.2.4 255.255.255.0
!
passwd 2KFQnbNIdI.2KYOU encrypted
access-list ANY extended permit ip any any
pager lines 24
mtu DMZ-7 1500
mtu DMZ-8 1500
mtu inside 1500
mtu outside 1500
icmp permit any DMZ-7
icmp permit any DMZ-8
icmp permit any inside
icmp permit any outside
no asdm history enable
arp timeout 14400
access-group ANY in interface DMZ-7
access-group ANY in interface DMZ-8
access-group ANY in interface inside
access-group ANY in interface outside
```

continues

Example 22-1 *Configuring Multiple Routing and Firewall Instances (Continued)*

```
route DMZ-7 10.0.13.0 255.255.255.0 10.0.7.1 1
route DMZ-7 10.0.15.0 255.255.255.0 10.0.7.1 1
route DMZ-7 10.0.17.0 255.255.255.0 10.0.7.1 1
route DMZ-7 10.0.19.0 255.255.255.0 10.0.7.1 1
route DMZ-7 10.0.3.0 255.255.255.0 10.0.7.1 1
route DMZ-7 10.0.20.0 255.255.255.0 10.0.7.1 1
route DMZ-7 10.0.14.0 255.255.255.0 10.0.7.1 1
route DMZ-7 10.0.16.0 255.255.255.0 10.0.7.1 1
route DMZ-7 10.0.18.0 255.255.255.0 10.0.7.1 1
route DMZ-7 10.0.4.0 255.255.255.0 10.0.7.1 1
route DMZ-7 10.0.5.0 255.255.255.0 10.0.7.1 1
route DMZ-7 10.0.6.0 255.255.255.0 10.0.7.1 1
route DMZ-7 10.0.10.0 255.255.255.0 10.0.7.1 1
route DMZ-7 10.0.12.0 255.255.255.0 10.0.7.1 1
route outside 0.0.0.0 0.0.0.0 10.0.1.1 1
timeout xlate 3:00:00
timeout conn 1:00:00 half-closed 0:10:00 udp 0:02:00 icmp 0:00:02
timeout sunrpc 0:10:00 h323 0:05:00 h225 1:00:00 mgcp 0:05:00
timeout mgcp-pat 0:05:00 sip 0:30:00 sip_media 0:02:00
timeout sip-invite 0:03:00 sip-disconnect 0:02:00
timeout uauth 0:05:00 absolute
no snmp-server location
no snmp-server contact
telnet timeout 5
ssh timeout 5
!
class-map inspection_default
 match default-inspection-traffic
!
!
policy-map global_policy
 class inspection_default
  inspect dns maximum-length 512
  inspect ftp
  inspect h323 h225
  inspect h323 ras
  inspect netbios
  inspect rsh
  inspect skinny
  inspect smtp
  inspect sqlnet
  inspect sunrpc
  inspect tftp
  inspect sip
  inspect xdmcp
!
service-policy global_policy global
Cryptochecksum:794ae09acb41892194902c24f5449373
: end
```

The configuration in Example 22-1 would not be something you would want to implement in a production environment, unless you need job security, but it does give you an idea of the flexibility of the host-chassis and FWSM.

Virtualization of FWSM contexts, LANs, and routing processes gives you tremendous flexibility in modifying existing services and deploying new services, especially because the entire previous example didn't require any physical cabling!

Summary

When designing a secure network infrastructure, the better understanding that you have of the operation and capabilities of all the devices that will be included in the solution will dramatically improve the success and security of the entire design. Take a methodical approach by determining the design requirements and considering the deployment options and placement of the FWSM. Also, don't avoid the documentation process as many of us do; this could be a life saver, or at least a job saver. Finally, to make the solution manageable, use the Keep It Simple method of design.

Reference

Cisco *Network Security Policy: Best Practices White Paper*, Document ID: 13601

CHAPTER 23

Design Scenarios

This chapter covers advanced design concepts using multiple features of FWSM and other networking technologies. These design scenarios help increase the availability and redundancy of the FWSM aligned with the network environment.

NOTE   The features of network virtualization with Layer 3 VPN technology are not covered in this chapter. The reader should know the concept of Layer 3 VPNs and routing protocols prior to reading this chapter.

Network virtualization is an efficient utilization of network resources through logical segmentation of a single physical network. The need for network virtualization occurs because of multiple factors:

- Network consolidation due to mergers and acquisitions.
- To minimize total cost of ownership (TCO) by sharing network resources while still maintaining secure separation between organizations or groups.
- Consolidation reduces the cost of operations.
- Regulatory compliance such as the Health Insurance Portability and Accountability Act of 1996 (HIPAA) and Sarbanes-Oxley (SOX).

Network virtualization with Layer 3 VPNs in an enterprise network requires security to be aligned with the network. It is common to place the FWSM in a Layer 3 Virtual Private Network (VPN) environment. The FWSM does not inspect Layer 3 VPN packets. This chapter will help the reader to understand the design scenarios to achieve this requirement.

Layer 3 VPN (VRF) Terminations at FWSM

The FWSM does not have any knowledge of the Layer 3 VPNs. The Layer 3 VPN services can be terminated at the Layer 3 next hop router connected to the FWSM. The FWSM interfaces can be configured to map different Layer 3 VPNs (Virtual Route Forwarding, or VRF), by associating the interface with the next hop Layer 3 device, where the VRF tag is removed. The removal of the VRF tag makes the FWSM receive regular IP packets. The Layer 3 VPN technology references MPLS Layer 3 VPN or multi-VRF technologies. Using this concept of terminating the Layer 3 VPN traffic, the FWSM can apply security rules to the traffic. The Layer 3 VPN traffic (defined in RFC 2547) and segregation of traffic are maintained across security domains.

What is a VRF?

A Layer 3 VPN is associated with separate routing/forwarding instances called VRF. Every VPN membership is defined as a VRF. A VRF consists of the following:

- An IP routing table derived from the Cisco Express Forwarding (CEF) table
- A separate routing protocol table for the Layer 3 VPN
- A set of interfaces that use the forwarding table

Network virtualization can be achieved by enabling the following:

- GRE tunnels
- Multi-VRF
- MPLS VPNs
- L2TPV3

These four solutions are well suited for network virtualization in an enterprise environment and can use Layer 2 or Layer 3 segregation technologies:

- **GRE tunnels:** Routing segregation can be achieved by running GRE tunnels across the administered infrastructure. GRE tunnels are good for a small deployment. For a large-scale deployment for network virtualization, the GRE solution is not recommended.

- **Multi-VRF:** VRF-lite is a Cisco feature that also goes by the generic name of multi-VRF. It virtualizes the routing domains by enabling a single routing device to support multiple virtual routers. This segregation has local significance only on the router. With VRF-lite, network managers enjoy the flexibility of using any IP address space for any given Layer 3 VPN, regardless of whether it overlaps or conflicts with the address space of other VPNs. This flexibility is beneficial in many scenarios.

- **MPLS Layer 3 VPNs:** Another way to partition a campus network is using MPLS-based Layer 3 VPNs. MPLS VPNs provide logical separation of networks on a common physical infrastructure. This provides a solution for campus separation by enabling a single routing device to support multiple virtual routers. IP address space for any given VPN can overlap with another VPN's address space.

- **L2TPv3:** Layer 2 Tunneling Protocol version 3 (L2TPv3) allows service providers and large enterprises with native IP core networks to offer high-speed Layer 2 tunneling or Layer 3 VPN segregation.

Figure 23-1 shows the logical flow of packets in a VRF through the FWSM with an example. Here the VRF in the outside security domain is depicted as RED. The Layer 3 VPN header information is removed at the Layer 3 next hop device connected to the FWSM. The packet enters the FWSM as an IP packet. After the packet leaves the FWSM in another security domain, the Layer 3 next hop device in the new security domain can add Layer 3 VPN definition to the packet. The packet can be placed in a new Layer 3 VPN or maintained in the old Layer 3 VPN.

Figure 23-1 *Logical Flow of Packets for VRF Termination Concept on Layer 3 FWSM*

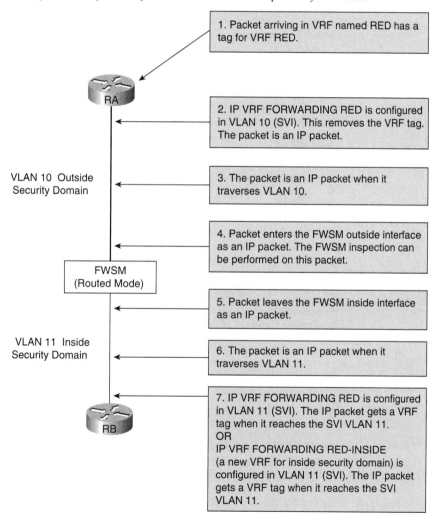

The outside interface in the switched virtual interface (SVI) is represented in VRF *out* (outside). The VRF *out* has its own virtual routing table.

The demilitarized zone (DMZ) is represented in the VRF *dmz*. The inside security domain is represented in the global routing table. The scenario in Figure 23-2 shows multiple VRF terminations at different security zones. The traffic from these VRFs flows to the global routing domain through the FWSM.

Figure 23-2 *VRF Termination on FWSM*

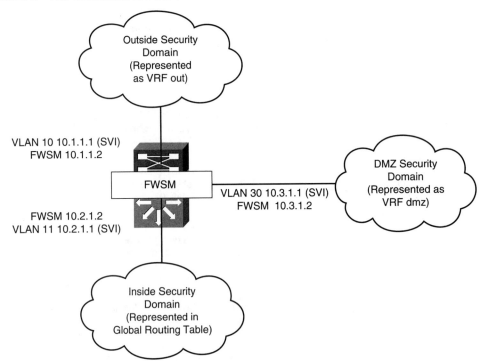

Because the FWSMs do not inspect labeled traffic, the key to pass the traffic through the security zones is to remove the Layer 3 VPN VRF tag from the packet before it reaches the FWSM. The IP packet traverses through the FWSM.

In this design, a single PFC is used for configuring a Layer 3 device for all security domains. The single PFC represents the Layer 3 next hop device at the outside and inside security domains. This is achieved by segregating the routing plane using VRF segregation.

In practical scenarios, multi-VRF using 802.1q or multiprotocol label switching (MPLS) can be used to extend these virtual domains across multiple Layer 3 hops.

Configuring the PFC

Follow the steps to configure Layer 3 segregation with multiple security domains on a single PFC. This configuration represents the PFC in Figure 23-2:

Step 1 Defining a VRF for each security domain:

```
ip vrf dmz
 rd 1:10
 route-target export 1:110
 route-target import 1:110
ip vrf out
 rd 1:1
 route-target export 1:101
 route-target import 1:101
```

Step 2 VLAN configuration on the switch:

```
vlan 10-13,20-24,30-31,34
```

Step 3 SVI configuration:

```
6504-E-1# show run interface vlan 10
Building configuration...
Current configuration : 82 bytes
!
interface Vlan10
 ip vrf forwarding out
 ip address 10.1.1.1 255.255.255.0
end
6504-E-1# show run interface vlan 11
Building configuration...
Current configuration : 59 bytes
!
interface Vlan11
 ip address 10.2.1.1 255.255.255.0
end
6504-E-1# show run interface vlan 30
Building configuration...
Current configuration : 82 bytes
!
interface Vlan30
 ip vrf forwarding dmz
ip address 10.3.1.1 255.255.255.0
```

Step 4 Static routes configuration:

```
ip route 0.0.0.0 0.0.0.0 10.2.1.2
ip route vrf out 10.2.0.0 255.255.0.0 10.1.1.2
ip route vrf out 10.3.0.0 255.255.0.0 10.1.1.2
ip route vrf dmz 0.0.0.0 0.0.0.0 10.3.1.2
```

Configuring the FWSM

The FWSM is configured as a single context routed mode. Some of the key elements to be noted in this configuration are the following:

- VLANs for the respective security domains
- Static translation
- NAT translation
- Access list
- Applying the access list to the interface
- Route statements

The following configuration represents the FWSM in Figure 23-2.

Example 23-1 *FWSM-A Configuration*

```
FWSM-A(config)# show run
: Saved
:
FWSM Version 3.1(3)6
!
hostname FWSM-A
enable password 8Ry2YjIyt7RRXU24 encrypted
names
! Configure outside interface parameters
interface Vlan10
 nameif outside
 security-level 0
 ip address 10.1.1.2 255.255.255.0
! Configure inside interface parameters
interface Vlan11
 nameif inside
 security-level 100
 ip address 10.2.1.2 255.255.255.0
! Configure dmz interface parameters
interface Vlan30
 nameif dmz
 security-level 50
 ip address 10.3.1.2 255.255.255.0
!
passwd 2KFQnbNIdI.2KYOU encrypted
ftp mode passive
!  Configure access list
```

Example 23-1 *FWSM-A Configuration (Continued)*

```
access-list 100 extended permit ip any any
access-list 100 remark this is for the outside
access-list 101 extended permit ip any any
access-list 101 remark this is for the inside
access-list 103 extended permit ip any any
access-list 103 remark this is for the dmz
pager lines 24
logging console debugging
logging monitor debugging
mtu outside 1500
mtu inside 1500
mtu dmz 1500
no failover
icmp permit any outside
icmp permit any inside
icmp permit any dmz
no asdm history enable
arp timeout 14400
! Configure translation statements
nat (inside) 0 0.0.0.0 0.0.0.0
nat (dmz) 1 0.0.0.0 0.0.0.0
static (inside,outside) 10.2.100.1 10.2.100.1 netmask 255.255.255.255
static (inside,outside) 10.2.1.1 10.2.1.1 netmask 255.255.255.255
static (inside,dmz) 10.2.1.1 10.2.1.1 netmask 255.255.255.255
static (dmz,outside) 10.3.1.1 10.3.1.1 netmask 255.255.255.255
! Reference the access list in the access-group command to be applied to the
! interfaces
access-group 101 in interface outside
access-group 100 out interface outside
access-group 101 in interface inside
access-group 101 out interface inside
access-group 103 in interface dmz
access-group 103 out interface dmz
! Configure routing statement with static routes
route outside 0.0.0.0 0.0.0.0 10.1.1.1 1
route inside 10.2.100.0 255.255.255.0 10.2.1.1 1
timeout xlate 3:00:00
timeout conn 1:00:00 half-closed 0:10:00 udp 0:02:00 icmp 0:00:02
timeout sunrpc 0:10:00 h323 0:05:00 h225 1:00:00 mgcp 0:05:00
timeout mgcp-pat 0:05:00 sip 0:30:00 sip_media 0:02:00
timeout uauth 0:05:00 absolute
no snmp-server location
no snmp-server contact
snmp-server enable traps snmp authentication linkup linkdown coldstart
telnet timeout 5
ssh timeout 5
console timeout 0
!
class-map inspection_default
 match default-inspection-traffic
!
policy-map global_policy
```

continues

Example 23-1 *FWSM-A Configuration (Continued)*

```
 class inspection_default
  inspect dns maximum-length 512
  inspect ftp
  inspect h323 h225
  inspect h323 ras
  inspect netbios
  inspect rsh
  inspect skinny
  inspect smtp
  inspect sqlnet
  inspect sunrpc
  inspect tftp
  inspect sip
  inspect xdmcp
 !
 service-policy global_policy global
 prompt hostname context
 Cryptochecksum:37b36406e10906d46d2da6d01071394b
 : end
```

Failover Configuration in Mixed Mode

Figure 23-3 illustrates the firewall configuration for multiple context modes. One of the contexts is in routed mode and the other is in transparent mode. VLANs defined in the FWSM are allowed on the trunk interface between the primary and secondary switches. The concept of Layer 3 VPN termination covered in the previous section is used to terminate security zones on the Layer 3 device.

Instead of using shared interfaces, the global routing table is leaked into the VRF outside. Each security context has its own VLAN in the VRF outside, instead of shared outside Layer 3 VLAN for both the contexts. The Department 1(DEPT1) and Department 2(DEPT2) security domains are represented as separate VRFs. If DEPT1 needs to access devices in DEPT2, the traffic first passes through the DEPT1 context; then it passes through the outside VRF and to DEPT2 context. In the same way, the traffic will traverse in the reverse direction. This removes the concept of a shared Layer 2 VLAN between contexts. In Figure 23-3, the context A and context A1 (standby) are in routed mode, and context B and context B1 (standby) are in transparent mode.

Figure 23-3 *Hybrid Firewall/Failover Configuration*

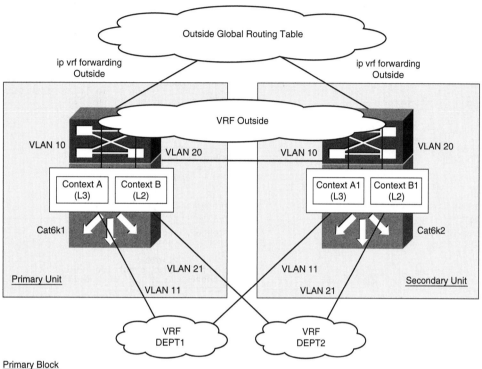

Primary Block

SVI VLAN 10 (VRF Outside) 10.1.1.1 HSRP VIP 10.1.1.10
SVI VLAN 20 (VRF Outside) 10.10.1.1 HSRP VIP 10.10.1.10
SVI VLAN 11 (VRF DEPT1) 10.2.1.1 HSRP VIP 10.2.1.10
SVI VLAN 21 (VRF DEPT2) 10.10.1.21 HSRP VIP 10.10.1.30

FWSM

Context A: VLAN 10 (Outside) Primary IP 10.1.1.3 Secondary IP 10.1.1.4
        VLAN 11 (Inside) Primary IP 10.2.1.3 Secondary IP 10.2.1.4
Context B: BVI-10.2.1.100 (Layer 2 Mode)
Failover VLAN : VLAN 50 Primary IP 192.168.1.1, Secondary IP 192.168.1.2
Failover State VLAN : VLAN 50 Primary IP 192.168.2.1, Secondary IP 192.168.2.2

Secondary Block

SVI VLAN 10 (VRF Outside) 10.1.1.2 HSRP VIP 10.1.1.10
SVI VLAN 20 (VRF Outside) 10.10.1.2 HSRP VIP 10.10.1.10
SVI VLAN 11 (VRF DEPT1) 10.2.1.2 HSRP VIP 10.2.1.10
SVI VLAN 21 (VRF DEPT2) 10.10.1.22 HSRP VIP 10.10.1.30

Table 23-1 shows the primary block switch and the secondary block switch configurations.

Table 23-1   *Primary/Secondary Block Switch Configurations*

Primary Block Switch Configuration	Secondary Block Switch Configuration
| ```
! FWSM VLAN configuration at
! the PFC
firewall multiple-vlan-interfaces
firewall module 9 vlan-group 9
firewall vlan-group 9   10,11,20,21,50,51
!VRF configuration for DEPT1
ip vrf DEPT1
 rd 1:2
 route-target export 1:102
 route-target import 1:102
! VRF configuration for DEPT2
ip vrf DEPT2
 rd 1:3
 route-target export 1:103
 route-target import 1:103
! VRF configuration for
! outside Security domain
ip vrf outside
  rd 1:1
  route-target export 1:101
  route-target import 1:101
!
interface Vlan10
  ip vrf forwarding outside
  ip address 10.1.1.1 255.255.255.0
  standby 1 ip 10.1.1.10
  standby 1 priority 150
  standby 1 preempt
! Associating the SVI in VRF
interface Vlan11
  ip vrf forwarding DEPT1
  ip address 10.2.1.1 255.255.255.0
  standby 2 ip 10.2.1.10
  standby 2 priority 150
  standby 2 preempt
  ! Associating the SVI in VRF
interface Vlan20
  mac-address 0000.0000.0001
  ip vrf forwarding outside
  ip address 10.10.1.1 255.255.255.0
  standby 1 ip 10.10.1.10
  standby 1 priority 150
  standby 1 preempt
!
 interface Vlan21
 mac-address 0000.0000.0021
 ip vrf forwarding DEPT2
 ip address 10.10.1.21 255.255.255.0
 standby 2 ip 10.10.1.30
 standby 2 priority 150
 standby 2 preempt
!
interface GigabitEthernet5/1
switchport
switchport trunk encapsulation dot1q
switchport mode trunk
no ip address
!
arp vrf DEPT2 10.10.1.1 0000.0000.0001 ARPA
arp vrf DEPT2 10.10.1.2 0000.0000.0002 ARPA
arp vrf outside 10.10.1.21 0000.0000.0021 ARPA
arp vrf outside 10.10.1.22 0000.0000.0022 ARPA
``` | ```
! FWSM VLAN configuration at
! the PFC
firewall multiple-vlan-interfaces
firewall module 9 vlan-group 9
firewall vlan-group 9   10,11,20,21,50,51
!VRF configuration for VRF DEPT1
ip vrf DEPT1
 rd 1:2
 route-target export 1:102
 route-target import 1:102
! VRF configuration for DEPT2
ip vrf DEPT2
 rd 1:3
 route-target export 1:103
 route-target import 1:103
! VRF configuration for
! outside Security domain
ip vrf outside
  rd 1:1
  route-target export 1:101
  route-target import 1:101
!
interface Vlan10
 ip vrf forwarding outside
 ip address 10.1.1.2 255.255.255.0
 standby 1 ip 10.1.1.10
!
!
! Associating the SVI in VRF
interface Vlan11
 ip vrf forwarding outside
 ip address 10.2.1.2 255.255.255.0
 standby 2 ip 10.2.1.10
!
!
! Associating the SVI in VRF
interface Vlan20
 mac-address 0000.0000.0002
 ip vrf forwarding outside
 ip address 10.10.1.2 255.255.255.0
 standby 1 ip 10.10.1.10
!
!
interface Vlan21
 mac-address 0000.0000.0022
 ip vrf forwarding DEPT2
 ip address 10.10.1.22 255.255.255.0
 standby 2 ip 10.10.1.30
!
!
interface GigabitEthernet5/1
 switchport
 switchport trunk encapsulation dot1q
 switchport mode trunk
 no ip address
!
arp vrf DEPT2 10.10.1.1 0000.0000.0001 ARPA
arp vrf DEPT2 10.10.1.2 0000.0000.0002 ARPA
arp vrf outside 10.10.1.21 0000.0000.0021 ARPA
arp vrf outside 10.10.1.22 0000.0000.0022 ARPA
``` |

Example 23-2 shows the primary FWSM system context configuration.

Example 23-2 *Primary FWSM System Context Configuration*

```
FWSM# show run
: Saved
:
FWSM Version 3.2(1) <system>
!
resource acl-partition 12
hostname FWSM
enable password 8Ry2YjIyt7RRXU24 encrypted
!
interface Vlan10
!
interface Vlan11
!
interface Vlan20
!
interface Vlan21
!
interface Vlan30
!
interface Vlan31
!
interface Vlan50
 description LAN Failover Interface
!
interface Vlan51
 description STATE Failover Interface
!
passwd 2KFQnbNIdI.2KYOU encrypted
class default
  limit-resource IPSec 5
  limit-resource Mac-addresses 65535
  limit-resource ASDM 5
  limit-resource SSH 5
  limit-resource Telnet 5
  limit-resource All 0
!
ftp mode passive
pager lines 24
! In the Failover configuration, the unit is a primary firewall

failover
failover lan unit primary
failover lan interface fover Vlan50
failover replication http
failover link flink Vlan51
failover interface ip fover 192.168.1.1 255.255.255.0 standby 192.168.1.2
failover interface ip flink 192.168.2.1 255.255.255.0 standby 192.168.2.2
no asdm history enable
arp timeout 14400
console timeout 0
```

continues

Example 23-2 *Primary FWSM System Context Configuration (Continued)*

```
admin-context admin
context admin
  config-url disk:/admin.cfg
! Define contexta and the VLANs associated with the context
context contexta
  allocate-interface Vlan10
  allocate-interface Vlan11
  config-url disk:/contexta.cfg
! Define contextb and the VLANs associated with the context
context contextb
  allocate-interface Vlan20
  allocate-interface Vlan21
  config-url disk:/contextb.cfg
!
prompt hostname context
Cryptochecksum:b6d0dd27e9719ebc2c46b88282a65540
: end
```

Example 23-3 shows the context A configuration (primary).

Example 23-3 *Context A Configuration (Primary)*

```
FWSM Version 3.2(1) <context>
!
hostname contexta
enable password 8Ry2YjIyt7RRXU24 encrypted
names
! Configure parameters for interface of outside security domain. Configure the
! standby IP address of the contexta in the secondary FWSM
interface Vlan10
 nameif outside
 security-level 0
 ip address 10.1.1.3 255.255.255.0 standby 10.1.1.4
! Configure parameters for interface of inside security domain. Configure the
! standby IP address of the contexta in the secondary FWSM
interface Vlan11
 nameif inside
 security-level 100
 ip address 10.2.1.3 255.255.255.0 standby 10.2.1.4
passwd 2KFQnbNIdI.2KYOU encrypted
! Configure access list
access-list 100 extended permit ip any any
pager lines 24
mtu outside 1500
mtu inside 1500
monitor-interface outside
monitor-interface inside
icmp permit any outside
icmp permit any inside
no asdm history enable
```

Example 23-3   *Context A Configuration (Primary) (Continued)*

```
arp timeout 14400
! Configure NAT
nat (outside) 1 0.0.0.0 0.0.0.0
nat (inside) 1 0.0.0.0 0.0.0.0
! Apply the access list to the interface using access-group command
access-group 100 in interface outside
access-group 100 out interface outside
access-group 100 in interface inside
access-group 100 out interface inside
! Configure default route
route outside 0.0.0.0 0.0.0.0 10.1.1.10 1
timeout xlate 3:00:00
timeout conn 1:00:00 half-closed 0:10:00 udp 0:02:00 icmp 0:00:02
timeout sunrpc 0:10:00 h323 0:05:00 h225 1:00:00 mgcp 0:05:00
timeout mgcp-pat 0:05:00 sip 0:30:00 sip_media 0:02:00
timeout sip-invite 0:03:00 sip-disconnect 0:02:00
timeout uauth 0:05:00 absolute
no snmp-server location
no snmp-server contact
telnet timeout 5
ssh timeout 5
!
class-map inspection_default
 match default-inspection-traffic
!
policy-map global_policy
 class inspection_default
  inspect dns maximum-length 512
  inspect ftp
  inspect h323 h225
  inspect h323 ras
  inspect netbios
  inspect rsh
  inspect skinny
  inspect smtp
  inspect sqlnet
  inspect sunrpc
  inspect tftp
  inspect sip
  inspect xdmcp
!
service-policy global_policy global
Cryptochecksum:5d298396be7b0e28ae274c14af178302
: end
```

Example 23-4 shows the context B configuration (primary).

Example 23-4 *Context B Configuration (Primary)*

```
FWSM Version 3.2(1) <context>
!configure the contextb in transparent mode
firewall transparent
hostname contextb
enable password 8Ry2YjIyt7RRXU24 encrypted
names
! Configure parameters for interface in the outside security domain for transparent
! mode
interface Vlan20
 nameif outside
 bridge-group 1
 security-level 0
! Configure parameters for interface in the inside security domain for transparent
! mode
interface Vlan21
 nameif inside
 bridge-group 1
 security-level 100
!
passwd 2KFQnbNIdI.2KYOU encrypted
! Define the access list
access-list 100 extended permit ip any any
access-list 100 extended permit udp any any
access-list 101 ethertype permit bpdu
pager lines 24
mtu outside 1500
mtu inside 1500
monitor-interface outside
monitor-interface inside
no asdm history enable
arp timeout 14400
! Apply the access list to the interface using access-group command
access-group 101 in interface outside
access-group 101 out interface outside
access-group 100 in interface outside
access-group 100 out interface outside
access-group 101 in interface inside
access-group 101 out interface inside
access-group 100 in interface inside
access-group 100 out interface inside
timeout xlate 3:00:00
timeout conn 1:00:00 half-closed 0:10:00 udp 0:02:00 icmp 0:00:02
timeout sunrpc 0:10:00 h323 0:05:00 h225 1:00:00 mgcp 0:05:00
timeout mgcp-pat 0:05:00 sip 0:30:00 sip_media 0:02:00
timeout sip-invite 0:03:00 sip-disconnect 0:02:00
timeout uauth 0:05:00 absolute
no snmp-server location
no snmp-server contact
snmp-server enable traps snmp authentication linkup linkdown coldstart
telnet timeout 5
```

Example 23-4 *Context B Configuration (Primary) (Continued)*

```
ssh timeout 5
!
class-map inspection_default
 match default-inspection-traffic
!
policy-map global_policy
 class inspection_default
  inspect dns maximum-length 512
  inspect ftp
  inspect h323 h225
  inspect h323 ras
  inspect rsh
  inspect smtp
  inspect sqlnet
  inspect skinny
  inspect sunrpc
  inspect xdmcp
  inspect sip
  inspect netbios
  inspect tftp
!
service-policy global_policy global
Cryptochecksum:7d29936fd297549850d3577af19b0de3
: end
```

Refer to Chapter 12, "Failover in FWSM," for configuring a standby FWSM unit.

Interdomain Communication of Different Security Zones Through a Single FWSM

Interdomain communication between various security zones has become very common, especially when firewalls are integrated in the data center environment.

Figure 23-4 illustrates a scenario in an enterprise network. The FWSM is configured for multiple context routed mode and VRF termination at the Layer 3 next hop to achieve zoning and routing segregations using the same device. In this scenario, consolidation is done when there is a requirement of a common security domain with multiple security domains, with restricted access.

Figure 23-4 *Communication of Different Security Zones in a Single FWSM with Multiple Context Mode*

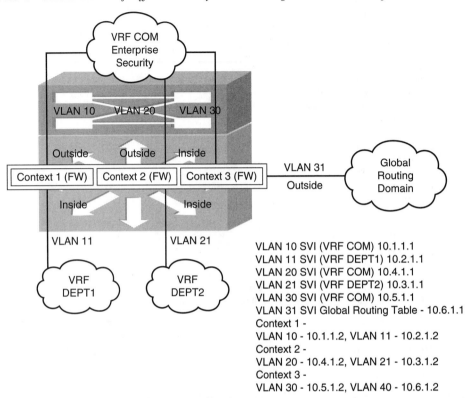

VLAN 10 SVI (VRF COM) 10.1.1.1
VLAN 11 SVI (VRF DEPT1) 10.2.1.1
VLAN 20 SVI (VRF COM) 10.4.1.1
VLAN 21 SVI (VRF DEPT2) 10.3.1.1
VLAN 30 SVI (VRF COM) 10.5.1.1
VLAN 31 SVI Global Routing Table - 10.6.1.1
Context 1 -
VLAN 10 - 10.1.1.2, VLAN 11 - 10.2.1.2
Context 2 -
VLAN 20 - 10.4.1.2, VLAN 21 - 10.3.1.2
Context 3 -
VLAN 30 - 10.5.1.2, VLAN 40 - 10.6.1.2

In Figure 23-4, the common security domain is represented in the VRF *COM*. The Department 1(DEPT1) and Department 2(DEPT2) security domains are represented as separate VRFs.

For the packet from DEPT1 to access DEPT2, it traverses through DEPT1 context, then to VRF COM, next to DEPT2 context, and finally reaches DEPT2's routing domain. This scenario assumes that the security policy allows the IP packet flow between the contexts. Figure 23-4 gives a hierarchy of security domains in a single FWSM and a Layer 3 device representing each security domain.

Configuring the PFC

PFC is configured as the Layer 3 next hop device from the FWSM on each security domain. This is achieved by segregating the routing tables using Layer 3 VPN technology. This configuration represents the PFC in Figure 23-4. Follow the steps to configure segregation of routing for each security domain:

Step 1 VRF representing each security domain:

```
ip vrf COM
 rd 1:1
 route-target export 1:101
 route-target import 1:101
!
ip vrf DEPT1
 rd 1:2
 route-target export 1:102
 route-target import 1:102
!
ip vrf DEPT2
 rd 1:3
 route-target export 1:103
 route-target import 1:103
```

Step 2 Enabling VLAN in the database:

```
vlan 90-92,100-101,325
```

Step 3 Configuring the SVI interfaces in different VRFs:

```
!
interface Vlan10
 ip vrf forwarding COM
 ip address 10.1.1.1 255.255.255.0
!
interface Vlan11
 ip vrf forwarding DEPT1
 ip address 10.2.1.1 255.255.255.0
!
interface Vlan20
 ip vrf forwarding COM
 ip address 10.4.1.1 255.255.255.0
!
interface Vlan21
 ip vrf forwarding DEPT2
 ip address 10.3.1.1 255.255.255.0
!
interface Vlan30
 ip vrf forwarding COM
 ip address 10.1.1.1 255.255.255.0
!
interface Vlan31
 ip address 10.6.1.1 255.255.255.0
```

Step 4   Firewall configuration at the PFC:

```
firewall multiple-vlan-interfaces
firewall module 4 vlan-group 3
firewall vlan-group 3  10,11,20,21,30,31
```

Step 5   Static route configuration:

```
ip route 10.1.0.0 255.255.0.0 10.6.1.2
ip route 10.2.0.0 255.255.0.0 10.6.1.2
ip route 10.3.0.0 255.255.0.0 10.6.1.2
ip route 10.4.0.0 255.255.0.0 10.6.1.2
ip route 10.5.0.0 255.255.0.0 10.6.1.2
ip route vrf COM 0.0.0.0 0.0.0.0 10.5.1.2
ip route vrf COM 10.2.0.0 255.255.0.0 10.1.1.2
ip route vrf COM 10.3.0.0 255.255.0.0 10.4.1.2
ip route vrf DEPT1 0.0.0.0 0.0.0.0 10.2.1.2
ip route vrf DEPT2 0.0.0.0 0.0.0.0 10.3.1.2
```

FWSM Configuration

The configuration in Example 23-5 represents the FWSM in multiple context mode. Refer to Figure 23-4.

Example 23-5   *Configuration of the System Context*

```
FWSM Version 3.1(3)6 <system>
!
resource acl-partition 12
hostname FWSMB
enable password 8Ry2YjIyt7RRXU24 encrypted
!
interface Vlan10
!
interface Vlan11
!
interface Vlan12
!
interface Vlan13
!
interface Vlan20
!
interface Vlan21
!
interface Vlan30
!
interface Vlan31
!
passwd 2KFQnbNIdI.2KYOU encrypted
class default
  limit-resource IPSec 5
```

Example 23-5   *Configuration of the System Context (Continued)*

```
  limit-resource Mac-addresses 65535
  limit-resource ASDM 5
  limit-resource SSH 5
  limit-resource Telnet 5
  limit-resource All 0
!
ftp mode passive
pager lines 24
no failover
no asdm history enable
arp timeout 14400
console timeout 0
admin-context admin
context admin
  config-url disk:/admin.cfg
! Define the contextA and the VLANs associated with contextA
context contextA
  allocate-interface Vlan10
  allocate-interface Vlan11
  config-url disk:/contextA.cfg
! Define the contextB and the VLANs associated with contextB
context contextB
  allocate-interface Vlan20
  allocate-interface Vlan21
  config-url disk:/contextB.cfg
! Define the contextC and the VLANs associated with contextC
context contextC
  allocate-interface Vlan30
  allocate-interface Vlan31
  config-url disk:/contextC.cfg
!
prompt hostname context
Cryptochecksum:c96ae291d4ebe9900c814120989cfd91
: end
```

Example 23-6 shows the configuration of the FWSM in contextA.

Example 23-6   *FWSM ContextA*

```
hostname contextA
enable password 8Ry2YjIyt7RRXU24 encrypted
names
! Configure interface parameters for the outside security domain
interface Vlan10
 nameif outside
 security-level 0
 ip address 10.1.1.2 255.255.255.0
! Configure interface parameters for the inside security domain
interface Vlan11
 nameif inside
 security-level 100
 ip address 10.2.1.2 255.255.255.0
```

continues

Example 23-6   *FWSM ContextA (Continued)*

```
!
passwd 2KFQnbNIdI.2KYOU encrypted
! Configure access list
access-list 100 extended permit ip any any
access-list 100 remark this is for the outside
access-list 100 remark this is for the outside
access-list 101 extended permit ip any any
access-list 101 remark this is for the inside
access-list 101 remark this is for the inside
pager lines 24
mtu outside 1500
mtu inside 1500
icmp permit any outside
icmp permit any inside
no asdm history enable
arp timeout 14400
! Configure NAT
nat (inside) 1 0.0.0.0 0.0.0.0
! Configure Static translation
static (inside,outside) 10.2.1.1 10.2.1.1 netmask 255.255.255.255
! Apply the access list to the interface using the access-group command
access-group 101 in interface outside
access-group 100 out interface outside
access-group 101 in interface inside
access-group 101 out interface inside
! Configure default route
route outside 0.0.0.0 0.0.0.0 10.1.1.1 1
timeout xlate 3:00:00
timeout conn 1:00:00 half-closed 0:10:00 udp 0:02:00 icmp 0:00:02
timeout sunrpc 0:10:00 h323 0:05:00 h225 1:00:00 mgcp 0:05:00
timeout mgcp-pat 0:05:00 sip 0:30:00 sip_media 0:02:00
timeout uauth 0:05:00 absolute
no snmp-server location
no snmp-server contact
telnet timeout 5
ssh timeout 5
!
class-map inspection_default
 match default-inspection-traffic
!
policy-map global_policy
 class inspection_default
  inspect dns maximum-length 512
  inspect ftp
  inspect h323 h225
  inspect h323 ras
  inspect netbios
  inspect rsh
  inspect skinny
  inspect smtp
  inspect sqlnet
  inspect sunrpc
  inspect tftp
```

Example 23-6 *FWSM ContextA (Continued)*

```
  inspect sip
  inspect xdmcp
!
service-policy global_policy global
Cryptochecksum:3127e35b248201054add298d9196640a
: end
```

Example 23-7 shows the configuration of the FWSM in contextB.

Example 23-7 *FWSM ContextB*

```
!
hostname contextB
enable password 8Ry2YjIyt7RRXU24 encrypted
names
! Configure interface parameters for the outside security domain
interface Vlan20
 nameif outside
 security-level 0
 ip address 10.4.1.2 255.255.255.0
! Configure interface parameters for the inside security domain
interface Vlan21
 nameif inside
 security-level 100
 ip address 10.3.1.2 255.255.255.0
!
passwd 2KFQnbNIdI.2KYOU encrypted
! Configure access list
access-list 100 extended permit ip any any
access-list 100 remark this is for the outside
access-list 100 remark this is for the outside
access-list 101 extended permit ip any any
access-list 101 remark this is for the inside
access-list 101 remark this is for the inside
pager lines 24
mtu inside 1500
mtu outside 1500
icmp permit any inside
icmp permit any outside
no asdm history enable
arp timeout 14400
! Configure NAT
nat (inside) 1 0.0.0.0 0.0.0.0
! Apply the access list to the interface using an access-group command
access-group 101 in interface inside
access-group 101 out interface inside
access-group 101 in interface outside
access-group 100 out interface outside
! Configure default route
route outside 0.0.0.0 0.0.0.0 10.4.1.1 1
timeout xlate 3:00:00
timeout conn 1:00:00 half-closed 0:10:00 udp 0:02:00 icmp 0:00:02
timeout sunrpc 0:10:00 h323 0:05:00 h225 1:00:00 mgcp 0:05:00
```

continues

Example 23-7 *FWSM ContextB (Continued)*

```
timeout mgcp-pat 0:05:00 sip 0:30:00 sip_media 0:02:00
timeout uauth 0:05:00 absolute
no snmp-server location
no snmp-server contact
telnet timeout 5
ssh timeout 5
!
class-map inspection_default
 match default-inspection-traffic
!
policy-map global_policy
 class inspection_default
  inspect dns maximum-length 512
  inspect ftp
  inspect h323 h225
  inspect h323 ras
  inspect netbios
  inspect rsh
  inspect skinny
  inspect smtp
  inspect sqlnet
  inspect sunrpc
  inspect tftp
  inspect sip
  inspect xdmcp
!
service-policy global_policy global
Cryptochecksum:0f2408e8ec439db20b84eec6e82e8fb8
: end
```

Example 23-8 shows the configuration of the FWSM in contextC.

Example 23-8 *FWSM ContextC*

```
hostname contextC
enable password 8Ry2YjIyt7RRXU24 encrypted
names
! Configure interface parameters for the inside security domain
interface Vlan30
 nameif inside
 security-level 100
 ip address 10.5.1.2 255.255.255.0
! Configure interface parameters for the outside security domain
interface Vlan31
 nameif outside
 security-level 0
 ip address 10.6.1.2 255.255.255.0
!
passwd 2KFQnbNIdI.2KYOU encrypted
! Configure access list
access-list 100 extended permit ip any any
access-list 100 remark this is for the outside
access-list 100 remark this is for the outside
```

Example 23-8 *FWSM ContextC (Continued)*

```
access-list 101 extended permit ip any any
access-list 101 remark this is for the inside
access-list 101 remark this is for the inside
pager lines 24
mtu inside 1500
mtu outside 1500
icmp permit any inside
icmp permit any outside
no asdm history enable
arp timeout 14400
! Configure NAT
nat (inside) 1 0.0.0.0 0.0.0.0
! Apply the access list to the interface using access-group command
access-group 101 in interface inside
access-group 101 out interface inside
access-group 101 in interface outside
access-group 100 out interface outside
! Configure default route
route outside 0.0.0.0 0.0.0.0 10.6.1.1 1
timeout xlate 3:00:00
timeout conn 1:00:00 half-closed 0:10:00 udp 0:02:00 icmp 0:00:02
timeout sunrpc 0:10:00 h323 0:05:00 h225 1:00:00 mgcp 0:05:00
timeout mgcp-pat 0:05:00 sip 0:30:00 sip_media 0:02:00
timeout uauth 0:05:00 absolute
no snmp-server location
no snmp-server contact
telnet timeout 5
ssh timeout 5
!
class-map inspection_default
 match default-inspection-traffic
!
policy-map global_policy
 class inspection_default
  inspect dns maximum-length 512
  inspect ftp
  inspect h323 h225
  inspect h323 ras
  inspect netbios
  inspect rsh
  inspect skinny
  inspect smtp
  inspect sqlnet
  inspect sunrpc
  inspect tftp
  inspect sip
  inspect xdmcp
!
service-policy global_policy global
Cryptochecksum:079cf249ee9a732e58b216770e97782f
: end
```

Dynamic Learning of Routes with FWSM

Placement of the FWSM is very important in the design. The routing information from one security domain to the other can determine the resiliency of the design. Following are some of the methods that can be used to learn the routes between security domains:

- **Method 1—Static routes:** The traditional method is to use static routes. The Layer 3 device at the inside security domain has a default route that points to the inside interface of the FWSM. (In case of a failover scenario, the static route will point to the IP address of the inside interface in the primary FWSM.) The firewall will have static routes for the inside subnets pointing to the inside VLAN's Hot Standby Router Protocol (HSRP) IP address. The FWSM will have a default route pointing to the outside VLAN's HSRP IP address. At the PFC, the outside security domain will have subnets defined in the inside security domain, pointing to the outside IP address defined in the primary FWSM (in case of redundancy). The route statements will be present in the inside security domain for the IP addresses in the outside security domain pointing to the primary FWSM's inside interface.

  The dynamic failover of routing traffic to the FWSM is achieved with static routes because the next hop IP addresses in the static routes point to the virtual IP address. The FWSM points to the virtual IP address of the primary HSRP of the VLAN, and the Layer 3 device has a static route that points to the primary FWSM's interface IP address for the respective domains. You should note that when using static routes, there is always a drawback of manual configuration in the network and firewalls for any changes in the network reachability. This is both time consuming and exhausting.

- **Method 2—Enabling a routing protocol on the FWSM:** Enabling a routing protocol on the FWSM is another way of routing packets. The FWSM can pass information about the routing next-hop IP address from one security domain to the other. The FWSM can be enabled with a routing protocol, such as OSPF, RIP, or BGP stub. For more information on implementing this solution, refer to Chapter 9, "Configuring Routing Protocols."

- **Method 3—Using BGP to carry routes between the domains:** In this method, static routes are configured for next hop reachability between the security domains. The static routes in the FWSM get the BGP session established between the Layer 3 devices in the security domains, and the packet forwarding in the Layer 3 domain will be based on BGP routing updates. BGP will rely on static routes for its session to be established. The FWSM will have routes defined only for IP addresses that will establish the BGP session between the Layer 3 devices in the security domains and for subnets of the network present in each security domain. The Layer 3 next hop device connected to the FWSM will also have static routes, for the BGP session to be established. BGP is configured in the Layer 3 devices of different security domains.

The FWSM should have TCP port 179 open in the security rule set. The BGP connection is established and carries the routing information from one domain to the other. FWSM does not participate in BGP routing.

- **Method 4—Routing updates through transparent firewalls:** The FWSM in this design is in Layer 2 mode. OSPF, BGP, and EIGRP are common routing protocols that are used to exchange routes between different security zones. FWSM in transparent mode can have two interfaces. The route exchange in this case will be between the two interfaces in the same bridge group. Intermediate System-to-Intermediate System (IS-IS) cannot be used to exchange routing information between two security domains in the transparent mode. The FWSM configuration will require the **access-list** command to permit the routing protocol ports. This methodology of route exchange is transparent to the FWSM.

Single Box Solution with OSPF

In Figure 23-5, the configurations for the Layer 3 device at the outside security domain, FWSM, and the Layer 3 device for the inside security domain are configured in a single chassis with the FWSM module. The concept of virtualization with Layer 3 VPNs is integrated as a solution with the FWSM. The following example with configuration will help you understand Method 4.

Figure 23-5 *Method 4 for Route Learning Across Security Domains with OSPF*

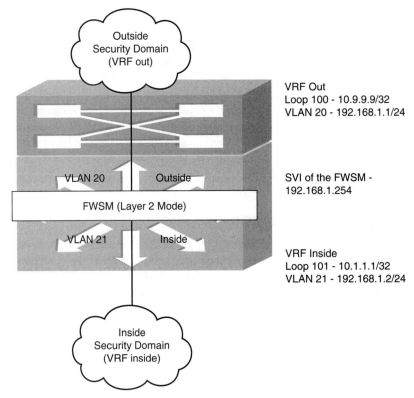

VRF Out
Loop 100 - 10.9.9.9/32
VLAN 20 - 192.168.1.1/24

SVI of the FWSM -
192.168.1.254

VRF Inside
Loop 101 - 10.1.1.1/32
VLAN 21 - 192.168.1.2/24

Example 23-9 shows PFC configuration of the Layer 3 next hop for the inside and outside security domains.

Example 23-9 *PFC Configuration*

```
! Define VLANs for the FWSM
firewall multiple-vlan-interfaces
firewall module 4 vlan-group 1
firewall vlan-group 1   10,11,20,21
ip subnet-zero
! define VRF for the inside security domain
ip vrf inside
 rd 1:2
 route-target export 1:102
 route-target import 1:102
! define VRF for the outside security domain
ip vrf out
 rd 1:1
 route-target export 1:101
 route-target import 1:101
```

Example 23-9 *PFC Configuration (Continued)*

```
! enable routing process associated with the outside security domain. The networks
! advertised in this routing process is configured in VRF out
router ospf 1 vrf out
 router-id 10.9.9.9
 log-adjacency-changes
 network 192.168.1.0 0.0.255.255 area 0
 network 10.9.9.9 0.0.0.0 area 0
 default-information originate always
! Enable routing process associated with the inside security domain. The networks
! advertised in this routing process is configured in the VRF inside
router ospf 2 vrf inside
 router-id 10.1.1.1
 log-adjacency-changesnetwork 192.168.1.0 0.0.0.255 area 0
 network 10.1.1.1 0.0.0.0 area 0
! The interfaces of the inside and outside security domains communicate with each
! other in the same subnet. The ARP statements are configured for the respective VRFs
arp vrf inside 192.168.1.1 0000.0000.0020 ARPA
arp vrf out 192.168.1.2 0000.0000.0021 ARPA
! Layer 3 next hop interface from the FWSM at the outside security domain
6504-E-2# show run interface vlan 20
Building configuration...
Current configuration : 141 bytes
!
interface Vlan20
 mac-address 0000.0000.0020
 ip vrf forwarding out
 ip address 192.168.1.1 255.255.255.0
 ip ospf network point-to-point
end
! Layer 3 next hop interface from the FWSM at the inside security domain
6504-E-2# show run interface vlan 21
Building configuration...
Current configuration : 144 bytes
!
interface Vlan21
 mac-address 0000.0000.0021
 ip vrf forwarding inside
 ip address 192.168.1.2 255.255.255.0
 ip ospf network point-to-point
end
! Loopback 100 is in the outside security domain and is the router-id of OSPF process
! enabled at the outside security domain
6504-E-2# show run interface loopback 100
Building configuration...
Current configuration : 109 bytes
!
interface Loopback100
 description outside
 ip vrf forwarding out
 ip address 10.9.9.9 255.255.255.255
end
```

continues

Example 23-9 *PFC Configuration (Continued)*

```
! Loopback 101 is in the inside security domain and is the router-id of OSPF process
! enabled at the inside security domain
6504-E-2# show run interface loopback 101
Building configuration...
Current configuration : 92 bytes
!
interface Loopback101
 ip vrf forwarding inside
 ip address 10.1.1.1 255.255.255.255
end
```

Example 23-10 shows FWSM configuration in transparent mode.

Example 23-10 *FWSM Configuration in Transparent Mode*

```
A# show run
: Saved
:
FWSM Version 3.1(3)6
! Configure the FWSM in transparent mode
firewall transparent
hostname A
enable password 8Ry2YjIyt7RRXU24 encrypted
names
! Configure the VLAN 20 for the outside security domain
interface Vlan20
 nameif outside
 bridge-group 1
 security-level 0
! Configure the VLAN 21 for the inside security domain
interface Vlan21
 nameif inside
 bridge-group 1
 security-level 100
! Configure the BVI interface
interface BVI1
 ip address 192.168.1.254 255.255.255.0
 !
passwd 2KFQnbNIdI.2KYOU encrypted
ftp mode passive
! Configure the access list
access-list 100 extended permit ip any any
access-list 100 extended permit udp any any
access-list 101 ethertype permit bpdu
pager lines 24
mtu outside 1500
mtu inside 1500
no failover
monitor-interface outside
monitor-interface inside
no asdm history enable
```

Example 23-10 *FWSM Configuration in Transparent Mode (Continued)*

```
arp timeout 14400
! Apply the access list to the outside interface using access-group command
access-group 101 in interface outside
access-group 100 in interface outside
access-group 100 out interface outside
access-group 101 in interface inside
access-group 100 in interface inside
access-group 100 out interface inside
! Configure default route needed for management purposes
route outside 0.0.0.0 0.0.0.0 192.168.1.1 1
timeout xlate 3:00:00
timeout conn 1:00:00 half-closed 0:10:00 udp 0:02:00 icmp 0:00:02
timeout sunrpc 0:10:00 h323 0:05:00 h225 1:00:00 mgcp 0:05:00
timeout mgcp-pat 0:05:00 sip 0:30:00 sip_media 0:02:00
timeout uauth 0:05:00 absolute
no snmp-server location
no snmp-server contact
snmp-server enable traps snmp authentication linkup linkdown coldstart
telnet timeout 5
ssh timeout 5
console timeout 0
!
class-map inspection_default
 match default-inspection-traffic
!
policy-map global_policy
 class inspection_default
  inspect dns maximum-length 512
  inspect ftp
  inspect h323 h225
  inspect h323 ras
  inspect rsh
  inspect smtp
  inspect sqlnet
  inspect skinny
  inspect sunrpc
  inspect xdmcp
  inspect sip
  inspect netbios
  inspect tftp
!
service-policy global_policy global
prompt hostname context
Cryptochecksum:4fb151060932dedd650b448bc02e456a
: end
```

Data Center Environment with the FWSM

The concepts covered in the previous sections change the perspective of the design principles for designing a data center. This brings the concept of virtualization through Layer 3 VPNs and the FWSM used together as a design solution.

In an enterprise customer environment, the current trend is consolidation of network infrastructure primarily to have reductions in the total cost of operation. Consolidation of the wide-area network (WAN) infrastructure is accomplished using Layer 3 VPNs.

This section goes through design details to consolidate the data center environment without using Spanning Tree. Here, multiple departments (for the same customer) can use the same switch/router/firewall in the data center environment and maintain separate security domains with traffic segregation.

There are two ways to achieve the desired design solution:

- Layer 3 VPN segregation (multi-vrf or MPLS) with Layer 3 FWSM in a multiple context mode.

- Layer 3 VPN segregation (multi-vrf or MPLS) with Layer 2 FWSM in a multiple context mode.

Method 1: Layer 3 VPN Segregation with Layer 3 FWSM (Multiple Context Mode)

The design has three logical blocks:

- Penultimate Hop Router
- Perimeter Device
- Distribution Block Device

These logical blocks are explained as follows:

- **Penultimate Hop Router:** This router removes the MPLS labels, in case MPLS Layer 3 VPNs are used for traffic segregation.

  This router maps VRF based on VLANs and communicates with the perimeter router. The traffic of each VRF will flow through the VLANs in the individual trunk. Mapping the untagged traffic to each VLAN will be sufficient to achieve the segregation between the penultimate hop router and perimeter device. The technology of vrf lite (multi-vrf) is used in the penultimate hop router to achieve route segregation.

- **Perimeter Device:** For the interface connected to each FWSM virtual context (routed mode), a new SVI interface in the respective VRFs is defined on the PFC. This makes all links point-to-point and binds the SVIs defined within a VRF as a segregated zone.

The firewall can also have more than two interfaces defined. The outside, DMZ, and the inside interfaces will be present in a separate VRF instance. You can consider a scenario where a department has a firewall in its infrastructure, separating two security domains before it is migrated into the shared infrastructure. In such a case, these security zones can be defined as a separate interface in the firewall virtual context (in routed mode), and the respective VRFs can be defined on the switch SVI.

The routing instance for these departments will be separate for the individual security zones because they will be associated with each VRF. If the traffic is inter-VRF, the packet will have to pass through the firewall before it reaches the routing instance of the next VRF. The routing protocol used in this example is OSPF.

The next step is to maintain the segregation when the packet passes from the perimeter device to the distribution block device. This can be done in one of the two methodologies:

— If the infrastructure is Layer 3 and multiple hops exist between the last Layer 3 device and perimeter device, multiprotocol BGP with LDP is used to carry the Layer 3 VPN to the downstream routers.

— In a single hop scenario, the VRF-lite (multi-vrf) can be used for each segregate domain. Figure 23-6 has a VRF-lite because most of the campus environments have single hop Layer 3 devices instead of multiple Layer 3 devices. Note that VRF lite can also be used across multiple Layer 3 hops mapped to the respective VLANs.

- **Distribution Block:** The distribution block is a Layer 3 device and is the last hop in the data center before the traffic hits the Layer 2 access layer. Each distribution block will have its own instance of Spanning Tree. Here the Spanning Tree instances will be based on the distribution block in the data center campus.

These two logical blocks are defined based on functionality:

- Segregation of traffic
- Firewall alignment based on traffic segregation

You can use a separate device representing each block or can combine these functional blocks based on requirements.

Figure 23-6 *Logical Explanation of Firewall Virtualization in a Data Center*

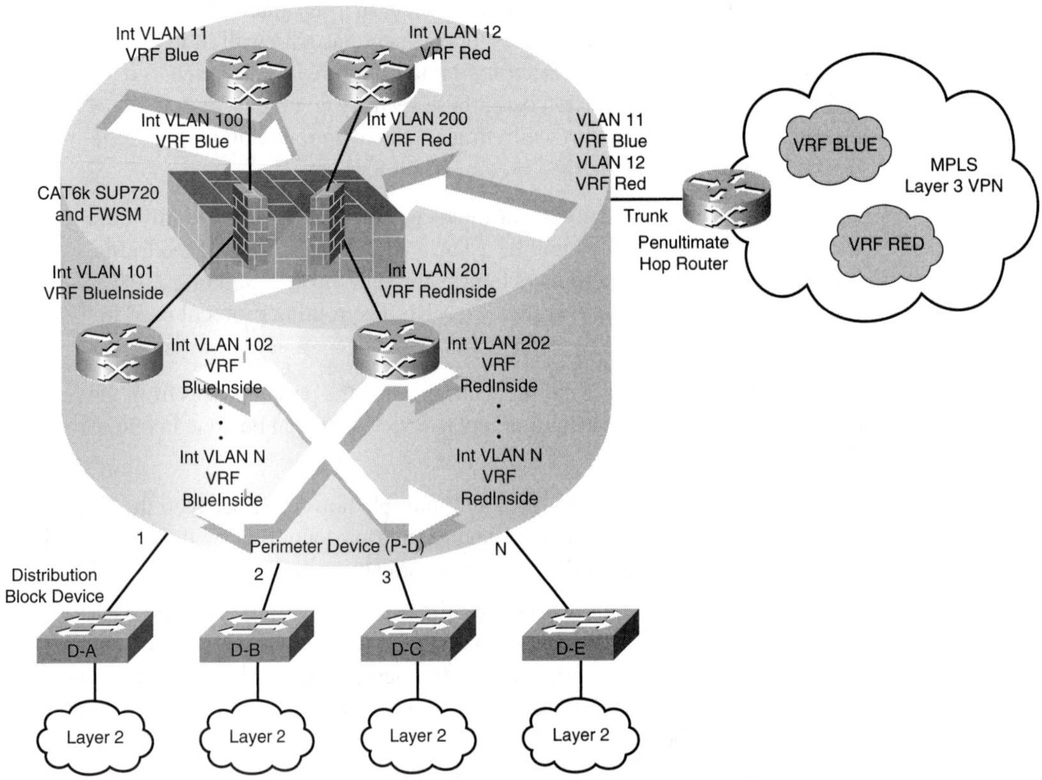

Method 2: Layer 3 VPN Segregation with Layer 2 FWSM (Multiple Context Mode)

In Figure 23-7, the router RB/RA represents a MPLS domain for the enterprise WAN campus, and the RC represents another MPLS domain for the inside security domain. This design aims to achieve this dynamic communication using the FWSM in transparent mode. RA and RB are in the MPLS domain (LDP neighbors). OSPF is used in RA, RB, and PFC for next hop reachability. The VRF custB and custA are transported through multiprotocol BGP (VPNv4) from RA to PFC. At the PFC, each VRF is terminated and is mapped to VLANs that are represented in the FWSM context. The FWSM context is in transparent mode.

Figure 23-7 *Virtualization with FWSM in Layer 2 Mode*

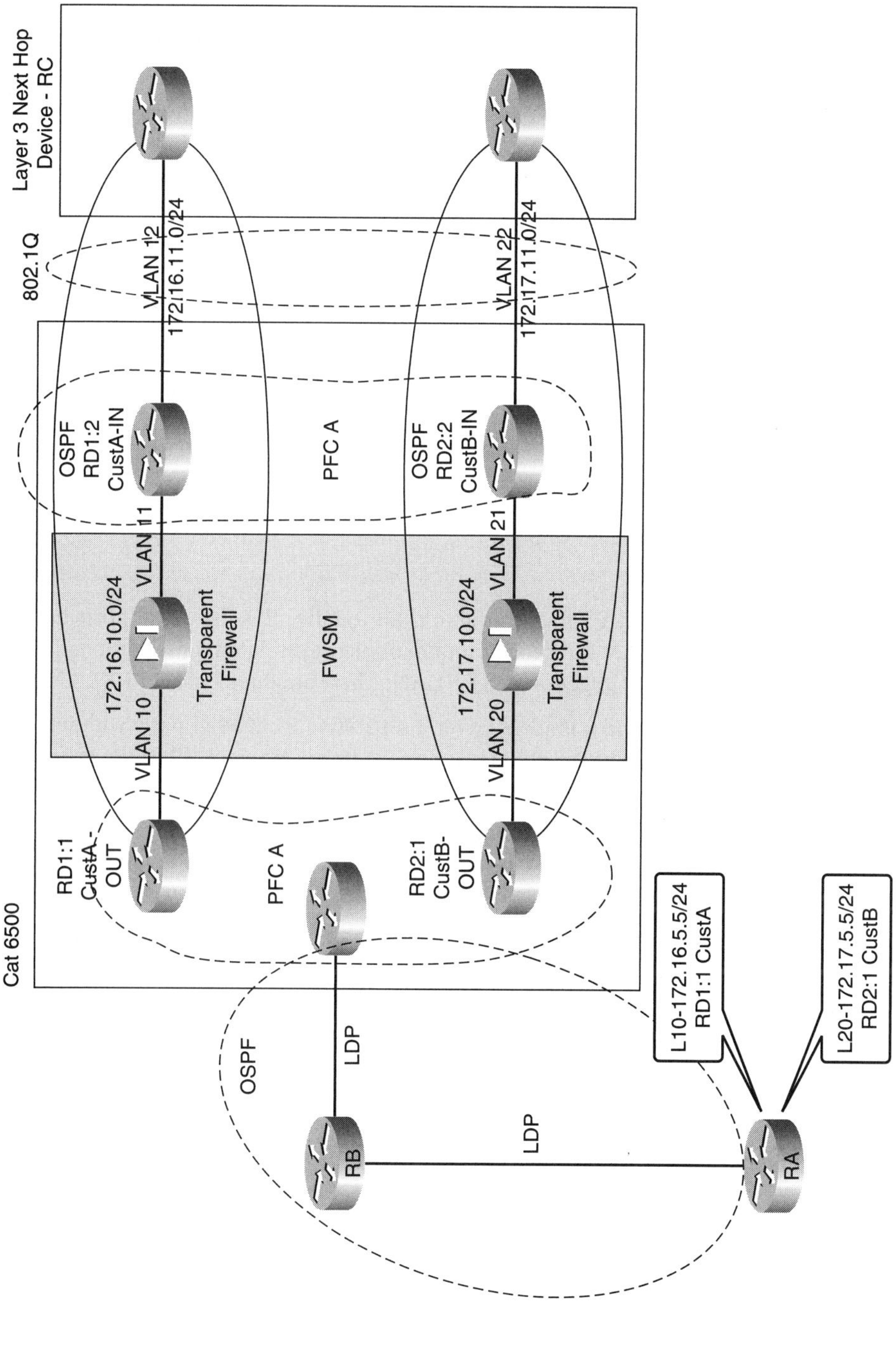

Multiple context transparent mode in the FWSM helps in dynamic route learning between the Layer 3 devices in each domain. Each context represents each VRF in the MPLS domain. From the outside VRF of the MPLS domain, a default route is advertised to the inside interface.

The inside interface of the FWSM is connected to a separate VLAN with the same subnet as the outside SVI. This inside VLAN is represented as VLAN 12 and this VLAN is mapped to a separate VRF. The VRF mapped to the inside VLAN is different from the outside VRF. This VRF for the inside interface is called the CustA-IN VRF for the respective customer. The outside security domain is represented as CustA-OUT VRF. An OSPF relationship will exist between the CustA-OUT VRF and the CustA-IN VRF because they are in the same subnet but different VLANs. This allows the route information to be dynamically learned across the two VRFs in separate MPLS domains across FWSMs. This example does not include the scope of using two FWSM modules across two chassis, which will help build redundancy to the design. This design gives the flexibility of having two MPLS domains to communicate across the firewall, with dynamic learning of the routes.

PVLAN and FWSM

What is PVLAN?

Private VLAN is a VLAN that is used to achieve Layer 2 isolation for hosts in the same subnet. A single VLAN can be split into multiple Layer 2 domains. Port configuration defines the domain segregation in a PVLAN. There are three types of PVLANs ports:

- **Isolated:** This has complete Layer 2 separation from other ports within the same PVLAN except for the promiscuous port. PVLANs block all traffic to isolated ports except traffic from promiscuous ports.

- **Community:** The hosts communicate among themselves and with their promiscuous ports. These interfaces are isolated at the Layer 2 domain from all other interfaces in other communities or isolated ports within their PVLAN.

- **Promiscuous:** Promiscuous ports can communicate with all interfaces, including the community and isolated ports within a PVLAN.

PVLAN Configuration in FWSM

The PVLAN concept was introduced in FWSM from 3.x code version onward. It is important for the switch code to be above 12.2.18SXFx version to integrate the PVLAN concept with the FWSM. Here x defines the version number. The primary VLAN of the PVLAN should be configured in the FWSM. No other special VLAN configuration is needed for PVLANs at the FWSM. Using PVLANs achieves Layer 2 segregation. This can be used in smaller DMZ designs where the servers in the DMZ within a single subnet need isolation. This helps to avoid major attacks in the DMZ security domain. Other virtualization techniques, such as Layer 3 VPN with MPLS labels or multi VRF, can also be used for Layer 3 segregation. These two techniques need a Layer 3 device.

In routed mode, the FWSM can act as a gateway between hosts on the PVLAN and the outside world. It secures the entire PVLAN itself from attacks initiated from the outside, and it stops malicious traffic originating from hosts on the internal PVLAN.

The concept of PVLAN facilitates pseudo security zones in a transparent firewall. The term pseudo is mentioned because these zones will not communicate with each other, but only with the inside interface. The inside interface is in promiscuous mode. The VLANs defined in a PVLAN represents the pseudo security zone.

Design Scenario 1 for PVLAN in FWSM

In this scenario, as shown in Figure 23-8, the FWSM is in single context routed mode. The inside interface of the FWSM is in VLAN 11. VLAN 11 is primary for the PVLAN (promiscuous mode). VLAN 12 and VLAN 13 are isolated VLANs. The hosts in VLAN 12 and VLAN 13 do not communicate with each other. This results in isolation of the traffic between the two hosts. VLAN 12 and VLAN 13 communicate with the host in VLAN 10 or the outside security domain through VLAN 11. The FWSM will need to have VLAN 11 defined only in its inside interface. By default, traffic from one interface cannot be routed through the same interface. The FWSM will also not allow the traffic to pass from the host in VLAN 12 to the host in VLAN 13.

Figure 23-8 *PVLANs and FWSM*

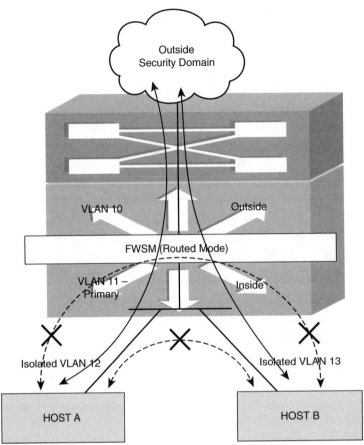

Design Scenario 2 for PVLAN in FWSM

In this scenario, as shown in Figure 23-9, the FWSM is in single context routed mode. VLAN 11 is the primary VLAN. VLAN 12 is an isolated VLAN and communicates only with the primary VLAN 11. VLAN 13 is defined as a PVLAN community and has two hosts. These two hosts, HOST B and HOST C, can communicate with each other through the switch.

Figure 23-9 *Using PVLAN Isolation with Host Communities*

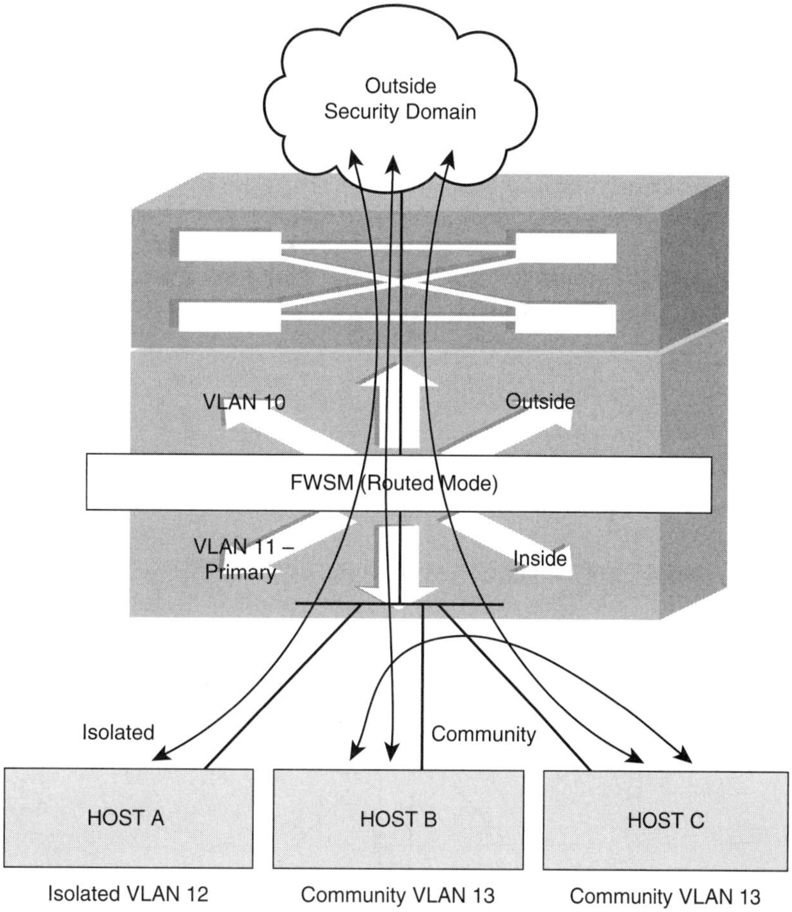

The following points represent the communication in Figure 23-9:

- HOST A (isolated VLAN) will communicate only with VLAN 11 and the outside security domain (based on the firewall policy).

- HOST B and HOST C can communicate with each other and will have access to the outside security domain (based on the security rule set) through VLAN 11 (inside interface of the firewall).

- HOST A cannot communicate with HOST B.

- The firewall (FWSM is in default configuration) will not route the traffic from HOST A to HOST B or HOST C.

Configuring PVLAN

The FWSM should have a 3.x code version or the preceding code, and the switch should have 12.2.18 SXF*x* version or the preceding code. Figure 23-10 shows the configuration of FWSM with PVLANs.

Figure 23-10 *Configuration of FWSM with PVLANs*

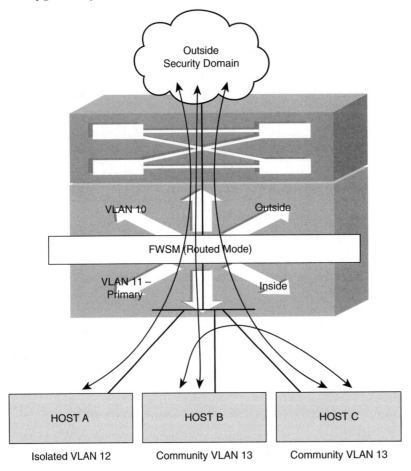

- VLAN 10 is the outside interface of the FWSM.
- VLAN 11 is the inside VLAN for the FWSM. It is also the primary VLAN (also referred as promiscuous VLAN) for the PVLAN in the PFC.
- VLAN 12 is a PVLAN—Isolated.
- VLAN 13 is a PVLAN—Community.
- VLAN 14 is a PVLAN—Community.

The sequence of configuring the PVLAN is important:

Step 1   Configure the primary PVLAN:

```
vlan 11
  private-vlan primary
  6504-E-1# show vlan private-vlan
Primary Secondary Type          Ports
------- --------- --------------- --------------------------------
  11                   primary
```

Step 2   Configure the secondary VLANs:

```
vlan 12
  private-vlan isolated
!
vlan 13
  private-vlan community
!
vlan 14
  private-vlan community
```

Step 3   Associate the secondary VLAN with the primary VLAN:

```
vlan 11
  private-vlan primary
  private-vlan association 12-14
```

To verify the association with the primary VLAN, enter the **show vlan private-vlan** command:

```
6504-E-1# show vlan private-vlan
Primary Secondary Type          Ports
------- --------- --------------- --------------------------------
  11      12       isolated
  11      13       community
  11      14       community
```

Step 4   Configure the SVI for the primary VLAN 11:

```
interface Vlan11
  ip address 10.2.1.1 255.255.255.0
  private-vlan mapping 12-14
```

To verify the Layer 3 mapping, enter the **show interface vlan 11 private-vlan mapping** command:

```
6504-E-1# show interface vlan 11 private-vlan mapping
Interface Secondary VLANs
```

```
--------  ----------------------------------------------------------
vlan11    12, 13, 14
```

Step 5 Configure host ports in the switch:

— CLI for host port configuration:

switchport private-vlan host-association *primary VLAN Secondary VLAN*
```
switchport mode private-vlan host
```

For example:

```
6504-E-1# show run interface g1/1
Building configuration...
Current configuration : 218 bytes
!
interface GigabitEthernet1/1
 description connection to cat6k2
 switchport
 switchport trunk encapsulation dot1q
 switchport private-vlan host-association 11 12
 switchport mode private-vlan host
 no ip address
end
```

To verify the switch port configuration, enter the **show interface g 1/1 switchport** command:

```
6504-E-1# show interface g 1/1 switchport
Name: Gi1/1
Switchport: Enabled
Administrative Mode: private-vlan host
Operational Mode: private-vlan host
Administrative Trunking Encapsulation: dot1q
Operational Trunking Encapsulation: native
Negotiation of Trunking: Off
Access Mode VLAN: 1 (default)
Trunking Native Mode VLAN: 1 (default)
Voice VLAN: none
Administrative private-vlan host-association: 11 (VLAN0011) 12
  (VLAN0012)
Administrative private-vlan mapping: none
Administrative private-vlan trunk native VLAN: none
Administrative private-vlan trunk encapsulation: dot1q
Administrative private-vlan trunk normal VLANs: none
Administrative private-vlan trunk private VLANs: none
Operational private-vlan: none
```

```
Trunking VLANs Enabled: ALL
Pruning VLANs Enabled: 2-1001
Capture Mode Disabled
Capture VLANs Allowed: ALL
Unknown unicast blocked: disabled
Unknown multicast blocked: disabled
```

— CLI for promiscuous VLAN port configuration:

switchport private-vlan mapping *primary-VLAN Secondary-VLAN*
switchport mode private-vlan promiscuous

For example:

```
6504-E-1# show run interface g1/2
Building configuration...
Current configuration : 218 bytes
interface GigabitEthernet1/2
 switchport
 switchport private-vlan mapping 11 13-14
 switchport mode private-vlan promiscuous
 no ip address
 media-type rj45
end
```

To verify the switch port configuration, enter the **show interface g 1/2 switchport** command:

```
6504-E-1# show interface g 1/2 switchport
Name: Gi1/2
Switchport: Enabled
Administrative Mode: private-vlan promiscuous
Operational Mode: private-vlan promiscuous
Administrative Trunking Encapsulation: negotiate
Operational Trunking Encapsulation: native
Negotiation of Trunking: Off
Access Mode VLAN: 1 (default)
Trunking Native Mode VLAN: 1 (default)
Voice VLAN: none
Administrative private-vlan host-association: none
Administrative private-vlan mapping: 11 (VLAN0011) 13 (VLAN0013) 14
  (VLAN0014)
Administrative private-vlan trunk native VLAN: none
Administrative private-vlan trunk encapsulation: dot1q
Administrative private-vlan trunk normal VLANs: none
Administrative private-vlan trunk private VLANs: none
Operational private-vlan: none
Trunking VLANs Enabled: ALL
Pruning VLANs Enabled: 2-1001
```

```
Capture Mode Disabled
Capture VLANs Allowed: ALL
Unknown unicast blocked: disabled
Unknown multicast blocked: disabled
```

Follow the steps to complete the PFC configuration:

Step 1 Follow the sequential steps to configure the PVLAN.

Step 2 Configure VLAN 10.

Step 3 Configure static routes.

Step 4 Configure the firewall VLAN group and the multiple interfaces command.

Example 23-11 shows FWSM configuration for Figure 23-10.

Example 23-11 *FWSM Configuration*

```
FWSM-A# show run
: Saved
:
FWSM Version 3.1(3)6
!
hostname FWSM-A
enable password 8Ry2YjIyt7RRXU24 encrypted
names
!
interface Vlan10
 nameif outside
 security-level 0
 ip address 10.1.1.2 255.255.255.0
!
interface Vlan11
 nameif inside
 security-level 100
 ip address 10.2.1.2 255.255.255.0
!
passwd 2KFQnbNIdI.2KYOU encrypted
ftp mode passive
same-security-traffic permit intra-interface
access-list 100 extended permit ip any any
access-list 100 remark this is for the outside
access-list 101 extended permit ip any any
access-list 101 remark this is for the inside
pager lines 24
logging console debugging
logging monitor debugging
mtu outside 1500
mtu inside 1500
no failover
icmp permit any outside
icmp permit any inside
```

Example 23-11 *FWSM Configuration (Continued)*

```
no asdm history enable
arp timeout 14400
nat (inside) 0 0.0.0.0 0.0.0.0
static (inside,outside) 10.2.100.1 10.2.100.1 netmask 255.255.255.255
static (inside,outside) 10.2.1.1 10.2.1.1 netmask 255.255.255.255
access-group 101 in interface outside
access-group 100 out interface outside
access-group 101 in interface inside
access-group 101 out interface inside
route outside 0.0.0.0 0.0.0.0 10.1.1.1 1
route inside 10.2.100.0 255.255.255.0 10.2.1.1 1
timeout xlate 3:00:00
timeout conn 1:00:00 half-closed 0:10:00 udp 0:02:00 icmp 0:00:02
timeout sunrpc 0:10:00 h323 0:05:00 h225 1:00:00 mgcp 0:05:00
timeout mgcp-pat 0:05:00 sip 0:30:00 sip_media 0:02:00
timeout uauth 0:05:00 absolute
no snmp-server location
no snmp-server contact
snmp-server enable traps snmp authentication linkup linkdown coldstart
telnet timeout 5
ssh timeout 5
console timeout 0
!
class-map inspection_default
 match default-inspection-traffic
!
policy-map global_policy
 class inspection_default
  inspect dns maximum-length 512
  inspect ftp
  inspect h323 h225
  inspect h323 ras
  inspect netbios
  inspect rsh
  inspect skinny
  inspect smtp
  inspect sqlnet
  inspect sunrpc
  inspect tftp
  inspect sip
  inspect xdmcp
!
service-policy global_policy global
prompt hostname context
Cryptochecksum:48794c0a97cda389441255764d5901b9
: end
```

Use the following command to verify PVLAN association with the primary VLAN in the
FWSM:

```
FWSM-A# show np 1 vlan 14 | in private Vlan
primary Vlan for private Vlan          : 11
FWSM-A# show np 1 vlan 12 | in private Vlan
primary Vlan for private Vlan          : 11
FWSM-A# show np 1 vlan 13 | in private Vlan
primary Vlan for private Vlan          : 11
```

Even though there is no configuration in the FWSM with the code supporting PVLAN
feature, when VLAN 11 (primary VLAN) is enabled in the FWSM, the NP 1 (Network
Processor) of the FWSM picks up all the PVLANs from the PFC.

Summary

This chapter covers options that readers can use to design a secured firewall infrastructure
aligned with network virtualization. The principles of high availability and resiliency are
achieved with a combination of features in FWSM and networking. Designing is an art, and
requirements give birth to innovation using a combination of features from various
technologies.

FWSM 4.x

CHAPTER 24

FWSM 4.x Performance and Scalability Improvements

The release of the 4.x code train offers some major improvements in performance and scalability. Trusted Flow Acceleration allows flows to bypass the Firewall Services Module (FWSM), achieving line-rate performance. The combination of the FWSM along with the Programmable Intelligent Services Accelerator (PISA) adds a new level of traffic inspection. The change in memory provisioning for both partitions and rule allocation has greatly improved how resources can be divided. Access list optimization also helps to improve the way that memory is utilized by consolidating overlapping access lists.

Increasing Performance by Leveraging the Supervisor

One of the most significant features to be released with the 4.x code train is the capability to offload flows to the supervisor, called Trusted Flow Acceleration. This capability dramatically increases the throughput of predefined types of traffic and requires a minimum code of 12.2(33)SXI on the supervisor.

Prior to Trusted Flow Acceleration, all traffic was required to flow through the FWSM; refer to Chapter 2, "Overview of the Firewall Services Module," for details. With the addition of Trusted Flow Acceleration, particular types of traffic defined by an access list can now bypass the FWSM entirely.

You may be asking yourself how this feature works. To get a better idea, the following list will give you an understanding of the packet flow:

1 The FWSM must first be configured for supervisor acceleration. This will function in either single or multiple context routed mode, but it cannot be in transparent mode, and the interfaces cannot be shared with interfaces on other contexts. Also, multiple FWSMs are supported in the same chassis.

2 When Trusted Flow Acceleration is configured, the supervisor takes ownership of the MAC address of the FWSM.

3 When a new session is initiated, it will go to the supervisor because the supervisor has ownership of the MAC address. Because no session entries exist, the supervisor redirects the connection to the FWSM.

4 The redirected traffic to the FWSM must match a predefined access list, which has been associated with the acceleration policy for that traffic to qualify for acceleration.

5 For TCP flows, the FWSM monitors the session for the completion of the three-way handshake. For User Datagram Protocol (UDP) flows, the FWSM watches for the return traffic.

6 Upon completion of a TCP or UDP session, the FWSM creates a flow entry on the supervisor.

7 Additional traffic from that session entering the host-chassis will now have a hardware entry and consequently bypass the FWSM.

Trusted Flow Acceleration takes advantage of NetFlow Ternary Content Addressable Memory (TCAM) space to create accelerated paths. TCAM space is specialized memory designed to provide high-speed forwarding lookups.

NOTE   TCAM space is specialized memory designed to provide high-speed forwarding lookups.

The following example shows how to configure the FWSM for supervisor acceleration in multiple-context mode and monitor the results. Use Figure 24-1 to see the traffic flow from a graphical perspective.

Figure 24-1 *Trusted Flow Acceleration*

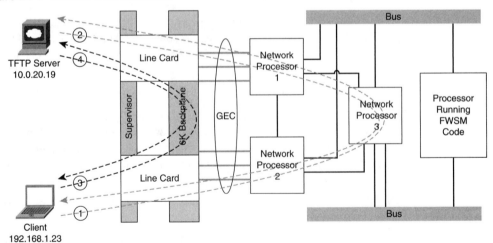

Step 1   The FWSM has been configured for multiple contexts. From the
"system" context, a context called **Accelerate** (arbitrarily chosen) was
added as shown; the key parameter to note is **service-acceleration**:

```
context Accelerate
  allocate-interface Vlan20
  allocate-interface Vlan21
  service-acceleration
  config-url disk:/Accelerate.cfg
```

Step 2   In the Accelerate context, an access list must be created to define
interesting traffic for Trusted Flow Acceleration. In this example, the
interesting traffic is a client on the inside (192.168.1.23) accessing a
TFTP server on the outside (10.0.20.19):

```
access-list SUP-ACCEL extended permit udp host 192.168.1.23 host
10.0.20.19 eq tftp
```

Step 3   A class map needs to be added that matches the previously created access
list:

```
class-map SUP-ACCEL-MAP
 match access-list SUP-ACCEL
```

Step 4   Next, a policy map with the associated class is configured with the **set
connection advanced-options service-acceleration** option enabled:

```
policy-map SUP-ACCEL-POLICY
 class SUP-ACCEL-MAP
  set connection advanced-options service-acceleration
```

Step 5   The service policy can be added to either an interface or set globally. In
this case, you want the policy to be more specific so it is applied to the
inside interface:

```
service-policy SUP-ACCEL-POLICY interface Inside
```

Step 6   After the connection is established between the client and server, within
the Accelerate context of the FWSM, the **show conn** command will
display the connection information. Notice the flag set to **N**, which
indicates that this connection is "service-accelerated". After enough
information is available for the FWSM to accelerate the flow, the byte
counter will no longer increment:

```
FWSM/Accelerate# show conn
1 in use, 1 most used
 Network Processor 1 connections
 UDP out 10.0.20.19:69 in 192.168.1.23:1178 idle 0:00:06 Bytes 3538 FLAGS
  - N
 Network Processor 2 connections
Multicast sessions:
```

```
Network Processor 1 connections
Network Processor 2 connections
```

Step 7 From the host-chassis, use the **show mls netflow ip sw-installed**
command to view the accelerated flows in the NetFlow TCAM table:

```
Host-chassis# show mls netflow ip sw-installed
Displaying Netflow entries in Active Supervisor EARL in module 5
DstIP         SrcIP         Prot:SrcPort:DstPort   Src i/f   :AdjPtr
------------------------------------------------------------------
Pkts          Bytes         Age   LastSeen  Attributes
--------------------------------------------------
192.168.1.23  10.0.20.19    udp :tftp   :1178       Vl20      :0x8003E
33512         18230528      101   21:43:12  L3 - SwInstalled
10.0.20.19    192.168.1.23  udp :1178   :tftp       Vl21      :0x8003D
33513         1541598       106   21:43:12  L3 - SwInstalled
```

As long as traffic is flowing between the client and server, the packet (Pkts) and byte (Bytes)
counter will continue to increment until the download is complete. You should also see that
there is both a client-to-server connection and a server-to-client connection, and both are
accelerated. If this was not the case, and the FWSM just saw the returning traffic, the
connection would be dropped.

There are some additional considerations when deploying Trusted Flow Acceleration.
When designing an infrastructure for high-availability and using Stateful Switchover
(SSO), Route Processor Redundancy (RPR), and FWSM failover, all the flows need to be
reestablished. Furthermore, the following features are not supported:

- Asymmetric routing
- DCF-enable line cards
- Multicast routing
- Shared interfaces
- Stateful failover
- Transparent firewall (single or multiple context)
- Virtual switching system (VSS)

CAUTION   When acceleration is used, none of the inspection engines on the FWSM are used, and TCP
state and sequencing is not checked. Additionally, this feature is available only when the
FWSM is in a "routed" mode. All packets that are fragmented have an IP option set or are
exceptions, such as packet errors, are also sent to the FWSM.

Trusted Flow Acceleration can be used for large file copies, backup traffic, bulk transfers, and so on, and can even be used when Network Address Translation (NAT) and/or Port Address Translation (PAT) is configured on the FWSM. With this feature turned on, there is no TCP sequence number or state information tracking. Application inspection is also not supported. With either the supervisor or FWSM failing, session information is not maintained and needs to be reestablished. Supervisor acceleration would be extremely beneficial in the datacenter but should be avoided where "untrusted" devices exist—for example, when connecting to the Internet.

Using the PISA for Enhanced Traffic Detection

PISA is a hardware subsystem of the Supervisor 32. The PISA has the capability to detect/classify protocols, and consequently make decisions on the FWSM to forward or deny traffic can be applied by application type. The PISA uses Network-based Application Recognition (NBAR) and Flexible Packet Matching (FPM) to classify traffic. Both NBAR and FPM use a process of "deep" packet inspection to determine traffic types. This looks beyond Layer 4 ports and into the data portion of the packet; therefore, applications using nonstandard ports can be detected. The minimum supervisor code requirement is 12.2(18)ZYA.

The following example uses Figure 24-2. As traffic begins to flow through the PISA, it may take several packets to identify and classify the traffic, depending on the application type. When the type of traffic is determined, the PISA encapsulates those packets in the pseudo-Generic Routing Encapsulation (pseudo-GRE) tunnel and forwards it to the FWSM. The pseudo-GRE headers add 32 bytes, so jumbo Maximum Transmission Units (MTU) larger than 1500 byte frame support should also be enabled. The FWSM and PISA must have a Layer 2 adjacency when the FWSM receives the packet; otherwise, it will be discarded. The FWSM strips the pseudo-GRE header and processes the packet in the fast-path according to how it was classified by the PISA, thereby providing the best possible throughput. The exception to this is for the first packet in a flow. In this case, it must pass the configured access list and/or other rules applied.

The fact that SUP-32+PISA is generally deployed at the access layer, and FWSM in the distribution or core, allows firewall security policies to be determined after classification and marking. This kind of deployment that uses PISA for application recognition and FWSM for policy control makes a compelling integrated story.

Figure 24-2 *PISA Deployment*

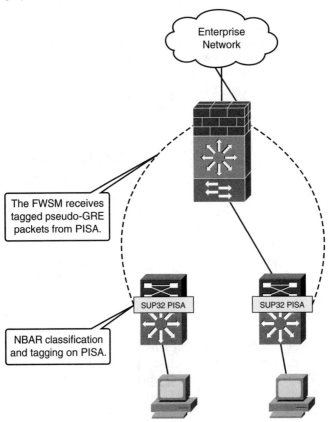

The connection between the host-chassis supporting the FWSM and the chassis with the Sup32/PISA should have jumbo frame support enabled.

There are two possible deployment scenarios to configure protocol discovery for the FWSM and Supervisor32 with a PISA (Sup32/PISA), which are Layer 3 (routed) and Layer 2 (switched) modes.

In Layer 3, or routed-access mode, the access ports are in different VLANs. The Layer 3 next hop is defined as a Switched Virtual Interface (SVI) on the access switch with the Sup32/PISA. The Sup32/PISA has a separate VLAN uplink connection to the FWSM in the upstream switch. Protocol discovery and port tagging will be done on the access-layer VLAN. All egress packets to the FWSM will be tagged leaving the Sup32/PISA switch.

NOTE   The Sup32/PISA and FWSM must be in the same VLAN.

Layer 2, or switched mode, can be configured using three methods. These modes are very similar in that there is a Layer 2 connection from the access layer (client access) and the FWSM. The difference is determined where the protocol inspection is performed. Protocol discovery can be done on the client side (downstream), on the FWSM side (upstream), or on the shared VLAN between the client and FWSM.

The following example uses a routed-access design, as shown in Figure 24-3.

Figure 24-3   *PISA Layer 3 Solution*

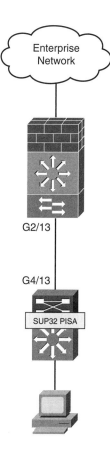

Step 1 Protocol discovery will be configured on the uplink of the Sup32/PISA switch. In this example, you will see GigabitEthernet4/13, as shown next:

```
interface GigabitEthernet4/13
ip address 10.1.1.1 255.255.255.0
ip nbar protocol-discovery
ip nbar protocol-tagging
```

Step 2 To determine whether protocol-discovery is working, use the **show ip nbar protocol-d interface g4/13 top-n** command on the Sup32/PISA switch. As you can see from the output, the PISA is doing its job.

```
sup32_pisa#show ip nbar protocol-d interface g4/13 top-n
```

```
GigabitEthernet4/13
                       Input                   Output
                       -----                   ------
          Protocol     Packet Count            Packet Count
                       Byte Count              Byte Count
                       5min Bit Rate (bps)     5min Bit Rate (bps)
                       5min Max Bit Rate (bps) 5min Max Bit Rate (bps)
          ------------ ----------------------- -----------------------
          telnet       3443681                 2764868
                       520354888               329109764
                       150000                  95000
                       153000                  98000
          http         938891                  1242007
                       609404867               116256355
                       175000                  33000
                       179000                  37000
          smtp         371298                  371356
                       47154846                29335504
                       13000                   8000
                       16000                   10000
          pcanywhere   445                     0
                       49872                   0
                       0                       0
                       0                       0
          aol          0                       0
                       0                       0
                       0                       0

                       0                       0
          appleqtc     0                       0
                       0                       0
                       0                       0
                       0                       0
```

Step 3   Configure the interconnect on the host-chassis with the FWSM as follows:

```
interface GigabitEthernet2/13
 switchport
 switchport access vlan 175
 switchport mode access
 spanning-tree portfast
```

Step 4   The interface configuration on the FWSM includes the name, security level, and IP address, as shown:

```
interface Vlan175
 nameif Inside
 security-level 100
 ip address 10.1.1.2 255.255.255.0
```

Step 5   Configure an access list used to identify interesting traffic.

```
access-list PROT-INSPECT extended permit tcp any any
```

Step 6   Create a class map and apply the previous access list.

```
class-map CLASS-INSPECT
 match access-list PROT-INSPECT
```

Step 7   Add a policy map statement matching the class map and defining which traffic types are to be permitted or denied.

```
policy-map POLICY-INSPECT
 class CLASS-INSPECT
  deny ftp
  deny smtp
  permit http
  permit telnet
```

Step 8   Apply the policy map to the inside interface.

```
service-policy POLICY-INSPECT interface inside
```

Step 9   Verify that the policy map is applied.

```
FWSM# show service-policy interface Inside
Interface Inside:
  Service-policy: POLICY-INSPECT
```

Step 10 Check that the protocol inspection is taking place, using the **show np 1 pisa** and **show np 2 pisa** commands. The output shows that you are indeed receiving GRE packets. Traffic is also being permitted and denied.

```
FWSM# show np 1 pisa
- - - - - - - - - - - - - - - - - - - - - - - - - - - - - - - - - - - - - - - - - - -
                  Fast Path PISA Statistics Counters (NP-1)
- - - - - - - - - - - - - - - - - - - - - - - - - - - - - - - - - - - - - - - - - - -
PISA GRE tagged packets received                      : 1983455
PISA tagged packets hitting a session                 : 1983455
PISA tagged packets permitted                         : 1792111
PISA tagged packets permitted first UDP               : 0
PISA tagged packets denied                            : 191344
PISA tagged packet not hitting PISA session           : 0


FWSM# show np 2 pisa
- - - - - - - - - - - - - - - - - - - - - - - - - - - - - - - - - - - - - - - - - - -
                  Fast Path PISA Statistics Counters (NP-2)
- - - - - - - - - - - - - - - - - - - - - - - - - - - - - - - - - - - - - - - - - - -
PISA GRE tagged packets received                      : 1968260
PISA tagged packets hitting a session                 : 1968260
PISA tagged packets permitted                         : 1778413
PISA tagged packets permitted first UDP               : 0
PISA tagged packets denied                            : 189847
PISA tagged packet not hitting PISA session           : 0
```

The PISA offers another level of inspection not found on the FWSM. By classification of traffic before it gets to the FWSM, it also helps the FWSM predefine how specific application types should be treated. Using the FWSM in conjunction with a PISA will notably improve the performance of the FWSM and the overall security posture of your organization.

Improving Memory

Rigid allocation of memory with code versions prior to 4.x required extensive thought and planning. The flexibility offered with 4.x code makes the management of the FWSM significantly easier.

Partitioning Memory

The 4.x code now has the capability to have memory partitions of unique sizes. For a quick refresher on what memory partitions are, see Chapter 5, "Understanding Contexts." Figure 24-4 shows how memory was allocated by dividing it equally among the total number of partitions. This posed some challenges for contexts associated with partitions that required additional resources. It was difficult to organize them in a manner that would take advantage of those resources efficiently. This is not the case with the 4.x code. Figure 24-4 shows how the allocation of resources in memory partitions has changed.

Figure 24-4 *Memory Partition Changes*

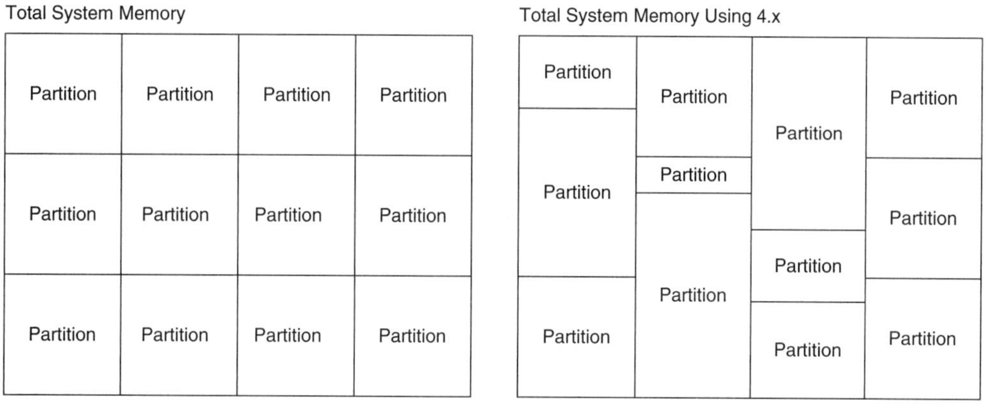

Step 1 From the system context, the allocation of memory can be viewed using the **show resource partition** command:

```
FWSM# show resource partition
                         Bootup      Current
    Partition  Default  Partition   Configured
    Number      Size      Size         Size
  -----------+---------+----------+-----------
       0       19219     19219        19219
       1       19219     19219        19219
       2       19219     19219        19219
       3       19219     19219        19219
       4       19219     19219        19219
       5       19219     19219        19219
       6       19219     19219        19219
       7       19219     19219        19219
       8       19219     19219        19219
       9       19219     19219        19219
      10       19219     19219        19219
      11       19219     19219        19219
```

```
backup tree   19219      19219       19219
----------+---------+----------+----------
   Total    249847     249847      249847


Total Partition size - Configured size = Available to allocate
       249847         -      249847     =           0
```

Step 2   The following example shows how to change (reduce) the partition size
of partition 1 to 1024.

```
FWSM(config)# resource partition 1
FWSM(config-partition)# size 1024
WARNING: The rule max has been reset based on partition size 1024.
The <size> command leads to re-partitioning of ACL Memory.
It will not take effect until you save the configuration and reboot.
```

Step 3   After the FWSM has been rebooted, the new changes have taken effect.
Notice that partition 1 has a partition size of 1024, and that now gives you
18,195 resources to allocate to other contexts.

NOTE   The FWSM must be rebooted for memory allocation changes to take effect.

```
FWSM# sh resource partition
                         Bootup      Current
Partition   Default    Partition    Configured
Number       Size        Size         Size
---------+---------+----------+----------
   0        19219       19219        19219
   1        19219        1024         1024
   2        19219       19219        19219
   3        19219       19219        19219
   4        19219       19219        19219
   5        19219       19219        19219
   6        19219       19219        19219
   7        19219       19219        19219
   8        19219       19219        19219
   9        19219       19219        19219
  10        19219       19219        19219
  11        19219       19219        19219
backup tree   19219     19219        19219
---------+---------+----------+----------
   Total    249847      231652       231652
```

```
Total Partition size - Configured size = Available to allocate
         249847         -      231652      =      18195
```

Partition allocating gives you a great deal of flexibility. Partitions that require fewer resources can now be reduced, consequently providing additional resources for other partitions.

Reallocating Rules

Within each one of the memory partitions is a subset of resources allocated to rules. These resources can also be divided according to the specific needs of each partition. Figure 24-5 shows how rules can be assigned within each of the memory partitions.

Figure 24-5 *Rule Reallocation*

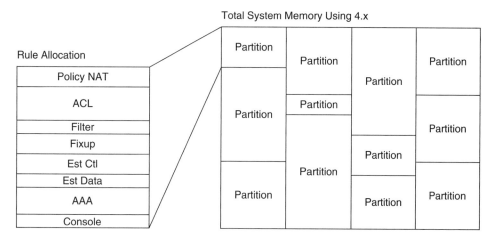

To view the resources allocated to a specific partition, use the **show resource rule partition** *number* command, as shown in Example 24-1.

Example 24-1 *Displaying Partition Resource Allocation*

```
FWSM# show resource rule partition 0
            Default  Configured  Absolute
  CLS Rule   Limit      Limit      Max
----------+---------+----------+---------
  Policy NAT    384        384       833
  ACL        14801      14801     14801
  Filter       576        576      1152
  Fixup       1537       1537      3074
  Est Ctl       96         96        96
  Est Data      96         96        96
  AAA         1345       1345      2690
```

continues

Example 24-1 *Displaying Partition Resource Allocation (Continued)*

```
Console      384        384        768
----------+---------+----------+---------
Total      19219      19219

Partition Limit - Configured Limit = Available to allocate
     19219      -       19219      =          0
```

As you can see from the output, 19,219 resources can be allocated among the eight groups, which are

- **Policy NAT:** Specifies the number of policy NAT entries.
- **ACL:** Sets the number of ACL entries, only limited by system resources.
- **Filter:** Identifies the number of filter rules.
- **Fixup:** Defines the number of application-inspection rules, also know as a fixup.
- **Est Ctl:** Signifies the number of established control commands.
- **Est Data:** Specifies the number of established data commands.
- **AAA:** Defines the number of AAA rules.
- **Console:** Identifies the total number of rules that apply to the FWSM in regard to management, including HTTP, Telnet, SSH, and ICMP.

From the output in Example 24-2, you can determine that additional ACL entries are needed.

Example 24-2 *ACL Resource Limit Reached*

```
FWSM/Cust-A(config)# access-list TEST-ACL per ip any host 10.1.4.254
ERROR: Unable to add, access-list config limit reached
ERROR: <TEST-ACL> element cannot be created
```

Step 1 The first step is to determine in which partition the context (Cust-A) resides. That is accomplished using the **show resource acl-partition** command. The output shows that **Cust-A** is in partition 1 and is not being shared with another context:

```
FWSM# show resource acl-partition
Total number of configured partitions = 12
Partition #0
    Mode              : non-exclusive
    List of Contexts    : admin
    Number of contexts    : 1(RefCount:1)
    Number of rules    : 1(Max:19219)
Partition #1
    Mode              : non-exclusive
    List of Contexts    : Cust-A
```

```
Number of contexts    : 1(RefCount:1)
Number of rules     : 294(Max:479)
```

Step 2   Using the **show np 3 acl count 1** command displays the resource allocation for partition 1. The display shows that the ACL rule count under CLS Rule Current Counts is 256, and the CLS Rule MAX Counts is 256. We hit the limit! There are a couple of options to free up resources. You could modify the memory partition, but that would require a reboot. The other option is to reallocate resources that are not being used to ACL rules.

```
FWSM# show np 3 acl count 1
-------------- CLS Rule Current Counts --------------
CLS Filter Rule Count      :            0
CLS Fixup Rule Count       :           32
CLS Est Ctl Rule Count     :            0
CLS AAA Rule Count         :            0
CLS Est Data Rule Count    :            0
CLS Console Rule Count     :            6
CLS Policy NAT Rule Count  :            0
CLS ACL Rule Count         :          256
CLS ACL Uncommitted Add    :            0
CLS ACL Uncommitted Del    :            0


---------------- CLS Rule MAX Counts ----------------
CLS Filter MAX             :           30
CLS Fixup MAX              :           80
CLS Est Ctl Rule MAX       :            5
CLS Est Data Rule MAX      :            5
CLS AAA Rule MAX           :           71
CLS Console Rule MAX       :           10
CLS Policy NAT Rule MAX    :           22
CLS ACL Rule MAX           :          256
```

Step 3   From the system context, in configuration mode, enter the following command:

```
FWSM(config)# resource partition 1
```

Step 4   Using the **rule** command, you are required to enter values for all the parameters. Four parameters can be entered for each:

— **A specific numeric value:** This must be between the minimum and maximum values.

— **Current:** Keep the current value unchanged.

— **Default:** Set the parameter to the default value.

— **Max:** Configure the parameter to the maximum allowed limit.

The following command line uses a combination of values. The most important is the acl limit; in this example it will be increased to 512:

```
FWSM(config-partition)# rule nat 10 acl 512 filter 20 fixup current est
max aaa 5 console max
```

Step 5   Using the **show np 3 acl count 1** command and looking at the CLS Rule MAX Counts, you can see how the specific parameters have changed:

```
FWSM# show np 3 acl count 1
---------------- CLS Rule MAX Counts ----------------
CLS Filter MAX             :          20
CLS Fixup MAX              :          80
CLS Est Ctl Rule MAX       :           5
CLS Est Data Rule MAX      :           5
CLS AAA Rule MAX           :           5
CLS Console Rule MAX       :          40
CLS Policy NAT Rule MAX    :          10
CLS ACL Rule MAX           :         512
```

There is now enough space to add some more ACL entries, without a reboot of the FWSM!

From the previous example, you can see how valuable it is to be able to dynamically modify the rule allocation. You may also consider lowering the size of the resources within a partition. That way you can easily adjust them without having to reboot the FWSM when you hit a limit. This will give you some time to consider more permanent changes by modifying memory partitions.

Optimizing ACL

Because memory space is a limited resource, and ACLs are the main contributor to the depletion of resources, the ACL optimization feature is a very welcome addition. As entries to access lists are added, removed, or modified, keeping track of all the changes and manually organizing them would be a management nightmare. Fortunately, the ACL optimization feature will review the existing ACLs and minimize the configuration, consequently saving memory resources.

The configuration in Example 24-3 contains an access list with 255 entries. Of those entries, 254 are host specific and one specifies the entire range.

Example 24-3   *ACL Optimization*

```
FWSM/Cust-B(config)# show access-list ACL_OPTIMIZATION
access-list ACL_OPTIMIZATION; 255 elements
access-list ACL_OPTIMIZATION line 1 extended permit ip any host 10.1.1.1 (hitcnt=0)
0x28d87d35
access-list ACL_OPTIMIZATION line 2 extended permit ip any host 10.1.1.2 (hitcnt=0)
0x68902d13
...
```

Example 24-3 *ACL Optimization (Continued)*

```
access-list ACL_OPTIMIZATION line 1 extended permit ip any 10.1.1.0 255.255.255.0
(hitcnt=0) 0xa0d2e6a1
...
access-list ACL_OPTIMIZATION line 254 extended permit ip any host 10.1.1.253
(hitcnt=0) 0x3f25ab70
access-list ACL_OPTIMIZATION line 255 extended permit ip any host 10.1.1.254
(hitcnt=0) 0x7fb31d4b
```

From the output in Example 24-3, there is a total of 255 ACL entries, 254 of which could be eliminated because they are more specific entries.

Step 1   To have the FWSM optimize the access list, enter the following command:

```
FWSM/Cust-B(config)# access-list optimization enable
ACL group optimization is enabled
```

Step 2   At this point, the access lists are optimized but not applied. To see what the FWSM did to the access list, use the **show access-list** *ACL_NAME* **optimization** command, as follows:

```
FWSM/Cust-B(config)# show access-list ACL_OPTIMIZATION optimization
access-list ACL_OPTIMIZATION;
255 elements before optimization
1 elements after optimization
Reduction rate = 99%
access-list ACL_OPTIMIZATION line 1 extended permit ip any 10.1.1.0
255.255.255.0 (hitcnt=0) 0x28d87d35
```

This access list may be a little unrealistic (okay, very unrealistic) but you get the idea of how it works. Because each of the host entries are a subset of the network, they were combined into a single access list. The reduction was an amazing 99 percent.

Step 3   You are not done yet! The access list has been optimized but not applied. You can copy the optimized access list to disk, flash, FTP or TFTP server, a system file, the startup-config, or in this example, the running-config as shown by the following command:

```
FWSM/Cust-B(config)# copy optimized-running-config running-config
Destination filename [running-config]?
FWSM/Cust-B(config)# Access Rules Download Complete: Memory
Utilization: < 1%
```

Chances are, the first few times you optimize the access list entries you will review them in detail, just like when you didn't trust your first calculator.

Step 4 Now that the access list has been applied, the configuration has changed to the following single-line ACL:

```
FWSM/Cust-B(config)# show access-list ACL_OPTIMIZATION
access-list ACL_OPTIMIZATION; 1 elements
access-list ACL_OPTIMIZATION line 1 extended permit ip any 10.1.1.0
255.255.255.0 (hitcnt=0) 0xa0d2e6a1
```

You may want to periodically use the optimization feature to check that you are not using up too much memory space for access lists. This feature will be a huge timesaver from the "old-fashioned" way of manually checking. Sometimes, features that automate processes tend to enable poor documentation habits; be sure to keep your records up to date to enable quicker troubleshooting and access to information for auditing.

Summary

Supervisor acceleration is one of the most significant features released in the 4.x code train. The capability to get "line-rate" throughput per flow is a drastic improvement over a 1-gigabit limit per flow. Leveraging the PISA to inspect traffic flows prior to the FWSM also increases throughput performance. Memory partitions, rule allocation, and ACL optimization help to make the best use of resources and grow as network requirements continue to grow. Understanding the intricacies of each of these features in this chapter will undoubtedly make you more successful in the design, implementation, and management of the FWSM and give you a better understanding of where the optimal placement of the FWSM should be in your network.

CHAPTER 25

Understanding FWSM 4.x Routing and Feature Enhancements

Several significant additions to the 4.x code enhance routing and other features. Some of these additions include Enhanced Interior Gateway Routing Protocol (EIGRP) routing, route health injection, and some additional security features and application inspection enhancements.

Configuring EIGRP

EIGRP has been a long-awaited feature for the Firewall Services Module (FWSM). With EIGRP support, the FWSM can be integrated into an existing EIGRP network, minimizing the need to redistribute routing information into other routing protocols. This reduces the complexity of managing multiple routing processes and simplifies the network design, especially within the datacenter.

Redistribution of routes between routing protocols can be difficult because each routing protocol exercises different methods to classify routes (cost). For example, RIP uses hop-count, OSPF uses a metric (single value), and EIGRP uses bandwidth and delay by default. When routing information is exchanged, the methods used to classify them are also lost. Consequently, routing loops can easily occur if you redistribute a route into one process, change the cost, and inject the route back into the first routing process. Use caution if you find yourself in this situation.

EIGRP is supported only in single-context mode and allows only one single EIGRP routing process. Unlike Routing Information Protocol (RIP) and Open Shortest Path First (OSPF), which cannot be enabled simultaneously, EIGRP and RIP or EIGRP and OSPF can be. Where additional security is required, when connecting to the Internet or other untrusted connections, an EIGRP process can be used on the inside and another routing process can be used on the outside.

NOTE   EIGRP is supported only in single-context mode.

Using Figure 25-1, the following example shows how EIGRP is configured to exchange routing information with the local network and extend the default route learned from the OSPF process exchanged on the outside interface to the local network. In the event the router on the outside stops forwarding the default route to the FWSM, the FWSM will remove the route from the local routing table, consequently removing the default route in the local network.

Figure 25-1 *EIGRP and OSPF Route Redistribution*

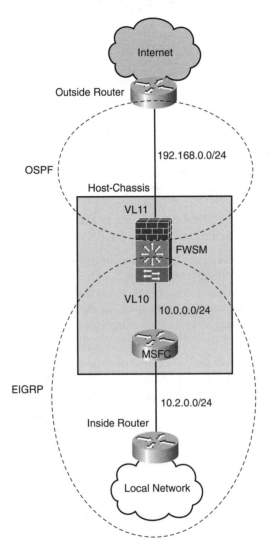

To enhance the security for the routing information exchanged on the outside, OSPF Message Digest 5 (MD5) authentication has also been configured.

Example 25-1 shows the configuration of the FWSM (only the pertinent information is shown).

Example 25-1 *EIGRP Route Redistribution*

```
interface Vlan10
 nameif Inside
 security-level 100
 ip address 10.0.0.2 255.255.255.0
 !
interface Vlan11
 nameif Outside
 security-level 0
 ip address 192.168.0.2 255.255.255.0
 ospf message-digest-key 1 md5 <removed>

router eigrp 1
 no auto-summary
 network 10.0.0.0 255.255.255.0
 redistribute ospf 1 metric 1000 2000 255 1 1500

 !
 !
router ospf 1
 network 192.168.0.0 255.255.255.0 area 0
 area 0 authentication message-digest
 log-adj-changes
 redistribute eigrp 1 subnets
 summary-address 10.0.0.0 255.0.0.0
```

As the output from the **show route** command shows in Example 25-2, the FWSM has learned about the routes from the local network via EIGRP. These routes are denoted with the letter "D," and the route from the outside has been learned via OSPF denoted with the letter "O."

Example 25-2 *EIGRP Redistributed Routes*

```
FWSM# show route
D     10.2.0.0 255.255.255.0 [90/26880256] via 10.0.0.1, 1:42:35, Inside
D     10.3.0.0 255.255.255.0 [90/27008256] via 10.0.0.1, 1:42:35, Inside
D     10.1.1.0 255.255.255.0 [90/130816] via 10.0.0.1, 1:42:35, Inside
O     10.0.0.0 255.0.0.0 is a summary, 1:42:43, Null0
C     10.0.0.0 255.255.255.0 is directly connected, Inside
D     10.4.0.0 255.255.255.0 [90/27008256] via 10.0.0.1, 1:42:35, Inside
C     192.168.0.0 255.255.255.0 is directly connected, Outside
O*E2 0.0.0.0 0.0.0.0 [110/1] via 192.168.0.1, 0:38:26, Outside
```

The FWSM is exchanging routing information with the Multilayer Switch Feature Card (MSFC) associated with the inside interface, as the output from the **show eigrp neighbors** command reveals in Example 25-3.

Example 25-3 *EIGRP Neighbors*

```
FWSM# show eigrp neighbors
EIGRP-IPv4 neighbors for process 1
H    Address                 Interface        Hold Uptime    SRTT   RTO  Q   Seq
                                              (sec)          (ms)        Cnt Num
0    10.0.0.1                Vl10             12  02:59:38 1  200    0   63
```

The OSPF adjacency has been established with the router on the outside interface, as the output from the **show ospf neighbor** command reveals in Example 25-4.

Example 25-4 *OSPF Neighbor*

```
FWSM# show ospf neighbor
Neighbor ID     Pri   State      Dead Time   Address       Interface
192.168.100.1    1    FULL/BDR   0:00:33     192.168.0.1   Outside
```

In Example 25-5, the last two lines from the **show ospf interface** command also indicate that the neighbor adjacency is using MD5.

Example 25-5 *OSPF Interfaces*

```
FWSM# show ospf interface
Outside is up, line protocol is up
  Internet Address 192.168.0.2 mask 255.255.255.0, Area 0
  Process ID 1, Router ID 10.0.0.2, Network Type BROADCAST, Cost: 10
  Transmit Delay is 1 sec, State DR, Priority 1
  Designated Router (ID) 10.0.0.2, Interface address 192.168.0.2
  Backup Designated router (ID) 192.168.100.1, Interface address 192.168.0.1
  Timer intervals configured, Hello 10, Dead 40, Wait 40, Retransmit 5
    Hello due in 0:00:03
  Index 1/1, flood queue length 0
  Next 0x0(0)/0x0(0)
  Last flood scan length is 3, maximum is 6
  Last flood scan time is 0 msec, maximum is 0 msec
  Neighbor Count is 1, Adjacent neighbor count is 1
    Adjacent with neighbor 192.168.100.1  (Backup Designated Router)
  Suppress hello for 0 neighbor(s)
  Message digest authentication enabled
    Youngest key id is 1
```

The challenges of complex redistribution scenarios from EIGRP to OSPF or RIP on adjacent routers are now eliminated with the capability of supporting EIGRP natively on the FWSM. Running EIGRP through the FWSM should be reserved for passing routing information internal to the network—for example, within the datacenter. This minimizes the impact of attacks targeting routing protocols.

The addition of EIGPR support makes the integration of the FWSM into networks taking advantage of the EIGRP routing protocol substantially easier, by not requiring the redistribution between routing protocols. When required, you still have the capability to redistribute routing information between routing protocols on the FWSM, but use caution that you do not cause a routing loop.

Configuring Route Health Injection

The FWSM has limited support for dynamic routing protocols when using "multiple-context" mode. Route Health Injection (RHI) has the capability of propagating routing information from individual contexts in routed-mode, including static routes, connected networks, and Network Address Translation (NAT) pools into the routing-engine on the host-chassis.

Because RHI has such a tight integration with the routing-engine, the minimum image needed on the Supervisor 720 and/or Supervisor 32 is 12.2(33)SXI.

RHI creates entries for static and directly connected routes in the MSFC.

Routes can be redistributed to any routing protocol: EIGRP, BGP, and so on.

RHI can also be used to advertise NAT pools into the MSFC.

RHI allows the FWSM to support more than one routing protocol in multi-context mode.

The following example shows how to propagate a default route into the routing-engine from a context on the FWSM.

Example 25-6 shows the configuration on the host-chassis.

Example 25-6 *RHI MSFC Configuration*

```
Host-Chassis(config)# firewall autostate
Host-Chassis(config)# firewall multiple-vlan-interfaces
Host-Chassis(config)# firewall module 9 vlan-group 9
Host-Chassis(config)# firewall vlan-group 9   10-100
Host-Chassis(config)# vlan 2-100,1000

Host-Chassis(config)# interface FastEthernet1/1
Host-Chassis(config-if)# switchport
Host-Chassis(config-if)# switchport access vlan 20
Host-Chassis(config-if)# switchport mode access

Host-Chassis(config)#interface FastEthernet1/2
Host-Chassis(config-if)# switchport
Host-Chassis(config-if)# switchport access vlan 21
Host-Chassis(config-if)# switchport mode access
```

The **firewall autostate** command sends messages from the host-chassis to the FWSM regarding the state of the VLANs associated with the FWSM. When an interface is configured to be in the same VLAN as the FWSM, and in the event that physical interface transitions to a "down" state, information can be propagated to the FWSM, consequently "downing" the interface associated with the FWSM. When this happens, the RHI will no longer be propagated to the routing-engine on the host-chassis.

Example 25-7 shows the configuration of the context on the FWSM (only pertinent information is shown).

Example 25-7 *RHI FWSM Configuration*

```
FWSM/RHI(config)# interface Vlan20
FWSM/RHI(config-if)# nameif Outside
FWSM/RHI(config-if)# security-level 0
FWSM/RHI(config-if)# ip address 10.20.20.1 255.255.255.0
FWSM/RHI(config)#interface Vlan21
FWSM/RHI(config-if)# nameif Inside
FWSM/RHI(config-if)# security-level 100
FWSM/RHI(config-if)# ip address 192.168.1.1 255.255.255.0
FWSM/RHI(config)# route Outside 0.0.0.0 0.0.0.0 10.20.20.254 1
FWSM/RHI(config)# route-inject
FWSM/RHI(config)# redistribute static interface Inside
```

Under the route-inject subsection, the **redistribute** command also offers another great feature. You can apply an access list to static routes, NAT pools, and connected networks redistributed to the routing-engine on the host-chassis, consequently providing very granular control over which routes are redistributed.

From the FWSM, using the **show route-inject** command, you can verify that the route is being propagated to the routing-engine on the host-chassis, as shown in Example 25-8.

Example 25-8 *RHI on the FWSM*

```
FWSM/RHI# show route-inject
Routes injected:
Address     Mask         Nexthop     Proto  Weight  Vlan
-------------------------------------------------------------
0.0.0.0  0.0.0.0  10.20.20.254     1      1     20
```

The host-chassis, using the **show ip route** command verifies that the route has been received, as shown in Example 25-9.

Example 25-9 *RHI on the MSFC*

```
Host-Chassis# show ip route
Codes: C - connected, S - static, R - RIP, M - mobile, B - BGP
       D - EIGRP, EX - EIGRP external, O - OSPF, IA - OSPF inter area
       N1 - OSPF NSSA external type 1, N2 - OSPF NSSA external type 2
       E1 - OSPF external type 1, E2 - OSPF external type 2
       i - IS-IS, su - IS-IS summary, L1 - IS-IS level-1, L2 - IS-IS level-2
       ia - IS-IS inter area, * - candidate default, U - per-user static route
       o - ODR, P - periodic downloaded static route
```

Example 25-9 *RHI on the MSFC (Continued)*

```
Gateway of last resort is 192.168.1.1 to network 0.0.0.0

C     192.168.121.0/24 is directly connected, Vlan121
C     192.168.1.0/24 is directly connected, Vlan21
S*    0.0.0.0/0 [1/0] via 192.168.1.1, Vlan21
```

You can see that this route shows up as "static". Now it can be redistributed into a dynamic routing protocol. In Example 25-10, we are using EIGRP.

Example 25-10 *Redistribution of RHI (Static) Routes on the MSFC*

```
router eigrp 1
 network 192.168.0.0 0.0.255.255
 no auto-summary
 redistribute static metric 1000 2000 255 1 1500
```

Downstream routers will now see that route in their local routing table, as shown in the output from the **show ip route** command in Example 25-11.

Example 25-11 *Downstream RHI Routes*

```
Downstream# show ip route
Codes: C - connected, S - static, R - RIP, M - mobile, B - BGP
       D - EIGRP, EX - EIGRP external, O - OSPF, IA - OSPF inter area
       N1 - OSPF NSSA external type 1, N2 - OSPF NSSA external type 2
       E1 - OSPF external type 1, E2 - OSPF external type 2
       i - IS-IS, su - IS-IS summary, L1 - IS-IS level-1, L2 - IS-IS level-2
       ia - IS-IS inter area, * - candidate default, U - per-user static route
       o - ODR, P - periodic downloaded static route

Gateway of last resort is 192.168.121.1 to network 0.0.0.0

C     192.168.121.0/24 is directly connected, FastEthernet2/0
D     192.168.1.0/24 [90/28416] via 192.168.121.1, 00:48:10, FastEthernet2/0
D*EX 0.0.0.0/0 [170/28416] via 192.168.121.1, 00:47:09, FastEthernet2/0
```

When the FWSM interface goes down, the static route being redistributed into the routing-engine on the host-chassis will be removed.

NOTE   The automatic route removal feature will not be available on the initial release of 4.01 but will be part of the first maintenance release (4.02).

To really take advantage of the dynamic nature of RHI, only one interface should be assigned to the VLAN. In Example 25-11, interface FastEthernet1/1 is assigned to VLAN

20. In the event FastEthernet1/1 goes down, typically due to an upstream device or interface failure, the associated VLAN interface will also go down. If multiple interfaces have been assigned to the VLAN, all must go down to take down the interface of the FWSM. This completely nullifies the use for any type of dynamic changes.

Figure 25-2 shows a diagram of how RHI can be used.

Figure 25-2 *RHI Usage*

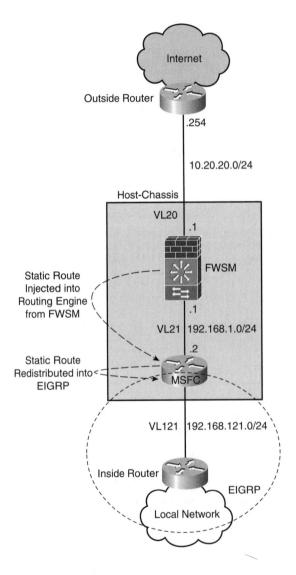

Although not really dynamic, it will automatically provide notification of the FWSM VLAN interface going down by removing the associated route. Something to be aware of is that it requires a physical failure. In the event the upstream had a Layer 3 problem, for example, the IP address changed, the VLAN interface would remain "up," but traffic would drop because the next-hop would not be available. One other notable item is that the routes are not Virtual Routing and Forwarding (VRF) aware, meaning that it will not function with MPLS or VRF-lite (at least not using 4.01 code). Propagating routes from the FWSM to the routing-engine on the host-chassis will be placed in the "global" routing table.

NOTE   Removal of routes using RHI requires that the VLAN on the FWSM must be down.

RHI helps to overcome the limitation that dynamic routing processes are not supported when the FWSM is operating the multi-context mode. Recognize that it requires a Layer 2 failure of the selected interface to retract routing information sent to the MSFC. Although some limitations exist, RHI is an excellent feature to have in your "tool kit."

Understanding Application Support

The release of FWSM 4.01 code introduces a very powerful feature with regular expressions. Regular expressions allow you to match a variety of parameters using strings or variables that you assign. Also, four additional inspection engines have been added: DCEPRC, ESMTP, HTTP, and SIP.

NOTE   For more information on DCEPRC, ESMTP, HTTP, and SIP, read on! The topics are covered later in this chapter.

Configuring Regular Expressions

If you have had an opportunity to work with Border Gateway Protocol (BGP), you may have been introduced to regular expressions. Regular expressions provide a way to match a group of characters using either an exact string match or by meta-characters that allow you to define a range, a character set, and so on. This feature can be used to match URL strings when inspecting HTTP traffic and perform an action based on a match, or perform an action on the traffic that does not match the regular expression.

The following configuration example shows how to implement regular expression matching. A client on the inside is connecting to a server on the outside. In this example, you will be inspecting the content for the permutation of the keyword "flash." If the keyword is found, the connection will be reset.

Step 1   The first step requires that you create a regular expression to match the specific content. Ensure that the regular expression command matches on the keywords of Flash, FLaSh, flASH, and so on:

```
regex URL_NOFLASH "[Ff][Ll][Aa][Ss][Hh]"
```

Step 2   Create and set a regular expression (regex) class map to match the regular expression (URL_NOFLASH):

```
class-map type regex match-any RESTRICTED_URL
  match regex URL_NOFLASH
```

Step 3   Add an inspection class map to match the previously created class map (RESTRICTED_URL):

```
class-map type inspect http match-all RESTRICTED_HTTP
  match request uri regex class RESTRICTED_URL
```

Step 4   Add a policy map to search through the body of the HTTP string. The numeric value of 48 specifies how many characters to search through. The maximum length of the string can be from 1 to 4,294,967,295 characters. Longer search strings will impact the performance of the FWSM. When a match is found, using the class map RESTRICTED_HTTP, the action assigned is to reset and log the connection:

```
policy-map type inspect http HTTP_PMAP
  parameters
    body-match-maximum 48
  class RESTRICTED_HTTP
    reset log
```

CAUTION   Longer search strings will impact the performance of the FWSM.

Step 5   Create and use a final policy map to match the policy map (HTTP_PMAP):

```
policy-map INSIDE_POLICY
  class inspection_default
    inspect http HTTP_PMAP
```

Step 6   Apply the service policy to the interface:

```
service-policy INSIDE_POLICY interface Inside
```

When a match is found, the following log message is generated:

```
%FWSM-5-415006: HTTP - matched Class 23: RESTRICTED_HTTP in policy-map
HTTP_PMAP, URI matched - Resetting connection from
Inside:192.168.1.23/3898 to Outside:10.133.219.25/80
```

Figure 25-3 shows a screenshot of what the client's experience would be without the service policy.

Figure 25-3 *Regular Expression Without the Service Policy*

Figure 25-4 shows a screenshot of what the client's experience would be with the service policy.

Figure 25-4 *Regular Expression with the Service Policy*

Notice now that the graphic has been removed from the display.

There is also a simple tool that you can use to test a regular expression from the command line. Use the following test command:

```
FWSM# test regex http://www.cIsCo123.com [Cc][Ii][Ss][Cc][Oo][0-9]
INFO: Regular expression match succeeded.
```

The first argument is the string, and the second argument is the match criteria. Notice that both upper and lowercase characters will match the string "cIsCo" but must be followed by a numeric value.

In the next example, the hyphen does not match a numeric value, consequently the match fails.

```
FWSM# test regex http://www.cIsCo-123.com [Cc][Ii][Ss][Cc][Oo][0-9]
INFO: Regular expression match failed.
```

Regular expressions are a very helpful tool that could be used to match on viruses, worms, questionable material, and so on. A maximum of 100 characters can be used in the regular expression; remember that implementing regular expressions will impact the performance of the FWSM.

Inspecting content within a packet and matching against a user defined regular expression is a very powerful feature. Because additional CPU cycles are required when you employ this feature, use caution that you do not overwhelm the processor on the FWSM. As an alternative to the FWSM for high-performance regular expression matching, consider using an Intrusion Prevention System (IPS).

Understanding Application Inspection Improvements

One of the primary functions of the FWSM is to provide application inspection, looking for protocol conformance, changing imbedded IP addressing, and so on. Increasing the capabilities of this feature only adds benefit to the services you are offering to your customers.

Domain Name Service (DNS) guard is a feature used when a client requests DNS information through the FWSM to a DNS server or servers. The default behavior of the FWSM is to allow only a single reply and drop any additional responses, consequently helping to prevent against DNS poisoning attacks. Although not recommended because of the possibility of exploiting the host, the FWSM can be configured to allow all responses using the following command:

```
FWSM/Context-A(config)# no dns-guard
```

As you may have noticed from the preceding command syntax, this command also works in multi-context mode.

Policy maps are covered in detail in Chapter 11, "Modular Policy," but the introduction of 4.01 includes additional support/enhancements for inspection policy and/or class maps for the following applications:

- **Distributed Computing Environment Remote Procedure Call (DCEPRC):** A protocol used across multiple computers to distribute the load. Policy map inspection is the new addition to 4.01.

- **Extended Simple Mail Transfer Protocol (ESMTP):** Added extensions to SMTP. The 4.01 code added the capability for application support and the capability to define inspection policy maps that match traffic using regular expressions.

- **HTTP:** A protocol used generally to transfer information across the Internet.

- **Session Initiation Protocol (SIP):** A signaling protocol used for voice communications over IP.

  The following options are available using policy maps with the previously listed protocols, as follows:

  — **drop:** Drops all packets that match the defined pattern.

  — **drop-connection:** Drops the packet and closes the connection.

  — **log:** Sends a syslog message.

— **mask:** Masks that portion of the packet that has been matched.

— **rate-limit:** Limits the rate of received messages.

— **reset:** Drops the packet; closes and resets the connection.

— **send-protocol-error:** Sends an error message when the packet does not match the ESMTP protocol.

The capability added with policy maps for DCEPRC, ESMTP, HTTP, and SIP adds tremendous functionality for the inspection of these protocols. With the option to drop, drop-connection, log, mask, rate-limit, reset, and send-protocol-error, for many of these protocols, the functionality also significantly improves.

Additional Support for Simple Network Management Protocol Management Information Base

Simple Network Management Protocol (SNMP) is used to get specific information from a device or to send it information for the purposes of configuration changes. Because the FWSM is a security device, you cannot send it information, but you can gather information for keeping track of interface statistics, packet counts, and so on. There have been two additions to the Management Information Base (MIB):

- ACL entries and hit counters located under CISCO-IP-PROTOCOL-FILTER-MIB

- Address Resolution Protocol (ARP) table entries located under IP-MIB

Table 25-1 shows the MIB additions with definitions.

Table 25-1   *FWSM 4.01 MIB Additions*

CISCO-IP-PROTOCOL-FILTER-MIB	cippfIpFilterTable	Command Line Interface (CLI) show run access-list
1.3.6.1.4.1.9.9.278.1.1.1.1.1	cippfIpProfileName	ACL name
1.3.6.1.4.1.9.9.278.1.1.3.1.1	cippfIpFilterIndex	Access Control Entry (ACE) line number
1.3.6.1.4.1.9.9.278.1.1.3.1.3	cippfIpFilterAction	Permit/Deny
1.3.6.1.4.1.9.9.278.1.1.3.1.4	cippfIpFilterAddressType	Either ipv4 or ipv6
1.3.6.1.4.1.9.9.278.1.1.3.1.5	cippfIpFilterSrcAddress	Source IP addr
1.3.6.1.4.1.9.9.278.1.1.3.1.6	cippfIpFilterSrcMask	Source IP mask
1.3.6.1.4.1.9.9.278.1.1.3.1.7	cippfIpFilterDestAddress	Destination IP addr
1.3.6.1.4.1.9.9.278.1.1.3.1.8	cippfIpFilterDestMask	Destination IP mask
1.3.6.1.4.1.9.9.278.1.1.3.1.9	cippfIpFilterProtocol	Protocol (IP/TCP/UDP/ICMP)
1.3.6.1.4.1.9.9.278.1.1.3.1.10	cippfIpFilterSrcPortLow	Src port low
1.3.6.1.4.1.9.9.278.1.1.3.1.11	cippfIpFilterSrcPortHigh	Src port high

Table 25-1   *FWSM 4.01 MIB Additions   (Continued)*

CISCO-IP-PROTOCOL-FILTER-MIB	cippflpFilterTable	Command Line Interface (CLI) show run access-list
1.3.6.1.4.1.9.9.278.1.1.3.1.12	cippfIpFilterDestPortLow	Dest port low
1.3.6.1.4.1.9.9.278.1.1.3.1.13	cippfIpFilterDestPortHigh	Dest port high
1.3.6.1.4.1.9.9.278.1.1.3.1.16	cippfIpFilterLogEnabled	Log enabled/disabled
1.3.6.1.4.1.9.9.278.1.1.3.1.17	cippfIpFilterStatus	ACL Active/Inactive
1.3.6.1.4.1.9.9.278.1.1.3.1.22	cippfIpFilterSrcIPGroupName	Src n/w object group name
1.3.6.1.4.1.9.9.278.1.1.3.1.23	cippfIpFilterDstIPGroupName	Dest n/w object group name
1.3.6.1.4.1.9.9.278.1.1.3.1.24	cippfIpFilterProtocolGroupName	Protocol object group name
1.3.6.1.4.1.9.9.278.1.1.3.1.25	cippfIpFilterSrcServiceGroupName	Src service object group name
1.3.6.1.4.1.9.9.278.1.1.3.1.26	cippfIpFilterDstServiceGroupName	Dest service object group name
1.3.6.1.4.1.9.9.278.1.1.3.1.27	cippfIpFilterICMPGroupName	ICMP object group
	cippflpFilterStatsTable	**CLI show access-list** *acl-name*
¬†1.3.6.1.4.1.9.9.278.1.1.1.1.1	cippfIpProfileName	ACL name
1.3.6.1.4.1.9.9.278.1.1.3.1.1	cippfIpFilterIndex	ACE line number within the ACL
1.3.6.1.4.1.9.9.278.1.2.1.1.1	cippfIpFilterHits	ACE hit-count
IP-MIB(RFC2011)	**ipNetToPhysicalTable**	**CLI show arp**
1.3.6.1.2.1.4.35.1.1	ipNetToPhysicalIfIndex	Interface number for the ARP entry
1.3.6.1.2.1.4.35.1.2	ipNetToPhysicalNetAddressType¬†	IP address type for the ARP entry
1.3.6.1.2.1.4.35.1.3	ipNetToPhysicalNetAddress	IP address for the ARP entry
1.3.6.1.2.1.4.35.1.4	ipNetToPhysicalPhysAddress	Media Access Control (MAC) address for the IP address

When using SNMP, avoid using ansnmp walk. This process will start at the top of the MIB tree and get the statistics for each MIB, until it gets to the end of the tree. Because SNMP is not performed in hardware, this will put an undue burden on the FWSM.

NOTE   Gathering SNMP information from the FWSM will increase the load. Get only specific information when necessary.

SNMP is a very valuable tool to gather statistics from the FWSM, and with the addition of ACL entries, ACL counters, and ARP table entries, it becomes an even better tool. Just remember not to overwhelm the FWSM with too many queries.

Miscellaneous Security Features

DHCP option 82 is typically used in service-provider networks. It adds location information that can be used to differentiate services between customers. A filtering enhancement was also added to support HTTPS with SmartFilter.

Dynamic Host Configuration Protocol Option 82

Option 82 provides location information from the Dynamic Host Configuration Protocol (DHCP) relay agent—in this case, the FWSM to the DHCP server. This information can be used to differentiate DHCP clients, consequently offering distinctive services on a client basis.

You can use two commands to enable DHCP relay. The first command specifies the DHCP server IP address and the interface where it is located. Optionally, the **dhcprelay server** *ip_address* command can be configured under the outgoing interface. The second line enables clients on the inside interface to send and receive DHCP information.

```
FWSM/Context-A(config)# dhcprelay server 10.20.100.25 Outside
FWSM/Context-A(config)# dhcprelay enable Inside
```

Option 82 can then be enabled on a specific interface, as shown by the following two commands:

```
FWSM/Context-A(config)# interface vlan vlan-number
FWSM/Context-A(config-if)# dhcprelay information trusted
```

Option 82 can also be enabled on all interfaces using the global command that follows:

```
FWSM/Context-A(config)# dhcprelay information trust-all
```

If you are currently using the FWSM as a DHCP relay agent, the addition of option 82 will be a simple addition. Also, when enabling option 82 globally, all interfaces are trusted except the interface that is configured as the dhcprelay (outgoing) interface.

DHCP option 82 adds location information to clients, which can be used to differentiate services. Although used primarily in service provider networks, it could all be used in enterprise networks to differentiate client services.

Smartfilter HTTPS Support

For those of you looking for HTTPS support from SmartFilter on the FWSM, it has now arrived with the introduction of 4.01. See Chapter 14, "Filtering," for configuration details.

Summary

The release of 4.x adds some very significant enhancements. The addition of EIGRP now provides the capability to integrate a FWSM into an EIGRP network without having to redistribute routes into other routing protocols. RHI allows static routes, NAT pools, and connected routes to be propagated to the routing engine on the host-chassis dynamically. Regular expressions give you the opportunity to match traffic based on custom signatures. Application inspection improvements and SNMP additions, option 82 support, and filter enhancements, make the FWSM an even better option to secure your valuable assets.

References

RFC 1869—*SMTP Service Extensions*

RFC 2011—*SNMPv2 Management Information Base for the Internet Protocol Using SMIv2*

RFC 3046—*DHCP Relay Agent Information Option 82*

N

T

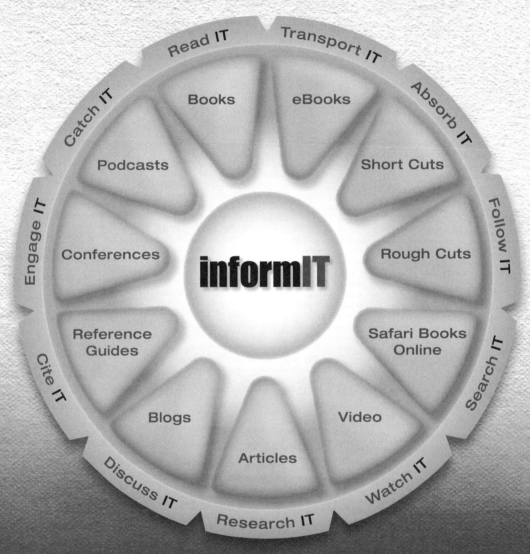

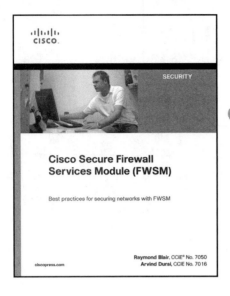

FREE Online Edition

Your purchase of **Cisco Secure Firewall Services Module (FWSM)** includes access to a free online edition for 120 days through the Safari Books Online subscription service. Nearly every **Cisco Press** book is available online through Safari Books Online, along with over 5,000 other technical books and videos from publishers such as Addison-Wesley Professional, Exam Cram, IBM Press, O'Reilly, Prentice Hall, Que, and Sams.

SAFARI BOOKS ONLINE allows you to search for a specific answer, cut and paste code, download chapters, and stay current with emerging technologies.

Activate your FREE Online Edition at www.informit.com/safarifree

> **STEP 1:** Enter the coupon code: 85HJ-D24I-WZH3-ZDHX-5HB4.

> **STEP 2:** New Safari users, complete the brief registration form.
> Safari subscribers, just login.

If you have difficulty registering on Safari or accessing the online edition, please e-mail customer-service@safaribooksonline.com